Liking, Loving, & Relating

CLYDE HENDRICK & SUSAN HENDRICK
University of Miami

Brooks/Cole Publishing Company

Monterey, California

Brooks/Cole Publishing Company
A Division of Wadsworth, Inc.

Printed in the United States of America
10 9 8 7 6 5 4 3 2 1

Library of Congress Cataloging in Publication Data

Hendrick, Clyde.
    Liking, loving, and relating.

    Bibliography: p.
    Includes indexes.
    1. Interpersonal relations. 2. Interpersonal
attraction. 3. Affiliation (Psychology) 4. Love.
5. Marriage. I. Hendrick, Susan, [date]–
II. Title.
HM132.H464 1983   302   82-14561
ISBN 0-534-01263-9

Subject Editor: *Claire Verduin*
Production Editor: *Patricia E. Cain*
Manuscript Editor: *Rhoda Blecker*
Interior and Cover Design: *Katherine Minerva*
Art Coordinator: *Judith Macdonald*
Illustrator: *John Foster*
Typesetter: *Holmes Composition Service, San Jose*

Liking,
Loving, &
Relating

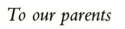

To our parents

Preface

In the past few years there has been an explosion of interest in the study of relationships, especially intimate, or close, relationships. Courses and seminars on close relationships have become popular at both undergraduate and graduate levels. Research interest has developed so rapidly that few suitable texts exist. Our purpose is to remedy the situation by providing a book that is broad in scope and appropriate for a variety of courses.

The parts of the book—Liking, Loving, and Relating—provide a certain conceptual order. In modern society, attraction, or liking, is viewed as a proper basis for the more intense sentiment of love; and love is viewed as the proper, legitimating condition for entering into the close relationship of marriage. We do not suggest a causal direction: the majority of people in Western societies construe the sequence in this way, and therefore we have organized the book accordingly.

Interpersonal attraction is a traditional subject of study in psychology and sociology. Part One, *Liking,* addresses these traditional interests. Chapter 1, "The Nature of Attraction," presents a relatively rigorous overview of concepts of attraction and analyzes the distinction between attraction as an internal, cognitive–affective response and attraction as it occurs in a behavioral, interactional context. This distinction provides the basis for both Chapter 2, "Attitudes and Attraction," which reviews traditional social-psychological approaches, and Chapter 3, "Affiliation and Attraction," which deals with several interactional aspects of attraction.

One correlate of the study of close relationships is a strong research interest in love and sexuality. Part Two, *Loving,* specifically addresses these interests in Chapter 4, "Love," and Chapter 5, "Sexual Love." Part Three, *Relating,* focuses on the dynamics of relationships. Chapter 6 details the processes involved in initiating, developing, and maintaining close relationships. Chapter 7 is devoted to marriage, which serves as a prototype for close relationships. Chapter 8, "Issues in Contemporary Relationships," deals with topics of intense current interest such as divorce, blended families, and dual-career couples.

For students who do not have much background in the concepts of modern social-science theory and research, the appendix discusses the nature of theory, hypotheses, and measurement, using material on attraction as a concrete example. The appendix concludes with an overview of issues involved in the study of close relationships.

Full consideration of attraction, love, and relationships requires discussion of a wide range of topics that span several disciplines. Included are topics as diverse as attitude similarity and attraction, beauty, friendship formation, mere exposure, self-presentation styles, the nuances of love, sexual behavior, dyadic processes (for example, negotiation, power, and conflict), divorce, and more. Supplemented by readings, the volume can serve as a text in a basic social-psychology course that considers human relationships as its central theme. The book will be most useful, perhaps, in specialized psychology and sociology courses on attraction, relationships, human sexuality, and marriage and family. It should also serve well as a basic conceptual background for counseling and clinical-psychology courses in marital therapy.

We are grateful to Keith E. Davis (University of South Carolina, Columbia) and John H. Harvey (Texas Tech University) for their helpful reviews of the manuscript. In a perfect world, these two individuals would review every author's manuscript! In addition, we thank the fine professional staff at Brooks/Cole for producing the book with a minimum of trouble—almost painless. Finally, our special thanks go to Sandi Racoobian and Shelley Slapion-Foote for their special efforts in flawless typing of the manuscript.

Clyde Hendrick
Susan Hendrick

Contents

Chapter 3   **Affiliation and Attraction   56**

Part Two   *Loving*   85

PART ONE

Liking

Chapter 1 develops fully the basic foundations of the study of attraction. The central concept is attraction, or liking, as a specific type of attitude, and cognitive–affective aspects of the attraction response receive detailed attention. The chapter also develops behavioral and interaction facets of liking in discussions of affiliation, roles, and relationships. Two classic theories of attraction—balance and reinforcement—are presented as examples of how theories of attraction work.

Chapter 2 develops the attitudinal, or "cognitive–affective," approach to attraction, drawing extensively from the laboratory tradition in which this approach originated. The relations between attraction and attribute similarity/dissimilarity, complementarity, reciprocity, desirable characteristics, and physical attractiveness are discussed, with examples of relevant social-psychological research for each type of relation.

Chapter 3 develops the interactional–affiliative approach to the study of attraction. Several functions of affiliation, as well as traditional variables such as propinquity and "mere exposure," are treated. Nonverbal aspects of behavior in interactions that also affect attraction are discussed. The chapter concludes with a consideration of styles of self-presentation and the relation of such styles to affiliation and attraction.

1

The Nature of Attraction

Gideon: A Modern Parable

Gideon's brain stirred. It was morning and time to leave the oblivion of night behind. Gideon started work at 8:30 A.M. sharp, as he did every day, Monday through Friday, week after week, year after year. His job was important; his title acronym was SORM—Specialist in Office Resources Management. In that role Gideon was responsible for inventory bookkeeping, ordering new supply stocks, filling orders, and periodic tabulation of total inflow of raw materials and outflow of finished products. High-level problem solving, often with advanced mathematics, was an important part of the job.

Gideon was efficient—very efficient—in his work. He worked rapidly and seldom made mistakes. Naturally, his office co-workers thought highly of him. Some of them were better at different kinds of skills from Gideon's, but Gideon was clearly the best in the office at what he did. He was, however, viewed by his co-workers as a little peculiar. The singleness of purpose and the speed with which he worked discouraged others from interacting with him for other than strictly business purposes. In fact, the bulk of his interaction with the other office staff members was by typed messages passed back and forth.

The truth is that Gideon was not friendly, but he was also not unfriendly. The whole concept of friendliness seemed alien to him, as if he lived in another dimension. Problem solving, accurate memory, and speed and efficiency of production summarized the meaning of existence for Gideon. He took no joy in his work, but he was not unhappy with it. A well-done job was a job well done, and then on to the next job with neither celebration nor remorse. Gideon accepted his nature, since he could not do otherwise, and his co-workers accepted him also. In fact, over time they became quite fond of him and occasionally expressed their sentiments toward him. It would probably be accurate to say that the others in the office felt more strongly about Gideon than he felt about himself.

Given that Gideon was such a formidable worker, one might expect some jealousy from the others, or perhaps some air of condescending superiority toward them on his part. But such was not the case. Gideon absolutely did not evaluate people, and in some measure this was the reason they were able to become attached to him. Gideon accepted people as they were, without judgment or comment.

Estelle and George were Gideon's closest co-workers. They dealt with him frequently, usually by written queries or instructions. They were in their late twenties and had worked in the office together for about five years. Both of them were intelligent, gregarious, charming people. In time George and Estelle became romantically involved with each other. They were discreet, but occasionally they expressed affection or touched tenderly when few other people were around. Gideon was unmoved; in fact, he was hardly aware of the office romance.

On one particular morning George came to work late. Estelle looked grim, as if she were deeply worried about something. She made a sharp comment to George and began to pace recklessly and angrily. She was unaware that she had bumped Gideon and was subsequently unaware that for once she had his full attention. Gideon was dazzled and confused by the events that occurred during the next half-hour. He was not used to the agitated speech that was springing from the lips of his two co-workers. The meaning of what they were saying was even more problematic. Estelle said things like "If you really loved me, you wouldn't have gone out with someone else." George replied "You have no right to be jealous; it's not what you think." After a while Estelle cried; George was trembling,

Later the tone of their voices changed. She said "I'm sorry." He touched her; she folded herself into his arms. They smiled at each other, kissed briefly, and left the room arm-in-arm. For perhaps the first time in his existence, Gideon was disturbed. A whole universe of meaning had passed before his senses, and he knew vaguely that he could not comprehend it and did not share in it. He tried repeating some of the words: love, jealous, emotional, care. But nothing happened. There was a void, an absolute neutral emptiness. Gideon's disturbance was due to his recognition of the discrepancy between the emotional life scenario that had just taken place and his own inner void. But Gideon didn't really want to change that inner void of evenness. It was part of his nature, and it was peaceful. Besides, the work tasks were urgently summoning him. Therefore he had to purge the life scenario he had seen. As his memory prepared to erase the emotional episode, he reflected briefly on how different he was from his co-workers. But it didn't bother him. Everything has its appointed nature and duties. His co-workers had their duties, activities, and emotions—and on the face of it, quite a disorganized hodgepodge they were. As for Gideon, he knew his tasks, and they were his whole life: calculate, compute, record, and then do it again. It is perhaps too much to say that Gideon liked his nature and his tasks. But if machines had feelings Gideon certainly would have been self-satisfied. Everyone agreed that Gideon was the best office computer in the entire city.

Lessons of the Parable

Gideon's ignorance about an everyday instance of love can be forgiven. He was not programmed to recognize or experience human emotions. For both good and ill we humans do not suffer from Gideon's particular defect. Our "programming" for emotional experience is detailed and highly complex. Most of our ongoing daily existence is seasoned with an emotional flavor. Some of life's greatest satisfactions come from the experience of emotion, but many of our miseries also stem from our capacity to be emotional. During the height (or depth) of Estelle and George's fight we can almost identify more strongly with Gideon. Who has not on some occasion desired a void instead of inner feelings, preferred the peace of emotional oblivion to the pain of dealing with strong emotion?

Such a sense of oblivion may occur for brief episodes on rare occasions. Otherwise, we live our lives in large measure from our gut feeling, experiencing, hating, loving, liking, and disliking. Attachment to other people, as an intrinsic emotional and orienting system of responses, begins during the first year of life (Cohen, 1976). To develop normally, infants must receive a rich mix of love and attention from other people. Most of the ebb and flow of our emotional life is related to the existence of other people. Most of them we do not know and will never see. Many are slight acquaintances; some we know well; and a select few are placed in a special category called "friends."

We experience a variety of emotions toward the people who fill our lives. With slight acquaintances there may be a neutral tone—no particular emotional feeling at all—whereas with people we know well we are seldom neutral in our feelings. Toward a few special people we label a complex set of feelings *love*. Because of our complexity it is possible to love a person at one time and detest that person at another time. It may even be possible to love and hate another person simultaneously. This condition, known as *ambivalence,* may occur with some frequency. In fact, Freud (1933, 1965) thought that ambivalence of emotions was an intrinsic part of human life (see also Jones, 1955). However, ambivalence is likely to be painful, and therefore most people attempt to keep their emotional feelings toward someone relatively consistent at a given time.

Although we experience many emotions toward other people, we can conveniently summarize those experiences by saying that we like some people and dislike others. Further, we like or dislike some people more intensely than others. As Figure 1-1 illustrates, we can list other people in terms of how much we like or dislike them. Liking and disliking can collectively be described by the concept *interpersonal attraction* or, simply, *attraction*. An examination of the scientific literature on interpersonal attraction shows that, although the concept of attraction is usually defined in terms of liking and disliking, textbook chapters on attraction nearly always concentrate on the positive pole, liking, while disliking is discussed in another chapter, frequently in a chapter on aggression. This separation may reflect peculiarities of textbook writers; however, the separation may also mean that, while defining liking and disliking as opposite poles of one dimension is conceptually pleasing, liking and disliking may in fact be very different dimensions. This answer has been suggested by Rodin (1978), who argued that liking and disliking

A social scientist interviewed children about their friends, acquaintances, and enemies. Careful questioning elicited the following descriptions, which have been translated into adult language.

I like Joan very much.
I dislike John very much.
I like Sam moderately well.
I dislike Sue to a moderate extent.
I like Allen slightly.
I dislike Alice slightly.
I feel perfectly neutral toward Gideon.

Based on these statements, a seven-step ruler, or scale, can be constructed on which the seven individuals are located. The individuals are listed from most disliked, through neutral, to liked. This order is a scale of measurement, and numbers can be assigned to each step. In this way internal subjective experiences can be partially quantified and brought into the domain of scientific research. Children might be presented just with the scale of stick figures, because they can easily translate the smile/frown dimension into liking. Adults would ordinarily use only the verbal labels in making ratings.

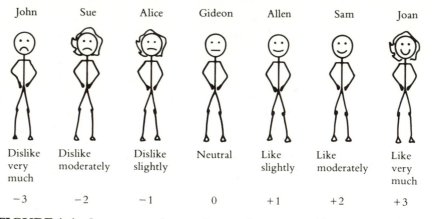

FIGURE 1-1 Interpersonal attraction can be measured because people can be described in terms of how much they are liked or disliked.

are really separate kinds of evaluative judgments. Rodin believed that the traits and qualities ascribed to disliked people are different in kind from the characteristics ascribed to liked people. The result is simply two "collections" of people, liked and disliked, rather than one collection that can be divided and placed on opposite ends of a single attraction dimension. We will concentrate mostly on the positive concept of liking and will have relatively little to say about disliking.

It was only about 20 years ago that social psychologists began to study attraction seriously. Perhaps because attraction is such a common, everyday occurrence, it simply was not considered worthy of study for many years. Now all that has changed. The explosion of research and theory on attraction and love has been so great that it would be impossible to summarize it all in one book. There are many questions that have been (or could be) researched. Some examples are shown in Box 1-1. The list is endless, and the answers to most questions would be immediately useful, because we are always involved in liking and disliking others, not to mention loving and hating them.

BOX 1-1   Examples of research questions about attraction and love. Answers to these questions would have great practical usefulness, because each question is relevant to nearly everybody.

1. Why do I like some people better than others?
2. Are some people intrinsically more likable than others?
3. Is it possible to learn to become more likable?
4. Are there secrets to being liked? For example, if I am deliberately very helpful to other people, will they like me better?
5. Are physically attractive people better liked than ugly people?
6. Do friends complement each other?
7. Am I most attracted to people similar to me?
8. How does the way I feel about myself affect the way others feel about me?
9. Is attraction the same as love, or are they different?
10. Can I both like and love someone at the same time?
11. Are true friends always loyal to each other?
12. Can I be "best friends" only with someone of my own sex?
13. Do people usually fall in love gradually, or does it happen all at once?
14. How do I know when I'm *really* in love?
15. Do romantic love and sexual desire always go together?
16. Is there one kind of love, or are there many kinds?

The Study of Attraction: Basic Concepts

Dimensions of Attraction

Four aspects of attraction may be seen in the previous discussion. Each aspect can be considered a dimension or factor relevant to the study of attraction.

   1. *Emotional states.* The involvement of the emotions in liking and disliking is obvious. Based on our feelings about others, we make judgments about them, good or bad, positive or negative. These judgments are essentially *evaluations* of others.
   2. *Beliefs about others.* This dimension was implicit in the previous discussion. It seems impossible to like or dislike someone without

knowing anything about that person. Usually, liking or disliking is related quite directly to the amount of knowledge one has about another person. The relation is not perfect, however, because we sometimes develop strong feelings based on limited information. Consider the following categories: Swede, Turk, Jew, Commie, right-wing Republican. Most people will have some feelings and beliefs about one or more of these terms. A set of beliefs prompted only by a category term is a *stereotype,* and the evaluative feelings accompanying it (which may be positive or negative) are *prejudice.* Stereotypes and prejudice are important in social life, but they will not receive much discussion in this book. Instead, the book focuses on beliefs and feelings about *specific, concrete persons,* rather than *abstract categories of persons.*

3. *Behavior toward others.* We not only have feelings toward others and beliefs about them, we also behave toward them. People call, stare, hit, and kiss, along with a few million other possible acts. We express our attraction as well as think and feel it. In fact, attraction unexpressed in actual behavior is hardly attraction at all. Behavior on the verge of open expression is usually called a *behavior tendency.*

These three dimensions of attraction—emotions, beliefs, and behavior—are roughly equal in importance. These three dimensions also define the concept of an *attitude,* and it will be convenient and conceptually satisfying to define attraction as one type of attitude, as we shall see in the next section. There is one final aspect of attraction.

4. *Interaction.* We not only behave or act toward others, we also react to them. A sequence of actions and reactions of at least two people toward each other is called *interaction.* A conversation is a prime example. Two people talk to each other face-to-face, taking turns and occasionally talking simultaneously. They are acting and reacting in turn and thus interacting. Interaction is wondrously complex, mundane, everydayish, yet vital to our existence as human beings. It is the basis not only for attraction, but for most of our other human attributes (for example, without interaction language would not exist). We assume therefore that face-to-face interaction is the original, primitive setting out of which most people's likes and dislikes emerge. This basic axiom does not deny that attraction also develops in other ways—falling in love from afar is a familiar example, and people also form strong likes and dislikes for actors and media personalities whom they have never met.

Attraction and Attitudes

The nature of attitudes.   The study of attitudes is an important part of social psychology. There are many approaches to the study of attitudes (for example, Fishbein & Ajzen, 1975; Himmelfarb & Eagly, 1974; Insko, 1967). The following definition summarizes the essence of many previous definitions of the concept.

> *Attitude*—an orientation toward or away from an object that may be described as having valence (positive, neutral, or negative). The orientation consists of a *cognitive* structure of beliefs and knowledge about the object, *affect* (emotion) felt and expressed toward it, and *behavior tendencies* to approach or avoid the object.

Attitudes may be held toward almost any object. The "object" may be an abstract concept such as mathematics, an issue such as a woman's right to have an abortion, a country such as the USSR, a style of music, and so on. Toward each object an individual holds a complex set of beliefs; feels positive, neutral, or negative; and behaves in certain consistent ways.

As an example assume the following position statement: "Women should have unlimited rights to abortion on demand." Suppose that you strongly agree with the statement; that is, you have a positive attitude toward the topic. In terms of the definition of an attitude, there are several things that should be predictable about you.

1. *Beliefs*—There are several propositions you might believe.

- Each person has the right to absolute control over his or her own body.
- A fetus is part of the mother and has no existence apart from her.
- A pregnant woman should have the same rights over her uterus as over any other body part, no more and no less.
- Until the fetus can survive on its own, it is the woman's property by virtue of being a part of her. Every person should have control over the disposition of personal property.
- Freedom of choice in abortion is no different in principle from freedom of choice in other important areas—for example, getting married, joining a church, or getting a divorce.

These various beliefs are the content or substance of the attitude object. As a set, the beliefs are what the attitude is about. Generally, a set of beliefs mutually reinforces and supports itself, but sometimes inconsistency occurs within a set.

2. *Affect*—Feelings toward the object (for example, right to an abortion) tend to be consistent with the nature of the beliefs about it. If someone believes in abortion, a speech against abortion may cause anger, and a strong pro-abortion stand by a local feminist group may cause positive feelings of happiness. An attitude scale may show strong evaluations on the issue. Thus, a position statement could be rated directly by circling the number from −3 to +3 that best describes one's

feelings on the issue. This type of rating scale is called a *Likert scale* after the name of the psychologist who invented it.

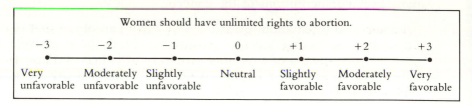

Notice that the form of the attitude scale is very similar to the liking rating scale shown in Figure 1-1. The principle is similar: people can be ordered on an evaluative scale of liking, and attitude objects can also be ordered on an evaluative scale of favorableness/unfavorableness.

3. *Behavior tendencies*—A positive attitude on the abortion issue may be expressed in many ways. Someone might join a local feminist group, wear a pro-abortion button, campaign for pro-abortion political candidates, write letters to a local newspaper, and work hard against the most visible anti-abortion spokesperson. In nearly all instances the various behaviors should be consistent with each other, consistent with the belief structure on the topic, and consistent with the direction of the affect.

Attraction as an attitude.   The example illustrates the importance of the concept of *attitude* in social life. We could hardly recognize our own society were it not for the complex hodgepodge of attitudes that people hold, toward objects and toward other people. Attraction is a special type of attitude, and the "attitude object" is another person. Thus attraction may be defined as follows, based on the earlier definition of attitude:

> *Attraction*—An orientation toward or away from a person that may be described as having valence (positive, neutral, or negative). The orientation consists of a *cognitive* structure of beliefs and knowledge about the person, *affect* felt and expressed toward him or her, and *behavior tendencies* to approach or avoid that person.

It is not always easy to distinguish statements about beliefs from statements about feelings. The two are sometimes combined and referred to as the *cognitive–affective component* of attraction, and contrasted to the *behavioral component*.

Cognitive and Affective Aspects of Attraction

The role of language in attraction.   Affect or feelings toward others and belief structures about them tend to be consistent in part because of the nature of language. We use linguistic terms to conceive and communicate characteristics of people and liking/disliking of them. Language refers to underlying qualities and characteristics, but language also seems to take on a life of its own. For example, the concept of a *trait* (for example, honest/dishonest) refers to a quality of persons. However, trait terms are also meaningful when they are considered abstractly. Each language has a great many trait terms to describe people. In English, Allport and Odbert (1936) counted 17,953 trait words, but it gets more complicated. If you are asked to rate how likable or dislikable each trait on a list is, you can do the task easily, and your ratings will agree well with other people's ratings. Lists of such words and their likability ratings have been compiled by researchers (for example, Anderson, 1968).

Traits are often arranged in pairs of polar opposites. Some examples are:

dishonest———honest
harsh———smooth
cruel———kind
ugly———beautiful
cold———warm

All the traits on the right-hand side are judged "good" or "likable" by most people, and the traits on the left-hand side are judged "bad" or "dislikable." If you are told that someone is honest, smooth, kind, beautiful, and warm, you will not have to ponder long to decide that you would like such a person. Thus the trait language used to describe a person and the language used to signify an affective evaluation are constructed, so to speak, to go together. We may have trouble deciding what specific behaviors mean (for instance, whether a given act is really honest), but we tend to agree well on the meanings of the trait terms themselves.

The relative consensus on the verbal meaning of specific trait words has led to several research traditions relevant to the study of attraction. Solomon Asch (1946) presented a list of trait words to students and asked them to form an impression of the person described by that list. Detailed sketches were written by the students, using other trait adjectives and personality terms. Students formed rather detailed impressions based only on an abstract list of no more than seven terms. Asch's work started a research tradition with trait words called *impression formation*.

When you considered the traits in the right-hand column of the preceding list, you were also essentially forming an impression of a hypothetical person possessing those traits. The almost immediate judgment of likability was a consequence of the overall impression. Extensive research during the past 25 years has found that liking/

disliking, or more generally positive/negative evaluation, is one of the more important consequences of forming impressions of people and of concepts.

Osgood, Suci, and Tannenbaum (1957) devised a new scale called the *semantic differential,* in an ambitious research program on the measurement of *meaning.* Examples of semantic-differential scales are:

Bad   ____ ____ ____ ____ ____ ____ ____ Good
Passive ____ ____ ____ ____ ____ ____ ____ Active
Weak   ____ ____ ____ ____ ____ ____ ____ Strong

An attitude object or person is rated on a great many scales. The opposing words for each scale serve as end anchors defining a rating dimension. A research subject rates a concept (for example, *mother*) by placing an "X" on one of the seven steps. An "X" next to "good" means mother is rated as "very good." An "X" on the middle step means mother is "neither good nor bad." An "X" next to "bad" means mother is rated as "very bad." The remaining steps are intermediate to those just described. Each pair of traits defines a meaning scale on which the "object" is to be located.

Using a great many scales and complex statistics, Osgood, Suci, and Tannenbaum found that there are three important dimensions (also called factors) of meaning used to describe most concepts. By far the most important dimension was *evaluation.* The good/bad scale is a pure example of this dimension. Other scales highly related to the dimension are kind/cruel, trustworthy/untrustworthy, honorable/dishonorable, and the like. The evaluative tendency seems to be a pervasive aspect of human life. This outcome is not surprising in light of our previous discussion. We are not neutral toward people we know. We respond affectively to them by liking and disliking.

The other two dimensions of meaning found by Osgood and associates were called *activity* and *potency.* Active/passive is a relatively pure measure of activity, and weak/strong is a measure of potency. For most concepts activity and potency were less powerful dimensions of meaning than evaluation, but they nevertheless remained quite important.

Sources of information about others.   It is clear that our cognitive structures about people depend on the nature and meaning of language structures and that evaluation is tied to those language structures. But that is not the whole story. Trait words describing others are important, but belief and knowledge structures about other persons are based on other types of information as well. Box 1-2 lists several of the important types of information we use in constructing our conceptions of people. If we know someone well, we know much more than the person's basic personality dispositions. We know about moods, various

BOX 1-2 Seven types of information about another person that help determine the degree of attraction toward that person.

1. Traits of other—Balance of positive over negative traits, consistency among the traits, relative predominance of one or a few "central" traits. Also mood changes.
2. Temperament of other—Style of expressing traits. May range from forceful to quiet.
3. Belief, attitudes, and values of other—Person holds vast array of beliefs and attitudes that are important in defining who a person is.
4. Socioeconomic status of other—Person holds membership rank in many groups: occupational, family, educational, religious, social, and so on. These statuses and the behaviors associated with them are important aspects of the definition of the person.
5. Physical appearance of other.
6. General relationship of other to self—The relationship of the other person to oneself on the five categories above is important. The crucial factor in attraction may be not the absolute values of category items but the relative similarity or difference between self and other person on the various items.
7. Interaction of self with other—Knowledge about another person builds most fully through interaction. Also, a new factor of egocentrism or self-interest is added in direct interaction, because the other person can impinge on self in ways not possible when self is a detached, unrelated observer.

beliefs and attitudes the other holds, money problems, love problems, and so on. We are also highly conscious of how the other person compares to us on many attributes, and we are particularly concerned with the implications for self of direct interaction with the other person.

It is clear that the information base for attraction is diverse and highly complex, consisting of many types of information. Some of the information is evaluatively loaded, and some is neutral. With that many sources of information it is natural that there should be some discrepancy or inconsistency in the conception of the other person. Sometimes it is a struggle to keep a coherent image of someone. Even our best friend may shock us by revealing a previously unanticipated facet of personality. Thus our cognitive structure about another person, although relatively stable, is always subject to revision and updating. Sometimes dramatic changes in conception are required.

It follows that our feelings of liking and disliking should also fluctuate over time. Information changes, and therefore evaluation changes. Changes in liking between two friends over a long time might well show a series of zigs and zags as they get angry with each other, make up, support each other, and so on throughout the course of their lives. Of course variation in liking/disliking should not be expected to mirror exactly each small change in the cognitive store of information. It is therefore still reasonable to view the cognitive basis of attraction as somewhat separate from the affective basis. Nevertheless, the two components are linked closely enough that for analytic purposes they can be treated as a single, complex unit.

Attraction and Behavior

The definition of attraction can be divided into sets of polar terms to lay bare the components of attraction.

General definition: Orientation away from——Orientation toward
Beliefs: Negative beliefs——Positive beliefs
Affect: Disliking——Liking
Behavior: Avoids——Approaches

"Approaches" seems to be consistent with "positive beliefs" and "liking," and "avoids" is consistent with "negative beliefs" and "disliking." The conception of *avoids/approaches* captures well the image of movement and action of one person with respect to another. It also includes the propensity or tendency toward action. Interpersonal behavior pertaining to attraction is so varied that it defies systematic classification. Such behavior can range from telling a third person you like X, to spending all your time with X, expressing affection for X, and the like. Nevertheless, we can conceive of two broad categories of behavior.

One category is *acts toward (or against) another person*. This conception provides the basis for *interaction* because, as we noted previously, interaction is at least two people acting in turn. The second general behavioral category is *association*, or *affiliation*. It is a broader category based on various types of complex interactions. This second category will be discussed in the next section.

When an act toward another person is examined more closely, it appears to have one or more of three basic components.

1. *Symbolic behavior*—Although this is usually oral conversation addressed to another person, it can also be a written message or perhaps drawings. A dead skunk presented to someone on a silver platter is a powerful symbolic message, probably representing disliking. Symbolic behavior used to express attraction is directed; it is oriented toward the other person *intentionally*.

2. *Physical movements*—Our bodies speak our likes and dislikes, sometimes eloquently, sometimes clumsily. The variety of physical movements involved in attraction is endless: a pat on the back, a caress,

a kiss, walking together, and so on. Some behaviors are done without awareness, and others are directed intentionally toward the other person. Actually, it is not so easy to separate conscious physical acts from symbolic acts, because human meaning is conveyed by both types of behavior. The example of the skunk represents a complex physical act, but its symbolic meaning seems to predominate. The middle finger of the hand thrown up in a certain gesture is currently an act of fixed symbolic meaning in our society, even though it is a completely physical expression of movement, without language involved. The meaning of overt behavior is highly dependent on its surrounding context. A pat on the back can mean many things. Its meaning depends on who does it, how hard it is, in what circumstances it occurs, and with what accompanying words. In general, however, the distinction between symbolic behavior and movements is usually made in terms of whether language is used or not.

3. *Unintentional behavior*—Much of our overt behavior is unintended. Yet this behavior is often meaningful, and information from it is used in assessing others and reacting to them. This type of behavior is sometimes called *nonverbal communication.* It functions almost as a type of language. One popular book, in fact, called it "body language" (Fast, 1970). The general assumption is that our nonverbal behavior, even though unconscious, is consistent with our underlying conscious feelings of liking or disliking and with our beliefs about another. There are many facets of such expression. Tonal quality of the voice may yield clues. Facial expressions, posture, physical orientation to others during interaction, and spatial proximity during interaction are some of the many interesting types of unintended nonverbal behaviors. We will consider such behavior as it relates to attraction in Chapter 3.

Interaction, Affiliation, and Attraction

Affiliation is "being together." Affiliation is based on physical interaction, but affiliation cannot be conceived adequately if it is restricted solely to physical interaction. Humans define themselves with respect to each other in many ways, of which ongoing interaction is only one. For example, Heider (1958) thought that relations between people can be divided into two generic classes. *Sentiment relations* include the various affective relations, especially liking and disliking. *Unit relations* are the various kinds of "belongingness" that people share—for instance, servant, boss, friend, and the like. More generally, the concept of *unit relation* is the generic term for a wide range of human relationships. In order to sort out some of the complexities in understanding affiliation and attraction, it will be useful to discuss interaction as the basis for affiliation, types of interactions, affiliation and relationships, and the concept of role relations versus person relations.

Interaction as the basis for affiliation.   A sequence of exchanged acts in a face-to-face situation by two or more people is the basic definition of *interaction* and thereby the basic way in which people affiliate with one another. Interaction also occurs in other ways: by telephone, letter, via third parties, and so on. However, these other modes of interacting seem less important in comparison to face-to-face interaction. The sociologist George Homans (1950) viewed interaction and attraction as intrinsically related. He stated several basic hypotheses:

1. The more nearly equal in status people in a group are, the more frequently they will interact with one another [p. 184].
2. Persons who interact frequently with one another tend to be similar to one another [p. 111].
3. If the frequency of interaction between people increases, their liking of each other will increase, and vice versa [p. 112].
4. The more frequently people interact with one another, the stronger their sentiments of friendship are likely to become [p. 133].

The mechanism that Homans (1961) used to explain why these hypotheses should be true was the concept of *reinforcement,* borrowed from B. F. Skinner (for example, 1938, 1953). Skinner believed that behavior is shaped by rewards and punishments. If a given act is rewarded, it should increase in frequency; if it is punished, its frequency should decrease. Presumably, positive feelings are associated with reward, and negative feelings with punishment. In Homans's view, human interaction on the average has a surplus of rewards over punishment. That is why we are so eager to affiliate with other people. In a given instance, of course, two people may be more punishing than rewarding to each other. In that instance interaction would be expected to break down, and the two would subsequently avoid each other.

Reward and punishment, or *reinforcement,* is a heavily used concept in social and behavioral science. It seems reasonable that most people most of the time do manage to extract more pleasure than pain from association with their fellows, and the result is the basic cornerstone of interpersonal attraction.

Types of interactions.   Ongoing, face-to-face interaction varies in several ways, but it depends on two basic structural features: the composition of the collection of people involved in the interaction and their purposes in coming together. Group composition can vary in many ways; perhaps the most basic way is *size*. A collection of two people functions differently from a collection of three. "Two's company but three's a crowd" is a relatively accurate folk proverb. A group of ten people would in turn be quite different from a group of three. The largest collection in which relatively intimate interpersonal interaction can transpire is a small group. Its number cannot be rigidly fixed, but somewhere between 12 and 20 people would be the upper limit. Beyond that size the collection is just that, a mere collection of people in one another's presence for their own individual purposes (such as a concert audience or sports fans). Our ability to process information is limited, and a dozen or so people is all that we have a chance to become acquainted with in a reasonable period of meeting time.

Even within a small group of a half-dozen people, affective relations are not quite the same as between a pair (also called a *dyad*). The larger group is more "public," very intimate conversations are more difficult, people have to wait longer to have their turn to talk, and so on. Further, larger numbers of people tend to develop a concept of themselves as a "group," and the group itself can be viewed as an object of attraction by the members. Members' desire to remain in the group and their attraction toward it has been called *group cohesiveness* (Cartwright & Zander, 1968). Thus it seems clear that the nature of the attraction bonds that form depends strongly on the size of the group. Other variables may be almost as potent—for example, sex composition, age distribution, and ethnic backgrounds of group members.

In addition to size and other background variables, the course of the interaction will be affected by the purpose of the individuals in coming together. People meet and groups form for many purposes: work tasks, sociability, competition, and so on. The actual dynamics of the way a group behaves should differ somewhat for each different purpose the group has. The difference in ongoing group processes should therefore affect the ways in which attraction develops within the group context.

One other dimension on which people in a group differ is *authority*, or *power*. One hypothesis is that strong affection or friendship can develop only between two people who have about equal power over each other. Other terms such as admiration or respect apply to superiors, but friendship does not. When two people of differing authority form bonds of friendship, as sometimes happens, the authority difference between them tends to erode. Large, formal organizations try to prevent people at different levels of authority from associating too closely. For example, military organizations have separate social clubs for officers and for enlisted men. The danger is real; an infection of intimate relations without regard to social rank could destroy the organization, because it would destroy the authority hierarchy on which the organization is based. Affection, friendship, and intimate relations tend toward mutuality of authority and power between the people involved in those relations.

Affiliation and relationships.   Affiliation is not based solely on physical interaction. Relationships also affect affiliation. *Relationship* is an abstract concept that may be conceived in many different ways and at different levels of complexity. There are a great many relationship terms, though not as many as there are personality-trait terms. Some examples of relationship terms are: citizen–foreigner, acquaintance–stranger, friend–nonfriend, family–nonfamily, club member–non-club member, and so on. These terms denote one's inclusion in or exclusion from a relationship in defined-membership classes. Other types of relationship terms imply stronger interaction connections between two people: husband–wife, parent–child, teacher–student, counselor–client, clerk–customer, and the like. Each pair is an example of a *role relationship*. A *role* is a socially defined set of expectations with rules for permissible and obligatory behavior that govern the relationship. For example, it is proper and expected that husband and wife will kiss passionately, but such behavior within any of the other role sets mentioned is considered improper.

Relationships may vary in how intimate/nonintimate they are. For example, husband–wife and parent–child are more intimate relationships than teacher–student, which in turn is more intimate than clerk–customer. *Intimacy* means the degree of closeness two people achieve. *Closeness* means both physical closeness (being together, touching) and psychological closeness. *Psychological closeness* can be defined informally as how many dark secrets two people are willing to share with each other. Stated positively, psychological closeness is based on personal self-disclosures between two people; the more they disclose and the greater the sanctity of topics discussed, the greater the intimacy.

Historically, the meaning of intimacy may have changed over the last 300 years. Gadlin (1977) noted that in Colonial times there was very little privacy, and people were almost continually under each other's surveillance. In spatial terms people were very intimate. However, the psychological sense of intimacy as sharing one's inner self with another did not exist, apparently because the strong sense of self as a unique entity did not exist then. Behavior, even between spouses, was more formal than today. For our generation psychological closeness to another is probably the most important component of intimacy.

It is usually assumed that the more intimate two people are, the more they will like each other. This assumption is true for a number of relationship types such as friends, spouses, and lovers, but it is not invariably true. For example, a client may reveal to a counselor the most intimate and anguishing of life's details, but it is improper for a deep attraction to develop between client and counselor. Their rules of interaction permit the most intimate of disclosures (communication intimacy) during the therapeutic hour but require somewhat aloof, formal relations otherwise (avoidance of physical or spatial intimacy). In fact, many counselors try not to see clients in other situations in order to avoid any transfer of emotions associated with therapy to other contexts. Such avoidance suggests an intuitive awareness that intimate communications in interaction do rather naturally tend to be associated with strong affective bonds.

Our concern is mostly with relationships—such as friends, lovers, and married couples—in which intimate behavior is positively associated with attraction. In such relationships the role definitions are broad enough so that the people have a great deal of behavioral freedom with respect to each other. They may show themselves to each other at their best and worst moments. They are free to talk to each other about practically anything, to chastise, forgive, comfort, protect, and care for each other. Such relationships may be defined as permitting a fuller range of oneself to be related to another self. In Martin Buber's (1958) conception such relationships have a larger proportion of *I-Thou* than *I-It* interactions.

Role relations versus person relations.   The concept of *role* was introduced and defined previously. Role is a very important concept in sociology; some sociologists would say that it is their most important concept. A few sociologists argue that all human relationships are role relationships, but most psychologists would probably not agree. Psychologists view an individual as possessing an organized pattern of traits, beliefs, values, and behavior styles that collectively may be called *personality*. Each individual also has a variety of role relationships; we are never just one thing. All the characteristics of the personality plus all the role relations one has define the person. One's own cognitive schema about one's personality and roles defines one's *self* or *self-concept*. Thus we view the concept of *person* more broadly than mere role relationships. We are persons first and bundles of roles second. One implication of this discussion is that our interactions with others vary on a dimension that may be called *formal role relations* at one end and *person relations* at the other end. Many formal roles (for example, clerk or customer) require rather rigid behavior patterns. One does not convey much sense of a full person within such a relation. Other roles are much more complex; they consist of subroles and provide very broad ranges for behavioral variation. Such relations almost require the full range of person commitment in order to endure. Imagine a husband and wife behaving toward each other in the rigid stereotyped ways of clerk–customer! Unfortunately, some couples do behave in almost such a manner; their marriages tend not to endure.

Despite the most careful attempts to sort out and define the various terms precisely, it is still possible for the richness of social life to provide conceptual puzzles. The human relationship of prostitute–client is common in most societies. It is also nearly always illegal. Why? One conceptual question that arises is whether this relationship is mostly personal or mostly a formal role relationship. The interaction basis is one of the most intimate in human life—sexuality. Yet there is a formal element involved: the client pays money to the prostitute much the same as the customer pays a clerk. But in a given case the client may talk in depth about life, and possibly the prostitute will also. Real affection is sometimes displayed, in addition to the raw fact of sexual intercourse. Yet, when the hour is over, both persons go their own way, perhaps never to meet again. The client becomes one more "john" to the prostitute, who becomes one more "whore" to the client. It all seems quite stylized, almost ritualistic. Yet two people have shared a rather extensive part of their persons with each other. Which was it, a person relationship or a role relationship? Perhaps society is confused, too; perhaps that is one reason why the relationship is illegal.

Theories of Attraction

During the past quarter-century psychological theories have tended to stress either *motivation* or *cognition*. For example, motivational versus cognitive theories of learning has a prolific history. Theories of attitude change also tend to stress either motivation (affect, drive reduction, reinforcement, and so on) or cognition (information processing, information integration, perceptual shifts, and the like). This preference for one type of theory over another most likely stems from philosophic and personality differences among social scientists. The difference is a preference, because a clear separation between cognition and affect cannot be made in the real world. Indeed, this chapter has linked cognitive and affective processes as one complex unit, because they cannot be readily distinguished in empirical reality. Nevertheless, it is useful to study the world analytically, as if it could be pulled apart strand by strand. One function of theories is to provide a definite perspective from which to view and interpret the world. It is the theorist's prerogative to take any creative approach desired and see where it leads.

To review, the two theoretical approaches to the study of attraction are:

1. *Cognitive*—Several varieties of consistency or balance theories, and recent versions of theories of attribution processes.
2. *Motivational*—Several different kinds of reinforcement theories.

We will first consider balance theory as an example of a cognitive theory of attraction and then consider two versions of reinforcement theory.

A Balance-Theory Approach to Attraction

Balance means harmony or equilibrium among elements in a set. There are several different balance theories, but all are based on an original theory proposed by Heider (1958). A version proposed by Newcomb

(1961) pertains most directly to attraction. Newcomb's theory, called the A-B-X model, consists of three conceptual elements: the actor A, whose perspective is being taken; another person B, perceived by A and related to A in some way; and object X, which may be another person. Actor A also perceives the relationship between B and X. For simplicity only two relationships are allowed—liking and disliking. The possible combinations of liking among A, B, and X are shown in Figure 1-2. Some examples may be helpful. In case 1, A likes B, and A likes X. It ought to follow that B also likes X. Since B does like X, the triad of three elements A, B, and X is in balance with respect to their liking relationships, as perceived by A. In case 4, A dislikes B and A dislikes X; both B and X are perceived by A as rascals. But two rascals ought to like each other. We see that B does like X, and the triad is balanced. Consider case 6 for an instance of imbalance. A likes B; perhaps they are friends. A also likes X. But A perceives that B dislikes X. This perception causes imbalance for person A. It is unpleasant to have two good friends who dislike each other.

Substance can be given to each of the other cases in Figure 1-2 in the same way. There is a simple rule that can be used to determine whether a triad is balanced or imbalanced. If the product of the three signs is positive, the triad is balanced. If the product of the three signs is negative, the triad is imbalanced. Balance theories assume that balance is a

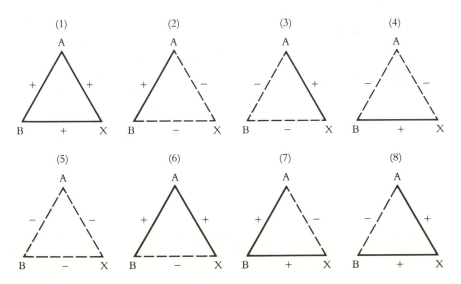

FIGURE 1-2. Examples of balance and imbalance. Solid lines represent liking; broken lines represent disliking. A triad is balanced if the product of the three signs is positive, and imbalanced if the product is negative. The four triads in the upper part of the figure are balanced; the four triads in the lower part are imbalanced.

natural state of affairs, intrinsically pleasant, and that imbalance is intrinsically unpleasant. When a situation is imbalanced in the perception of A, there is a motive to restore balance, or a "strain toward symmetry" (Newcomb, 1961). Of course, the situation can be schematized from person B's point of view, and B may or may not perceive the situation in the same way that A perceives it. If both people perceive imbalance, however, there should be strong pressures to restore the balance, and persons A and B usually will communicate about the unpleasant state of affairs. For example, in case 6, person A might try to persuade person B to like X. If the persuasion is successful, all three signs become positive, and the triad is balanced. However, person B might try to persuade person A to dislike X. If B is successful, balance would be restored in this way, because the triad would then have two negative signs and one positive sign.

There is some evidence supporting a balance approach to attraction (Miller & Norman, 1976), although it is not as strong as some would like. Most of the relevant studies have used paper-and-pencil ratings of abstract situations. One intruding variable is that subjects tend to be very concerned about agreement and attraction between persons A and B and will often sacrifice overall balance to ensure that relations between A and B are positive.

Balance theory can be applied directly to the concept of *attraction* in the following examples. Suppose Pam (A) is an ardent supporter of the Equal Rights Amendment (ERA) and feels very good about her stance. Suppose also that Joan (B) is opposed to the ERA (X). Pam may infer that Joan will dislike or disapprove of Pam's attitudes, so it is expected that Pam may dislike Joan. A balanced triad (one positive, two negative signs) is preserved in this way. Suppose, instead, that Joan, like Pam, supports the ERA. Pam will infer that Joan will approve of Pam's attitudes, and therefore Pam likes Joan. Balance is maintained because all the relationship signs are positive. As another example suppose that Neil (A) has a very positive self-concept (X) and that he perceives that Mark likes and respects him. Neil should in turn like Mark because liking of Mark implies a balanced relationship. If Neil dislikes himself, however, and Mark likes Neil, then the only way a balanced triad can be achieved (unless Neil and Mark discuss things) is for Neil to dislike Mark. Thus we have the anomalous prediction that persons of low self-esteem—that is, those who dislike themselves—will dislike persons who like them. This prediction does hold under some conditions.

Aronson and Cope (1968) conducted an interesting experiment that tested case 3 shown in Figure 1-2. This situation may be described by the hypothesis "My enemy's enemy is my friend," the title of Aronson and Cope's article. In the experiment subjects (A) wrote essays that purportedly were measures of creativity. The experimenter (B) informed subjects that the essays were uncreative, but the evaluation was given very harshly to half the subjects and very pleasantly to the other half. Just after the appraisal of the essays, the experimenter's supervisor (X) called the experimenter out of the room and delivered either a blistering condemnation or lavish praise for a report the experimenter had written. The experimenter returned to the room and sent the subject to the psychology office to get his or her credit points. The departmental secretary administered a questionnaire and also asked the subject if he or she would be willing to make phone calls to recruit local residents as subjects for the supervisor to use in a research project that the supervisor was conducting. The number of phone calls the subject was willing to make was the primary variable of interest.

The results are shown in Table 1-1. The results indicate that subjects were willing to work more for a supervisor who treated a harsh experimenter harshly (my enemy's enemy is my friend) than for a supervisor who treated a pleasant experimenter harshly (my friend's enemy is my enemy), or for a supervisor who treated a harsh experimenter pleasantly (my enemy's friend is my enemy). Another balance prediction that was confirmed was that a relatively large number of calls would be made for a supervisor who treated a pleasant experimenter pleasantly (my friend's friend is my friend). Since the supervisor's treatment of the experimenter was unrelated to the experimenter's treatment of the subject, the results offered relatively pure and striking support for balance theory.

TABLE 1-1   Mean number of phone calls volunteered on behalf of supervisor

Experimenter's behavior to subject	Supervisor's behavior to experimenter	
	Harsh	*Pleasant*
Harsh	12.1	6.2
Pleasant	6.3	13.5

From "My Enemy's Enemy Is My Friend," by E. Aronson and V. Cope. In *Journal of Personality and Social Psychology*, 1968, *8*, 8–12. Copyright 1968 by the American Psychological Association. Reprinted by permission.

Balance theory can account for the results of many attraction experiments and undoubtedly is applicable to many everyday situations, particularly situations in which three-person "triangles" are involved. This approach has not received as much attention as reinforcement theories. More recent research (for instance, Insko & Adewole, 1979) has tested sophisticated hypotheses in very complex experimental designs. Eventually there may be a comprehensive cognitive theory of attraction based on the balance approach.

Reinforcement Theory and Attraction

Reinforcement theories are most closely associated with learning theories. Two general types of learning theories have been developed: theories of classical conditioning and theories of instrumental conditioning. In *classical conditioning* any stimulus (the conditioned stimulus) associated physically or in time with an unconditioned stimulus (one that "naturally" elicits some type of "unconditioned" response) will, on repeated pairings, come to elicit a conditioned response similar in form to the unconditioned response. When a dog is presented with food and a bell is rung simultaneously, the dog will, after several pairings of food and bell, start to salivate when the bell is rung alone. Food is the unconditioned stimulus and salivation is the unconditioned response. The bell is the conditioned stimulus, and the salivation elicited by the bell is the conditioned response. *Instrumental conditioning* is exhibited when any response that is closely followed by a reinforcer becomes more frequent over time. A rat in a Skinner box given a food pellet for pushing a bar will push the bar more and more frequently in order to obtain additional food pellets. The reinforcer of food for a hungry rat is said to control the behavior of bar pressing.

We will consider two specific reinforcement theories of attraction: a reinforcement–affect theory (Byrne, 1969; Clore & Byrne, 1974; Lott & Lott, 1974) and a gain/loss theory proposed by Aronson (1969).

Reinforcement–affect theory.   In its classical form reinforcement theory assumes that attraction toward a person is an internal response, often shown in overt behavior occurring any time an individual experiences reward in the presence of that person (Lott & Lott, 1974, p. 172). A hungry individual presented with food (unconditioned stimulus) will experience pleasure (unconditioned response) upon its consumption. A person associated with the food consumption is a conditioned stimulus for the hungry individual. The pleasure derived from the food will be attached to the person who is present. Thus attraction to the person is in this case a classically conditioned response. Dislike for another person may possibly be conditioned in the same way if the unconditioned stimulus is aversive. For example, it has been shown that attraction to strangers based on written descriptions is reduced in hot and crowded environments (Griffitt, 1970; Griffitt & Veitch, 1971). Presumably the negative feelings caused by the heat and crowding were directly conditioned to the stimulus stranger, with the result of relative disliking. Kenrick and Johnson (1979) pointed out that aversive environments may cause disliking only for abstract strangers, but a real, in-the-flesh stranger may be liked better in aversive than in normal environments. Other people who are physically present may help to reduce the negative feelings caused by stressful events; this stress reduction is pleasant. The result may in fact be conditioned liking for the people present.

Attraction can also be instrumentally conditioned. For example, a mother who praises a child is administering a reinforcement. In time the child will learn to work hard for such reinforcements. By the time people are adults, they regard expressions of social approval as potent sources of reward, and they become attracted to individuals who express approval of them. Byrne (1969) has developed the reinforcement model of attraction most completely. The general assumption is that "attraction toward X is a function of the relative number of rewards and punishments associated with X" (Byrne, 1969, p. 67). The formulation is general since X can be almost anything—a nonliving object or another human being. Rewards and punishments vary widely. What is punishment for one person may be rewarding for another. It is assumed, however, that the divergence of rewards and punishments for adults can be traced back to association with the direct physical experience of pleasure and pain in infancy and childhood.

Byrne (1969) proposed a *law of attraction,* which states that attraction toward X is a positive linear (or direct) function of the proportion of positive reinforcements received from X. The law of attraction was first formulated to account for the effects of similarity and dissimilarity on attraction. In reinforcement-theory terms, why is similarity so often a positive reinforcer and dissimilarity a negative reinforcer? (Here we assume the reinforcement value of similarity; specific evidence will be considered in Chapter 2.)

One answer to this question was provided by White (1959), who proposed that people have a very general need to be competent in dealing with their environment: a need to understand, cope with, be effective in, and master the wide array of problems and puzzles that life poses for us. White named this general need state the *effectance motive.* In terms of social relations, to be competent means to be able to understand other people, to predict their actions, to have a sense of certainty about one's own actions, and in general to exist in a meaningful and integrated flow of life with other people. Much of the reality that we experience is social reality (Festinger, 1950)—socially defined and arbitrary—in contrast with the reality of the physical world. Should you eat fried chicken with your fingers or with your fork? Nature does not tell you what to do; social convention dictates the correct choice. Given the arbitrary nature of social convention, the definition of *social reality* lies in people's opinions, attitudes, and values. If another person holds the same attitudes and values that you hold, that person validates your version of social reality (Festinger, 1954). In such validation the similar other bolsters your sense of competence in dealing with the social world. The person provides satisfaction for your effectance motive. Dissimilarity can be threatening to one's social definition of the world and calls into question one's competence in dealing with the world. Such negative arousal of effectance is very unpleasant. One way of reducing the unpleasantness is by relative rejection of the person. Thus similarity/dissimilarity on various attributes serves as a powerful source of reinforcement, which results in various degrees of attraction.

Many stimuli can serve as reinforcements for attraction. Complementarity of personality needs or social roles may result in mutually reinforcing behavior. Self-disclosure may be reinforcing to another because it implies trust in the other and may in turn stimulate disclosure from the other. Many verbal reinforcements may be exchanged during the course of mutual self-disclosure. Positive or negative evaluations of one's behavior or performance may be powerful rewards or punishments, respectively. These issues are discussed in detail in Chapter 2.

One interesting issue is the question of which is most rewarding: a constant series of positive evaluations received from another person, or an initial negative series of evaluations followed by a positive series of evaluations. A similar question may be posed for punishment. Is a constant series of negative evaluations more punishing than a series that begins positively, but turns negative over time? The effects of the sequencing of evaluations on attraction was studied by Aronson (1969) and his students in a series of experiments designed to test what is called the gain/loss model of attraction.

Gain/loss theory.   In an initial experiment Aronson and Linder (1965) proposed that gain or loss of esteem from another person is a more potent source of reward and punishment than constant praise or criticism. The prediction was that a person who provided a gain in esteem would be better liked than a constant rewarder, and a person who provided a loss in esteem would be more disliked than a constant punisher.

The experiment was rather complex; it involved an experimenter and two female subjects (one of whom was a confederate of the experimenter). Through an elaborate sequence of explanations and deceptions, a scenario was developed that allowed the confederate (posing as a subject) to give evaluations of liking for the subject on several different occasions. The real subject was made aware of these evaluations, which differed, or varied in four ways. In one condition the confederate was always positive (constant positive condition) in her statements about the subject. In the second condition the confederate was always negative (constant negative condition). In the third condition the confederate started off negative, but gradually became quite positive over seven sessions (the gain condition). In the fourth condition the confederate started off positive, but gradually became negative (the loss condition). In this experiment the sequence of evaluations of the subject by the confederate was what is called the manipulated independent variable. The dependent variable, or the variable to be studied, was a measure of the real subject's attraction toward the confederate. The scale ranged from −10 for dislike to +10 for like. The subject liked the confederate much more in the constant positive condition (6.42) than in the constant negative condition (2.52), as might be expected. Of special importance was the finding that the confederate was liked more in the gain condition (7.67) than in the constant positive condition and was disliked more in the loss condition (.87) than in the constant negative condition. As predicted, change in evaluations received from another had a more potent effect on attraction than constancy of evaluations. The gain/loss theory was neatly supported.

One may reasonably ask why gain or loss exerts a strong effect on attraction responses. Aronson (1969) gave several possible explanations:

1. *Anxiety reduction*—Negative evaluation from others causes anxiety. The gain condition is one of strong anxiety reduction, with consequent high positive feelings toward the evaluator. Likewise, a positive evaluation that changes to negative stimulates a great deal of anxiety, more so than continuous negative evaluation.

2. *Competence*—If an evaluator changes his or her opinion over time, it may be due to the efforts of the person being evaluated. In the gain condition a positive sense of competence would be created, but in the loss condition the opposite effect might occur.

3. *Discernment*—The change in opinion of the evaluator over time may imply that he or she is a discerning individual. In the gain condition the discernment works in the "right way" to prove that one is indeed a worthy individual. Unfortunately, in the loss condition the discerning evaluator proves that one is perhaps a dolt after all. The evaluation in the loss condition hurts very much and may cause intense rejection of the evaluator.

4. *Contrast*—Positive things that follow negative things may seem even more positive by way of contrast. The same reasoning applies to negative things that follow positive things.

All these explanations may be involved to some extent in accounting for gain/loss effects. A large number of relevant experiments have been conducted during the past decade (for example, those reviewed in Mettee & Aronson, 1974). Generally, the gain effect is easier to obtain than the loss effect (Clore, Wiggins, & Itkin, 1975). However, since the research findings have been somewhat ambiguous, at present there is still uncertainty as to exactly how gain and loss effects determine attraction ratings.

If we put gain/loss theory in everyday terms, we realize that, if we are consistently friends or consistently enemies with someone else, our attitudes toward that person are fairly stable. If, on the other hand, a previous enemy begins making overtures of friendship and appears to like us, we may be initially wary but we are likely to be pleased also. But, if a friend begins treating us shabbily, we are likely to react with hurt and very deep anger. We suffer deeply when we are betrayed by a friend.

Summary

Attraction between people is a complex action system with belief (cognitive), emotional (affective), and behavioral components. The emotional component is manifested in liking and disliking; the belief component is manifested by a structure of knowledge about another person; the behavioral component consists of both behavioral tendencies and direct actions toward others. This approach views attraction as a type of attitude, with the attitude objects as concrete persons. Other kinds of attitudes are about abstract entities and objects, such as political issues or ethnic groups. Face-to-face interaction is the basis for the occurrence of attraction in daily life. Through interaction we learn to attribute evaluative meaning to others. Evaluation is a pervasive aspect of life, and liking/disliking others is only one of the more important facets of evaluation. Our concepts are so value laden that the cognitive and affective components of attraction are almost invariably yoked to each other. One result is that the two components tend to be linked as one complex "cognitive–affective component," and overt behavior tends to be split off as a relatively separate component.

The consideration of attraction and affiliation leads to questions about the nature of groups and to the study of relationships among people. The concept of role is one approach to the study of relationships. Many roles are rigid and prevent a full expression of the person. The relationships of most interest allow a broad range of behavior, full expression of the personality, and a high degree of intimacy. Husband–wife and parent–child are examples of such broad relationships.

Theories of attraction tend to have either a cognitive or a motivational orientation. Newcomb's A–B–X model, a variant of Heider's balance model, is an example of a cognitive theory. Two reinforcement theories serve as examples of motivational theory: reinforcement–affect theory, and the gain/loss model.

2

Attitudes and Attraction

This chapter is concerned with attraction as a type of attitude, or at least with the cognitive–affective aspect of an attitude. The focus is primarily on the feelings and thoughts that one person holds toward another person and secondarily on behavior. To some extent this approach conveys the impression that attraction is a process of being lost in thought about another person. This focus is indeed an important part of the scientific study of attraction. However, to study attraction as all thought and no action would be sterile. Chapter 3 provides a needed balance by examining the behavioral–interactional–affiliative aspect of attraction.

Similarity and Attraction

The proverb "birds of a feather flock together" can be translated into the research hypothesis "The more similar two people are on any of a wide variety of attributes, the more attracted to each other they will be." This hypothesis, or more generally the relationship between similarity and attraction, has received extensive research.

Social psychologists study attraction primarily through laboratory experiments. Most attitude research tries to find situations or variables that will change an attitude. Another way of stating the matter is to say that researchers attempt to manipulate independent variables to cause an attitude to change. With this approach to the study of attitudes, attitude change is often viewed as a dependent variable. Given that attraction is thought of as a type of attitude toward specific persons, it is natural for researchers to treat attraction as a dependent variable and search for independent variables that will cause greater or lesser degrees of liking (the attraction response). Often these experiments use relatively impoverished stimulus situations to try to achieve control. Manipulation of independent variables by written material is common, and research subjects are often asked to rate strangers they never meet. There is nothing wrong with this approach, especially in the early development of an area of scientific research. However, one should keep in mind that such well-controlled laboratory examples may or may not be used to generalize to ongoing social life. Therefore it is wise to apply mentally results of such experiments to everyday examples. This commonsense test will sometimes suggest further research or qualifications of research results. On occasion common sense will be surprised, but eventually it must be satisfied, or else research findings are not likely to be accepted.

A number of independent variables thought to affect attraction have been studied. Several of the more important ones are: similarity, complementarity, reciprocity, self-disclosure, desirable characteristics, and physical attractiveness. Our concern is to examine the evidence in favor of or against the similarity–attraction hypothesis in daily life as well as in the scientific laboratory. We would also do well to inquire about the limit of the hypothesis—that is, to ask under what conditions it breaks down.

An Example from Everyday Life

Miami, Florida, is ethnically diverse. The three major groups are Black, Hispanic, and Anglo. Each group consists of several subgroups. For example, Hispanics include Puerto Ricans, Chileans, Colombians, contingents from every country in Central America, and Cubans; the predominant language of these groups is Spanish. Anglos have migrated to Miami from many places, and a variety of dialects can be heard: New York twang is as common as a midwestern drawl. Blacks also have migrated to Miami from many other areas, including Haiti, and they too speak with a variety of accents.

Miami is *not* a melting pot. The three major groups tend to live in different, well-defined geographical areas. In fact, one section of Miami is even called "Little Havana" due to a high concentration of Cubans. In the spring of 1980 two events occurred at the same time that had considerable consequence for the area. (1) A savage riot confined to Black areas resulted in several deaths and millions of dollars in property damage. The riot's ostensible cause was the acquittal of several White policemen charged with brutality in the slaying of a Black man. The riot caused enormous apprehension in the Anglo and Hispanic communities. (2) An excess of 100,000 Cuban refugees arrived over a one-month period in Key West, Florida, on a freedom flotilla, an armada of many hundreds of small boats. This vast immigration was against official government policy. Although many thousands of refugees were settled in other areas of the country, the majority were destined for Miami. Many Anglos were heard to declare that within six months all the refugees would find their way back to Miami.

Among Anglos the large immigration of Cubans caused at least as much anger and resentment as the ghetto riot. The sentiments expressed conjured up endless hordes of Spanish-speaking immigrants inundating the Anglo culture. Some resentment was also expressed in the Black community. The reservations were mostly economic; unemployment was high in the Black community, and the influx of immigrants meant increased competition for scarce jobs.

Both Spanish and English had been approved as official languages of Dade County in 1973. In July of 1980 a petition was circulated for a November election ballot issue to make English the only official language. As might be expected, the petition originated in the Anglo community. A group within the Hispanic community organized almost immediately to defeat the petition drive. Despite disclaimers by Anglos, many Hispanics felt that ethnic prejudice was behind the petition. That November, voters approved English as the only official language.

Miami, circa 1982, could well be described as an arena in which three cultures clash. Why? What happened to the liberal idea that contact with other cultures is enriching? Careful listening to Anglo complaints about Hispanics provides one very general answer—*they are different*. Many specific complaints are made by Anglos: inconvenient language differences (with an unwillingness to learn English), aggressive behavior, poor driving, noisy parties, loud radios late at night, offensive style of dress, and pushy behavior. Most of these complaints can be translated into one generic complaint—they are dissimilar to me, my habits, my beliefs, and my values. Such dissimilarity is somehow a threat. It is uncomfortable to live with, and it creates ill will and even active dislike.

Miami is probably no different from any other large city where diverse ethnic groups are thrown into contact with one another. People seem to prefer to associate primarily with others from their own ethnic group, and to some extent they dislike and avoid people from different ethnic groups. The general observation from daily life seems to be that people like "their own kind" and relatively dislike the others. This general inclination is called *ethnocentrism,* and it is common to the human condition. Ethnocentrism may be one manifestation at the cultural level of the similarity–attraction hypothesis; the more similar others are to us on a wide variety of attributes, the more we like them. This informal example of ethnocentrism provides intuitive support for the similarity–attraction hypothesis. However, it is not rigorous evidence, because ethnic conflict is probably caused by many factors. For hard evidence the hypothesis should be subjected to the test of scientific research.

Evidence from the Laboratory

There are two main types of evidence for the hypothesis. In one type researchers simply measure both similarity and attraction to see if the two variables go together, or covary. The measure of the natural covariation of two variables is called *correlation*. The second type of evidence is provided by the laboratory experiment, in which the researcher manipulates the independent variable (in this case similarity) to find out whether it is causally related to the dependent variable (attraction).

Extensive correlational evidence supporting the similarity–attraction hypothesis goes back many years (Byrne, 1971). For example, data show that spouses are more similar in opinions and preferences than unmarried couples. Friends have also shown substantial correlations between various beliefs and values. One problem with much of this research is that it is unclear what causes what. Similarity may have been a causal variable in the formation of friendships and marriages, but the hypothesis that people become more similar as a result of association is equally plausible. The traditional cliché that correlation does not demonstrate causation applies equally well in this case.

During the past two decades, several researchers have conducted vigorous research programs on attraction, assessing the similarity–attraction hypothesis with well-controlled laboratory experiments. Donn Byrne has been a particularly active scholar in this area. His research was so extensive that an entire volume was required to summarize it (1971), and he has done much more work since then.

Most of Byrne's experiments have followed a standard experimental procedure. Subjects (usually college students) first complete a questionnaire designed to measure their attitudes or personality dispositions. One frequently used measure is a 56-item Survey of Attitudes. Based on the subject's responses, a questionnaire is constructed that is either very similar or very dissimilar to the subject's questionnaire. The bogus questionnaire, which is attributed to another person, is presented to the subject for evaluation. The subject's task is to form an impression of and rate the person on several items on a form called the Interpersonal Judgment Scale. The two critical items are personal feelings and willingness to work within an experiment. The sum of the ratings of these two items is considered a measure of attraction toward the hypothetical stranger.

This procedure allows precise variation in the degree of similarity of the subject to the hypothetical stimulus person. One variable that proved to be of major importance was the proportion of similar attitudes shared by the subject and stranger. An extensive study by Byrne and Nelson (1965) found that, as the proportion of similar attitudes increased, attraction as measured by the Interpersonal Judgment Scale increased in almost perfect proportion. A graph of the relationship is shown in Figure 2-1. In fact, the relationship could be described quite well by an equation: $Y = 5.44X + 6.62$, where X is the proportion of similar attitudes and Y is the dependent variable, attraction. Such a relationship is called a *linear function,* and if very precise, the relationship may be called a scientific law. (See the section on "Hypothesis Testing" in the Appendix for further discussion of linear functions.) Byrne believed that his data were precise enough so that he could speak of the relationship as an empirical law of attraction.

The strong relationship between similarity and attraction has been found for many other types of similarity as well. These include similarity on economic background (Byrne, Clore, & Worchel, 1966), personality characteristics (Byrne, Griffitt, & Stefaniak, 1967), and self-esteem (Hendrick & Page, 1970). Variation in similarity on almost any dimension seems to work.

One issue of interest is whether the strong relationship between simi-

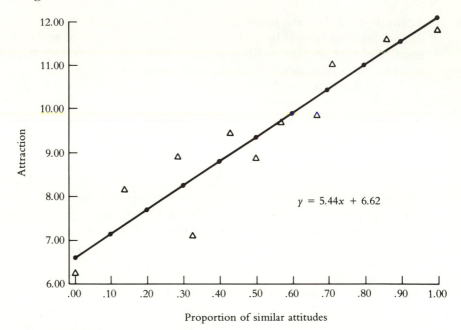

FIGURE 2-1   Attraction toward a stranger as a linear function of proportion of similar attitudes. *(From "Attraction as a Linear Function of Proportion of Positive Reinforcements," by D. Byrne and D. Nelson. In* Journal of Personality and Social Psychology, *1965, 1, 659–663. Copyright 1965 by the American Psychological Association. Reprinted by permission.)*

larity and attraction found in the laboratory translates directly into everyday life. The best guess is that the translation is not perfect. In daily life people often discuss their attitudinal disagreements. Most social occasions are defined as positive or at least peaceful. Therefore there are presssures on people to get along with each other and not to disrupt the fabric of the social occasion. This general norm of peacefulness is sometimes called the *strain toward consensus.*

It may be that, when people do disagree openly, the opportunity to reply will result in fewer negative feelings than when no reply can be made. Engaging the other in reply sets up an interaction bond in which the other is oriented to and treated as a person, rather than as an anonymous stranger. The chance to reply also gives one the opportunity to change the other person's attitude, to make it more similar to one's own. Several experiments have shown that the opportunity to reply to a disagreeing stranger results in less-negative attraction ratings. For example, Brink (1977) manipulated the subjects' opportunity to reply to a disagreeing stranger by creating four different experimental conditions:

1. No reply (standard control condition).
2. Uncommunicated reply (a reply was formulated but not delivered).
3. Reply only to the experimenter.
4. Reply directly to the dissimilar stranger.

The results showed that attraction ratings for the stranger were about equally negative in conditions 1, 2, and 3, but were more positive in condition 4. Other data suggested that subjects in condition 4 thought that they might have persuaded the stranger to change his or her attitude.

The experiment by Brink suggests that there are boundaries or limits to the strong similarity–attraction function shown in Figure 2-1. One value of scientific procedure is that it can be used to discover the conditions under which a hypothesis is true, as well as the conditions under which it is false. It is natural for attraction researchers to search for conditions under which attraction is unrelated to similarity, and even conditions under which an inverse relation is obtained (that is, those in which increases in similarity lead to decreases in attraction).

Limits: A Reversal of the Similarity–Attraction Relation

A few studies have found such reversals. One example will illustrate the reasoning for this approach to attraction research. Hendrick and Brown (1971) first had subjects complete a form that measured their introversion or extroversion. Subjects then evaluated two stimulus strangers who had purportedly completed the same questionnaire. One stranger was extremely extroverted; the other, extremely introverted. The sample of subjects that was retained for analysis included 32 extroverts and 32 introverts. Thus subjects evaluated two strangers, one of whom was dissimilar and the other similar to themselves in introversion/extroversion. There were several dependent variables in addition to a rating of liking.

The results of the experiment are shown in Figure 2-2. The results indicate that on all the measures extroverted subjects preferred similar extroverts to dissimilar introverts. However, on measures of "liking," "interesting at a party," and "preference as a leader," introverted subjects rated the dissimilar extroverted stranger more favorably than the similar introverted stranger. Such a reversal did not hold for ratings of "reliable friend" and "honest and ethical." On these measures introverts preferred a similar other, the same as did extroverts.

There are other conditions under which the positive similarity–attraction relationship does not hold. However, the great bulk of the research finds such a relationship. It is fascinating to ponder why we treasure similarity so dearly.

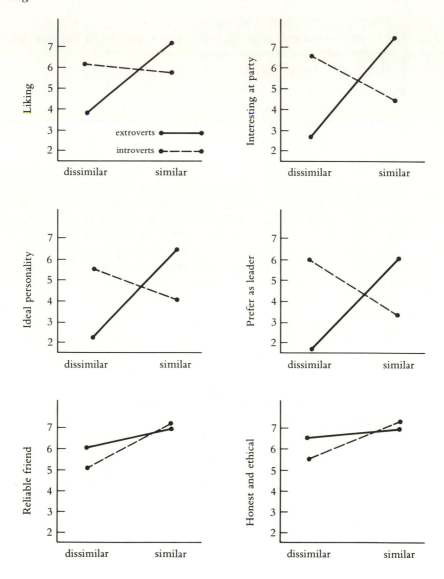

FIGURE 2-2   Similarity/Dissimilarity in Extroversion/Introversion. Each dependent variable plotted as a function of the subjects' extroversion/introversion and personality similarity/dissimilarity to the stimulus strangers. *(From "Introversion, Extroversion, and Interpersonal Attraction," by C. Hendrick and S. R. Brown. In* Journal of Personality and Social Psychology, *1971, 20, 31–36. Copyright 1971 by the American Psychological Association. Reprinted by permission.)*

Why Is Similarity So Important?

Four types of answers have been given for this question (Huston & Levinger, 1978). (1) Similarity is directly reinforcing. This answer is most often given and was considered in Chapter 1. (2) Similarity bolsters one's own sense of rightness, goodness, or self-concept. Similarity helps confirm that one is after all the very center of the universe. This answer relies on the concept of competence (or effectance) also discussed in Chapter 1. (3) Similarity anticipates a good future. Knowledge of another's similarity may cause anticipations that actual future interactions will be positive. This answer seems to be a special case of the first answer. (4) Similarity is related to attraction only because it happens to be correlated with the affective (emotional) value of another person's attributes. A few studies have purported to separate similarity from the affective value of information. Apparently it can be done in a few selected cases, and in those cases similarity is unrelated to attraction. However, it is questionable whether such separation occurs in the real world.

Complementarity and Attraction

The notion that opposites attract has existed for a long time. The basic concept is that people who differ on some attribute or on two different attributes are able to provide satisfactions to each other in ways that would not be possible if the difference did not exist. Such attributes may range from basic personality dispositions or psychological needs to relatively simple behaviors. One common example is the pair of personality needs of *nurturance* and *succorance*. A person with a strong nurturance need desires to take care of, nurture, or otherwise fuss over another person. A person with a strong succorance need desires to be taken care of and nurtured by another person. Two people, one high in nurturance and the other high in succorance, would be complementary on this pair of needs. They would satisfy each other's needs because expression of those needs in behavior toward each other would result in mutual reciprocity of behavior given and received as each expected and desired. Two persons high in the need for succorance would not be compatible in this way, because each would want to be taken care of by the other in ways the other could not give. However, it is not so clear that two persons high in nurturance would not be good for each other. They might well gain much satisfaction by alternating in active nurturant roles.

Most of the research on complementarity has focused on personality needs, such as nurturance/succorance. Most of this research has been concerned specifically with friendship formation and marital choice. Interest in the latter undoubtedly stems from our occasional perceptions of two married people who seem most unsuited for each other, as different as night and day, but yet seem quite happy with each other. One basic question would seem to be, given that similarity is generally important, in what situations or under what conditions would complementarity be expected to also enhance attraction?

Research on Complementarity

There have been many theories about complementarity. In modern social science research, Robert Winch (1958) has been one of the strongest advocates of a theory of complementary needs. Winch believes that need gratification of one person by another automatically leads to attraction. His approach therefore follows a type of reinforcement theory.

Winch does not deny the importance for mate selection of initial similarity on such variables as age, socioeconomic status, race, and educational level. However, such variables only create selection possibilities; they do not determine actual marital choices. Actual choice is made on the basis of personality needs that require fulfillment. There are two types of relevant needs.

Type I. The *same* need is gratified in both person A and person B because the need exists at different levels of intensity. An example of type-I needs might be one person with a high need for dominance and a second person with a low need for dominance (Seyfried, 1977).

Type II. The needs are *different* in type, but are of about the same intensity. The nurturance/succorance example given earlier is an example of a type-II need.

Winch's research used young married couples. This research will be discussed in more detail in Chapter 6. Unfortunately, there have been problems in replicating experiments that have found complementarity effects (for example, Murstein, 1971; Levinger, Senn, & Jorgensen, 1970). Apparently such effects are more sensitive to disruption than the more robust similarity–attraction relationship. Yet the idea persists that complementarity is important. Harrison and Saeed (1977) analyzed 800 lonely-hearts advertisements of both men and women. The content of the ads showed meshing of some needs. "Women were more likely than men to offer attractiveness, seek financial security, and seek partners who were older than themselves. Men were more likely than women to seek attractiveness, offer financial security, and seek partners who were younger than themselves" (p. 259). If complementarity is part of our culture, the question is why the phenomenon is so elusive in the laboratory.

Sex-Role Expectancy Rather than Personality Traits

Most research on complementarity has focused on personality needs. Seyfried and Hendrick (1973) suggested that the focus has been on the wrong variable. The important variable may not be personality needs at all, but *sex-role expectancy*. To a considerable extent males and females live in different cultural worlds, and they have different life roles. Our society has a set of general expectancies about the appropriate roles and behaviors for each sex, although the expectancies seem to be slowly changing. However, a female is still expected to bear children and be their major caretaker. A male is by and large still expected to be the major breadwinner while the female raises the children. Very often the attitudes and values concerning the two sex roles imply contrasting or complementary behavior. It would raise no eyebrows if Jane said "When I marry, I will enjoy preparing all the meals for my family." However, if John made the same statement, many people would consider him a little peculiar.

Our sex-role expectancies imply different role behaviors for males and for females. We expect complementary role behavior from someone of the opposite sex and are attracted (in part) to a member of the opposite sex on that basis. We are relatively unattracted to a member of the opposite sex who expresses sex-role attitudes which are appropriate for our own sex. Also, we will like a member of our own sex better when that person expresses sex-role attitudes appropriate to his or her sex and will be relatively unattracted to a person of our own sex who expresses sex-role attitudes more appropriate to the opposite sex.

To test this reasoning, Seyfried and Hendrick (1973) had male and female subjects complete a Masculine/Feminine Preferences Test that contained a number of items similar to the one on meal preparation. The subjects then formed impressions and rated their attraction toward two strangers who had ostensibly completed the same test. One stranger expressed strong masculine preferences; the other stranger expressed strong feminine preferences. Half the strangers who expressed masculine preferences were represented as males, and the other half of the strangers were represented as females. Likewise, half the strangers expressing feminine preferences were represented as females, and the other half were represented as males. Thus subjects rated their attraction toward strangers who expressed appropriate sex-role attitudes (that is, masculine male stranger and feminine female stranger), as well as strangers who expressed inappropriate sex-role attitudes (feminine male and masculine female).

The mean (or average) attraction ratings for both male and female subjects are shown in Table 2-1. These means indicate that the results were as predicted. Masculine males and feminine females were well liked by subjects of both sexes. However, feminine males were rejected

TABLE 2-1   Mean attraction ratings in the Seyfried and Hendrick study

Sex-role attitude of stranger	Male subjects		Female subjects	
	Sex of stranger			
	Male	Female	Male	Female
Masculine attitude	4.85	3.67	4.75	3.00
Feminine attitude	2.75	4.03	2.52	4.15

Note: The higher the mean, the more attraction toward the stimulus person.

From "When Do Opposites Attract? When They Are Opposite in Sex and Sex-Role Attitudes," by B. A. Seyfried and C. Hendrick. In *Journal of Personality and Social Psychology*, 1973, *25*, 15–20. Copyright 1973 by the American Psychological Association. Reprinted by permission.

by both male and female subjects. There was more tolerance for a masculine female, although such a person was not liked as well as the masculine male. The data also show a positive bias toward the masculine male, who was consistently liked better by subjects of both sexes than the feminine female. There is also a hint in the data that females have some small measure of freedom to become like males in their sex-role attitudes, but that males are most unfree to become like females.

The Seyfried and Hendrick study demonstrates that sex-role attitude is one basis for complementary attraction. We are attracted to someone of the opposite sex who expresses sex-role attitudes opposite or complementary to our own. However, if the other person is of the same sex, we prefer similarity—we want the person to hold the same sex-role attitudes that we hold. Thus it would appear that roles and role relationships are the variables that should receive the most intensive study with regard to complementarity and attraction. Some authors have claimed that our recent sexual revolution will eventually promote unisex attitudes and behaviors. It will be of great interest to see whether the complementarity of attraction based on contrasting sex-role attitudes will continue to exist in a decade or so.

Reciprocity and Attraction

To *reciprocate* means literally to give and take or exchange mutually. People engage in reciprocal behaviors endlessly, ranging from the exchange of physical commodities to subtle sentiments, expressions of approval, and love. It seems reasonable that reciprocity of at least some behaviors is related to the development of attraction. In fact, Lickona (1974, p. 35) believes that "reciprocity is at the heart of human attraction" and is "a central dynamic in human attraction, with meaning for everything from making conversation to making love."

Reciprocity in human behavior has been viewed as highly significant for social life by many scholars. A sociologist, Alvin Gouldner (1960), hypothesized a universal positive *norm of reciprocity* with two components: (1) people should help others who help them, and (2) people should not hurt others who help them. There is also a negative form of the norm, though perhaps not as universal, that people should repay harm and injury in kind (an eye for an eye, a tooth for a tooth).

Reciprocity of Liking

Almost by definition a friend is someone who likes you. It is a popular truism that we tend to like someone who likes us. Most of us have at one time or another been informed by an acquaintance that so-and-so likes us. It is almost impossible not to have an immediate feeling of warm regard for so-and-so. We reciprocate the other's perceived liking for us with liking for the other. Reciprocity of liking depends upon the fact that having someone like us is a potent source of reward. Only in a society in which people have a strong need for the approval and esteem of others would perception of their liking have such a strong effect. Berscheid and Walster (1969) concluded that we do indeed live in such a society. Advertising presents the message in a massive way; if you will buy and use brand X, other people will approve of you and like you.

If liking from another is a reward, then, when a person receives information that he or she is liked by the other, he or she should reciprocate that liking. Backman and Secord (1959) tested this hypothesis by forming small discussion groups of subject strangers who, prior to the initial meeting, were individually informed that (bogus) personality-test information indicated that certain other members of the group would be highly attracted to the subject. An informal group discussion was held at the first meeting. Afterward the experimenter told the group that they might eventually be divided into two-person groups. Each member was asked to rank the three other members of the group for preference as a discussion partner. The entire group continued to meet for six sessions, and the same ranking of preferred discussion partners was obtained after the third and sixth sessions. The results showed that at the end of the first session, subjects clearly preferred as potential discussion partners the other group members whom the experimenter had indicated (falsely) would like them. However, this preference had disappeared by the third group meeting. Subjects were no more likely to choose expected likers than other members of the group as a discussion partner. Thus the anticipation of liking stimulated initial reciprocal liking. However, the experimenters chose the designated liker at random, and as the sessions went on the actual attributes of specific individuals made more of an impact, as might be expected. Backman and Secord's (1959) experiment is important because it demonstrates that people tend to reciprocate initial anticipated liking. If the feelings are genuine, very often the interaction should be rewarding enough so that over time strong mutual attraction will develop.

Liking and Reciprocity of Other Types of Behavior

One interesting issue is, given that two people like each other, whether that liking will cause them each to benefit the other in exchanges of other types of behaviors. Current experimental evidence suggests that the answer is no. Stapleton, Nacci, and Tedeschi (1973) induced pairs of female subjects to either like or dislike each other by manipulating their perceptions of similarity or dissimilarity of beliefs. One subject was actually a confederate of the experimenter. In the second phase of the experiment the confederate gave "points" of experimental time to the subject either one, five, or nine times out of ten trials. Before each trial the subject estimated the probability that the confederate would give points on the next trial. After the ten trials roles were exchanged and the subject was allowed to administer points to the confederate for ten trials. Afterward the subject rated her liking for the confederate. Results showed that the subject reciprocated points strictly on the basis of how many points the confederate had given her. The subject's level of initial attraction toward the confederate did not affect the point allocation to the confederate. However, the stinginess or kindness of the confederate in giving points did cause changes in the subject's attraction toward the confederate. Subjects who were initially highly attracted to the confederate remained high when the confederate was generous, but decreased their liking when the confederate was stingy with the points. Subjects initially low in attraction toward the confederate remained low when the confederate was stingy, but increased their liking when the confederate was generous.

Tedeschi (1974) reviewed several other experiments that showed similar results. Apparently, attraction (at least as manipulated by laboratory experiments) does not generalize to benefits given another person. Instead, subjects seem to follow a strict reciprocity rule that is particular to the given task involved. If anything, the reciprocal reward level of the task will change the liking or disliking for the other person.

Self-Disclosure and Attraction

People differ in how much they will disclose about themselves. Topic areas vary in intimacy, and what is intimate or nonintimate may vary in different places and at different times. Most of us will talk in detail to both friends and strangers on nonintimate topics. However, how much we will disclose on intimate topics depends upon our personality dispositions, the situation, and our sex. Jourard (1964) constructed a self-disclosure scale and found that people differ widely in how much information they will divulge about themselves. There are also sex differences; females in our society tend to disclose more than males. Situational constraints on disclosure are also apparent. Some situations are defined as appropriate for high disclosure and others are not. It is appropriate to reveal the most intimate details of your life to your psychiatrist; the same intimate detail related to your classmates will get you into trouble.

Jourard (1964) believed that there is an optimum level of self-disclosure. To fully know oneself, it is necessary that a few significant other people know the core of one's being. To be nonintimate with all other human beings is to be alienated from oneself and not to know oneself. On the other hand, an individual who discloses self to everyone encountered is likely to be viewed as egocentric, maladjusted, and to be avoided. The modern phenomenon of the weekend encounter group, sensitivity training, and the like may have increased the number of "instant disclosers." It is uncomfortable (and boring) to be trapped for two hours at a party by a person who insists on revealing all the squalid details of his or her life with great gusto and even pride. For most of us such instant intimacy seems inappropriately fast; we prefer a much more guarded and leisurely pace in spilling our insides to the outside world.

Reciprocity of Self-Disclosure

There is some consensus that exchange of intimate disclosures is necessary for the development of close relationships (Levinger, 1974; Derlega, Wilson & Chaikin, 1976). Some mutuality or reciprocity of the disclosure may be required for strong attraction to emerge. Self-disclosure processes in marriage are discussed in Chapter 7.

Numerous experiments demonstrate that fairly high levels of reciprocal self-disclosure between two strangers can be achieved in experimental periods of an hour or less. Nearly all this research has used an experimental confederate as one of the strangers. Derlega, Wilson, and Chaikin (1976) questioned whether such a reciprocity effect would occur between already well-established friends, so they designed an experiment to include both stranger pairs and friendship pairs. The variable of interest—the behavior to be tested—was the amount of self-disclosure a subject revealed in response to either a low or high intimate note received from the partner. The results showed that when the other was a stranger/confederate, subjects gave intimate self-disclosures if the stranger gave an initial intimate self-disclosure, but low self-disclosures if the stranger gave an initial low self-disclosure. However, when the other was a friend, subjects gave low self-disclosures regardless of the level of intimacy that the friend disclosed. Thus the precise reciprocity of self-disclosure that has been observed many times between strangers does not automatically occur between good friends. By the time two people have become close friends, they have probably outgrown the need for tit-for-tat matching of disclosure. They have long since disclosed fully, up to the level of that particular friendship. If one of the pair feels a strong need to disclose at a given time, the other feels no necessity to reciprocate. The discloser may instead need sympathy, comfort, advice, or some behavior other than reciprocal disclosure.

Davis (1976) uncovered some interesting aspects of the disclosure process. Students in a class were arbitrarily paired in same-sex pairs and engaged in a disclosure exercise. Results showed that within the session intimacy of disclosure increased over time, and the two members of the pair tended to match each other on level of disclosure. However, matching was not achieved by an equally mutual reciprocity. There was a process of role differentiation in which one person took the lead in disclosing, and the other person in the dyad followed in disclosure. The leader was also generally the more disclosing member of the pair. The disclosure process appears to be more complicated than a rote matching of level. Some degree of mutual disclosure allowing deep knowledge of the other person seems necessary for strong attraction to develop. Once a friendship is formed, however, routine reciprocation of disclosure is no longer needed or expected. During the acquaintance phase, disclosure is not an automatic process. Rather, it is a process of delicate negotiation, with one person assuming the lead, which is in turn reciprocated, which in turn stimulates another exchange initiated by the leader.

Degree, Content, and Timing of Self-Disclosure

The discussion of reciprocity of disclosure in the acquaintance process implies that self-disclosure is related to liking. Several experiments have found such a relation. For example, Worthy, Gary, and Kahn (1969) found that a person who disclosed intimate information about self was better liked than one who disclosed superficial information. Content and similarity of the self-disclosures between two people also influence liking. The content must indicate some basis of value, belief or personality similarity, or need complementarity (Daher & Banikiotes, 1976). If such bases do not exist, mutual disclosure will cease, and the interaction will probably be broken off.

Timing and sequencing of self-disclosure also seem to affect attraction (for example, Archer & Burleson, 1980; Jones & Gordon, 1972;

Wortman, Adesman, Herman, & Greenberg, 1976). The results of these studies are complicated. Sometimes it is better to reveal negative information about oneself early in the interaction; under other conditions, negative information is best not disclosed until late in the interaction. Clearly, self-disclosure is a complex variable that can affect attraction in different ways. The last word on the subject has obviously not been spoken by the researchers.

Desirable Characteristics and Attraction

It is generally true that we like people with pleasant or agreeable characteristics better than people with unpleasant characteristics (Aronson, 1969). One example is the study by Hendrick and Brown (1971) discussed previously. On most of the measures both introverted and extroverted subjects preferred and were more attracted to the extroverted stranger. In our society extroverted outgoingness seems to be a highly valued trait. Introverts preferred this ideal on some (but not all) of the measures instead of opting for similarity.

The propensity to be attracted to others with highly valued traits poses an interesting dilemma with regard to similarity. Giving ourselves the benefit of the doubt, most of us have moderately positive amounts of desirable traits. Suppose we meet someone who has these traits in superabundance. Will we like that person more or less than someone else who has the same level of the traits that we do? An interesting ambivalence is created.

John F. Kennedy was an immensely popular president. He was youthful, handsome, very intelligent, rich, and had a beautiful wife. The Bay of Pigs fiasco in Cuba early in his presidency was characterized by Aronson (1969, p. 148) as "one of history's truly great blunders." Yet Kennedy's personal popularity increased immediately after the debacle. Why?

Aronson reasoned that, if someone has too many good qualities or too much ability, that person may be threatening to us. If someone of outstanding ability commits a blunder, however, the person is reduced to our own stature, merely human, therefore similar, and our attraction for the person may increase. To test this reasoning, Aronson, Willerman, and Floyd (1966) performed an experiment in which subjects listened to a tape recording of a student ostensibly trying out for a College Quiz Bowl. The questions posed by the interviewer were very difficult. The candidate answered either brilliantly, demonstrating superior ability, or rather ineptly, demonstrating only average ability. For half the subjects the tape ended at the end of the interview. However, the other half of the subjects heard the student near the end of the interview commit the clumsy blunder of spilling a cup of coffee all over himself. In this way four experimental conditions were created. A student of superior or average ability either committed a clumsy blunder, or no such blunder occurred. After the interview tape was finished, subjects rated on several scales how much they would like the candidate.

The results are shown in Table 2-2. The higher the mean, the more attracted the subjects were toward the candidate. The results were as predicted. When the superior candidate spilled coffee on himself, he was liked more than in any of the other conditions. However, when the average candidate made the same blunder, he was relatively disliked. In the no-blunder condition the candidate of superior ability was liked somewhat more that the candidate of average ability, as might be expected.

TABLE 2-2 Mean attraction ratings of candidates in the Aronson, Willerman, and Floyd study

	Clumsy blunder	*No blunder*
Superior candidate	30.2	20.8
Average candidate	−2.5	17.8

Note: The higher the mean rating, the more attractive the candidate.

Adapted from "The Effect of a Pratfall on Increasing Interpersonal Attractiveness," by E. Aronson, B. Willerman, and J. Floyd. In *Psychonomic Science,* 1966, *4,* 227–228. Copyright 1966 by the Psychonomic Society. Reprinted by permission.

Demonstration of clumsiness apparently made the candidate similar to the subjects, since everyone makes such blunders once in a while. The positive effect of similarity apparently added to the positive effect of superior ability to create a highly liked candidate. Based on the results for the average candidate, however, the moral seems clear for the rest of us. If we spill coffee on ourselves, we should expect to be perceived as merely clumsy oafs—unless we can convince people around us quickly that we are really brilliant!

One important possibility is that the superior candidate might have been perceived as less able when he spilled the coffee. However, Mettee and Wilkins (1972) found that intelligence and respect ratings did not differ between the superior condition in which coffee was spilled and the superior condition in which it was not spilled. Thus high ability with a little blundering thrown in appears to be an attraction-producing formula.

One desirable characteristic of others is the tendency to evaluate the world (and other people) positively rather than negatively. However, nearly everyone has known a "grouch" that one is well advised to avoid. Folkes and Sears (1977) posed the issue as: Does everybody like a liker? In a series of experiments these researchers had subjects rate their liking for stimulus persons who varied in the proportion of positive to negative evaluations they gave of a set of attitude objects. Reciprocity was not at issue since the subjects would not see the stimulus persons. Results showed that stimulus persons giving predominantly positive evaluations were liked best. The result remained true even when attitude similarity was held constant. Apparently everybody does like a liker.

Physical Attractiveness and Attraction

Physical attractiveness, particularly of members of the opposite sex, is of considerable interest in everyday life and probably always has been. It is a curiosity that social-psychological researchers developed a late interest in physical attractiveness, in the mid-1960s. Perhaps the neglect was due to the bias of general psychology toward environmental determinants of behavior; physical beauty is a constitutional variable not very receptive to stimulus manipulations (Aronson, 1969; Berscheid & Walster, 1974b). In any event the situation has now changed dramatically; there has been an explosion of research interest in physical attractiveness and its effects. Most of this work has been concerned with heterosexual attraction.

We will consider two questions. (1) Are people of similar attractiveness attracted to each other? (2) Do beautiful people prosper more than ugly people? An answer of "yes" to the first question would confirm what is called the *matching hypothesis*—people at about the same level of social desirability, including physical attractiveness, tend to pair off: ugly with ugly, average with average, and beautiful with beautiful. A sociologist, Erving Goffman (1952, p. 456), eloquently stated one version of the hypothesis: "A proposal of marriage in our society tends to be a way in which a man sums up his social attributes and suggests to a woman that hers are not so much better as to preclude a merger or a partnership in these matters."

The second question is more complex, and consists of an interrelated set of three issues. (1) Is there a general physical attractiveness stereotype? That is, do people often assume the truth of the hypothesis that *what is beautiful is good* (Berscheid & Walster, 1974b)? (2) If there is a physical attractiveness stereotype, then beautiful people may receive favored treatment in life, or *beautiful people have better interactions*. (3) If attractive people have richer, more rewarding interactions, it is possible that they develop better self-concepts and more adept social skills. In other words, *beautiful people are better people*. Each of these possibilities will be considered.

The Matching Hypothesis

An experiment by Walster, Aronson, Abrahams, and Rottmann (1966) was conducted to test the matching hypothesis. The researchers ostensibly conducted a "computer dance," in which 376 males were paired with 376 females, presumably on the basis of personality test information collected at an initial session to which subjects reported to sign up for the dance. In fact, males were randomly paired with females for the upcoming dance. The subjects had been surreptitiously rated on physical attractiveness at the first session. The researchers hypothesized that pairs who by chance were of the same social desirability level would be more satisfied and attracted to each other than pairs of unequal social desirability. On the night of the dance the couples danced and talked a couple of hours. Then males and females were separated during intermission and asked to complete a questionnaire assessing their date. Results showed that the only variable determining how much a subject liked his or her date, wanted to see the date again, and how often the man asked the woman for future dates was the physical attractiveness of the date. The more physically attractive the date, the more he or she was liked. Thus Walster et al. (1966) did not find support for the matching hypothesis.

Berscheid, Dion, Walster, and Walster (1971) considered the possibility that the matching hypothesis failed in the earlier study because the dates were literally assigned to subjects. Few risks of rejection for that date existed, and subjects could focus on their desire to retain an attractive date for the future. However, in the usual world of courtship, men and women have to choose actively and do run the risk of rejection. Given such risk, people may tend to play it safe and approach only others who are at about the same level of attractiveness.

Berscheid et al. conducted two experiments to test whether the chance of rejection would affect the attractiveness level of requested dates. In one experiment subjects thought they were signing up for a computer date. Half the subjects were led to believe that their prospective dates would have the opportunity of turning them down after a brief meeting. The other half were led to believe that they would attend the dance with their assigned partners. Subjects then rated the characteristics which they desired in their dates. The results showed that the possibility of rejection by the date had no effect at all on the ratings. However, subjects' ratings of desired level of physical attractiveness was related to the subject's own level of physical attractiveness. The more attractive the subject, the higher the required level of attractiveness of the date. Thus this experiment found some support for the matching hypothesis.

The second experiment conducted by Berscheid et al. was similar to the first except that subjects selected a prospective date from a set of six photographs of members of the opposite sex. The models for the photographs varied in their physical attractiveness. Once again the possibility of rejection by the date did not affect the preferred level of attractiveness of the date. However, the more attractive subjects chose the more attractive photos for dating choices significantly more than did the less attractive subjects, and this difference was found for both male and female subjects. The results also provided support for the matching hypothesis.

Several other experiments have found some evidence for the matching hypothesis. For example, Murstein (1972) took photographs of 99 couples who were either engaged or going steady and had judges rate the attractiveness of each member of a couple. A control set of photographs was formed by randomly pairing the male and female photographs. The results showed that the difference in attractiveness between male and female for couples engaged or dating was significantly less than the difference in attractiveness of randomly formed pairs. The inference is that actual couples tend to match each other more closely in attractiveness than would occur if couples were instead formed on a random basis.

More recent work by Murstein and Christy (1976) found that middle-aged, middle-class couples tended to be matched on physical attractiveness. Similar results were obtained by Price and Vandenberg (1979) for samples of married couples from both mainland United States and Hawaii. Cash and Derlega (1978) extended this approach to same-sex friends and found that for both sexes friends were more closely matched in attractiveness than randomly formed pairs.

Although there are some discrepancies in the evidence, there is a tendency for people of similar physical appearance to select each other as romantic partners and as friends. However, the literature also indicates a very strong tendency to prefer highly attractive others, regardless of one's own physical attractiveness. People want to be associated with other beautiful people.

What Is Beautiful Is Good

It perhaps seems only common sense that more physically attractive persons will be preferred as dating and mating choices. However, there is another research tradition which goes back half a century (Berscheid & Walster, 1974b) in which people consistently rank looks much lower in importance than other qualities, such as sincerity, personality, character, and the like, when asked to list the prized qualities of a prospective date or mate. Such studies are in contradiction with the strong preference for physical attractiveness found in the research on computer dating.

At one level there seems to be a cultural dictum that we should not be dazzled by good looks, that we should not judge a book by its cover. This dictum may be especially salient when people are simply asked to list another person's desirable personal attributes. However, there may also be an opposing cultural dictum that what is beautiful is good (Berscheid & Walster, 1974b), and this dictum may be especially salient when one is actually exposed to attractive stimulus persons or to their photographs.

If there is a tendency to believe that what is beautiful is good, then in effect there exists a physical attractiveness stereotype in which beautiful people are assumed to be more intelligent, interesting, successful, and so forth. Dion, Berscheid, and Walster (1972) conducted an experiment to determine if such a physical attractiveness stereotype exists. They had male and female college students study the photographs of three people (one physically unattractive, one average, and one attractive), and rate each person on a large number of characteristics. Half the subjects of each sex rated same-sex photographs, while the other half rated opposite-sex photographs. The researchers expected that when subjects rated same-sex photographs, there might be a jealousy effect for the very attractive photograph with some resulting derogation in the ratings.

The results showed that the more physically attractive stimulus persons were judged to have more socially desirable personalities, greater occupational success, marital happiness, general social and professional happiness, and total happiness in life than were the less attractive stimulus persons. There was no evidence for a jealousy effect. Dion et al. concluded that their evidence suggested that a physical attractiveness stereotype exists and that it is compatible with the thesis that what is beautiful is good.

Sigall and Landy (1973) provided further evidence for the stereotype in male subjects. The researchers had groups of three subjects report to the laboratory. In actual fact two of the subjects in each group were confederates of the experimenter. There was one male and one female confederate. Half the time the female confederate was very attractive, and the other half she was made up to appear unattractive. In addition half the time the two confederates represented themselves as being together and the other half as two strangers reporting for the experiment. After a brief period the experimenter led the male confederate and the actual subject to separate cubicles. The subject was asked to rate the male confederate on several scales. The results showed that when the male confederate was associated with an attractive female, he made a much more favorable overall impression and was better liked than when he was associated with an unattractive female or when the female was merely present but the male confederate was thought to be unassociated with her. These results were obtained from both male and female subjects. Sigall and Landy concluded that there is a *radiating effect of a beautiful woman* on a man who is associated with her. The desirable qualities of the beautiful woman transfer to the male in terms of other people's perceptions of him. In a second experiment by Sigall and Landy (1973), when actual male subjects were placed in the role of the male confederate of the first experiment and asked to predict how others would rate them, they essentially predicted the radiating beauty effect. Thus not only is beauty good, but it may rub off on a lucky member of the opposite sex who happens to be associated with the beautiful person. The strong preference for association with attractive others is therefore very understandable. Beauty is treated by our society as a valuable commodity.

More recent studies have provided further evidence for the physical attractiveness stereotype. Landy and Sigall (1974) had subjects rate the quality of an essay and the writer's ability when a photograph of the writer (which varied in attractiveness) was attached to the essay. The results showed that more attractive persons received more favorable ratings on their essays, and these ratings were independent of the actual quality of the essay, which had been experimentally varied. It appears that beauty can bias judgment of the quality of the beautiful person's work in a positive direction.

Bar-Tal and Saxe (1976) presented some evidence that the physical attractiveness stereotype has different effects for males and females. Male and female subjects rated photographs of couples who were purportedly married, and who were either similar or different in level of physical attractiveness. Female spouses tended to be evaluated independently of their husband's level of physical attractiveness. However, evaluations of male spouses were related to the level of the wife's attractiveness, especially when there was a difference in level of attractiveness. In fact, an ugly man married to a beautiful woman was apparently perceived as "really having something going for himself" since he was rated as having the highest income, most occupational status, and most professional success compared to other combinations of male/female pairs. Apparently the radiating effect of beauty found by Sigall and Landy (1973) is most potent when transferred from females to males, but relatively weak when the direction is from males to females. The physical attractiveness stereotype is probably somewhat stronger and more coherent in our society for females than for males.

Some evidence for a jealousy effect was found by Krebs and Adinolfi (1975) among male dormmates, and by Dermer and Thiel (1975) who had females who varied in attractiveness rate photographs of females of variable attractiveness. The latter result was due to females low in attractiveness downgrading the character ratings of the most attractive photos. Over all subjects, however, unattractive female photographs were given undesirable personality ratings (what is ugly is bad), and attractive female photographs were given desirable personality ratings (what is beautiful is good). The jealousy effect is not as strong a result as the data showing that beautiful is good.

The preference for beauty starts early in childhood. Several studies have shown that attractive children receive better behavior and personality ratings from both adults and other children than unattractive children receive. The preference for beauty was demonstrated strongly by Dion (1977), who had children aged three to six depress a button for five-second slide exposures of a child's face. The children pressed an average of 72 times to see attractive faces, but only 36 times for unattractive faces.

Why should physically attractive people be rated more favorably on their various traits? Adams (1977) suggests that there is a "dialectic" between outer appearance and inner processes. We are whole persons, and there is a strain toward consistency of conception of a unified whole. Therefore outer appearance and inner qualities interact and reinforce each other in circular fashion. Solomon and Saxe (1977) give a much more mundane answer: physical appearance affects person ratings so strongly because it is the most readily available source of information. Other characteristics, such as intelligence, should have equally strong effects if made equally salient. Solomon and Saxe were able to provide some evidence for this conjecture.

It may be some time before we know the full story about why beauty has such a strong impact. However, one immediate implication is that if beauty is good, it probably is treated better as well.

Beautiful People Have Better Interactions

If beautiful people are assumed to have better inner qualities, they should have more rewarding interactions than average people. In a word life provides beautiful people an interactional bonus. There is evidence for the hypothesis. Reis, Nezlek, and Wheeler (1980) had freshman college students keep a journal record of their interactions over an eight-month period. Some of the results were:

1. For both males and females satisfaction with opposite-sex interaction increased over time for the more attractive students.
2. Attractive males spent more time in conversations and less time in other activities than average males. Attractive females spent more time on dates and at parties than average females.
3. Physically attractive males spent more time socializing with the opposite sex and less time with their own sex than their average counterparts. The result was not the same for female students. The data were complex, but overall it appears that more attractive freshmen had a more interesting first year of college.

Snyder, Tanke, and Berscheid (1977) conducted an excellent laboratory study to determine if the beautiful-is-good stereotype actually affects ongoing interaction between the sexes. Pairs of unacquainted male and female students were recruited for an experiment on "becoming acquainted." The male called the female for a ten-minute phone conversation. Actual attractiveness of male and female pairs was unrelated, but in half the cases the male thought the girl was beautiful (via a fraudulent photo) and in the other half that she was homely. Their conversation was recorded and each subject rated the partner on several scales. Some of the results were:

1. Males had a more favorable stereotype of the beautiful females after viewing their photographs.
2. Independent raters who listened only to the males' part of the telephone conversation judged the males who thought they were talking to beautiful females as more social, sexually warm and permissive, interesting, attractive, and the like than males who thought they were talking to homely females.
3. Independent raters who listened only to the females' part of the telephone conversation judged the females who were thought beautiful by their male partners as more sociable, poised, sexually warm, and outgoing.

Thus the initial stereotype in the men's minds became reality in the behavior of the women. The perceived beauty or homeliness of the females affected the telephone interaction of the males, which in turn affected the quality of the interaction of the females. These data show quite clearly that beautiful people do have better interactions.

Are Beautiful People Better People?

If the stereotype that beautiful is better leads to better interactions beginning in early childhood, it is reasonable that this social bias might become a self-fulfilling prophecy. A lifetime of such rewarding interactions might result in attractive people having higher self-esteem, more positive personality characteristics, and more refined social skills. Beautiful people might in fact become better people. There is some evidence (for example, Berscheid and Walster, 1974b) that physically attractive people do have somewhat better self-esteem. Goldman and Lewis (1977) found moderate correlations between attractiveness and social skills. Chaiken (1979) found that physically attractive people were more persuasive, in part because they had better communication skills. The research on this question is just beginning. Nevertheless, the available evidence suggests that beauty works as a character-building device—beautiful people have a chance to become better people.

But Is It Fair?

Social scientists are uncomfortable with the pattern of the data emerging from research on physical attractiveness. It isn't fair! But no one has claimed that life is fair. It is also clear that beauty is just one of many variables. It has some effect, but it is not overwhelming. When all is said, action probably speaks louder than beauty. Perhaps the ugly must work harder to succeed, but one hopes that in the end hard work will prevail. Eleanor Roosevelt was a homely woman, yet she was beloved by millions. She developed a warm, strong personality in spite of, and perhaps partially because of, her physical appearance. It is well to remember that in the race between the tortoise and the hare the tortoise won. There are a lot of tortoises in the world; most of us are. We tortoises should gracefully forgive the beautiful people their beauty. There is really nothing to forgive; beautiful people cannot help being the way they are.

Summary

Many variables affect attraction, but six independent variables have received the most attention.

1. *Similarity*—The more similar two people are on a variety of attributes, the more they tend to like each other. Much research, using a technique developed by Byrne, has confirmed this hypothesis. There are boundary conditions, however, and under a few conditions the positive relationship between similarity and attraction can be broken up or even reversed.

2. *Complementarity*—Opposites attract under some conditions, but the relation is not as robust as the similarity-attraction relation. Recent research on complementarity of sex-role relationships shows more promise for a solid relation than older research which focused on personality needs.

3. *Reciprocity*—To reciprocate means to exchange. If person A hears that person B likes A, it is most difficult for A not to reciprocate the liking. In general, liking between two people tends toward reciprocity. Observation of this tendency led Gouldner to propose a universal norm of reciprocity.

4. *Self-disclosure*—Self-disclosure is associated with liking. Disclosure may also itself serve as a stimulus for liking. Self-disclosure tends to be reciprocal between two people, especially strangers getting acquainted.

5. *Desirable characteristics*—People are attracted to others who have socially valued attributes. Extremity of preferred attributes may increase dissimilarity, however, relative to average persons. Therefore a highly desirable person who occasionally blunders may be better liked than one who does not blunder at all.

6. *Physical attractiveness*—There is considerable evidence that people who are in a relationship (such as spouses and dating couples) tend to be more similar in level of beauty than random pairs, supporting the matching hypothesis. There is also evidence that people prefer to associate with attractive people and attribute good traits to them (what is

beautiful is good). As a result of stereotypes about them, beautiful people often do have more rewarding interactions. There is some evidence that more attractive people develop better self-esteem and social skills than average people.

3

Affiliation and Attraction

Authors are often tempted to divide attitudes and behaviors into discrete categories. Their hope is to put the intellectual and emotional aspects of a concept such as attraction into one neat conceptual box called *attraction as an attitude,* and the behavioral–interactional aspects of attraction into another conceptual box called *attraction as affiliation.* The goal is to clarify once and for all the nature of attraction. No such luck!

The real world of human behavior does not come in neat, self-contained bundles. Such conceptual schemes may help clarify, but they are not *the* reality. In Chapter 2 we discussed the cognitive–affective correlates of attraction, and in the present chapter we will discuss some of the behavioral aspects of attraction, such as affiliation, nonverbal behavior, and modes of self-presentation. Of course none of these topics is really discrete and self-contained; all are interrelated, because life flows as one interconnected contextual fabric.

Let us suppose, for example, that Susan and David are two first-year medical students. They are assigned to the same laboratory group for anatomy class, begin dating, and are very attracted to each other by the end of their first year of medical school. What factors influenced their growing attraction? First, Susan and David are in anatomy class together (proximity) because both are in their first year of medical school (similarity). Each finds the other reasonably pleasant-looking (physical attractiveness) and also mutually helpful when preparing for exams (reciprocity). David is a physically affectionate, "touching" person (type of nonverbal behavior), and, although Susan is less demonstrative, she likes David's openness (complementarity). When they first begin to date, Susan and David each tries to make a good impression and be positive most of the time (mode of self-presentation), but as they become closer, each reveals more positives *and* negatives to the other (self-disclosure).

The process of building a relationship is not simple and is affected by many factors. In this chapter we deal with some of the factors that affect liking in an interactional context. The emphasis on behavior versus attitude is relative, depending mostly on the focus of the research. For example, traditional research on the functions of affiliation points to inner emotional correlates such as anxiety reduction, social comparison, and loneliness. However, other research traditions explore environmental and sociological variables associated with affiliation, such as spatial proximity, effects of sheer physical exposure, age, sex, social class, and so on. Another research tradition has examined nonverbal behavior and its relation to affiliation and attraction. This focus takes into account the basic fact that humans are physical beings and that despite the importance of symbolic behavior, interaction is ultimately a physical activity. Much interesting research exists on the use of space in affiliative behavior, unconscious bodily activity (body language), the use of the eyes in interaction, and facial signals of approval/disapproval and other inner states. People differ in how they present themselves to others for interaction, and how closely they monitor their presentations. Thus self-presentation styles, degree of self-monitoring, and ingratiation tactics become important interactional variables that affect the course of social affiliations and attraction between people. We explore these topics in detail.

Affiliation: Traditional Viewpoints

While the word *attraction* is derived from Latin root words involving pulling together, *affiliation* comes from root words referring to son or to being as close to someone as to a son. Thus in some sense attraction may be seen as a force which draws people together, while affiliation is the behavioral act of coming together. Researchers in social psychology have viewed affiliation in several different ways.

Affiliation as Anxiety Reduction

Stanley Schachter's (1959) now classic experiments with students at the University of Minnesota were concerned with the effects of anxiety on affiliation. Schachter attempted to induce anxiety in his student subjects by telling them that they were going to receive a series of electric shocks. Students in a *high anxiety* condition were told that the shocks would be quite painful, though there would be no permanent physical damage. Students in a *low anxiety* condition were told that the shocks would be slight and merely produce a tingle on the skin. After receiving information about the impending shock, each subject was told that there would be a ten-minute wait before the shocks would be administered and was given the opportunity to wait alone for the ten minutes or to wait with someone else. The high-anxiety subjects more often chose to wait with someone else, while the low-anxiety subjects more often chose to wait alone. Schachter concluded that people who are anxious will be more likely to seek out other people (affiliate) than will nonanxious people. Numerous studies have replicated Schachter's findings, though some authors contend that fear rather than anxiety is the principal impetus for affiliation (Sarnoff & Zimbardo, 1961). One of Schachter's influential conclusions was that a person's order of birth affects his or her tendency to affiliate under high-anxiety conditions. When experiencing high anxiety, firstborn (or only) children tended to affiliate more than later-born children. Although research on birth order and affiliation has only sometimes found a relationship (Cottrell & Epley, 1977), there is some everyday logic to firstborns' affiliating in high-anxiety situations. Firstborn (or only) children sometimes have a more focused relationship with parents than do those born later (at least for a while). Perhaps firstborns are used to more attention and supervision, whereas others are used to greater autonomy and independence.

Perhaps firstborns are more aware of possible hazards in a high-anxiety situation and are thus more likely to seek out the companionship and comfort of other people.

Affiliation as Social Comparison

At first Schachter did not know why anxious subjects affiliated. Were they simply looking for distractions? Or did they want to compare their reactions to others' reactions? In a second experiment in the series Schachter informed *all* subjects that they were to receive intense electric shocks. The subjects were then divided randomly into two experimental conditions. Subjects in one condition were given the choice of waiting alone for ten minutes before the experiment started or waiting with other students who were participating in the same experiment. Students in another condition could either wait alone or with students who were not involved in the experiment but were merely waiting to see their faculty advisers.

The results of the study clearly indicated that subjects affiliated in this context for reasons of social comparison rather than distraction. Students who could wait with others who were in the experiment strongly preferred to do so rather than wait alone. Subjects in the other condition chose to wait alone rather than with students who were not in the experiment and whose emotional state was probably quite dissimilar. The old saying that misery loves company has often been applied to this experiment, although that statement was qualified by Rabbie (1963), who found that subjects did not want to wait with others who were *extremely* fearful. Perhaps a tendency to look for a role model is present, so that fearful subjects would rather be with someone who is similarly fearful or less fearful (since their own fear might diminish) rather than with a very fearful other (since their own fear might increase). Schachter basically concluded that people tend to affiliate to make social comparisons with others when they are in a somewhat new and unfamiliar emotional state and/or when the overall situation is ambiguous. In their review of the research on affiliation and social comparison processes, Cottrell and Epley (1977) concluded that fear prompts affiliation, which in turn reduces the fear. The evidence regarding the effects of other emotional states and situations on affiliation is mixed.

What does all this research evidence mean to you as a student? If the present academic term goes smoothly for you, your anxiety will probably not be unduly aroused. Suppose, however, that one of your courses is particularly difficult and the professor's tests for the course are difficult, unpredictable, and sometimes even off the wall? You might become a bit anxious and seek out other students in the course to talk with about the material. You might organize a study group which prepares together before every course exam. Chances are good that you would not want students in the study group who have either no interest in or no worries at all about the course, but you would also be averse to including someone so uptight about the exam that he or she cried and paced the floor. In other words you might affiliate with other persons who are in a situation and emotional state similar to your own.

Affiliation and Loneliness

The need to affiliate and be with others is counterbalanced by the need to be alone, to withdraw from social interaction. Withdrawal from interaction may be voluntary, as in the maintenance of privacy, or involuntary, when the individual may feel withdrawn, isolated from others, and lonely. Loneliness has become a popular area of research in social psychology within the past few years; in fact, a whole chapter is devoted to loneliness in a recently published social psychology text (Middlebrook, 1980). In trying to define loneliness, we might assume that being lonely is synonymous with being alone, but most of us have on occasion felt lonely even when we are with others. What is lonelier than a large party where we know very few people? In addition being alone may be a lonely experience for some people and not for others. To some degree loneliness is in the eye of the beholder, since, as Peplau and Perlman (1979) point out, loneliness is not defined so much by an individual's level of social interaction as by the difference between his or her *desired* level of interaction and the *actual* level of interaction. For example, Veronica is a quiet, studious undergraduate who sees very few people during an average day. And she likes it that way. Victoria, on the other hand, is another undergraduate who has left her parents and five brothers and sisters and is living away from home for the first time. She also sees very few people during an average day, but she is miserably lonely. Individuals vary in their needs for social interaction, but when any individual's needs are far from being met, that person is likely to experience loneliness.

Although most of us have experienced loneliness at one time or another, certain groups of people are particularly vulnerable to loneliness. Married persons do not report high levels of loneliness, but lonely feelings increase in the widowed and divorced, and the aged are particularly beset by loneliness (Middlebrook, 1980). Middlebrook distinguishes between emotional loneliness and social loneliness. Emotional loneliness involves the lack of intimate (usually pair) relationships and the absence of deep communication and mutual understanding. Social loneliness refers to the absence of a support system or social network, a lack of enjoyable activities and people with whom to do them.

Both individual and societal factors may precipitate loneliness. In Chapter 2 we discussed variables that influence attraction. If similarity or physical beauty can foster attraction, then differences or ugliness can inhibit attraction and contribute to loneliness. People who are homely, handicapped, shy, or socially unskilled may suffer greater loneliness.

People low in self-esteem may consciously or unconsciously avoid others, because they are afraid of rejection or negative evaluation, and some individuals may choose to be lonely rather than take the kinds of interpersonal risks which are necessary to form close relationships.

Although personal factors influencing loneliness may not be much different from the past, societal factors have changed radically. An individual no longer lives and works in the bosom of a family; family and work lives are often widely separated, sometimes by as much as an hour-long commute. In our technological urban-based society, the individual's opportunity to relate to nature is greatly diminished. A marital relationship is not the inviolable bond which it once was. Changing sex roles, working women, divorce, and increased mobility all contribute to upheaval in marriage. Families do not spend as much time together as they used to, and family time in the home involves passive activities rather than interactional ones (for instance, watching television rather than playing Scrabble). The dinner hour is less a forum for family communication than a chance to grab a quick meal and then race out again. Yet the loss of meaningful interaction in marriage and the family is superseded by the anonymity of much of our present society. No longer do our daily errands consist of chitchat and personal exchanges with the butcher, the local pharmacist, and the little old lady at the drygoods store. Now our meat is prepackaged in cellophane, and we have to push a buzzer to summon the butcher. We are likely to be merely a prescription number at our local pharmacy, and instead of just adding new prescription costs to our account, we pay by check, supported by a local driver's license and two credit cards. Our dark and somewhat musty-smelling drygoods store has been totally replaced; now we have everything from large discount and department stores to exclusive boutiques. But no little old ladies sell us merchandise as they call us by name and ask us how our family is getting along. Many of us are employed by large corporations who give competitive salaries and comprehensive benefits, but who unceremoniously move us across the country every two or three years and who neither know nor care about the consequent loneliness that we experience. Although as a people we have benefitted greatly from the technological explosion of the twentieth century (for example, improved nutrition and medical care), life is a tradeoff, and we have lost many valuable things in our move toward modernity.

Although many factors influence loneliness, what does loneliness itself influence? Loneliness is often highly correlated with depression, and although the two appear to be somewhat different constructs (Weeks, Michela, Peplau, & Bragg, 1980), both loneliness and depression "probably share some common origins" (p. 1238). Loneliness may also lead to both illicit and legal drug abuse (Middlebrook, 1980), since boredom, depression, and loneliness may precipitate such reactions as alcoholism.

Probably the most serious reaction to intense loneliness (and other negative psychological factors) is suicide, and "suicide is not a rare event. Statistics show that from 25,000 to 60,000 Americans kill themselves yearly; and at least 200,000 try and fail" (Middlebrook, 1980, p. 542). If loneliness can play even a part in as destructive an event as suicide, then it surely deserves our attention. Different events may cause lonely feelings at different ages; examples are given in Figure 3-1.

Although there are few sure cures for loneliness, several authors have suggested methods of coping with it. Peplau and Perlman (1979) suggest various cognitive methods of handling loneliness. An individual can alter his or her real level of interaction with others, desired level of interaction, or perceptions of the differences between the two levels—a "power of positive thinking" approach. The authors also note that individuals who feel they personally have the power to change their lonely situation are able to cope with loneliness more effectively. Middlebrook takes a more behavioral approach, suggesting that after one accepts one's loneliness and becomes aware of what events trigger lonely feelings, practical actions include calling a friend, doing a physical activity, and pampering oneself in satisfying and positive ways.

Affiliation: Traditional Variables

There are several commonsense factors that influence affiliation—factors such as how close together people live and work and how often

Age	Experience
3	A toddler has been given full-time care by his mother, and when his mother takes a job outside the home, he feels abandoned and lonely for a time.
10	A child moves with her family from Ohio to Florida and leaves her best friend behind. For several months she has no one to confide in, and she feels lonely.
15	An adolescent boy feels pressure from his parents to be "good" and pressure from his peers to try out all kinds of new behaviors such as drinking. He sometimes feels he has nowhere to turn and is very lonely.
20	A college transfer student is away from home for the first time. She misses her family, but knows no one her own age who is experiencing the same feelings. She is lonely.
35	A successful businessman with a wife and children finds out his father has died. Even after active mourning has ceased, the man keenly feels the loss of his parent and the now overwhelming burden of being the head of the family. He feels vulnerable and lonely.
50	A full-time wife and mother sends her last child off to college. The house seems quiet and the days empty. She is very depressed and lonely.
65	A retired couple moves to Arizona to start a new life. They leave their family and friends back in the East and know no one in their new area. For a while, they feel quite isolated and lonely.

FIGURE 3-1   Loneliness across the life cycle

they see each other. Homans (1950) noted that, given a general basis of positive interaction, the more frequently two people interact, the more they will like each other. To create this general basis of positive interaction, individuals tend to form relationships with others who are similar in age, sex, and race (Nahemow & Lawton, 1975), and who in addition live in fairly close proximity.

Propinquity

Propinquity means proximity or nearness, and it is used in attraction/affiliation research to refer to spatial proximity. Spatial proximity is a necessary condition for affiliative behavior to occur. We have all heard the phrase that whatever special or wonderful thing we are looking for in life is probably right in our own backyard; this saying basically refers to propinquity. There is extensive evidence that propinquity within residential areas or housing units is associated with friendship choices and marital selection.

One problem with propinquity is that it may not itself cause attraction and affiliation. It is what people do when they are in proximity to each other that is probably most important in causing affiliation–attraction. However, we will review some evidence that "mere exposure" to another, even without real interaction, may enhance attraction toward the other.

Another problem with the propinquity research is that often propinquity is only a correlate, not a genuine independent variable in which people are randomly assigned to rooms or housing units. To the extent that people self-select their living quarters, causal inferences about spatial proximity and attraction are difficult to make. Any observed relationship might actually be caused by several other unknown variables.

One classic study which did more or less use random assignment was reported by Newcomb (1961). The acquaintance process of 17 male students was observed over a semester. The men agreed to live in a fraternity-like house and complete weekly questionnaires in exchange for free rent. The students were quartered on the second and third floors of a three-story home. Altogether there were three single rooms, four doubles, and two triples. The 17 students were selected to be relatively homogeneous in personal characteristics and were randomly assigned to rooms. Thus it was pure chance whether a student lived alone in a single room, or together with someone else. The experiment was repeated again during the following year with a new sample of 17 male students.

Newcomb predicted that at the beginning of the semester, roommates would be more attracted to each other than to other members of the house, and that this heightened level of attraction would be maintained throughout the semester. The reasoning was impeccable, but unfortunately empirical reality has a way of spoiling conceptions. For the first year attraction was no higher between roommates than other pairs. However, during the second year, attraction between roommates was initially higher than attraction between other pairs, and this higher level of attraction lasted for the entire semester. It was not clear why the prediction held for the second group but not for the first group of students.

An interesting test of the propinquity–attraction hypothesis was conducted by Segal (1974). A questionnaire was mailed to 52 students (all male) in the Training Academy of the Maryland State Police. The students, who had known each other for six weeks, were asked to name their three closest friends on the force. Of importance was the fact that students were assigned to rooms and seats in classes on the basis of the alphabetical order of their last names. Thus propinquity was based on the accident of one's birth name, and in this sense came close to serving as a true independent variable. The results showed that alphabetical ordering did have a strong effect on friendship choices. A total of 65 friendship choices was made, and of these, 29 (45 percent) were given to trainees adjacent to the chooser's name in alphabetical order. Segal concluded that propinquity contributes to attraction, but noted that the trainees were very similar to each other on a large number of variables. It may well be that propinquity is a powerful variable only when people in a geographical area are all relatively alike.

Nahemow and Lawton (1975) pursued the topic of similarity and propinquity by examining spontaneous friendship development in a housing project in New York. They found that proximity and similarity of race and age were significant predictors of friendship and also that when a subject indicated a friendship with someone in a different age or racial group, that person tended to live closer to the subject. The authors reasoned that propinquity may be less essential when people are similar, but may be necessary when people form friendships with different others.

Most researchers have assumed that interaction is the true causal variable that mediates the propinquity-attraction relationship. Newcomb assumed that roommates would more likely exchange intimate disclosures than nonroommates, and that such exchanges would build mutual trust, and thus greater attraction. Berscheid and Walster (1969) noted that proximity increases the probability that the two people will acquire information about each other. People tend to present desirable "social fronts," hence the preponderance of information acquired should be positive. A second point is that proximity increases the probability of receiving rewards or punishments from others, and if people generally give more rewards than punishments, proximity would be expected to lead most often to attraction and affiliation.

The fact that people do punish each other, however, leads to another hypothesis—that proximity can lead to disliking and hating others

(Berscheid & Walster, 1969). This possibility was studied by Ebbesen, Kjos, and Konecni (1976). The subjects of their study lived in a condominium complex in southern California. Nearly all the 183 subjects who were interviewed were married housewives. Subjects were asked to list their choices of three people in the complex whom they liked, three people whom they disliked, and three people whom they saw most often at social gatherings. The results indicated that dwelling proximity was related to both liking and disliking. Of the three choices for liking, 61 percent of the liked others lived in the same building attachment. The same result held true for social contacts; 55 percent of a subject's social contacts lived in the same area. However, the same result also occurred for disliked people; 56 percent of the other people that subjects disliked lived in the same area.

Ebbesen et al. (1976) presented additional data that showed the longer subjects had lived in the condominiums, the less important proximity was in determining where their best friends lived. In contrast, length of time subjects had lived in the area was unrelated to proximity of disliked others. Apparently, quite different dynamics underlie propinquity–liking and propinquity–disliking. The authors posited an "environmental spoiling" hypothesis to account for the development of dislikes. We tend to dislike others who allow their dogs to deface our lawns, who park in front of our driveways, and who keep us awake at night with loud parties and stereos. A second interview study tended to confirm the environmental spoiling notion for disliked persons. In contrast, reasons for liking persons were most often attributed to personal characteristics of the chosen person.

The evidence seems to indicate rather clearly that when propinquity is related to attraction, it is the quality of the interaction that mediates liking and disliking, and not propinquity per se. The intriguing question remains, however, as to whether mere association or exposure to another person, with no interaction with him or her will result in enhanced attraction.

Mere Exposure and Attraction

Zajonc (1968, p. 1) proposed the general hypothesis that "mere repeated exposure of the individual to a stimulus is a sufficient condition for the enhancement of his attitude toward it." Although the hypothesis refers to a stimulus which may be an inanimate object as well as a person, we are interested in the possibility that simple repeated exposure to another person, without any interaction, will make us more attracted to that person.

Zajonc found support for his hypothesis with a variety of objects, including Chinese characters, nonsense syllables, and photographs of human faces. The general procedure was to present slides of specific objects within a class (for example, the Chinese characters) either 1, 2, 5,

10 or 25 times, and afterward ask subjects to rate each object on a good/bad or pleasantness/unpleasantness scale. The findings indicated that the more frequently an item had been presented, the more favorably it was rated. This basic result was obtained for several different types of stimuli, including human faces.

An experiment by Saegert, Swap, and Zajonc (1973) provided strong evidence for the mere exposure effect by varying the number of encounters between female subjects in a situation designed *not* to bring attention to frequency of exposure. Subjects were ostensibly participating in an experiment in which they tasted and rated noxious-tasting liquids such as quinine water or pleasant liquids such as Kool-Aid. The experiment was conducted in a series of small cubicles. Each subject completed a total of 25 taste-tests. During the tests each subject was shifted from cubicle to cubicle in such a way that a cubicle was shared with another specific subject for either none, 1, 2, 5, or 10 of the taste-tests. Subjects were instructed not to talk or make faces or other gestures so as not to disturb each other. Subjects were told that they would rotate across cubicles with each other because of the predetermined order in which the taste-tests were conducted, and that the rotation was necessary because the large bottles containing the fluids were too heavy to shift around.

Half the subjects tasted bitter liquids; the other half, pleasant ones. The variation in taste was considered as a context variable to test one possible explanation that increased liking with increased frequency is a classically conditioned phenomenon in which an object more frequently experienced in a pleasant setting is better liked, and an object experienced in an unpleasant setting is more disliked.

After the taste-tests were finished, the subjects congregated in a large room, sat facing each other in a semicircle, and completed a variety of ratings, including favorability of their impressions about each other. The results showed clearly that the more frequently a subject had been exposed to another subject, the more attractive the other subject was. Whether the subjects tasted pleasant or noxious substances did not affect the attraction ratings, indicating that the mere exposure effect occurred even within a moderately negative context of having to taste bad substances.

In an experiment involving the effects of repeated exposure and attitude similarity on self-disclosure and interpersonal attraction, Brockner and Swap (1976) found that subjects were slightly more attracted to others with similar attitudes. However, they rated people more positively when they had been exposed to them more often, regardless of whether their attitudes were similar or dissimilar to the subject's own attitudes. Thus there is some evidence that mere frequency of exposure, a factor which is involved in propinquity, can create a degree of attraction between persons.

Sociometric Measurement

The measurement as well as the causes of attraction–affiliation represent a challenge to social-psychological researchers, and one method for measuring attraction is the *sociogram*. A sociogram is a pictorial attempt to show behavioral relations. Moreno (1934) presented one of the first systematic measures of interpersonal attraction. He believed that likes and dislikes within a group are central aspects of social life. He simply asked each person in a group to choose and reject others according to some specified criterion, such as "which people do you like and dislike most as friends," or "as work partners." Such choices and rejections can be schematized simply in a sociogram, an example of which is shown in Figure 3-2. Persons are represented by circles, solid arrows indicate attraction choices, and dotted arrows indicate rejections. Two arrows between two persons mean mutual choice or rejection.

The pattern shown in Figure 3-2 is interesting. It is clear that there are two major subgroups with four people per group who all mutually like each other, but do not care much for members of the other subgroup.

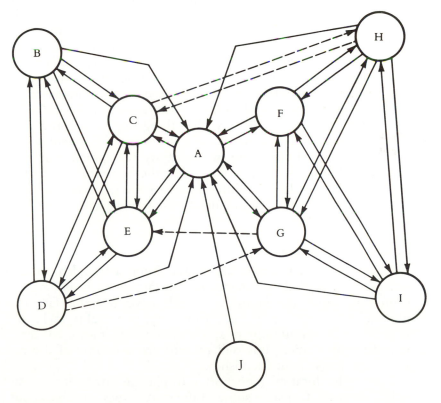

FIGURE 3-2   Hypothetical sociogram of members of a group's choice and rejections of other members of the group

Person A is called a *sociometric star* since everyone likes him or her. We might also surmise that person A has a leadership function within the group; indeed, one might well sympathize with the delicate emotional balancing that A must perform to keep the two cliques at peace with each other. We might also reasonably be pessimistic about the long-term survival of the group as a group. It should also be noted that person J was not chosen by any other person in the group. This person is an *isolate*. We cannot know why the person is an isolate from the sociogram alone. In most cases, however, it would be a safe bet that the lot of J is not a happy one.

The set of likes and dislikes shown in Figure 3-2 symbolizes the *attraction structure* of the group in bold relief. It might take an interviewer many hours or days of delicate interaction with group members to deduce this attraction structure that the sociometric researcher was able to obtain in five minutes. It is clear that the sociogram is a very useful tool of measurement in some situations. Sociometric devices have been widely used in both research and practice. At one time it was rather common for elementary school teachers to construct sociograms of their class. Teachers could identify children who were isolated, as well as the potential disruptiveness of a clique formation. With this information in hand the teacher was better able to proceed as a diplomat in group relations. One fascinating use of the sociogram is to repeat its construction over time. For example, a teacher might construct the sociogram several times during the year. The changes in attraction structure over time provide a literal description of the shifts (or stability) of interpersonal relations within the group during the year.

Of course the sociogram is only useful to the extent it accurately reflects real-life choices, and in one study (Chapman, Smith, Foot, & Pritchard, 1979) researchers found that the behavioral and sociometric choices of the children involved were somewhat different. In other words, the children did not really choose to play with the kids they said they would choose.

Friendship Formation

The process of developing and maintaining a friendship can be very complex. It depends on demographic factors such as age, sex, race, economic status, and location, as well as on personal factors such as physical attractiveness, attitude similarity, personality style, and interests. We will not attempt to summarize the literature concerned with friendship formation, but will merely discuss some of the recent research findings about friendship.

Geographic location is purported to play an important role in friendship formation. Consider some of the stereotypes we have about people in various parts of the United States: Southerners are friendly and hospitable; New Englanders are reserved; Californians are open, but a bit "way out." The size and density of one's location also affect friendship formation.

Specifically, a theory called the *linear development model* states that as number of population and density of settlement increase in a given location, there will be a commensurate weakening of kinship ties and investment in the community. The *systemic development model,* on the other hand, proposes that a community is an organism with a "life of its own" that will change, but not necessarily weaken, when population and density increase. In a survey study in England Kasarda and Janowitz (1974) found that the most significant influence on one's development of social bonds in a community is length of residence in the community. They concluded that "location in communities of increased size and density does not weaken bonds of kinship and friendship . . . nor . . . result in a substitution of secondary for primary and informal social contacts" (p. 338). In a conceptually related study, Franck (1980) interviewed graduate-school newcomers in urban and nonurban university settings. Although for the first seven to eight months in a new community, nonurban residents had more satisfying friendships than urban residents, after that time, the differences in satisfaction levels virtually disappeared. The urban friendships in fact seemed more intimate. On the basis of this and other studies, Franck concludes that fear, distrust, uncertainty, and stress, which are greater in the urban than in nonurban settings, make it somewhat harder to initiate personal contacts with other people. But once such contacts are begun and developed, urban friendships may be deeper and more intimate than those in nonurban settings.

Why do people become friends? Are your friends similar to you or different from you? Or do you have different types of friends—people whom you like but who may not especially like each other? Werner and Parmelee (1979) obtained responses to attitude and activity preference surveys by students and their partners (friends). The authors discovered that friends were no more similar in attitudes than were stranger pairs, but they were much more similar than strangers in *activity preferences.* Friends liked to do the same things. Booth and Hess (1974) examined cross-sex friendships—friendships with members of the opposite sex—finding that more men than women report cross-sex friendships (35 percent to 24 percent), the number of women's cross-sex friendships declines with increasing age, and cross-sex friendships of married persons have less reported emotional involvement and amount of contact than do similar friendships among single persons.

Shulman (1975) surveyed close relationships, including friendships, at various points in the life cycle. He conceptualized close relationships as a network including kin, friends, and neighbors. Younger adults tended to be less involved with kin than older adults, with widowed and divorced persons relying on relatives and single persons relying on friends for social support. Single people experienced the most change in the support network. The importance of friends waxed and waned over the life cycle, with friends proportionately more significant when there was less involvement with kin or with one's own children. La Gaipa (1977) proposed a multidimensional approach to the study of acquaintance and friendship, with self-disclosure, helping, similarity, positive regard, strength of character, and authenticity all differentially important at different stages of the relationship. In an extension of La Gaipa's work Davis and Todd (1982) constructed ideal examples of friendship and love relationships and assessed the similarities and differences between the two. Although the two relationships appear to be similar in many ways, there is an aspect of exclusivity and sexuality that is common to love, but not to friendship. Davis and Todd constructed relationship assessment scales based on their ideal examples and in three different studies found support for the validity of both their scales and their theory.

Children's friendships are the focus of a recent interesting book by Rubin (1980). Rubin used both descriptive and empirical data to illustrate friendship formation of children and to discuss developmental and environmental influences on those friendships.

Nonverbal Aspects of Attraction–Affiliation

Humans appear to have some fairly specific nonverbal rules and regulations for interaction. First, there seem to be implicit rules by which people space themselves with respect to each other. Others sometimes violate these rules, resulting in flight or other forms of territorial behavior. Humans also use their bodies in complex and varied ways in interaction. Facial expressions, eye contact, and touching all have definite communicative value. We will examine briefly some of these varied correlates of affiliation–attraction.

Personal Space and Affiliative Behavior

Personal space denotes a general area of research and thinking which includes concepts such as interaction distance, territoriality, population density, and crowding. In addition to the breadth of the area itself there has also been breadth in the conceptual approaches to the study of personal space (Baldassare, 1978). Early research on personal space was more concerned with cultural and environmental influences on territoriality and interaction distance, while modern societal pressures have forced a growing concern with population density and crowding. Since our emphasis is on intimate pair relationships rather than on social groups, we will be concerned primarily with interaction distance and territoriality–privacy.

Anthropologist Edward T. Hall (1966) coined the term *proxemics* to designate the scientific study of *interaction distance*. Hall recognized the importance of spatiality in human behavior, but felt that we are often unaware of our use of space. He complained about our lack of awareness in a memorable analogy, stating that we treat space like we treat sex: it's there, but we don't talk about it. Hall's work continues to influence the study of spatial behavior (Hayduk, 1978).

Hall's (1966) major contribution was the identification of four major spatial zones of human interaction: *intimate, personal, social,* and *public*. The four zones are appropriate for different situations and signify different types of social relationships. The *intimate zone* extends from physical contact to about 18 inches separating two people. Both lovemaking and fighting can occur within the intimate zone. In general people in public spaces separate themselves further than the limits of the intimate zone, since two people within this zone in space are assumed to be intimately related to each other psychologically and perhaps sociologically (they might, for example, be married).

Social life is such that strangers must occasionally inhabit each other's intimate space, such as on crowded elevators or buses. There is an unwritten rule that in such a situation, one should ignore one's neighbor and stand erect with slightly tensed muscles. For example, when standing on a crowded bus that lurches and swings two people into bodily contact, it would be considered extremely inappropriate to simply relax one's body and enjoy the contact. The rule seems to be that when two strangers are forced by circumstance to inhabit each other's intimate space, they are supposed to behave so that psychologically they seem farther apart.

The *personal zone* extends from about 18 inches to 4 feet. This zone is used by people in fairly intense social interaction, which is mostly conversational in nature. The personal zone is the zone of friendship and convivial interaction.

The *social zone* extends from about 4 feet to 12 feet. Within this zone people tend to relate to each other formally, such as in business interactions, negotiating sessions, and so on. In general social distance seems preferred when the two people are linked in some kind of official role relation, but do not have extensive familiarity with each other as persons beyond that role relation.

The *public zone* extends from about 12 to 25 feet. Communication within this zone tends to be formal, as in public lectures, plays, and musical performances. Communication is usually one-way, with one person (or group) presenting a performance of some kind which is observed by a passive audience. Beyond the outer limits of 25 feet, contact with another person as a person is rapidly lost. It is a strange sensation to watch people on the sidewalk below from the observation deck of a tall building. You know that they are people, but they look like an army of orderly moving ants. To fully experience another individual as a person, humans seem to require physical closeness.

The four interaction zones are not immutable, and in fact preferred interaction distances differ widely across cultures. For example, English-speaking people tend to maintain privacy about their body and its direct effects, such as breathing on someone or trying to prevent the smell of one's body from intruding into someone else's nose. In contrast, Arabs tend to interact at closer distances. Smell is important, and according to Hall, Arabs consistently breathe on people when they talk. "To smell one's friend is not only nice but desirable, for to deny him your breath is to act ashamed" (Hall, 1966, p. 160).

When people from two different cultures interact, some amusing things can happen. For example, there is the story about the Arab and the Englishman who were trying to carry on a conversation in a hallway. The Englishman was trying to maintain his proper civilized distance of 5 feet; the Arab preferred 2 feet. Whenever the Arab approached too closely, the Englishman would subtly back away to his comfortable distance. The Arab, uncomfortable with that distance, would move closer. The result was that, at the end of an unsatisfactory 15-minute conversation, the Arab had backed the poor Englishman down a long corridor. From the Englishman's point of view, the Arab persisted in entering his personal space too closely, leading to a mild flight reaction. Misunderstanding of cultural expectations of appropriate interaction distances can lead to many strange and sometimes hostile results. Expectancies of norms for proper spatial behavior do develop, and people react strongly when these norms are violated.

People tend to mark or personalize their spaces in various ways. For example, if you are studying in a library in a preferred location, you will probably leave some possessions to mark your chair and table when you have to leave temporarily. You are also likely to be annoyed if a stranger comes and sits in the chair next to your chair if there are many unoccupied tables in the immediate vicinity. Although it is a public area, you feel that the stranger has violated your personal space in some sense. Several researchers have observed how people react to such violations (for example, Shaffer & Sadowski, 1975; Sommer, 1969) and have found that the typical response to this sort of casual spatial invasion is flight.

In observing spatial invasion in a field setting (a streetcorner), Smith and Knowles (1979) found that subjects tended to be more threatened by a stranger who invaded their personal space for no apparent reason. Thus if I am jogging in a local park and a stranger dressed in shirt, jeans, and loafers begins running right next to me, I may well feel threatened. If that same stranger has on shorts and jogging shoes, I am likely to be a bit more comfortable. A slightly unorthodox study conducted in a men's lavatory (Middlemist, Knowles, & Matter, 1976) studied the relation between the proximity of a confederate to a subject using a urinal and the onset and persistence of the subject's urination. Basically, the closer the confederate stood to the subject (adjacent versus distant urinal), the greater the delay in onset and steadiness of the subject's urination. The authors believe that invasions of personal space cause physiological arousal which acts to inhibit urination.

Some of the most interesting research on personal space is concerned with *privacy* and its relation to territoriality. (Privacy in the context of relationship development will be discussed in Chapter 6.) Vinsel and her colleagues (Vinsel, Brown, Altman, & Foss, 1980) studied 73 freshmen at the University of Utah, photographing the room decorations in the students' dormitory rooms and administering several paper-and-pencil instruments to each student. The authors then waited for a year to see which students remained at the university and which students dropped out of school. They found that the students who remained at the university originally had more varied and effective means for regulating their privacy in the dormitory. They had better methods of retaining control over both their time and their personal space. They also had more positive attitudes toward the university and were more effectively integrated into local student and community life. The needs for privacy and for certain defined boundaries of personal space are significant in human behavior. Also significant are the ways in which we use our bodies to interact with one another.

Body Language

The term *body language* was popularized by Julius Fast (1970) in a book by that title and is an informal way of designating a vast area of research on nonverbal communication. Body language is treated in some respects like verbal language in that it is structured and has communication value. Strictly speaking, nonverbal communication includes all aspects of behavior that communicate messages to someone else, other than the verbal meaning of words. It is convenient, however, to divide nonverbal communication into two general classes. One class is concerned directly with the body and the messages which the body mediates. The other class is concerned with the physical possessions which belong to the person, such as clothing, jewelry, briefcases, handbags, and so on. Physical possessions help designate the wealth and status of a person and in this way define permissible relationships vis-à-vis other persons. Thus one's possessions are often a potent nonverbal communication device.

With respect to the body as a medium of communication, it is convenient to arbitrarily distinguish between the head and the rest of the body. The study of the head has itself spawned several diverse areas of study. The issue of facial expressions and whether or not they have universal cross-cultural meanings has received much attention (see, for example, Ekman, 1972). What has been called "the language of the eyes" has also been studied in considerable detail (by, for one, Exline, 1972). Other research has concentrated on the voice, particularly nonverbal messages communicated by the voice's tone and intensity. When we speak of body language, we mean many things. The general posture, position, and orientation of the body may provide rich interpretive cues to an observer. The body in action also communicates messages. Hand gestures and their many meanings come readily to mind. The movement of the arms and legs when one is seated or the movement of the body when one is walking are also often scrutinized for their unspoken meanings.

Birdwhistell, an anthropologist, made early and important contributions to the study of bodily movement. His work is summarized in *Kinesics and Context* (1970). The term *kinesics* denotes a science of bodily movement that he is trying to develop. Birdwhistell searches for basic movement structures, from which more complex movements can be constructed. Since most of us are more concerned with interpreting behavior or movement at the level of everyday life, it may be difficult to see the usefulness of the elementary movement units isolated by Birdwhistell.

The value of the general approach can be illustrated by what Scheflen (1965) calls quasi-courtship behavior in psychotherapy and other interaction situations. After extended observations Scheflen was somewhat surprised to find courtshiplike elements in most types of interactions; not only between lovers, but also in such situations as psychotherapy sessions, business meetings, and parties. Since few of these interactions ended in actual sexual behavior, it seemed reasonable that there also were qualifying signals that changed the function of the courtshiplike behaviors.

According to Scheflen there are three basic elements of kinesic behavior in the courtship situation: courtship readiness, positioning for courtship, and actions of appeal or invitation. Courtship readiness is indicated by high muscle tone, erect posture, bright eyes, and variable skin color. Preening behavior, such as stroking the hair, rubbing the body discretely, or adjusting clothing slightly may occur. Positioning for courtship involves strong attention between two people. Usually they will face each other directly, lean toward each other, and screen other people out of the field of attention. In this position the two people may adopt an intimate mode of conversation. Actions of appeal or invitation follow positioning for courtship. Language may become soft and hushed. Other behaviors may include making flirtatious glances, gazing extensively, cocking one's head, and rubbing one's hip or thigh.

Women may cross their legs to slightly expose the thigh, turn the wrist or palm outward as an invitational gesture, and so on. Men may spread their legs apart slightly, hook their thumbs in their belts with fingers pointed toward the crotch, and the like.

In an actual courtship situation the sequence described above (along with the proper words at the proper time) eventually leads to interesting and rewarding sexual encounters. However, it is surprising that these same courtship elements exist in a great variety of noncourtship situations. Scheflen argues persuasively that we interject *behavioral qualifiers* that serve to define the situation as quasi-courtship and not as the real thing. For example, some reference may be made verbally or nonverbally as to the inappropriateness of the present context for courtship. A head movement or glance at a third person, or even a pretended third person, may effectively signal inappropriateness of the courtship elements. Other signals may include incongruent postures. For example, two people may sit facing each other directly, but turn their bodies slightly away from each other. Another type of incongruence may involve saying soft, courtshiplike words, but leaning back away from the other person instead of toward him or her. The list of possibilities seems endless; the key point is that discrepant elements intrude in some way to block the progression toward courtship and define the situation as merely one of quasi-courtship.

Scheflen (1965) noted that such quasi-courtship behaviors occur quite extensively in psychotherapy and are often consciously used by the therapist as an effective interaction tool. Properly modulated, quasi-courtship is a stimulant to social interaction. It is based on sexuality, but the effect is to increase attractiveness, attentiveness, sociability, and readiness to relate to others. Essentially, the sexual drive is harnessed or sublimated to some optimal state between immediate sexual preoccupation and total sexual inhibition. Freud saw such diffusion of sexuality as the basis for civilization, cooperation, creativity, and social interest. Thus it is perhaps not so unexpected that the study of body language, starting basically from a nonsexual perspective, should find a sexual tinge in many of our movements and actions.

Even when sexuality or courtship is not an issue in a relationship, nonverbal behavior can have a potent effect on relationship formation. In a comprehensive review of studies on expressive behavior, Cappella (1981) notes that even in the establishment of the infant–parent relationship, infant and adult styles of nonverbal interaction are important. Foot, Smith, and Chapman (1979) viewed 9-year-old children in various kinds of dyadic relationships and found that children in pairs with friends showed more matched nonverbal responses than children paired with strangers. In other words, children who were friends were more alike nonverbally.

Facial Expressions of Emotion

Facial expressions can be used to "manage" human interactions by initiating or terminating behavior sequences and by influencing the progression of sequences. The face offers complex rather than unidimensional information, and Ekman, Friesen, and Tomkins (1971) have developed a coding system for six emotions which seem to be at the base of most facial expressions: surprise, fear, anger, disgust, happiness, and sadness. It appears that different areas of the face are important in displaying different kinds of emotions, and Ekman, Friesen, and Ancoli (1980) found that spontaneous facial expressions not only accurately depicted what subjects were feeling at a particular time, but could differentiate between levels of intensity within a particular emotion. In other words, facial expressions showed how happy or how sad a subject felt. Brunner (1979) notes that smiles can be a real part of conversation, encouraging a listener in much the same fashion as do verbal statements such as "yah" and "un-hunh."

Researchers have recently begun to document the differences between men and women in encoding (sending) and decoding (receiving and interpreting) nonverbal messages. Hall (1978) reviewed 75 studies of nonverbal behavior and determined that females are significantly better than males at all ages at decoding nonverbal communications. Although both genetic predispositions and socialization influences have been posited as reasons for female skill, no single cause has been isolated. Noller (1980) conducted an ingenious study in which 96 spouses (48 couples) delivered ambiguous messages to each other. Spouses were rated on how accurately they could convey messages to and interpret messages from their partners. The author found that wives were significantly better at encoding nonverbal communication, especially when it was positive rather than negative. Couples were divided into groups high and low in marital satisfaction, and the husbands in the higher marital satisfaction group were better at encoding and decoding and sent more positive messages than did husbands in the other group. Because wives in the two groups did not strongly differ in their abilities, it appeared that husbands' skills in nonverbal communication were particularly important in relation to a couple's marital satisfaction.

Visual Interaction

The glance, the stare, lingering eye contact, and other forms of visual interaction are very important in everyday life. Eye contact is a frequent topic in literature, where two distinct themes exist. One approach views eye contact as a mechanism of dominance and evil acts, while the other approach views eye contact as a means of conveying preference and affection.

These themes are echoed by actual research results, since there is some evidence that eye contact can be aversive and a stimulus to either flight or fight. Ellsworth, Carlsmith, and Henson (1972) found that automobile drivers as well as pedestrians crossed an intersection faster when stared at than did subjects in a control condition not involving staring. The aversion caused by the steady stare may be general across primates, particularly between males. Exline (1972) reported one study in which a male experimenter stood directly in front of the cage of male rhesus monkeys and either stared directly at the eyes of the monkey or first established eye contact and then dropped the gaze deferentially. The monkeys reacted to the fixed stare with threat displays and sometimes charged to the front of the cage as if to attack. No such behavior occurred when the experimenter dropped his gaze. It appears that it really is impolite to stare, and the reason why may be part of our evolutionary heritage.

In humans prolonged eye contact can also indicate positive regard for another person. Simmel (1924) emphasized the role of mutual glances in establishing meaningful interpersonal relations. Shelley and McKew (1979) noted that the dilation of the pupils of the eyes of a woman denotes sexuality and sexual attractiveness to males viewing pictures of her.

There are two prevailing theories which attempt to account for visual interaction behavior. Argyle and Dean's (1965) *affiliative–conflict model* states that the level of intimacy in pair interaction is influenced by such factors as eye contact, interaction distance, intimacy of conversation topic, and smiling. In any interaction there are forces moving the participants toward greater intimacy while other forces hold the participants back. Delicate negotiation between the participants results in an *equilibrium point,* where the forces are in balance and where the participants hope to feel comfortable. On a very simple level Argyle and Dean postulate that if two persons establish a comfortable degree of eye contact, interaction distance, and other factors in a given context, if one factor such as eye contact is increased, another factor such as distance will increase to maintain the balance of intimacy. Thus increased eye contact heightens the intimacy while increased distance lessens it, and a balance is maintained. Argyle and Dean's theory has also been called the *equilibrium model of intimacy*.

Patterson's (1976) *arousal model of intimacy* proposes that the participants in an intimate couple experience some degree of physiological arousal. When one of the participants (person A) changes his or her intimate behavior, the other participant (person B) will experience heightened arousal. If person B identifies the arousal with positive emotional feelings, he or she will move the interaction to greater intimacy, while an identification with negative emotional feelings will bring about a decrease in interaction intimacy. To return to the example in the preceding paragraph, if two persons establish a comfortable degree of eye contact and then person A suddenly increases the amount of eye contact, person B will respond in one of two ways. If the emotional context is positive, person B may move even closer to A and thus reciprocate in raising the intimacy level even higher. If the context is negative, however, B will probably move farther away from A to compensate for the eye contact.

Self-Presentation and Affiliation–Attraction

We have learned that humans affiliate for many reasons, including anxiety or fear, loneliness, and the need for social comparison. Affiliation is influenced by environmental factors such as propinquity or similarity of activities, and the affiliation process is subtly interwoven with such changes in nonverbal behavior as increased eye contact and more relaxed body language. Nonverbal behavior is part of a larger construct called *self-presentation behavior,* which refers to the way in which we present or offer ourselves to the world at large in our various social roles. Self-presentation potentially includes everything we say and do: accent, use of language, apparent intelligence, grooming and physical appearance, affect (smiling, frowning), posture and body positions, and so on. Whenever we interact with other people, we are engaging in self-presentation, but some of us more actively employ various strategies of self-presentation in order to influence the way in which we are perceived by others. Such strategy is called *impression management.* Certain social or professional roles seem to require a considerable amount of impression management—for instance, movie performer, political figure, fashion model, or university president. One common thread in these roles is their visibility to the public. We can perhaps be much less concerned about influencing others' perceptions of us when we are in private than when we are in public. When we refer to familiar social settings where we can relax and just "be ourselves," we are really talking about settings where we can present ourselves without much conscious control over our behavior and where we don't have to worry about the impression we are making. There are times, however, when we are in rather private settings and yet monitor our behavior very carefully as we try to make a good impression. One such setting is courtship.

Self-Presentation Styles

Christy is a very pretty, popular college junior. She's a good student, well-liked by other girls, and dates frequently. One reason Christy is so sought after for dates is that she likes many different activities and is flexible from situation to situation. For instance, when Christy dates Bob, they usually go to a sporting event such as a football or basketball game and may sit for hours in a cold stadium. But Christy is a good sport! When she goes out with Mark, they go to art galleries or foreign films and frequently end up drinking wine and discussing art until late into the night. When she dates Tom, however, Christy knows that they will spend most of the evening dancing at a disco club. In each of the settings Christy dresses differently and exposes a different facet of her personality, yet she seems equally at home in all three. Is Christy really a flexible person with wide interests, or is she merely a good impression manager?

On the other hand, Christy's roommate Peg is a somewhat different person. Peg is also well-liked and a good student, but she dates only one or two fellows on a limited basis and usually confines her activities to concerts or shows on the campus or to study dates at the library. Peg dresses pretty much the same in every setting (jeans and a blouse) and is quietly humorous most of the time. Is Peg really a consistent, focused person, or is she just a good impression manager?

In addition to controlling our own self-presentations, we must deal with other people's self-presentations every day. We form impressions of other students, professors, salespersons, physicians, television personalities, and so on on the basis of how we interpret the selves they present to us. Such interpretation would be an overwhelming task if it did not largely occur on an intuitive level. Many of our impressions are formed without a great deal of conscious thought.

The conscious aspects of our self-presentation may be influenced by factors such as our need to be liked by someone else, the status differences between ourselves and someone else, and the degree of our dependence on another person (Figley, 1979). Self-esteem can also influence a person's style of self-presentation in a given situation, since Cialdini and Richardson (1980) found that students who had been subjected to an ego-deflating experience were more likely to favorably describe their home university (build themselves up) and to unfavorably describe a rival university ("put down" their rivals). Thus, when we have had a self-deflating experience, we particularly need to make ourselves feel worthwhile again. In fact, Walster (1965) found that women whose self-esteem had been temporarily lowered were more receptive to the attentions of a potential date than were women whose self-esteem had been temporarily raised. If we lose in one area of our lives, we will often try harder to win in another area.

The way in which we present ourselves is also influenced by whether or not we expect to see another person again. In one experiment participants tended to evaluate other people more positively (even when the other people were quite dislikable) if future interpersonal contact was anticipated (Tyler & Sears, 1977). Of course at times we may change our evaluation only to have the new evaluation become the true one. For instance, if I know I'll be seeing Tom again, I may evaluate Tom more highly and may even be nicer to him when we're together. In turn, Tom responds pleasantly to me, and we actually become quite friendly. Snyder (1981) describes the same process in relation to our impression management when we actually "come to believe our own performances" (p. 99). One example of this is the midwestern farm girl who becomes a Hollywood star, with all the suitable trappings. Within a fairly short time, the girl ceases to just *act* like a star, she *is* a star. She has become her own performance.

Baumeister (1982) proposed that there are two main reasons why we engage in self-presentation. First, we may present ourselves so as to impress a certain group of people (pleasing an audience). Second, we may be trying to make our public image or public self consistent with our ideal self; Baumeister calls this "self-construction" (p. 3). These two self-presentation motives are related to various things, including giving and receiving help, conformity, influence, reactance, attitude expression and change, receiving evaluation, aggression, attribution, task performance, ingratiation, and emotions.

In addition to the various possible styles of self-presentation there are various levels of skill in managing one's self-presentation. As we noted, some people appear to change their behavior from one context to another, while other persons are the same across several contexts. One psychological concept which deals with the differences in how people monitor their verbal and nonverbal self-presentation is *self-monitoring*.

Self-Monitoring

Snyder has been the primary developer of research on self-monitoring (see, for example, his work in 1974 and 1979) and divides individuals into high and low self-monitors based on their scores on the Self-Monitoring Scale (1974). High self-monitors are particularly sensitive to the various personal and environmental cues in a situation, and they use these cues to influence their own behavior. High self-monitors are thus not only skilled at figuring out what kind of behavior is appropriate in a certain situation, but are also incredibly good at supplying it. High self-monitors can effectively convey a wide range of emotions by both verbal and nonverbal means, and although they may not always be authentic in what they portray, high self-monitors are usually perceived as quite convincing.

Low self-monitors, on the other hand, seem to be unaware of or at least not influenced by the external cues in a social situation. Low self-monitors present themselves in ways which accurately reflect their true attitudes and values—in a sense they "march to their own drummer"—and they behave much the same from one situation to another.

As you might expect, high self-monitors are better impression managers than are low self-monitors; they know just what to do to get people to think well of them. High self-monitors will often go to considerable lengths in order to be well thought of by others, and in one case (Elliott, 1979) actually paid money to gain information about the people with whom they were going to interact and thus more judiciously manage their own self-presentation. High and low self-monitors differ in their ability to conceptualize a situation, according to Snyder and Cantor (1980). High self-monitors are more adept at seeing the external, environmental factors in the situation, but low self-monitors can more easily respond to internal, dispositional factors. One study conducted with high and low self-monitors (Dabbs, Evans, Hopper, & Purvis, 1980) revealed that high self-monitors are (not surprisingly) more facile and effective speakers in an interaction, and that high and low self-monitors communicate quite well when paired. The principle of complementarity operates, with high self-monitors doing most of the talking and low self-monitors most of the listening.

If we look at Christy and Peg, the college students mentioned earlier, we can probably describe Christy as a high self-monitor and Peg as a low self-monitor. Christy is sensitive to the social situation and seems to tailor both her appearance and her personality to fit the occasion. It is also very important to her to be popular, and she is. Peg does not seem particularly responsive to external cues, but rather appears consistently governed by internal attitudes and values in nearly all situations.

Self-monitoring and the larger topic of impression management will continue to be studied, since most of us are consistently curious about how effectively we come across to other people and how accurately they come across to us. However, at times we are less concerned with the accuracy of our self-presentation than with our ability to make another person like us.

Ingratiation

Ingratiation refers to the specific techniques of impression management that we use to increase another person's liking for us. Jones (1964) has studied ingratiation in depth and has proposed four sets of tactics which are typically used in ingratiation attempts.

1. *Compliments*—This technique is just what it says: compliments and flattery. We tell another person all the things we like about him or her (sometimes embellishing reality a bit), and we usually leave out any criticism which might come to mind. If we do criticize at all, it is over a relatively minor point and only serves to highlight the praise we're offering.
2. *Self-presentation*—In Jones's taxonomy this refers to presenting the most positive picture of ourselves we can, maximizing our strong points and minimizing our weaknesses. This aspect of ingratiation is typically used during job interviews.

3. *Conformity in opinion and behavior*—In this instance we make sure we agree with the person whom we are trying to impress. (High self-monitoring behavior would be very helpful when using this tactic.)
4. *Rendering favors*—This fairly simplistic but effective technique involves both giving gifts to and doing favors for the person with whom we are trying to ingratiate ourselves.

Ingratiation is a strategy practiced by all of us at one time or another. Whenever we have especially wanted or needed to be liked by someone else—a friend, a date, a potential employer, or even our psychology professor—we have probably used one or more of the techniques just described.

One of the most interesting and compelling situations where all the impression management techniques can be and are used is courtship, an exciting, sometimes rather delicate experience during which we want to put our best foot forward. For example, Connie and Hal have been dating for about a month. Each likes the other and is trying hard to make the relationship work. Although Hal doesn't like to make plans ahead of time, he is trying to plan specific dates with Connie well in advance of the time they usually go out. He is also showing up for dates on time, something rather new for Hal. Connie is trying to dress up for dates (since Hal hates jeans) and is accommodating to Hal's modest income by suggesting study dates instead of expensive dinners. Both Connie and Hal monitor their own and each other's behavior and spend a fair amount of time discussing their relationship. They both try to do nice things for each other (render favors) and to praise each other (give compliments). They are so anxious to be agreeable and to avoid conflict (conformity in opinion and behavior) that they often end up playing the game of "What do you want to do, I don't care, what do you want to do?" If they continue courting, they will probably gradually reduce their self-monitoring and allow a few negatives to creep into the relationship. There is an old saying that "you don't really know someone until you've lived with them," and this really refers to the high self-monitoring (and very pleasing) behavior that occurs during courtship but that sometimes abruptly changes after a couple is married.

Ingratiation is only one technique of self-presentation, and Jones and Pittman (1982), although noting that ingratiation is undoubtedly the most commonly used technique, have presented several other basic self-presentational strategies. These strategies include *intimidation* (using threat and fear), *self-promotion* (emphasizing one's competence), *exemplification* (serving as an example or moral model), and *supplication* (throwing oneself at the other's mercy). These strategies are not mutually exclusive and may sometimes be used effectively in combination.

Impression management and specific offshoots such as self-monitoring and ingratiation are not inherently bad or good. They can be used to facilitate the interpersonal relationships that make the world go 'round or to manipulate and distort impressions and subsequent relationships.

Summary

Affiliation is the process of joining together in pairs or in groups. Affiliation is complex and occurs for many different reasons. Some people affiliate with others to reduce anxiety or fear in a negative situation, and it has been proposed that firstborn children affiliate more readily than others in high-anxiety situations. The need for social comparison has been proposed as another reason for affiliation, since people will often choose to be with others who are "in the same boat." This may be one reason why self-help groups like Alcoholics Anonymous or T.O.P.S. have become increasingly popular.

Some individuals affiliate because they are lonely. Loneliness means different things to different people and is primarily influenced by the difference between an individual's desired level of interaction and his or her actual level of interaction. Widowed, divorced, and aged persons are particularly vulnerable to loneliness. Changes in marital relationships and family structure, as well as the increasing mobility and anonymity of modern society all increase loneliness. Loneliness is related to such negative behaviors as alcoholism and suicide, but it can be ameliorated through various cognitive and behavioral strategies (for example, increasing one's communication with friends and acquaintances).

Many environmental factors influence affiliation. People often form relationships with others who are similar in age, sex, and racial background, and who live or work in close proximity. Proximity can influence disliking as well as liking, since people who have negative interactions and live close to each other may grow to dislike each other more and more strongly. Mere exposure can in some cases lead to greater attraction and thence to affiliation. Sociograms have been effectively used in many settings to measure attraction between persons in a group. Sociograms can be used with both adults and children.

Friendship formation is influenced by a wide variety of demographic and personal factors. Length of residence in a community appears to be highly related to one's investment in and satisfaction with the community, and although friendships may form more slowly in urban than in nonurban settings, the urban friendships may eventually be deeper and more intimate. People who are friends tend to have similar activity preferences. Friendships may wax and wane in importance at different ages and different stages of the life cycle.

Humans communicate as extensively through their nonverbal as their verbal behavior. People relate to others at different distances, being physically close in some settings, such as dating, and far apart in others (like speaker to audience). Different cultures also have different norms for the use of personal space. If people violate our personal space a typical reaction is flight, since such invasions may cause unpleasant physiological arousal. Body language is an important mode of communication. Courtshiplike body language occurs in many types of personal and business interactions and even in psychotherapy sessions. Facial expressions are also important in nonverbal communication, and females are typically better than males at both giving (encoding) and interpreting (decoding) facial expressions which accurately reflect underlying emotions. Eye contact is so important that it is even a popular theme in literature. Although prolonged eye contact is a positive factor in intimate relationships, staring between strangers can cause aversion. Two contemporary theories that attempt to explain visual interaction are the equilibrium model of intimacy and the arousal model of intimacy.

Individuals vary in how conscious they are of their style of self-presentation. When we try to actively influence others' impressions of us, we are engaging in impression management. Our style of and reasons for certain self-presentations may be affected by our need to be liked, our current level of self-esteem, and whether or not we expect to see that person again. Individuals usually monitor their behavior, and high self-monitors are responsive to the external cues in a social situation and often behave differently in different situations. Low self-monitors respond primarily to internal cues. If we strongly wish another person to like us, we may try to ingratiate ourselves with that other person. Ingratiation tactics include giving compliments, presenting a positive self, conforming in opinion and behavior, and doing favors for the other person. We all use impression management techniques at one time or another in our lives.

PART TWO

Loving

Previous discussion of attraction sets the stage for consideration of love, on the assumption that in modern Western society liking is one basis for the development of love relationships. Love seems to be in some respects similar conceptually to attraction, but it may differ in critical respects.

Chapter 4 analyzes love from a social-psychological perspective. The roots of love originate in parent/child interaction, and learning to love in early childhood is probably necessary in order to experience love as an adult. Recent researchers, such as Zick Rubin, have tried to distinguish liking from loving. Berscheid and Walster, using Schachter's theory of emotion, have pursued the distinction fruitfully, although controversy remains. One problem is that there are many theories of love. Three examples of theories are discussed: an exchange approach, Tennov's recent "love as limerence" theory, and John Alan Lee's color-wheel analogy. Love preoccupies nearly everyone at one time or another, causing misery as well as happiness. Chapter 4 concludes with consideration of some of the problems of love and a brief practical section on how to fall out of love.

People are preoccupied with sex perhaps even more than with love. Chapter 5, "Sexual Love," begins with a discussion of the interrelation of value to fact in the study of sexuality, using the issue of sex with love versus sex without love as an illustration. The nature of scientific research on sex is outlined, and this discussion blends into consideration of substantive issues of change in sexual attitudes and behavior over the past generation. Sexual aspects of the self and sexual interactions receive detailed attention. Sexual behavior always occurs within a social context, and Chapter 5 concludes with overviews of some important contextual variables, including communication, conflict, boredom and novelty, fantasy and erotica, and sexual aggression.

4

Love

I feel neutral about you.   I feel neutral about you.
I like you a little.   I love you a little.
I like you very much.   I love you very much.

In everyday life "I love you" and "I like you" mean quite different things to most people. The difference seems obvious until you try to say exactly what it is. The two parallel progressions listed above both seem equally natural. Loving and liking flow along together as strong correlates, if not two sides of the same coin. However, other arrangements of sentences seem to reveal clear differences between the two. For example, consider the following pairs of sentences:

1. I love only you.
   I like only you.
2. I love you more than anyone else in the world.
   I like you more than anyone else in the world.
3. I love you to the breadth and depth my soul can reach.
   I like you to the breadth and depth my soul can reach.

"I love only you" is considered highly appropriate when uttered in the right context to the right person. "I like only you" would be considered by most people to reveal a stunted personality and an inability to relate properly to people. How would you feel if someone confessed that he or she liked only you in the whole world? Probably your desire to escape would be stronger than your feelings of flattery.

The next two pairs of sentences indicate that the language of love does differ somewhat from the language of liking, and it is this type of difference that probably leads most people to conclude that loving and liking are different emotional states. In everyday life we may like many people, but love only a few of them. It is also not unheard of for a couple to declare their love for each other even as they clearly and actively appear to dislike one another.

Despite these differences, most people hold the belief that if you love someone you should also like that person. That is, liking or attraction should be an underlying basis for the development of love. This commonsense notion is indeed a major assumption of this book—attraction is a basis for love, and love is one basis for intimate relationships. Thus love is similar to but not quite the same as attraction. They are similar in emotion, except that love involves stronger feelings. But love also includes a deep emotional commitment, and such commitment involves increased attention to, interest in, and idealization of the loved person. Such commitment also leads to stronger desires to be with the other and for exclusiveness in the relationship. Thus liking may be the basic core of feeling in love but love also involves other dimensions not involved in liking.

There are many kinds of love, perhaps as many as there are different kinds of people to be loved. There is the love of parents for children, of children for grandparents, of brothers and sisters for each other, and so on. Each love relationship is different, and each has its own unique aspects. One type of love that preoccupies most people at some time in their lives is love for one (or more) members of the opposite sex. Romantic love has a profound impact on nearly everyone's life. It is enormously important from a social-psychological point of view, because it instigates and guides heterosexual relationships, often resulting in the societal institution of marriage.

Love begins in the cradle. Without love and care we would all perish as infants. It is likely that the intense romantic attractions of adult life are related to the experiences of love in early childhood, and we thus begin at the beginning of love, at the very roots of its origins.

BOX 4-1   Examples of some of the great loves of history and literature

ANTONY AND CLEOPATRA, who defied convention and Julius Caesar in order to be together. As Antony lay dying, his last words were to Cleopatra:

I am dying, Egypt, dying; only
I here importune death awhile, until
Of many thousand kisses the poor last
I lay upon thy lips.

Shakespeare's *Antony and Cleopatra,* Act IV: Scene xiv

ROMEO AND JULIET, the young star-crossed lovers, probably the ultimate tragic romantics:

But, soft! What light through
yonder window breaks?
It is the east, and Juliet is the sun . . .
See, how she leans her cheek upon her hand!
O, that I were a glove upon that hand,
That I might touch that cheek!

Shakespeare's *Romeo and Juliet,* Act II: Scene ii

DAVID AND BATHSHEBA:

And it came to pass in an eveningtide, that David arose from off his bed, and walked upon the roof of the king's house: and from the roof he saw a woman washing herself; and the woman was very beautiful to look upon. . . . And David sent messengers, and took her; and she came in unto him, and he lay with her.

The Bible, II Samuel 11:2,4

King David wanted Bathsheba for himself, so he sent her husband, Uriah, to the front lines of battle in the Israelite war. Uriah was killed, and David and Bathsheba were married.

ELIZABETH BARRETT, spinster and semi-invalid, left her family home to marry poet Robert Browning. She became a famous poet herself and wrote one of the best-known love sonnets of all time.

> How do I love thee? Let me count the ways.
> I love thee to the depth and breadth and height
> My soul can reach, when feeling out of sight
> For the ends of Being and ideal Grace.
> I love thee to the level of every day's
> Most quiet need, by sun and candle light.
> I love thee freely, as men strive for Right;
> I love thee purely, as they turn from Praise.
> I love thee with the passion put to use
> In my old griefs, and with my childhood's faith.
> I love thee with a love I seemed to lose
> With my lost saints—I love thee with the breath,
> Smiles, tears, of all my life!—and, if God choose,
> I shall but love thee better after death.

The Poetical Works of Elizabeth Barrett Browning. Sonnet XLIII.

The Roots of Love

It is obvious that most infants become attached to their parents over time, usually more strongly to the mother than to the father. Several years ago psychologists explained the attachment process in terms of various learning theories. Because the parents are constantly associated with feeding, changing, and comforting the infant, psychologists presumed that parents become *conditioned stimuli* associated with the satisfaction of these basic biological needs. In the language of learning theory, parents become *conditioned reinforcers,* because of the constant conjunction of their activities with the satisfaction of basic drives. In this view the development of love is second hand, a derivative of a satisfied stomach and a contented bowel.

Today we know that these previous views are too simple minded. The need for love and affection may be just as basic and primitive as the need for food. Further, love does not develop as a simple consequence of stimulus association, but emerges out of the rich interaction between parents and infants.

Mother—Infant Interaction

Careful observational studies of humans and other primates, especially monkeys and chimps, indicate that mothers do not simply care for their infants. Rather, they *interact* with them almost from birth (Hofer, 1975;

Hartup & Lempers, 1973), with the infant's behavior affecting the mother (Lewis & Rosenblum, 1974). Mother and infant, and to a lesser extent father, form an *interactional system*.

Infant cries and smiles are powerful activators of adult behavior. Several authors (for example, Morris, 1971) have suggested that the strong adult responses to smiling and crying may be a biological heritage of our species. No less an authority than Darwin believed that the infant smile has definite survival value because it elicits strong attentional responses from adults. Thus cries and smiles are infant response patterns that make an early contribution to the interaction system.

The interaction system changes over time because the infant grows rapidly. Humans and other primates extensively hold and fondle the infant. Such *contact comfort* is apparently vital to the welfare of the infant and is pleasurable to the mother. Many authors believe that this early physical touching and holding is the true root of love. For example, Harlow (1974) coined the concept *organic affection* to describe the infant monkey's need to cling to its mother long before it can recognize her. In fact, soft, warm terrycloth models served the basic need to grasp and hold almost as well as real mother monkeys.

Human infants also obviously derive much comfort from being held, rocked, and patted. Thus, touching and holding—physical contact— may be the physical basis for the development of emotional attachments, or as it is sometimes called, the development of a *pair-bond* (Money, 1980).

After the first few weeks of life being held and touched are supplemented by vocal activities which soon affect behavior. Within a few months parent and child engage in many obvious *reciprocal behaviors* (Schaffer, 1971), such as gazing, vocalizing, and imitating each other's physical movements. In brief mother and infant develop a moderately complex interaction system. It is out of the complexity of this interaction system with its basis in physical contact that true affection originates.

The Development of Attachment

The term *attachment* was used by Bowlby (1958) to describe the observed fact that a mother and infant try to maintain physical closeness to each other. The term is now also used to describe the inferred feelings of affection—or love—that develop between infant and adult.

The development of attachment is a complex achievement (Ainsworth, 1973) that goes through roughly four phases during the first year of life (Cohen, 1976). During the first few months the infant responds positively to the contact comfort provided by any adult. But at about the age of three months the infant becomes more responsive to its mother than to other people. Between six and nine months of age the infant becomes strongly attached to its mother. The baby makes active efforts to be near her and protests strongly when she is absent. At this time the infant also develops a fear response to strangers. A little later, at approximately nine to 12 months of age, fear of strangers decreases somewhat, and the infant may develop an attachment to other familiar people, especially the father.

The attachment process is striking to observe. It can develop very rapidly, although infants vary considerably in this regard. The preparatory work of holding, caring for, and providing a rich, safe environment during the first six months seems necessary to stimulate brain development to the point where an emotional attachment can develop. Because attachments to people develop about the time the infant develops a sense of the permanence of objects in general, it seems reasonable to conclude that the attachment bond, or the potential for it, is an innate part of the human heritage. We are not unique, however, since the same bonding process occurs in the other primates and, indeed, in practically all mammals.

Sequencing of Attachment

Physical contact is an important initial condition for the development of attachment to mother in the second half of the first year. It may well be that mother/infant attachment is in turn important for the development of normal human relations as one matures. The consensus of scientific thinking is that the effects of one developmental stage carry over into the next one.

The Harlows (1966, 1970; Harlow, 1974) have studied the development of love in several species of monkeys for many years. The Harlows' detailed work shows the importance of sequencing in developmental stages. In the infant monkey the first stage of "organic affection" develops within a few weeks into a stage of attachment to and comfort-seeking from its mother. As the infant matures and learns to play, it moves into a stage in which its mother represents general solace and security. Slowly, peers become more important, and there is a relative disattachment from the mother monkey. The peer friendships and play of early adolescence are important in the later development of heterosexual relationships. Monkeys without the experience of peer socialization have considerable difficulty in mating in adulthood.

A developmental sequence seems to occur approximately as follows:

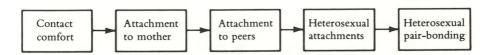

This sequence implies that the attraction between the sexes leading to mature adult sexual relations can be traced step by step back to the initial physical contact between mother and infant in the first few days of life. According to this conception the creature love of an enfolding mother is the root of all love.

There is good evidence involving monkeys and some evidence involving humans that the growth of love does follow such a sequence, with each later stage dependent upon an earlier stage. Infant monkeys reared in isolation cannot have successful heterosexual relations if the period of isolation lasts beyond about six months. Such monkeys do not know how to play with peers, and they are consequently inept in adult sexual relations.

Human infants cannot be reared in complete isolation. However, infant humans can be socially and emotionally deprived by their parents even though their physical survival needs are met. Such children are apathetic and slow to respond. Sometimes such children exhibit glandular disturbances which slow physical growth, a condition called *deprivation dwarfism* (Gardner, 1972). When given proper social attention, such infants usually grow rapidly.

Deprivation dwarfism is an extreme example of love starvation. More typically, unloved infants develop into forlorn (but sometimes aggressive) children with few or no playmates. Peer isolation in turn sets the stage for a lonely adolescence and perhaps a lonely adulthood. Most authorities agree (see, for instance, Shaffer, 1979) that human infants need rich stimulation from loving interactions in order to develop normally. The social stimulation does not have to come from a specific person (a father may, for example, serve as a fine surrogate mother), but it may be necessary for the infant to develop an attachment to at least one person.

If an attachment to another human fails to develop in the first two years of life, it is questionable whether the person will be able as an adult to develop a deep love attachment. Research and comparisons with other primates do suggest that without learning to love as an infant, it is very difficult—perhaps impossible—to learn love as an adult. The genesis of and capacity for adult heterosexual love quite likely does have its beginnings in mother's arms, with the first stirrings of organic responsiveness to her warm touch and soothing voice. It is perhaps part of the meaning of being a loving creature (or at least a loving mammal) that the creature must first love its creator, its mother, intrinsically, instinctively, and without reservation.

Love through the Ages

The strong recent emphasis by behavioral scientists on the origins of love in infancy is, of course, not really new. At the turn of the century Sigmund Freud hypothesized that children go through a series of psychosexual stages leading, by the age of 3 to 5, to a complex identification with the same-sex parent. This process in boys is called the Oedipus complex after the mythical king of Thebes who killed his father and married his mother. In girls an assumed similar process is called the Electra complex. The reasoning is that the male child develops sexual desires for his mother, finds these desires very threatening, represses them, and identifies with his father, thereby possessing the mother symbolically or vicariously.

Freud's theorizing is well known. What is not so often realized, however, is that the Oedipus myth is ancient. Its very age suggests that early societies were aware of the subterranean family love affair. Regardless of whether the parent/child love bond is specifically sexual in nature, the early myths recognized the dynamic power of love in family origins and the potential for trouble in later life that these strong emotional bonds can cause.

One aspect of the emotional bonding process of family life is the incest taboo, which is nearly universal across all cultures and has existed throughout recorded history. Social scientists most commonly accept some version of psychoanalytic theory that explains the incest taboo as a permanent defense mechanism resulting from the resolution of the Oedipus or Electra complex. However, there are at least a dozen theories about the origins of the incest taboo (Murstein, 1974b), and none is completely satisfactory.

Recent research suggests that the taboo is broken with some frequency. In summarizing several surveys, Herman (1981) noted that approximately 10 percent of all women report a childhood sexual experience with a relative, and 1 percent of all women report father/daughter incest. Herman believes that incest represents an extreme exaggeration of traditional patriarchal control patterns.

Love, Sex, and Marriage

The nature of love is not fully independent of patterns of sexual behavior and marriage customs. Thus learning to love parents in infancy may, in societies with autocratic male dominance of the family, lead to erotic sexual behavior, especially between father and daughter. While rare, incestuous behavior does suggest a link between emotional closeness, physical intimacy, and sexual behavior. In this sense incest is a perversion of what we today consider the natural order of things in the relations between the sexes.

During the latter half of the twentieth century the norm seems to be that boy and girl meet, interact, and discover common interests, backgrounds, and family values. They begin to like each other. There is also physical attraction, which may develop either rapidly or more slowly. Liking plus attraction leads to increased interaction. If the feelings develop further, at some point the couple define themselves as in love. Being in love automatically sanctions serious consideration of marriage. Sexual activity may or may not have begun before marriage, but it most likely is linked closely with the couple's perception of being in love.

Therefore, in today's average couple, liking and good companionship go together and are causally related to falling in love, and quite often to full sexual expression of that love. Falling deeply in love is in turn a good, reasonable basis for marriage. Further, some would say that deep and committing love is the *only* valid basis for marriage. Love, sexual expression, and marriage are all closely interconnected. The progression seems so natural, so inevitable, that one may feel quite sure the creator ordained human nature in this way.

The truth is that our current conceptions are recent phenomena and did not exist throughout most of recorded history. Marriage and sexuality have always been linked, but the relationship of love to marriage and to sexual expression has varied very widely over the past few thousand years.

Love as the basis of marriage is an eighteenth-century invention that gradually grew in influence in the Western world until it has become the predominant view in the twentieth century (see Stone, 1977). Love in ancient Greek marriage was unknown, perhaps unthinkable (Bullough, 1976; Murstein, 1974b). Women then were not educated and were considered inferior in almost all respects to men. Good companionship could be had only with other well-educated males or with a rare female courtesan. One result was that love often bloomed between males; classical Greece had a large incidence of male homosexuality. Marriage was a necessary drudgery to produce children and create one's estate, but the real joy in life was in male companionship. Presumably, females felt equally negative about marriage, but they left few written records.

The most adequate general statement is that love was not a real basis of marriage until the late middle ages. In most societies marriages were arranged by the parents (usually fathers), and women were considered legally and morally inferior to men. Sexual intercourse, as a facet of love between equals, could have existed only in rare instances. A small change occurred in the middle ages, when some authorities began to write of a companion role for the wife in addition to the usual wifely roles of sex, procreation, and domestic worker (Murstein, 1974b).

Between roughly 1000 and 1300 A.D. a new concept emerged, called *courtly love*. It was also mostly a male invention. Elements of this new behavior pattern were emotional exultation, adoration, and intense total pursuit of the beloved. Courtly love had little to do with marriage and probably not much to do with overt sexual behavior. Typically a knight, usually married, would be love struck at the glimpse of a fair lady, who was most likely also married to a nobleman. Then there would ensue what might become years of intense courtship, the object of which was to win the lady's favor. The ultimate favor was physical contact, some caresses, and perhaps occasionally actual intercourse. Between strenuous bouts of combat and other daring feats for his lady, the

BOX 4-2   Courtly love

Courtly love originated in the songs and poetry of troubadours—wandering men who traveled from manor to manor in the middle ages, earning food and lodging by entertaining the lord and his court. These minstrels sang of the blessings of love freely chosen. Since marriage was not free (always arranged), free, spontaneous love could only occur outside marriage with someone else's marriage partner. As the lore developed, however, this love was idealistically pure, not adulterous. It involved esteem for the noble lady, inspiration to great feats for her, respect for her virtuous qualities, and courtesy in interaction with her. The results were supposed to be ennoblement of the male from a rather loutish brute at best to heights of self-sacrifice, pure thoughts, and loving consideration of his chosen lady.

This ideology was translated into behavior patterns, first by the troubadours and later by other members of the noble classes. In time courtly love evolved into a stylized set of behavioral stages (Murstein, 1974b). Initially, the love-struck male could only worship from afar as a hopeful aspirant. He might, for example, crouch in hiding for many hours to catch a glimpse of the lady. At some point he moved to the stage of supplicant by various subtle acts that caught the lady's attentions. After some period of time, perhaps months, she might send him a positive sign, which allowed him to enter the stage of courtship. During this period a profuse number of songs and poetry were composed for the lady. These were delivered in semiprivate situations as well as more public gatherings. Symbolic acts, such as fighting in tournaments or going on long crusades to prove one's valor, were often part of the ritual. The last stage of courtship, if it occurred, was admittance to the lady's private chamber, during which kisses and embraces might be exchanged and occasional love-making might occur. Since the lady was invariably married to a powerful lord, the last stages of the courtship were necessarily discreet.

Specific forms of courtly love evolved somewhat differently in different countries. The golden age was the twelfth century. In France the emphasis was more explicitly on love and its effects. One of the most famous troubadours, Bernard de Ventadour, fell in and out of love many times, each time repeating the courting ritual and leaving behind large quantities of rather mediocre love lyrics.

Bernard's lifestyle epitomized the *concept* of love as his true quest. Each new lover embodied part of the ideal, but Bernard was in love with the concept of love itself and was thus doomed to an eternal quest.

In Germany courtly love was more strenuous, involving the concept of service to the woman. One of the most famous German troubadours, Ulrich von Lichtenstein, devoted many years of his life to the courtship of a married princess. To win her favor he had his harelip corrected, suffered her ripping out a handful of his hair, cut off his finger and sent it to her in a velvet case (proof of his service), and worked his way from Venice to Vienna in a dazzling series of tournaments in which he broke 307 lances, unseated several opponents from their horses, and was never unseated himself. Fifteen years into the courtship the lady yielded and saw Ulrich privately, but history does not tell us his final reward. Shortly afterward, the pair parted company.

During his strenuous life, Ulrich nevertheless managed to find time to marry and have several children! Quite clearly, sexual release was not the goal of courtly love. Whatever the complex of esoteric and stylized behaviors involved in courtly love, it forged a new conception of woman—that of a creature of great value, one who is worth effort, sacrifice, devotion, and intense emotional attachment—in short, a creature worthy of passionate love.

knight would go home to visit his wife, have sex with her, and see his children. It never occurred to him to cherish, idealize, and desire intensely his own wife in the same ways he dreamed of the fair lady.

Courtly love was highly stylized and ritualized. As a social form it could not endure. However, courtly love did give general support to the concept that a woman could be intensely cherished, loved, and adored by a man. It also spawned a wide range of tender and solicitous behavior forms that men would express toward women. These forms have evolved, but still exist today, denoted by the term "courting."

Courtly love was a precursor to full emotional love between the sexes, and during the Renaissance and the Reformation periods (about 1500–1615 A.D.) the notion of a love marriage developed. Of course there were great conflicts between advocates of the traditional arranged marriages and the scandalous advocates of love marriage. But the idea of marriage for love was a concept whose time had begun to arrive.

The past 350 years may be viewed as a slow ascendance of the notion of love as the basis for marriage. At first it was only one basis and not the most important one at that. Other bases—status, family alliances, economic security—remained more important; these are not totally insignificant even today. One important issue was the relative importance of the individual. Our current emphasis on the value of the individual human being has slowly gained ground over the past several hundred years. Though difficult to prove, it seems likely that the growth and elaboration of love could not have occurred until the concept of the individual as someone uniquely important and distinct from his or her family background had emerged. In other words, the ability to love another intensely required the related concept of that individual as a full person of intrinsic worth who has dynamic, self-determining attributes.

Modern Love

During the past two centuries conceptions of love have shifted and changed, but grown irreversibly in the direction of love in marriage through individual choice of the marriage partner. Slowly, people began to recognize that need satisfaction and personality characteristics of the other sex were important to the success of love. Similarity of backgrounds and values was also recognized as important, because they reduced conflict potential between the partners. During this century the importance of communication has been discovered, and successful love is viewed as an accomplishment of ongoing communication in interaction.

The growth of love as a basis for marriage became something of a cult that reached its heyday in the 1950s. During the past two decades there have been rapid changes in mores regarding sexuality. Today sexual expression outside a loving marriage is not stigmatized as it was twenty years ago. Love is still important, no doubt central in the relations of most men and women, but the tendency described previously may have weakened just enough so that the relationships between love, sexual expression, and marriage patterns may be moving toward independence once again—or at least relatively more independence than two decades ago.

The lessons of history teach us that the relationships between the sexes have been slowly but constantly evolving. Each generation feels that the mores it was born into are permanently fixed. But even during each generation's lifetime there are enough changes to cause problems. What is "real" love? Is sex okay if you are in love? Or is it okay if you really like someone? These and similar questions are the cutting edge of uncertainty for today's young generation. Such questions probably would have been meaningless two centuries ago, and three centuries ago the last two questions could have caused the questioner serious legal and religious problems.

One of the more recent concerns of youth has been to sort out the various meanings of love and friendship. Love has matured in the last 2000 years, but it can still be problematic and troublesome. Therefore trying to decide how it differs from mere liking, if it does, is a useful thing, important in interpersonal relations in everyday life.

Liking and Loving

Liking is related to loving, but it also seems different. Zick Rubin (1970, 1973, 1974) was one of the first social scientists to study the similarity and difference between the two concepts in a rigorous way. Rubin (1970) viewed love conceptually as "an attitude held by a person toward a particular other person, involving predispositions to think, feel, and behave in certain ways toward the other person" (p. 265). This definition is very similar to our general definition of interpersonal attraction. This was intended; both love and liking are best viewed conceptually as an attitude. The research problem for Rubin was to determine whether the two concepts are different in the ways they really occur in people's behavior.

In order to study this issue Rubin developed two questionnaires (or scales), one to measure liking and the second to measure romantic loving. The results from responses to the two scales would be used to decide whether liking is really different from loving, or whether the two scales seem to measure the same thing. Constructing the scales was a challenging and difficult job, because it was necessary to construct a fair test. A fair test required that items for the two questionnaires be selected in an unbiased way, so that the scales could either be unrelated or highly related, depending on what the true state of nature is. It would probably be possible to choose sets of items that proved no difference between liking and loving, or other sets of items that proved a complete difference. Such an initial bias in item selection would really be a form

FIGURE 4-1 Must you like someone to have sex with him or her? *(Copyright, 1981, Jules Feiffer. Reprinted with permission of Universal Press Syndicate. All rights reserved.)*

of scientific cheating and would not inform us about love versus liking in the real world.

Given these considerations, it will be useful to specify more precisely the criteria that Rubin followed in the development of the love scale and the rationale by which liking could be distinguished from romantic love.

1. Since the content of the questionnaire items would constitute the conceptual meaning of romantic love, the items should be based on current popular and theoretical conceptions of love.
2. Answers to the questionnaire items should indicate that they are measuring a single underlying attitude of love. Operationally, all of the items should be highly intercorrelated.
3. A parallel questionnaire measuring liking must be developed. All the items should also be highly intercorrelated. However, if love and liking are separate or independent concepts, then the correlation between the love questionnaire and the liking questionnaire should be fairly low.

A large number of items were initially obtained and sorted by judges into love and liking categories. From this procedure 70 items were obtained, rated by students in an introductory psychology course, and evaluated by methods that estimated their correlation, or relation to each other. This analysis resulted in 13 items for a love scale and 13 items for a liking scale. Example items for each scale are shown in Table 4-1. The love items seem to tap affiliation and dependence needs, desire to care for the other, exclusivity, possessiveness, and intimacy toward

TABLE 4-1   Sample items from Rubin's love scale and liking scale

Sample love-scale items
1. If I could never be with _____, I would feel miserable.
2. If I were lonely, my first thought would be to seek _____ out.
3. I would forgive _____ for practically anything.

Sample liking-scale items
1. I think that _____ is unusually well adjusted.
2. _____ is one of the most likable people I know.
3. _____ is the sort of person whom I myself would like to be.

Note: Each scale contains 13 items. High correlations exist between items within each scale, and only a modest correlation exists between the two scales. For example, neither scale includes an item on attractiveness, since this item could pertain equally to love or liking. Therefore, love and liking, as measured by the two scales, should be relatively independent of each other.

From "Measurement of Romantic Love," by Z. Rubin. In *Journal of Personality and Social Psychology*, 1970, *16*, 265–273. Copyright 1970 by the American Psychological Association. Reprinted by permission.

the other. The liking items tap favorability of evaluation, respect, perceived similarity, maturity, intelligence, admirability, and likability.

The two questionnaires were tested and retested by recruiting 158 couples to complete them. Subjects also completed the questionnaires again by rating a close, same-sex friend. Each item on the questionnaire was rated on a nine-point scale.

The results provided some support for Rubin's distinction between loving and liking. For females the love scale had an average correlation between items of +.84; the liking scale had an average correlation between items of +.81. However the correlation between the total liking and loving scales was only +.39. The results for males showed average correlations between items of +.86 for loving and +.83 for liking. However, the correlation between liking and loving was also quite high, +.60. Rubin suggested that women may distinguish more sharply between liking and loving than men do.

Some interesting differences in average ratings emerged between males and females. These means are shown in Table 4-2. The means shown are for total scores, which were computed by adding a subject's responses to all 13 questions on a scale. Men and women showed the same overall level of love for each other, and women liked their partners as much as they loved them. However, men liked their female partners less than they loved them, and also liked the partners less than the partners liked them. This difference may have been because men tended to get higher ratings than women on liking-scale items such as intelligence, good judgment, and leadership potential. Both sexes loved their best friend of the same sex considerably less than they loved their romantic partner of the opposite sex. They liked their best friend of the same sex considerably more than they loved him or her, but still somewhat less than they liked their romantic partner.

Rubin's evidence is not completely convincing that love is different from liking because of the high correlation between the two scales for

TABLE 4-2   Means for loving and liking in Rubin's study

	Women	Men
Love for partner	89	89
Liking for partner	88	85
Love for friend	65	55
Liking for friend	80	79

males. However, it is a good first attempt to operationalize and scientifically distinguish between the two sentiments. More recent research by Dermer and Pyszczynski (1978) provided additional evidence for the validity of the distinction. These authors were puzzled by the absence of any reference to sexual behavior in the love scale. The authors reasoned that sexual interest and romantic feelings of love should be highly related. If some stimulus, such as erotic literature, prompted a sexual response, feelings of love for one's lover should be stronger after reading the erotic passage than before reading it. College males who said they were currently in love served in the experiment. Some of the males were assigned to read a "Collegiate Fantasy," which dealt in explicit detail with the sexual behavior and fantasies of a college woman. The rest of the men served in a control condition and read a rather dull article on the courtship and mating behavior of herring gulls. Afterward both groups of men completed several scales, including abbreviated versions of Rubin's liking and love scales. Results showed that men reading the erotic passage had significantly higher love scores (for the person they were in love with) than men who read about herring gulls. However, there was no difference in the liking scores (for the loved one) between the two groups. These results show that the love scale was differentially sensitive to the erotic manipulation, but the liking scale was not. Therefore, these data provide additional validation for the distinction between liking and loving.

It seems reasonable to conclude that people do in fact distinguish between liking someone and loving that person. Rubin's research is of value in providing some empirical evidence on the matter. Yet, because emotions are very difficult to distinguish in concrete terms, it is still unclear exactly how the emotional aspects of these two states differ. It is even possible that the emotional aspect of liking and loving does not differ. Rubin's work may only show that the cognitive or belief aspects (Chapter 1) of the two concepts are different. It is possible that the basic inner emotional state, including physiological arousal, may be the same for many types of emotional experiences and that all that differs is the individual's interpretation of the situation. Given emotional arousal, love and liking—and the perceived difference between the two—may be more in the head than in the loins. We next examine this interesting interpretation of passion and romantic love.

Emotions and Passionate Love

Falling in love is a fitting description of an experience that almost everyone has at least once and usually several times. To fall into love is to fall into a profound set of emotional experiences. There may be a range of physical symptoms such as dry mouth, pounding heart, flushed face, and knotted stomach. The mind may race, and fantasy, especially about the loved one, is rampant. Motivation to work, play, indeed for anything except the lover, may fall to zero. As the love feelings develop, strong feelings of passion may occur. In fact, passionate love is essentially the same as romantic love, except that the focus is more specifically on the emotional intensity and sexual passion.

Clearly, love is closely connected to emotional states and feelings of passion. But how? There are many theories of emotion. We will examine one theory proposed by Stanley Schachter. This theory was used in a clever way by Ellen Berscheid and Elaine Walster to explain passionate love.

Schachter's Theory of Emotion

Suppose that John can drink exactly one cup of coffee in the morning with no ill effects. If he drinks two cups of coffee, he gets jittery, his hands tremble, and his heart palpitates. When this happens, he berates himself for being a dunce and swears that it will never happen again. The extra caffeine creates a state of physiological arousal.

One morning John had breakfast with a business acquaintance. The conversation was intense, and without John's awareness the waiter refilled his coffee cup. John drank two cups of coffee, but he left the meeting thinking that he had drunk only one cup. In fifteen minutes he will get jittery and his heart will start palpitating. An interesting question arises—how will John explain his arousal, knowing that he drank only one cup of coffee? Two different but equally plausible scenarios of John's experiences 15 minutes later are described below.

Possible scenario 1:   After John left the business acquaintance, he walked across the street to the catalog department of a department store to pick up an item he had ordered the week before. The clerk waiting on him appeared somewhat surly and seemed to take forever in the stockroom looking for his order. While John was waiting, his hands began to tremble and his heart began to palpitate. John's thoughts were on the clerk. Very shortly he became aware of his inner arousal. He soon decided that he was angry—in fact, very angry—at the clerk for taking so long. In fact, he actually conceptualized a fitting label in his mind for the clerk: "no-good S.O.B." When the clerk returned, John was quite short and snapped at him, much to the clerk's surprise.

Possible scenario 2:   After John left the business acquaintance, he walked across the street to a barber shop to get a shave. A young and attractive female barber shaved him. After the shave was under way for a few minutes, John's hands began to tremble and his heart began to palpitate. He was very aware of the presence of the young woman, and at the same time became aware of his inner arousal. John soon decided that he was attracted to the woman; in fact, he concluded that he was becoming sexually aroused. A potentially embarrassing erection began to occur. As the shave ended, John took the gamble and asked the lady out that evening. He was disappointed when she responded that she does not socialize with customers.

In each scenario John experienced heightened physiological arousal caused by excess caffeine. In neither case was he aware of the true cause of his arousal. The arousal was *unexplained*. John used the environmental situation in which he found himself to infer situational cues which might be relevant to his arousal. On the basis of those cues he made a decision about the causes of his arousal. Making such a decision, or an attribution, was equivalent to labeling himself as experiencing a certain emotional state. The attributed emotional states were very different in the two scenarios because the two situations were very different. In the first possible scenario John attributed his arousal to the clerk's behavior and experienced the emotion of anger. In the second possible scenario John attributed his arousal to the lovely woman and experienced the emotions involved in sexual arousal.

In each scenario the initial state of physiological arousal was identical, but the emotions attributed to the arousal state were quite different. These scenarios suggest that, in general, the experience of emotion is heavily dependent on the attributions that people associate with their inner arousal in a given set of situational circumstances. It is precisely this kind of thinking that led to the development of Schachter's (Schachter & Singer, 1962; Schachter, 1964) theory of emotion. According to the theory, an emotional state depends on two variables, which may be expressed as a simple verbal equation:

$$\text{Emotional State} = \text{Unexplained Physiological Arousal} + \text{Relevant Situational Cues}$$

This theory was created in an attempt to integrate two earlier conflicting theories of emotion. Before the turn of the present century William James suggested that people have direct physiological reactions to the perception of stimulating events, and that awareness of bodily changes as they occur *is* the emotion. Phrased differently, we feel happy because we laugh, sad because we cry. This theory, which came to be known as the James-Lange theory of emotion, directly equated inner physiological states and their changes with emotion. The theory implied that different emotional experiences should have different physiological states and that a direct manipulation of bodily state should also directly manipulate emotional experience.

The Cannon-Bard theory of emotion was developed later in opposition to the James-Lange theory. The Cannon-Bard theory proposed that emotional experience and physiological arousal are relatively independent of each other, with each controlled by different central nervous system processes. This theory was based on Cannon's (1929; cited in Schachter, 1964) strong critique of the James-Lange theory, as follows:

1. Separation of the viscera from the central nervous system does not destroy emotional behavior.
2. The same physiological changes seem to occur in very different emotional states.
3. The viscera are insensitive to subtle changes.
4. Visceral changes are too slow to be the direct cause of emotional feeling.
5. Artificial production of physiological changes naturally associated with strong emotional states does not cause such states.

In reviewing the two theories, Schachter and Singer (1962) concluded that both physiological arousal and a cognitive label (or attributed cause) based on situational cues were necessary for a full emotional experience. Neither arousal alone nor the cognitive label alone was sufficient to cause an emotional state.

Passionate Love

In Chapter 1 we saw that reinforcement theories are widely used to explain interpersonal attraction. We like people who provide rewards for us and dislike people who punish us. Many theories explain love in the same way. However, in the previous section we reviewed the work of Rubin, which argued for and provided some evidence that liking and loving are different phenomena.

Berscheid and Walster (1974a; Walster, 1971) also felt that there are real differences between liking and loving. Some of those purported differences are:

1. Liking relationships seem to depend upon actual rewards; with love, fantasy and imagined gratifications may occur out of all proportion to the number of actual rewards received.
2. Liking and friendship often grow over time, but romantic love seems to become diluted with the passage of time.
3. Liking is consistently associated with good things (positive reinforcers), but passionate love seems to be associated with conflicting emotions, as witnessed by teenagers' frequent question of whether it is possible to love and hate someone at the same time.

Based on these apparent differences, Berscheid and Walster argued that passionate love is not just intense liking and that reinforcement theory does not account for passionate love very well, because such love seems to be a strong mix of both rewards and punishments. Instead, they selected Schachter's theory of emotion as the best conception to explain passionate love.

In order to explain passionate love, the same two conditions must hold that are needed to account for any emotional state:

1. The individual must be intensely aroused physiologically.
2. The cues in the situation must dictate to the individual that passionate love is the appropriate label for his or her feelings.

Both conditions are necessary. One will not experience passionate love unless physiologically aroused, but, given arousal, it is still not love unless the individual labels it love. If the situation is such that it is reasonable to attribute the aroused state to passionate love, then the individual will experience love. However, "as soon as he ceases to attribute his arousal to passionate love, or the arousal itself ceases, love should die" (Berscheid & Walster, 1974a, p. 363).

There are several negative as well as positive experiences which can generate a state of arousal: fear-provoking stimuli, social rejection, and sexual frustration. There is some evidence that such negative states can be interpreted as passionate love; for example, the rejected suitor sometimes redoubles the intensity of passion after rejection. The frequent arousal of fear and anger in war also seems to stimulate passionate love. In his fascinating account of life as a soldier in wartime, Gray (1959) devoted a chapter to love in war. He wrote in a letter to a friend in 1944 that "the Greeks were wise men when they matched the god of war with the goddess Aphrodite. The soldier must not only kill, he must give birth to new warriors" (p. 70). The increased intensity of eroticism during war of both men and women is vividly described (Gray, 1959, p. 73).

> If we are honest, most of us who were civilian soldiers in recent wars will confess that we spent incomparably more time in the service of Eros during our military careers than ever before or again in our lives. When we were in uniform almost any girl who was faintly attractive had an erotic appeal for us. For their part, millions of women find a strong sexual attraction in the military uniform, particularly in time of war. This fact is as inexplicable as it is notorious. Many a girl who had hitherto led a casual and superficial existence within a protective family circle had been suddenly overwhelmed by intense passion for a soldier met by chance on the street or at a dance for servicemen. It seems that the very atmosphere of large cities in wartime breathes the enticements of physical love. Not only are inhibitions on sexual expression lowered, but there exists a much more passionate interest of the sexes in each other than is the case in peacetime. Men and women normally absorbed by other concerns find themselves caught up in the whirlpool of erotic love, which is the preoccupation of the day. In wartime marriages multiply and the birth rate increases. We can

safely assume that the number of love affairs, if they could be reduced to statistics, would show an even greater rate of expansion.★

Berscheid and Walster's theorizing would predict such an effect. The rigors of soldiering in wartime would tend to keep soldiers in a state of general physiological arousal. The context and situation are very different from peacetime, and the mere sight of a woman may be a sufficient stimulus to define the situation as one appropriate for passionate arousal.

Positive as well as negative experiences may generate the necessary physiological arousal. For example, sexual arousal during the excitement phase is physiologically very similar to the physiological responses of fear and anger. Thus sexual gratification should be and probably is a direct source of passionate love. Any activity which generates a sense of danger and excitement may serve as an arousal stimulus. In fact, many people value passionate love just because it is a source of excitement, which is positively valued.

It seems reasonable to conclude that a wide variety of experiences, both positive and negative, can generate a state of physiological arousal which can serve as one of the necessary conditions for a state of passionate love to exist. We are taught as children how to label our feelings in a wide variety of situations. By the time we are adults, we have an idea of the appropriate emotion to experience in most situations. The turmoil experienced at the funeral of a relative is unlikely to be experienced as sexual arousal instead of grief; such feelings are inappropriate at a funeral. The physiological excitement experienced after a half-hour of vigrous kissing is unlikely to be interpreted as grief; social learning dictates that you label the excitement as sexual arousal. The state of physiological arousal may be quite similar in both situations; the difference in labeling dictates what emotion will be experienced.

Berscheid and Walster's theory of passionate love is interesting, though as yet incomplete (Murstein, 1980). It could possibly account for the development of such sexual practices as masochism and sadism as accidents of mislabeling states of arousal during the course of socialization. It is presently unclear what types of arousal are conducive to labeling as sexual arousal or passionate love, and what types are not. For example, loud and prolonged noise is physiologically aversive. It is most unlikely that one could learn to interpret the physiological response to noise as passion. Likewise the ongoing experience of intense pain may be incompatible with labeling as passion. However, the quick reduction of physiological arousal just after the offset of an aversive stimulus may be quite conducive to the experience of passion. In fact, Kenrick and Cialdini (1977) criticized the theory on just this point: the

★From *The Warriors: Reflections on Men in Battle,* by J. G. Gray. Copyright © 1959 by J. G. Gray. (New York: Harper & Row Publishers, Inc., 1959.) Reprinted by permission of the author.

reduction or offset of aversive stimulation is reinforcing. For example, lovers' quarrels are very unpleasant. But if they kiss and make up, the unpleasant emotional state ends, and the termination of negative feelings may reinforce feelings of love.

We must leave open the question of whether Berscheid and Walster's theory of passionate love can be accounted for by principles of reinforcement. However, they deserve much credit for drawing attention to the turbulence of passionate love. Phenomenally, love is often an alternation between ecstasy and despair, which is much stronger than in ordinary liking. Love is often both pleasure and pain. Further, the intensity of passionate love does seem to diminish over time in a way not quite true for liking. Although the expression is seldom applied to liking, love can die.

When Passion Dies

The intensity of a new romantic love seldom endures more than a few weeks or months. Many popular books and articles propose means for rekindling love's fire. After the intensity settles into a warm glow, what then? What replaces passionate love? Walster and Walster (1978) proposed two general kinds of love: passionate love and companionate love. The latter is "the affection we feel for those with whom our lives are deeply intertwined" (p. 9). If a relationship is built on a sufficient number of shared endeavors and positive experiences, presumably after passionate love withers, a steady state of enduring companionate love will take its place. If such experiences are not available, the love affair will often terminate.

Walster and Walster did not hold out much hope that the binding effects of passionate love can be maintained indefinitely. The mix of emotions in passionate love is based on several factors, some positive and some negative.

1. Need for attention and security.
2. Need to be understood and accepted.
3. Need to be taken care of.
4. Excitement of getting to know someone.
5. Excitement of sexual experience.
6. Frustration of misunderstanding and miscommunication.
7. Uncertainty and unknown aspects of the loved one.
8. Jealousy of the loved one's time and attention.
9. Anxiety and fear about the outcome of the new relationship.
10. Anger at the loved one for the pain caused by the intensity of the relationship.
11. Overwhelming, consuming, preoccupation with the loved one in thought, fantasy, and deed.

A cold, detached look at the list may suggest the question, "Who wants it anyway?" Apparently most of us do at one time or another.

Careful consideration of the list suggests several reasons why the initial intensity of passionate love inevitably wanes. Several needs, such as security and understanding, are reasonably more satisfied the better one knows the other person. His or her behavior is increasingly more predictable, and uncertainty about the person goes down. There should be fewer misunderstandings. At the same time there is an adaptation to the presence of the other, and the sheer excitement of mere physical presence extinguishes to some extent. The loved one is increasingly seen as the real "grub" he or she must be as a biological human being. Humans also need sensory variety and new stimulation. Thus the single-minded preoccupation with the other eventually gets tiring and then boring. The rest of the world, such as one's job and relatives, are increasingly insistent on their share of attention. At some point, either weeks or months later at most, the madness breaks; the loved one gets demoted to the status of one of many prized objects in the mind, rather than filling it completely. At this point the transition from passionate to companionate love is in progress.

What's wrong with companionate love? Actually, nothing, except that we humans are seldom fully satisfied with what we have. The security, understanding, predictability, and mutual acceptance is great, and for many people it is enough. However, security, understanding, predictability, and acceptance are not the same as excitement, and many people crave, even demand, excitement from their romantic relationships. In short, the lovely attributes of companionate love are exactly those attributes that may lead to boredom for some people.

The secret that each couple needs to discover is: (1) how to steadily build the solid virtues of companionship (2) without loss of the ability to periodically refuel the fires of passion. The secret is far from easily discovered. There is no answer to this dilemma at present other than commonsense suggestions, such as varying routines, seeking out exciting environments together, programming in ample romance time, and so on. While these are undoubtedly valid suggestions, they are not very precise and do not speak to the tempo or unique needs of specific couples. Research that focuses on ways to keep the balance between passionate and companionate love will be very welcome in the years ahead.

Approaches to Love

The research by Rubin discussed in a previous section suggests that liking is different from loving, or at least different from passionate loving. Berscheid and Walster's theory of passionate love seems to capture part of the everyday conception of romantic love. This theory suggests that liking may be explained by reinforcement theory but that passionate love requires another cause, because mutuality of reward and punishment does not necessarily exist in passionate love as it does in ordinary liking. However, Kenrick and Cialdini argued that reinforcement theory can explain the complexities of passionate love just as well as Berscheid and Walster's version of Schachter's theory of emotion.

One of the great difficulties in understanding love is that no single theory of love is well supported by scientific evidence. Different theories and research traditions yield different concepts. The best one can do is to examine the various approaches to love; each may contain valuable nuggets of wisdom that will help us understand love better.

To accomplish this aim we examine briefly three very different approaches to love. The first, exchange theory, uses concepts from reinforcement theory to explain every aspect of love. The second approach, love as limerence, is a recent development similar in some respects to Berscheid and Walster's theory of passionate love. The third approach views love as a style of the personality of the individual lover. Styles may be as varied as the colors of a rainbow, suggesting a classification analogy, the colors of love.

Love as Exchange

Blau (1964) defined love as the extreme case of intrinsic liking, rooted in interpersonal *exchange*. Exchange theory (Homans, 1961; Thibaut & Kelley, 1959) is a type of reinforcement theory based on the analogy of the marketplace. In the marketplace people exchange goods and services and incur rewards and costs during the process. When the rewards and costs are in balance or proportional the exchange is *equitable,* or mutually satisfactory.

The interaction between two people in a market situation is explicitly practical and ultimately useful. Such a relationship is said to be *extrinsically* motivated. Many interaction relationships, such as those between lovers, are intrinsically motivated. That is, the people involved exchange positive behaviors and sentiments for their own sake; the exchange is an end in itself, not a means to obtain other kinds of rewards. Friends, lovers, and spouses are examples of relationships presumed to be motivated primarily by intrinsic considerations.

The major assumption of exchange theory is that intrinsic relationships can be analyzed as a type of exchange in the same way as extrinsic relationships. Many people object to this approach as crass, arguing that it profanes and cheapens ultimate human experiences. A more reasoned scientific approach would urge suspense of judgment until the evidence is in. Thus we should instead ask, perhaps skeptically, just how well the theory can account for the complexities of love. Toward this end we examine the development of a love relationship as "the extreme case of intrinsic liking" (Blau, 1964, pp. 76–85).

The early stage of love can be quite painful. The other person intrudes into one's thoughts and causes emotional stirrings, and there is great uncertainty about how he or she feels. If the growing attraction is openly expressed, one reveals his or her growing dependence on the partner and runs the risk of rejection. Therefore during the early stage of love, each partner has a vested interest in not revealing the full extent of his or her feelings. The social ritual known as flirting provides a means to move beyond the stage of uncertainty, at the same time minimizing the costs if failure should occur.

> Flirting involves largely the expression of attraction in a semi-serious or stereotyped fashion that is designed to elicit some commitment from the other in advance of making a serious commitment oneself. The joking and ambiguous commitments implied by flirting can be laughed off if they fail to evoke a responsive cord or made firm if they do so [Blau, 1964, p. 77].

As the relationship moves beyond the initial stage, lover's quarrels may occur. Such quarrels test the strength of the relationship. One or both partners in effect engage in a temporary withdrawal from the relationship. If the temporary termination is sufficiently painful, the partners make up and in this way express a renewal and deepening of commitment to the relationship.

During the growth of the relationship the lovers exchange many rewards. These range from gift-giving, which is effective mostly because of its symbolic value, to shared expressions of each other's intrinsic values (I love you because you are you). The perception of increasing attachment by the partner is itself a powerful reward and may stimulate a reciprocal increase in attachment. Giving favors and presents and exerting efforts for the partner are all signs of love. The self-perception of doing these many things may work to promote self-attributions of love for the other (I keep saying I love you; therefore I must really love you).

The proper progression of the love relationship requires a nicely balanced degree of mutuality. The more in love one is, the more one wants to please the other. Therefore the partner less deeply involved in the relationship has a power advantage over the other, which may lead to exploitation in various ways. Some slight imbalance of power may actually solidify a relationship, since the more-committed partner will make extra efforts to please the less-committed partner, which may really please him or her so that a further surge in commitment may be stimulated. Too much of a power difference, or exploitation of it, may eventually cause frustration to exceed the level of reward the less-powerful member obtains from the relationship. The resulting quarrels can terminate the relationship.

Love never occurs in a social vacuum. It is an exchange relation whose value is socially defined. The value of the relationship is in part defined by how valuable the partner is perceived to be in other potential love relationships. If the partner is desirable for many other potential partners, his or her value is enhanced for the current one. If the one in progress is the only one potentially available for the partner, his or her value is depreciated proportionately.

The value of the relationship also depends on the availability cues that the partner gives off. If the partner is too eager and expresses much commitment too early, the other is likely to assume that the partner's value is low on the love market and depreciate it accordingly. Closely related to perception of value is the importance of timing or sequence in the growth of the relationship. If one person's love grows much faster than the other's love, the other may be scared off if he or she does not feel ready for that degree of commitment. Alternatively, great unevenness in commitment may lead to exploitation. Thus there are pressures on both persons not to get in too deeply or at least not much more deeply than the other. But there are also counter pressures to express one's love for the direct rewards to be experienced and to satisfy expectations created in the earlier stages of the relationship.

The social network around the couple helps define for them an acceptable sequence of steps toward a permanent relationship. The specifics of the sequence and their timing vary across social classes, age groups, and geographical areas. However, there are general norms of timing. A man proposing marriage when first meeting a woman may be considered a little peculiar. A man proposing marriage 15 years after a relationship begins is also not likely to be taken very seriously. Whatever the particular social norms governing timing, it seems crucial that the deepening commitment progress at roughly a mutual pace. If not, as in any other exchange relation, one member of the trading pair will get an inequitable deal, and the transaction will cease.

Even though an intrinsic love relationship can be analyzed as if it were an extrinsic relationship, it may be important for the lovers to perceive their relationship as fully intrinsic. If the lovers begin to view their relationship as based on extrinsic rewards, their feelings of love may wane. Seligman, Fazio, and Zanna (1980) tested this idea in a clever laboratory experiment. They recruited college couples who had been dating one year or less and tried to manipulate the cognitive set of the participants. The students, working individually, were first asked to complete open-ended sentences containing either the phrase *because I* or *in order to.*

Example: I date my boyfriend/girlfriend *because I* . . .
I date my boyfriend/girlfriend *in order to* . . .

Previous research had shown that the phrase *because I* led to an intrinsic cognitive set, but *in order to* led to an extrinsic set. Presumably the first set induced students to think of inherent aspects of the relationship, and the second set induced a focus on useful aspects. This manipulation was also reinforced by asking students to rank a group of reasons for dating the partner. Students who completed *because I* sentences ranked a group of intrinsic reasons; students who completed *in order to* sentences ranked a group of extrinsic reasons.

After these activities all students completed Rubin's liking and loving scales. Students given an extrinsic cognitive set scored only about 50 on the love scale. However, students given an intrinsic cognitive set scored 61, a score that was the same as for a control group who had not received the manipulation. These results showed that focusing students' attention on extrinsic aspects of their relationship caused a moderation in their expressions of love. There were no differences in liking scores across experimental conditions, providing additional support for the distinction between liking and loving.

The study by Seligman et al. (1980) demonstrates that it may be important for people to believe that they love for intrinsic reasons. These results provide incidental insight into the aversion that many people have for exchange theory: we are not *supposed* to love for extrinsic reasons. When the students were made aware of possible extrinsic reasons, they actually lowered their love scores.

This interesting experiment does not, however, address the theoretical issue of whether exchange theory can fully account for love relationships (regardless of whether people like the theory or not). Clark and Mills (1979) gave a negative answer. They distinguished between *exchange* and *communal* relationships. In exchange, benefits are given with the expectation of receiving a benefit in return. In a communal relationship the partners assume that each is concerned about the other, and they have a positive attitude about providing benefits based on the *need* of the other. In a communal relationship, such as between lovers or in a family, the benefits given and received are not part of an exchange because each partner is responding to need, and thus no obligation to return a specific benefit is incurred. As a matter of fact, "in a communal relationship, the idea that a benefit is given in response to a benefit that was received is compromising, because it calls into question the assumption that each member responds to the needs of the other" (Clark & Mills, 1979, p. 13). In two experiments these authors were able to provide considerable support for their distinction between exchange and communal relations.

Considerable doubt remains about whether exchange theory, which explains well much of everyday life, can fully account for the mysteries of romantic love. Certainly Berscheid and Walster did not think so. Other recent research has found romantic love peculiar and different enough from other types of love so that it requires a new concept, called "limerence."

Love as Limerence

Dorothy Tennov (1979) coined the term *limerence* to describe a state of being in love or falling in love. In Tennov's view this state is clearly different from liking, and also different from loving if loving is defined as caring and concern for another. Care and concern are actions or interactions freely given. Limerence is an intense state of cognitive and emotional experience. Tennov focused on the experience, rather than on the relationship between persons, because most of the important aspects of limerence seem to reside in ideas or fantasies one person holds about another person, the *limerent object*. Some people are in a state of limerence much of the time, others some of the time, and other people never experience the state at all.

Limerence may begin as no more than a twinge of feeling. If conditions are right, it may develop rapidly and grow to enormous intensity. In full flower the state of limerence is characterized by a number of attributes:

1. Persistent, intrusive thinking about the limerent object (LO), who will usually be a possible sexual partner.
2. Intense longing for reciprocation of feeling from LO.
3. Fluctuation of mood that depends on the perception of LO's actions and his or her probable reciprocity.
4. Inability to be limerent toward more than one person at a time.
5. Temporary relief from intense longing whenever there is perceived reciprocation from LO.
6. Shyness in LO's presence; fear of rejection, especially in periods of uncertainty.
7. Intensification of feelings under adverse circumstances.
8. Exquisite sensitivity to LO's actions, and constant interpretation of minute behaviors so that they appear favorable.
9. Physiological responses, such as chest constriction ("heartache"), especially when uncertainty is high.
10. Buoyancy of spirit whenever LO appears to reciprocate.
11. Intensity of focus and feelings that pushes other concerns into the background.
12. Idealization of LO's positive qualities and avoidance of his or her negatives.

Many people, perhaps most, can recognize falling head over heels in love. It is important to stress that limerence is a state of mind. A full-blown limerent reaction can occur even when there is no actual relationship with the limerent object (LO). Limerence feeds on the potential of a relationship and the uncertainty about whether one will develop or last. The feelings of LO are a relatively independent matter; in fact, poor LO may be totally unaware that he or she is the object of such intense longing.

In most cases limerence eventually declines to a low level. Tennov suggested that in a typical case it would take about two years to run its course. In instances where a real relationship develops, limerence may be transformed into the genuine caring and concern that Tennov defines as love. In other cases limerence toward one LO may start to extinguish and then be transferred to another. For others it may extinguish for several years and then flare full force again toward some new LO.

Sexual attraction seems to be an essential component of limerence, but it is not the main focus. LO is such a cherished fantasy that the poor limerent would often feel guilty if lustful thoughts were projected onto such a beloved object. The object of desire is for reciprocity, not for sex per se. A sexual response from LO symbolizes reciprocity and is therefore valuable as a strong sign of what the limerent desires most.

Tennov's research and theorizing led her to conclude that love, limerence, and sexual passion are relatively independent of each other. Love (as caring and concern) and sexual attraction can exist without limerence; basically, any one of the three—love, limerence, or sex—may exist without the others.

After some threshold level is passed, limerence is involuntary. In fact, an individual in this state may often curse his or her fate. Most limerents reported that the state was of value, a cherished experience. However, much anguish was also experienced because of the uncertainty. The lack of control over feelings and the obsessional thought patterns are also worrisome and at times scary. A long bout with preoccupation may lead to exhausted boredom, which can switch immediately to joy if a proper signal comes from LO (for instance, a phone call).

The concept of limerence captures well the madness of love that has preoccupied poets, philosophers, and ordinary people since time immemorial. The concept helps sharpen our ideas of romantic love and provides a more thoughtful perspective on the intense emotional attachments that many people develop. Understanding the state of limerence may increase our tolerance of others who are in the state, as well as of ourselves. This understanding may in turn help us learn to minimize the negative aspects of the experience. For example, knowing that limerence thrives on uncertainty can serve as a directive to acquire accurate information about the other as rapidly as possible. Interaction with the other in a variety of contexts will stimulate a more well-rounded image of the other, instead of the fantasy image in the limerent's mind. In general a twinge of limerence suggests an active, rather than a passive, approach toward the other. Active information acquisition and interaction with LO will either cut short the limerent fantasy or provide a more reality-oriented basis for an ongoing relationship with that person.

Not everyone experiences limerence. In fact, Tennov discovered the conception because her best friend had never experienced the state and was totally mystified by it. Limerence is one style of loving experienced by some people some of the time. There may be more styles, each different from the other, but each equally legitimate as a mode of feeling and expressing human love.

The Colors of Love

In an attempt to develop a classification of the different types of love, John Alan Lee (1973, 1976) developed an extensive research program based on an interview questionnaire format called the Love Story Card Sort. The questionnaire was given to Canadian and English subjects under age 35. The card sort consisted of 170 questions, each on a separate card, about a love relationship. For each statement card a series of answer cards was provided from which the subject selected one or more answers most appropriate for him or her. Two examples are:

21. After X and I started going out together, the other person I was going out with . . .
    a. remained deeply involved with me, so that I was going out with two people and falling in love with both of them.
    b. remained a good friend, but we both knew it wasn't "love."
    c. was very upset. We went on seeing each other for a time, then broke off.
    d. broke off with me right away.
    e. was dropped by me.
    f. other
    g. remained unaware of the fact that I was dating X.
43. The night after I met X . . .
    a. I could hardly get to sleep. For a long time I lay there thinking.
    b. I dreamed about X.
    c. I woke up earlier than usual the next morning and started to think about X.
    d. I slept quite normally.
    e. I wrote a letter to X (or telephoned).

The subject was asked to focus on one major love relationship that might be in progress or might have occurred in the past. The card sort essentially allowed the subject to tell the story of the love relationship, how it started, what the problems and satisfactions were, whether other people were involved, the intensity of each partner's feelings, the various behaviors, the development of the relationship, and how it terminated (if it had).

In analyzing the data, Lee discovered that there are many types of love relationships. These types could be described well by analogy to a color wheel (thus the colors of love). There were three primary types (colors) of love relationships, named *eros, ludus,* and *storge.* Still other people's love styles were best described as compounds or mixtures of the three primary types. The three most important compound types were named *mania, pragma,* and *agape.*

The six types were suggested by the findings. They are *ideal types* in the sense that no individual would match a type perfectly. Nevertheless, a brief description of the types indicates that they represent different and distinct types of love relationships people actually experienced.

1. *Eros.* The erotic lover is ready for love and accepts the risks it involves; in fact, the erotic type considers love as life's most important activity, although not worth self-damage or destruction. There is a definite physical stereotype that the erotic lover prefers. Strong approval and attraction toward the other person is usually aroused during the first meeting. This attraction has a strong physical component, which is expressed verbally and by touching. Considerable contact is desired, daily if possible. There is pleasant anticipation about the other and very little anxiety about the relationship. The erotic lover attempts to develop a quick rapport with the partner which includes openness, honesty, and sincerity in the relationship. The erotic lover wants the relationship to develop mutually, but does not demand mutuality from the partner. Finally, the erotic lover enjoys intense emotions and seeks early sexual relations with the partner. An erotic lover tends to focus exclusively on the partner, but is neither possessive nor afraid of rivals.

2. *Ludus.* Ludic love is love practiced as a game or pleasant pastime. It was developed into something of a skilled art form in the courts of European aristocrats in preceding centuries, but it still survives as a value orientation toward love held by many people. Ludic love is best played with several partners in ongoing relationships. A ludic type does not make deep emotional commitments, likes a variety of physical types, and can easily switch from one type to another. A ludic lover does not become overly excited when first meeting the partner; life goes on as usual. Too frequent contact with the partner is avoided in order that intense feelings can be avoided. The ludic person will be very wary of a partner who begins to get too intense and will try to help the partner retain a sense of self-control and detachment. The game is to be played for mutual enjoyment, and this requires just the right level of intensity; too little or too much by either partner may unbalance the relationship. Lies and insincerity are justified as part of the rules of the game, although there is no desire to hurt the other person. A ludic lover is not jealous or possessive and may encourage the partner to have other relationships to help keep their own relationship at the required delicate balance. The ludic lover enjoys sex and variety in sexual activity, but tends to consider sex good fun, not a means to deep emotional rapport.

3. *Storge.* "Storge is love without fever or folly, a feeling of natural

affection such as you might have for a favorite brother or sister. An unexciting and often uneventful kind of loving, storge is rarely the stuff of dramatic works or romantic novels" (Lee, 1973, p. 77). This type of love develops most often in communities where people know each other over long periods of time. The storgic lover considers love as the basis of society and the family. Love is not expected to be exciting, but rather an extension of friendship. There is no preferred physical type. One should get to know the partner gradually and incorporate the partner into more and more of life's activities. The relationship is generally relaxed, because there are no strong emotions to control. There is a tendency to share interests and activities, but to avoid expression of direct feelings about the relationship. The storgic person tends to be shy about intense contact and sexual behavior, assuming that after full commitment any sexual difficulties will be worked out. Love is not exciting to the storgic lover, but it is solid, incorporated into the ongoing flow of life.

4. *Mania*. The components of mania overlap considerably the traditional conception of romantic love. In fact, over the centuries literature has smeared together elements of both manic and erotic love under the general rubric of romantic love. However, Lee's evidence indicated that mania was something quite different from eros. Manic love is a compounding of eros and ludus. The typical manic type yearns for love, yet expects it to be painful. There is no set preference for physical types, and the search is often for a contradictory set of qualities in the partner. Ambivalence or dislike toward the partner may be felt upon the first meeting. However, the manic lover soon becomes preoccupied and even obsessed with thoughts of the partner. There is much imaginative construction of a future with the partner, but it is fraught with anxiety. The desire to see the partner frequently is intense, and frustration of this desire causes much unhappiness. There is a sense of loss of control over feelings. If no particular problems exist, the manic lover will create them in order to intensify feelings, but then periodically struggle to get his or her feelings under control. The manic lover tries to force the partner into greater expressions of love and affection and is very possessive. The mutual frustrations which are created often prevent enjoyment of intimacy. The manic lover can convince himself or herself that life without the partner's love is not worth living (although suicide seldom occurs) and will abuse himself or herself in order to win the partner's love. Mania rarely ends happily.

5. *Pragma*. "Pragma is the love that goes shopping for a suitable mate, and all it asks is that the relationship work well, that the two partners be compatible, and satisfy each other's basic or practical needs" (Lee, 1973, p. 124). The pragmatic lover is looking for contentment and a mate with whom he or she is well suited. This quest means similarity on many characteristics and perhaps some complementarity of satisfac-

tion of emotional needs. The pragmatic type will be predisposed to select a familiar partner, such as a worker at the office. The calculation involved in the selection process is similar to the calculating intent of ludus, but the purpose of long-term, compatible companionship is more like storge. The pragmatic type wants to avoid emotional extremes; get to know the partner well over time; expects a measure of reciprocated affection without forcing it; believes that sexual compatibility is important, but that any problems can be worked out mutually; and that, although a satisfactory mate is an important part of life, no particular person is worth too much sacrifice to achieve one's love objectives. Pragmatic love is well described by its name—it is first and foremost practical.

6. *Agape.* Agape as a concept comes from the Christian tradition:

> When Saint Paul wrote to the Corinthian members of the early Christian church telling them that love is patient and kind, not jealous or boastful, not arrogant or rude, does not insist on its own way, but believes all things and endures all things, the Greek translation for love was *agape*. This concept of love implies a duty or obligation to care about the other person, whether you want to care or not, and whether the love is deserved or not. Agape is "gift love," without ulterior motives and with no strings attached. It is completely altruistic and deeply compassionate [Lee, 1973, p. 139].*

Given the lofty requirements of agapic love, it is no wonder that Lee found no pure types in this research. Agapic love is more cognitive than emotional, and it has difficulty in knowing what to do with sexuality. Since the body is thought of as the temple of the spirit, sex would have to be a lofty, sacramental act. But given the biological nature of the act, it is difficult to keep the emotions uninvolved. The ultimate consequence is that advocacy of agapic love tends to go with a philosophy of sexual abstinence. The early Christian church attempted a natural experiment in which both sexes lived and slept together without sexual contact. The point was to shun pleasures of the flesh, but to enjoy the spiritual ecstasy of closeness to another human. As Lee (1973, p. 144) noted, enough pregnancies resulted from this experiment so that it was discontinued. The church continued to downplay sexuality over the centuries, and intercourse for pleasure alone was forbidden. Sex was permissible only as an act of procreation. The struggle between the reality of biology and the equally real ideal of agapic love has continued unabated for some 2000 years.

Although the color-wheel analogy should not be taken too seriously, Lee's typology represents a definite advance, because it is based on solid

---

*From *The Colors of Love: An Exploration of the Ways of Loving,* by J. A. Lee. Copyright © 1973 by J. A. Lee. (Ontario : New Press, 1973.) Reprinted by permission of the author.

evidence. The typology lends itself well to future research, and recent work (Lasswell & Lobsenz, 1980) has used a more efficient question-naire version of the card sort.

It should be noted that the types of love relationships might best be considered as love styles (Lee, 1976). Although an individual may have a strong preference for one style over another, the styles are not fixed in the genes. A person's preferred love style may change over a lifetime or even during the course of a given love relationship. Indeed, an individual may be involved in an erotic relationship with one person and a ludic or other type of relationship with a second person.

Lee's typology of love styles clarifies Tennov's concept of limerence. The description of the manic lover, possibly with components of the erotic lover, is very similar to Tennov's description of the state of limerence. People who never experience limerence are most likely pragmatic or storgic types. Thus Lee's approach makes sense of falling madly in love as one of a range of love styles. Although the most publicized form of love over the centuries, it is not universal, and it is no more or less valid as real love than the other styles.

The Miseries of Love

We cannot live without love, or at least we cannot live well. To love and be loved is considered one of life's more precious experiences, and one who misses out on love misses one of the supreme values of life. Such sentiments are common and are strongly held by nearly everyone. At the same time it is clear that negatives are also associated with love. The ecstasy of limerence cannot escape agony as a traveling companion. Parents dote on their children, but what child has not caused much grief for his or her parents? For that matter, what parents have not caused pain for their children? In brief, in this arena, as in others, life poses a tradeoff. The joy of love can seldom be lived without the experience of pain.

The Pains of Love

Ultimately love creates pain because of our basic human condition, because we are social animals who cannot survive alone, because others are necessary to satisfy our needs, and because of mortality—our own and that of those we love. Love of another person links one's own fate to the fate of that person. This basic linkage makes us dependent on the other. The nature of dependency varies widely, but no love relationship is free of it. To be dependent on another means that the other has power to please or displease, to help or hurt, and sometimes even the power of life and death itself. If the other person loves us, we have a degree of power and control over that person, and that can be scary. To have power over another life means to be responsible to some degree for that life. Young parents with their first infant often have brief moments of panic when they realize the awesome responsibility that they bear. Young lovers contemplating marriage may pause at the responsibility implied by "to love and cherish until death do you part."

The mutual dependency and power involved in a love relationship sets the condition for negative outcomes. Intimate human relationships seem to prosper best when there is equity or mutuality in the exercise of power and control. Reaching and maintaining mutuality is not decreed by fate; it requires effort at best and in many relationships is impossible to achieve. Lack of reciprocity is always a potential threat to a love relationship. The miseries of unrequited love are well known. Even in the beginning stages of a love relationship there may be painful uncertainty about the degree of reciprocity, more perhaps than in later stages. Loss of the relationship is always possible, through either death or abandonment by the partner.

Thus the nature of life itself creates conditions that make misery a potential outcome intrinsic to loving. Some of our most painful emotional experiences flow from the miseries of love.

1. *Uncertainty*—Lack of certainty about important events and persons is painful. We may be uncertain about our own value, about the other person, or about our relationship to that person. The aversiveness of uncertainty causes attempts to reduce it. Such attempts may be unproductive, leading to altercations, wasted time, and feelings of unhappiness.

2. *Ambivalence*—Ambivalence means to feel two ways—for example, to love and hate—at the same time. Freud believed that all human relationships contain a degree of ambivalence, whose inherent contradictions cause it to be painful. We are seldom unreservedly positive or negative toward someone. Generally, it is impossible for any extended interaction not to be at least mildly punishing, even though on the whole the interaction may be rewarding. Our response systems are specific enough so that we feel good about the positive aspects of the interaction and bad about the negative aspects. In this way the seeds of ambivalence may be sown in any interaction. As a matter of fact the uncertainty inherent in a new relationship, because it is painful, serves as a punishment. In effect the other punishes us because he or she is a condition or cause of the uncertainty. The negative emotional feelings caused by the uncertainty may persist even after the uncertainty itself is reduced to a low level.

3. *Obsessive preoccupation*—If you have ever had a tune run through your mind over and over, you have experienced a mild, ordinary obsession. Everyone gets preoccupied from time to time with a thought that seemingly will not go away. It can be irritating, annoying, and boring. When the obsession is another person, especially someone we are falling

in love with, it can be unbearably acute. The person is in mind constantly or intrudes into mind at inappropriate times. Obsession with one person upsets the needed variety of mental life, and when it is linked with uncertainty about the other person, the anguish of the obsession can be extreme.

4. *Jealousy*—Almost everyone has experienced jealousy at one time or another. One child may be jealous of another, or one parent may be jealous of the attention given to a child by the other parent. The most common form of jealousy arises between two people in a romantic love relationship. Jealousy is not a simple emotion. Most basically, jealousy is a fear of losing something or someone of great value (Clanton & Smith, 1977). Feelings of jealousy vary: some people feel mostly fear or anxiety; others feel anger or rage. Jealous rage has in many instances led to the murder of a loved one. In past years jealousy was sometimes considered a sign of love, although intense jealousy was thought pathological. During the past decade there has been a trend toward the value that jealousy is unhealthy and is a sign of deficit, rather than proof of love. Consequently, many people feel guilty when they experience jealousy, although it is doubtful whether fewer people experience jealousy today than in previous years.

Most people who have experienced strong jealousy, obsessive thought about another, or uncertainty about a relationship can readily agree that these are unpleasant experiences. The consequences of love can indeed be painful.

There is much literature, both popular and scientific, on the nature of love and how to succeed in a love relationship. However, there are few guides on how to deal with the miseries of love. We could use a set of procedures to help people extricate themselves from a love relationship that has gone sour. In a word there ought to be ways to fall out of love.

How to Fall out of Love

The propensity to love may be part of our heritage. But we *learn* to love specific other people. Since we learn to love specific others, the possibility exists that we may also be able to learn *not* to love them, or to fall out of love. In an interesting book Phillips and Judd (1978) described several techniques that may help an individual recover from the pains of love. Phillips, a psychotherapist, has based the techniques on one approach to psychotherapy, *behavior therapy*. Behavior therapy relies on simple principles of learning, such as repetition and reward, as a means of helping people change their ways of thinking and behaving. The techniques work best in situations in which a relationship has fully terminated, such as a broken love affair or a divorce.

The simplest and most general technique is *thought stopping*. This technique is most useful for someone who is obsessively preoccupied with thoughts of the missing partner. Basically one has to set his or her mind to say "stop" whenever thoughts of the other person intrude. This may be difficult; therefore, one should make a list of very pleasant activities that do not involve the other person. As soon as the unwanted thought intrudes, the person gives the self-order to stop and substitutes a pleasant item from the list. It takes practice, but in many cases intrusive thoughts of the other become less frequent over time, usually within a few days or weeks. The idea is that the pleasant thought (from the list) serves as a reward for stopping a thought about the other person. Repeated reward strengthens a habit, in this case the habit of not thinking about the other. Over time the obsessive preoccupation with the other should drop to a low level as the habit of not thinking about him or her grows stronger.

Thought stopping may be supplemented by *silent ridicule*. Because the absent person may be idealized to an extreme degree, silent ridicule allows construction of a fantasy that cuts the lost lover down to size. For example, one girl who was dropped by a macho boyfriend found solace in imagining him wandering through a store in a diaper sucking a bottle of milk. In an alternate fantasy he flexed his powerful biceps, which then sagged like a balloon losing its air. Silent ridicule is a charming means of reducing the other to merely human proportions. It also requires practice, preferably several times a day.

In conjunction with thought stopping and silent ridicule, one may wish to create a program for building a positive self-image. Self-esteem is often low after a relationship ends; indeed, one may feel worthless. Making a list of productive tasks, doing them, and rewarding oneself generously for task accomplishment is a good ploy. Basically it is doing systematically what we often do automatically in daily life, such as going to a movie after an afternoon of hard study.

Behavior therapy techniques may even be helpful for jealousy, but they grow more complex and are best done under the guidance of a professional skilled in their use. One general approach is called *systematic desensitization*. First, the therapist questions the client, constructing one list of situations that cause jealousy and another list of situations that do not. The list is arranged in hierarchical order from situations that cause no jealousy, a little jealousy, and so on, to the situation that causes the most intense jealousy. Next the client learns deep-muscle and mental relaxation exercises that can take some time to master. After deep relaxation has been learned, the therapist will slowly introduce items from the jealousy list, starting with the most neutral items. The client works up the list in imagination until he or she feels a twinge of jealousy, then backs off and proceeds again. In time the therapist will be able to work through most if not all of the list with the client. The idea is that deep relaxation is a response incompatible with the intense emotional feelings involved in jealousy. Gradually, through repetition, the thoughts and feelings of jealousy are neutralized by keeping them weaker than and associated with the relaxation. In time even intense jealous feelings may be lessened this way.

Systematic desensitization will not work for everybody. If it fails, a somewhat extreme technique called *covert sensitization* may be used. This technique involves associating aversive thoughts and images with the image of the person one wants to forget. For example, one man imagined the woman who jilted him as covered with vomit. A girl imagined her ex-boyfriend spewing pus from his mouth and penis. The idea is that if highly aversive images are habitually associated with the other person, in time thinking of that person will become aversive. Consequently, one also avoids thinking of the other person to avoid the unpleasant imagery. Covert sensitization is a heavy-duty technique and should only be used with skilled guidance.

These various techniques are means of getting another person out of mind. In so doing, they reduce the pain of unrequited or jilted love. Undoubtedly these techniques will not work with everybody, but many people have found them effective.

Summary

The roots of love extend backward to the infant's experience of physical contact with the adult caregiver. The child develops obvious attachment to its mother during the first year of life. If conditions prevent this early development of love, the child may be unable to develop a love relationship as an adult.

Currently, love is viewed as the proper basis for marriage. Historically, this was not true, and it is only within the last few hundred years that the concept of *married love* developed. The emergence of courtly love in the eleventh century provided a conception of women as objects who could be cherished by a man, and this conception was eventually linked to the romantic love of a partner. The separateness of love, sex, and marriage were gradually fused, and the fusion probably reached its height in the 1950s.

Recent social-psychological research, especially by Rubin, has attempted to show that liking is different from loving. The difference is difficult to demonstrate, because the two concepts have much in common and overlap in everyday life. Nevertheless, this research has had some success.

Berscheid and Walster argued that reinforcement theory can explain liking, but not loving, because the latter does not seem to depend that closely on rewards and punishments. Instead, these authors used Schachter's theory of emotions as a means to explain passionate love. In Schachter's theory an emotional state requires two conditions: unexplained physiological arousal and relevant situational cues that one uses to label experience. If one is in a state of (unexplained) physiological arousal and a cue occurs that suggests passion, the state will be interpreted as passionate arousal or love. When the cues change or the arousal decreases, love should decrease as well.

The theory of passionate love is only one of several approaches to romantic love. Recent theoretical approaches include exchange theory, limerence, and the colors of love. The exchange approach analyzes intrinsic relationships, such as love or friendship, in the same way it would analyze extrinsic trading relations. It is based completely on the analogy of the marketplace. Tennov coined the term *limerence* to describe the inner state of pleasure and turmoil that occurs in falling in love. This concept seems to capture well the experience of love that many people have. Through an extended research program Lee discovered six distinct types of love relationships or love styles: eros, ludus, storge, mania, pragma, and agape. Each type is a valid approach to love. The recognition of several different love styles helps explain why there has been so much confusion about what love "really is"; it is not any one unique way of feeling and thinking, but rather several ways.

Love causes misery as well as pleasure. Misery is intrinsic to love because of uncertainty in developing a relationship, our natural ambivalence toward other people, the obsessive preoccupation that often goes with love, and the jealousy that love relationships may entail. It would be helpful to learn how to fall out of love, and there are several recently developed techniques for reducing the misery of love.

5

Sexual Love

The title of this chapter would be considered inappropriate by many people. They would argue that the chapter should be just "Sex" or "Sexuality," thus suggesting that sex and love have no necessary connection with each other and may even be independent phenomena. The previous chapter noted the historical variation in the connections between love, sex, and marriage and concluded that today love is considered the most appropriate norm or basis for sexual interaction with another person.

This issue of the relation between love and sexuality needs to be explored in some detail. We are sexual beings, and a substantial portion of adult life is filled with issues of sexual desires, pleasures, problems, and pains. The very intensity that sexuality has as part of our humanity guarantees that it will be a focus of attention. Further, sexuality is for most people interpersonal; it takes two, in contrast to satisfaction of other needs such as eating or elimination. The fact that sex is mostly interpersonal opens it to all the complexities and problems of interpersonal relations—problems of equity or fair trade, power struggles, self-pleasure versus care for the other, territorial possession of property rights, to name a few of the most important.

In general it seems that the more important an area of life, the more it is surrounded by rules of conduct, moral sanctions, and ethical considerations. The ethical issues involved in playing a game of checkers do not seem very compelling to most people. The ethical issues involved in playing a sex game are very different. In fact, some people would strongly object to the use of the word *game* in conjunction with sex. Such people would also object in principle to the ludic lover (Chapter 4). However, even if we strip away religious issues and basic ethical questions about whether sex is good or evil and simply assume that it is always good, we still have many problems needing resolution. For example, what is the purpose of sex as part of human experience? Is sex a means to an end or an end in itself? If sex can be a means, are certain means proper and others improper? For example, can sex be a means of intense communication? Is it okay for a sex act to be no more significant than a two-person mutual masturbation? What really is a good sexual experience?

Clearly there are many questions involved in a discussion of sexual interactions. It is very difficult for most of us to separate what *is* or could be (facts) from what *ought* to be (ethics). One can at least be sensitive to such difficulties. The purpose of the first section is to help create such a sensitive perspective, not by providing the answers, but by bringing into focus some of the many questions.

Sexual Love versus Loveless Sex: The Problem of Purpose in Sex

If love is viewed as an intense, enduring attitudinal complex toward another person—including active behavioral components such as commitment, care, and trust—then there is no *necessary* connection between love and sexual interactions. Peter Koestenbaum in *Existential Sexuality* (1974) argues that the meaning of sexuality is that of a free human choice. This statement is in line with the philosophy of existentialism, which stresses that freedom to choose is the primary attribute of the human condition. It follows that the interconnections between the four basic aspects of the sexual side of life—sex, love, marriage, and children—depend upon value definitions. An individual (or an entire society) may view all four elements as tightly interconnected or as totally independent. Logically, sex does not necessarily imply love, nor does love imply sex. Despite the logical independence, one can still wonder whether love makes for better sex and whether sex enriches love. Koestenbaum seems to imply that love confers on sexuality an enrichment of meaning that sexual experience would not otherwise have. But what is this meaning? In what ways can the experience of sexual encounter vary from time to time and person to person?

The Nature of Sexual Experience

It has been said that sex begins as an itch in the loins. This descriptive phrase recognizes the ultimate biological nature of sexuality; like other bodily needs it is programmed into our brain. In Freudian terms the sex need is an instinct with energy sources in the body. The aim of sex is the release of energy; this release is experienced as pleasure. The object toward which release is sought is learned in humans and may be highly variable. For most people the object is a member of the opposite sex, but occasionally it may be something as peculiar as Aunt Matilda's old shoe.

Most of us learn by adolescence to have that "itch" for the opposite sex, although a significant percentage of the population shows a basic homosexual orientation. The quality of sexual experience can vary enormously. A sexual encounter may be viewed as no more significant than an evening snack, no more than scratching the itch. At the other extreme, the encounter may be viewed as a cosmically significant spiritual merging of two souls. For two well-practiced sexual partners, sex on one occasion may be a mildly interesting release from frustration, on another occasion a tender affirmation of love, and in other instances a total, explosive merging of two personalities so that the two seem to become one. It is possible to be bored and still have an orgasm; it is also possible to be highly aroused and yet have orgasm remain elusive.

The awareness of one's sexual partner can be quite variable. During a sex act some people focus so intently on their own sensations that their partner becomes peripheral. Others may focus so intently on the partner that they are largely unaware of their own sensations. Feelings of dominance and submission during sex are important for many people. In some cases total dominance may be a goal, independent of the desires of the other. Society can define that extreme situation as forcible rape. Even the quality of an orgasm varies widely. At one extreme it may feel so mild that there is uncertainty as to whether it actually happened. At the other extreme orgasm convulses an individual's entire being, in rare instances leading to a momentary loss of awareness.

Given that sexual experience can vary so widely, does it make any sense to ask about its meaning? Many people would answer yes. Given the overwhelming importance of sex, we want to understand it and give it meaning within some kind of conceptual scheme. Most major religions and many secular theories attempt to define the scope and purpose of sexuality. One interesting attempt by Michael Kosok (1971), a phenomenologist—a person who studies concrete facts or events— views sex as an evolutionary phenomenon that unfolds through four idealized historical stages.

1. In the beginning (before the fig leaf) humans mated with a simple animal awareness that involved a harmony of opposites and no consciousness of conflict. Presumably this is the way other animal species still mate today.

2. Humans eventually became self-conscious. The unity of opposites was broken when self-awareness occurred. The sex act then became a blind attempt to join the other person and to become the other. Kosok uses the interesting phrase *attempts to devour the other* as descriptive of this self-aware mating. Because mating was still based ultimately on our animal nature, Kosok describes this self-aware attempt to mimic the original animal act as *fucking*.

3. Humans eventually created a vast artifice called civilization. All behavior became regimented into rules and defined into social roles. Sexuality was harnessed within the role of marriage and became a dignified form of role playing called *intercourse*. Self-consciousness was carried over into the sex act, which was performed properly, appropriately, and legitimately. Kosok believes that society now alternates between fucking and intercourse. The former, because it stems from our animal nature, poses a threat to civilization; the latter ultimately does not fully satisfy our primal urge. Kosok's solution is:

4. A loving sexual unity in which both people somehow remain separate and yet become one. The two are joined together in the primal passionate act, but with a balanced respect for each other that allows individuality and uniqueness to be preserved.

Thus Kosok views the human dilemma of the meaning of sexuality as solved when love is fused with the biological drive. This is just one view, of course, and Kosok does not really tell us how such delicate fusion occurs. Others argue that sex can be just as rich and fully human without love.

Sex with and without Love

Philosopher Russell Vannoy (1980) carefully explores the arguments for sex both with and without love. Some of the themes for sex with love include:

1. Sex with love makes the experience deeply personal, because love joins two whole persons and not just two bodies. Sex alone is only pleasure, but sex with love makes the experience both pleasurable *and* meaningful.
2. Sex with love ensures that the lover will relate to you as a person, and not only as a sex object.
3. Sex with love is incorporated into the continuity of life with the loved person. Present sexual love is continuous with the past and can with reasonable security be expected to flow into the future.
4. Sex, like fine wine, becomes better over time with a person you love. Love provides a motive for each partner to maximize the pleasure of the other partner.
5. Sex with love can be a form of communion, or a communication with the other in a language beyond words.
6. Love often serves as a stimulant to desire for sex with the loved one. In this sense love is an aphrodisiac. This argument is somewhat weak because while many people find sex difficult unless they love the other person, many others are equally capable of desire and sex without any hint of love.

Although there are many advantages to sex with love, Vannoy's intent is to present a strong case that sex without love is equal or superior to sex with love. Several arguments are presented for sex without love. Sex with a relative stranger precludes feelings of jealousy or possessiveness. In addition one has no obligation to perform unless one feels like it. In a full love relationship, sex becomes to an extent a duty to the beloved. Along with obligations may go performance anxieties; one need feel no anxiety if the relationship is temporary. Further, sex with a relative stranger allows a focus on the "appetitive" aspects of sex for its own sake. This focus may be diffused if the complexities of love are involved.

All these reasons are preliminaries in the argument because they tend to imply a relative stranger rather than a long-term partner. The strongest argument in favor of sex for sex's sake and against sex for love may be stated in terms of means versus ends.

Perhaps the most basic difficulty of using sex to express love is that one is often merely using sex as a means to an end: expressing love, rather than enjoying sex for sex's sake. The focus tends to be on the emotions of love rather than lust itself. The sensual aspects of sex thus

BOX 5-1 Older women make better lovers—in Ben Franklin's opinion. The reasons are part of a pseudoletter to a friend. Franklin says marry but concludes that, if you must take a lover instead, choose an older woman. He justifies with eight reasons.

Ben Franklin said that older women make better lovers:

1. Because they have more Knowledge of the World and their Minds are better stor'd with Observations, their Conversation is more improving and more lastingly agreable.
2. Because when Women cease to be handsome, they study to be good. To maintain their Influence over Men, they supply the Diminution of Beauty by an Augmentation of Utility. They learn to do a 1000 Services small and great, and are the most tender and useful of all Friends when you are sick. Thus they continue amiable. And hence there is hardly such a thing to be found as an old Woman who is not a good Woman.
3. Because there is no hazard of Children, which irregularly produc'd may be attended with much Inconvenience.
4. Because thro' more Experience, they are more prudent and discreet in conducting an Intrigue to prevent Suspicion. The Commerce with them is therefore safer with regard to your Reputation. And with regard to theirs, if the Affair should happen to be known, considerate People might be rather inclin'd to excuse an old Woman who would kindly take care of a young Man, form his Manners by her good Counsels, and prevent his ruining his Health and Fortune among mercenary Prostitutes.
5. Because in every Animal that walks upright, the Deficiency of the Fluids that fill the Muscles appears first in the highest Part: The Face first grows lank and wrinkled; then the Neck; then the Breast and Arms; the lower Parts continuing to the last as plump as ever: So that covering all above with a Basket, and regarding only what is below the Girdle, it is impossible of two Women to know an old from a young one. And as in the dark all Cats are grey, the Pleasure of corporal Enjoyment with an Old Woman is at least equal, and frequently superior, every Knack being by Practice capable of Improvement.
6. Because the Sin is less. The debauching a Virgin may be her Ruin, and make her for Life unhappy.
7. Because the Compunction is less. The having made a young Girl miserable may give you frequent bitter Reflections; none of which can attend the making an old Woman happy.

8(thly and Lastly). They are so grateful!!

Thus much for my Paradox. But still I advise you to marry directly; being sincerely Your affectionate Friend.

tend in many such cases to be sacrificed to tenderness, something which has its own worth and beauty, to be sure, but which may not be the central focus many sexual partners would prefer [Vannoy, 1980, p. 28].

It is true that sex can serve many purposes beyond itself; that is, sex can become an instrument to accomplish something else. Some of these additional purposes are quite familiar: to relieve tensions and frustrations, to control or dominate another person, to prove that one is liberated, to overcome loneliness or boredom, to please another person, to lose oneself in another, and occasionally to get revenge against some third person.

It is easy enough to view these reasons in a somewhat negative light, but consider the following additional purposes sex can serve: to procreate, to prove one's love or convey feelings of love, to communicate emotions, or to attain a type of spiritual harmony with the universe. These purposes seem perfectly valid to most people. Vannoy's point is that even these reasons make sex an instrument for something else. His argument is that sexual experience is valid as an end in itself; it does not have to point beyond itself to anything else. Further, sexual experience may be most deeply satisfying when people are able to value it as its own end. One does not have to treat another person poorly or with disrespect just because what one values most with the other is sexual interaction.

Comment

In the abstract Vannoy's arguments make good sense. But, in fact, human life is an intricate web. We seldom do anything for itself alone. For example, how often do we eat as an end in itself, for the sheer pleasure of eating? We eat to satisfy hunger, to socialize with friends, to conduct business, to bring the family together as a unit, and so on. Rarely do we just eat for the pure end of eating per se. The same holds true for most other bodily functions and many if not most social actions. Thus it seems unlikely that most people will be able to make sexual experience an end value, independent of other aspects of life.

Yet there is value in Vannoy's point. Sex may become too instrumental, fraught with anxiety and life's complications. There is an intrinsic goodness to sexuality that ought not to get lost in the interconnecting web of life. The authors' value choice is that it is possible to have good sex, even excellent sex, without love. However, the *best* sex occurs within the context of love, which in turn will nearly always involve a relationship with another with both sexual and nonsexual aspects. The trick is to make sex an end in itself within the larger end of a cherished love relationship.

It should be clear that this statement is an ethical choice and not a statement of fact. As in other central areas of life the meaning and purpose of sex in life must be questioned and answered by each individual within his or her own social context. The answers lie in the realm of value choices, not in empirical facts.

The Study of Sexuality in the Twentieth Century

There are now several volumes available on the general history of sexuality (for example, Bullough, 1976) or on specialized sex-related topics such as rape (Brownmiller, 1975). Our focus will be on the twentieth century, and that focus must necessarily be highly selective. We will note some of the complexities of sexuality as a field of study and provide an overview of modern approaches to research in this field.

Complexities of Sexual Behavior

Sexual behavior, perhaps more than other types of behavior, can be studied from many perspectives and at different levels of analysis. Sexual behavior is biological behavior, and while anatomy may not be destiny, it is clearly important. Further, the firm biological base for sexuality exhibits itself regularly throughout the animal kingdom. Comparison of sexual functioning among animal species or between humans and other species is one valid approach to research (Ford & Beach, 1951). The way rats copulate (Bermant, 1961), the role of chemicals called pheromones in sex (for example, Connor, 1972), and the control of sexual expression by hormones at different phylogenetic levels (Beach, 1969) are small samples of literally hundreds of areas of research on sexuality. The direct study of human copulation has occurred only in the past two decades (Masters & Johnson, 1966).

There is much interest in the biological aspects of human sexual functioning. Contraception, pregnancy, abortion, and sexually transmitted diseases are researched extensively in such fields as medicine, physiology, genetics, and immunology. Extensive discussions on these topics occur in the mass media, homes, classrooms, and social gatherings. Because the physical aspects of sexual dysfunctions currently are receiving attention (Masters & Johnson, 1970), sex clinics and sex therapy (for example, see Kaplan, 1974) have become popular.

Treatment of sexual dysfunction does not exist solely at the biological level. Many experts have noted that personality issues are often involved in such sexual problems as impotence, frigidity, and premature ejaculation. Since sexual behavior usually involves two people, personality issues in sexuality are quickly joined by interpersonal issues, ultimately based on the attempts of people to live together in sexual harmony and (it is to be hoped) happiness. Much marriage counseling and psychotherapy are related in one way or another to the interpersonal difficulties that people experience in their sexual behavior.

Sexuality is also societal and cultural as well as interpersonal. Sexual customs differ across societies and within social classes in a given society. Such differences often lead to discussion, controversy, and clashing ideologies. One good example is the present continuing controversy over abortion. A Supreme Court ruling several years ago essentially made abortion a constitutional right of the individual, and state laws against abortion were voided. Some of the population is strongly opposed to that decision and has proposed several anti-abortion amendments to the Constitution. The abortion debate will undoubtedly continue throughout the 1980s.

This controversy also makes clear that other cultural subsystems—law, religion, ethics, and codes of morality—are highly involved with the sexual subsystem of behavior at nearly all levels of existence—biological, interpersonal, and societal—except perhaps for the most basic anatomical and cellular levels. The issue of sex with or without love discussed previously is only one of a wide range of sexual issues in which moral concerns become intertwined with scientific theories and factual descriptions.

Research on Sexuality: Modern Approaches

We tend to be interested in any topic connected with sex. As it turns out, the history of scientific research on sex is quite an interesting topic in its own right, much more interesting, for example, than the history of research on cockroaches or flatworms. Two general conclusions may be drawn from the history of scientific research on sex, a history that began less than 100 years ago.

1. *Feedback effects of scientific knowledge.* Science searches for causes and facts. The act of scientific research itself, and the results that research obtains may have on society a feedback effect that changes the way people behave (Gergen, 1973). The feedback principle seems to work especially strongly in the study of sexual behavior (Byrne, 1977b, p. 22). Because of the intense interest in the topic, research results on sexuality are disseminated rapidly into the general culture via newspapers, magazines, and television, and the results may in turn influence public opinion, attitudes, and even sexual behaviors (Gagnon, 1975). Changes in opinion and attitudes may then set the stage for new kinds of sex research, which previously would have been forbidden. In fact, one author (Robinson, 1976) believes that the effects of certain

research—such as that of Kinsey and of Masters and Johnson—has been dramatic, creating a modernization of sex.

2. *The gradual lifting of sexual taboos*. A taboo is a restriction on something and can be applied to aspects of bodily functioning (Money, 1980), and taboos on various aspects of sexual functioning extend far back into prehistory. One taboo was severe restrictions on discussion of sex. In the nineteenth century sex was not mentioned in most social settings. It was something out there (Gagnon, 1977), something to be done in secret, guiltily, and never talked about. This taboo and many others have weakened, in part due to the social feedback effects of sex research. Change occurs unevenly, however. We may be bombarded by novels, plays, and movies rife with sexual content and have so-called hard-core media easily available in any large city. Yet it has only been since 1964 that general courses in human sexuality were introduced into college curricula (Wrightsman & Deaux, 1981). Sex education in public schools is still an issue of dispute in many areas, and people are still arrested and prosecuted for purveying pornography. Indeed, the National Commission on Obscenity and Pornography, appointed by President Lyndon Johnson in 1968, had its report soundly rejected by President Richard Nixon and the Congress in 1970 on moral grounds (Byrne, 1977a). Thus taboos have lifted somewhat, but you can still quite easily get yourself arrested for indecency. Stroll down any busy street in the nude, and you can reasonably expect to land in jail, even though you have hurt no one and have made no sexual advances. The old taboo on public exposure of the genitals (Ford & Beach, 1951) is still very much with us.

The Victorian era, in the nineteenth century, was gripped by many sexual taboos. The most famous sex researchers of that century were Havelock Ellis (1899) and Richard von Krafft-Ebing (1886/1894), and their work dealt mostly with clinical case studies of abnormal sexual functioning. There were negative reactions, but the work was tolerated because it dealt with *them*—dissimilar, abnormal people (Byrne & Byrne, 1977). In contrast, Freud's bold theories (see, for example, Freud, 1905/1962) stated that the roots of normal functioning are sexual, and that small children have sexual feelings. The firestorm of condemnation he evoked gradually died down as Freudian psychoanalysis became a respectable medical specialty.

During the next 30 years some social scientists timidly developed innocuous survey instruments, and reports on cross-cultural sexual practices and animal sexuality (such as Ford & Beach, 1951) were accepted with relative calm. The work of Alfred Kinsey (Kinsey, Pomeroy, & Martin, 1948) created sensational public reaction (Victor,

1980). Kinsey and his co-workers interviewed more than 15,000 males in detail and showed that the sexual practices of American males departed widely from cultural mythology about such practices. A similar study on females a few years later (Kinsey, Pomeroy, Martin, & Gebhard, 1953) also created quite a stir. These books were roundly condemned, but they also became best-sellers.

The effect of Kinsey's work was to break the powerful taboo on talking about sex, at least to the extent that it became acceptable to talk in detail to a sex researcher. And in the last 30 years sex research has blossomed into thousands of studies in many scientific disciplines. Social scientists have developed carefully designed interviews and sex questionnaires. Most of the research, including Kinsey's, used volunteer subjects. The issue of a biased sample is a real issue for any research that hopes to generalize to the population at large. In general, however, descriptive data from large studies tend to be consistent, and the actual error rate is relatively small.

Against this background it now seems inevitable that Masters and Johnson (1966) would arrive on the scene and actually study sexual intercourse in the laboratory. Their work received wide attention, but did not create the furor of earlier research, partly because of the effects of that earlier work in establishing the acceptability of sexual research. Today the technology of sexual research is well developed. It is possible to measure sexual arousal directly, for example, by the penile plethysmograph (Geer, 1975) and the vaginal plethysmograph (Geer, Morokoff, & Greenwood, 1974).

It is clear that the possibilities for sexual research have come a long way in the past hundred years. Just how far may be illustrated by a story told by a famous sexologist, who swore that it was true, although he was slightly drunk at the time. In 1882 a young Bostonian named Tom Peepers decided to do a scientific study of sex. He knocked on a door in a well-to-do neighborhood and asked the lady if he could talk to her about her sex life. She screamed, and the neighbors came running to help. When she told them what had happened, they promptly hanged Peepers from the nearest tree.

In 1982 a young sociologist, John Peepers (actually the great-great-grandson of Tom Peepers), was conducting a survey of sexual practices among the middle class, again in Boston. He knocked on a door, asked the lady for an interview, and proceeded with a detailed three-hour interview of the most intimate aspects of the lady's sexual behavior. At the very end he asked a few demographic questions to correlate with the sex-history data. When Peepers asked about her annual income, the lady became very indignant: "How dare you, that's a very personal, private matter—get out of my house!"

The Sexual Revolution: Reality or Myth?

During the past several years expressions of popular culture suggest that a radical social change has occurred in sexual behavior. The gist of this so-called revolution is that "everyone's doing it," and if they aren't now, they soon will be. Is this popular sentiment mostly myth, or is it a reality? If reality how much have the sexual mores changed? Has there really been a sexual revolution at all? Stated specifically, in what ways have attitudes and various sexual behaviors changed over the last two to three decades, and what are the consequences of those changes?

Changes in Sexual Attitudes

Most authorities agree that there has been a shift toward more permissive sexual attitudes. Permissiveness means tolerance for the sexual ideas and behavior of other people and, to a varying extent, of oneself. Several indicators of such shifts in attitudes exist. Byrne (1977b) sketched the trend toward permissiveness for erotic materials. He found that in several media—fiction, magazine photographs, and motion pictures—the trend is toward more explicit portrayal of sexuality. This change, plus such phenomena as topless and bottomless waitresses and the easy availability of hard-core porn, suggests that society's attitudes have evolved toward greater acceptance of an erotic environment.

In the early 1970s Hunt (1974) was commissioned by the Playboy Foundation to conduct a national study of sexual attitudes and behavior. Hunt attempted to represent the total population in over 2000 interviews. Hunt's data suggested more liberal attitudes in several respects. Some of the findings were:

- Seventy-five percent or more of males and females believed that schools should offer sex education.
- Eighty percent or more of both sexes did not think the male should always initiate intercourse.
- Half the sample disagreed that "most men want to marry a virgin."
- About half the sample disagreed that "homosexuality is wrong."
- Depending on the emotional relationship between partners, roughly one-third to over 80 percent of the sample believed that premarital sex is acceptable.
- The great majority of the sample did not feel that anything is wrong with masturbation.
- The majority of the sample favored legalized prostitution.
- The majority favored legal abortions.
- Two-thirds or more felt that mate swapping is wrong.
- About three-fourths of the sample disagreed that oral sex is wrong.
- About 60 percent of the sample disagreed with the statement "anal intercourse between a man and a woman is wrong."

To the extent that this sample represents the population, the findings suggest that permissive attitudes are widespread for most sexual behaviors, except mate swapping.

The change in attitude about premarital chastity has been studied carefully and is the most fully documented of all attitude changes. A number of recent studies (Clayton & Bokemeier, 1980) show more positive attitudes toward premarital sexuality and less negative attitudes or guilt about engaging in it. This change holds for national samples (Hunt, 1974) as well as for samples of college students. For example, King, Balswick, and Robinson (1977) found that between 1965 and 1970 the percentage of a college sample who believed that premarital sex is immoral dropped from 33 percent to 14 percent for males and from 70 percent to 34 percent for females.

These findings suggest that females are approaching males in expressed permissiveness. This suggestion received support by Bell and Chaskes (1970), who made comparisons for college females in 1958 and again in 1968. It is interesting that of those females who had premarital intercourse, the percentage feeling guilt declined considerably. Whether or not they felt they went too far depended on the specific nature of the relationship.

	1958	1968
Sex while dating	65%	36%
Sex while going steady	61%	30%
Sex while engaged	41%	20%

Other studies show similar results.

It seems clear that attitudes toward premarital sex and other practices have become more permissive. However, that could mean that people talk about sex more freely without a corresponding change in overt sexual behavior (see Chapter 1). In general we would expect changes in expressed attitudes to correspond to behavior changes, but correspondence is not guaranteed, and the case must be documented.

Changes in Sexual Behavior

One of the most powerful results of the Kinsey surveys was the finding that people engaged in more sexual activities than popular culture assumed to be the case. The nineteenth-century taboo on talk about sex carried over partially into the 1940s.

The two Kinsey et al. volumes (1948, 1953) are enormous, containing tremendous amounts of data. As a baseline it is interesting to note the incidence of premarital intercourse that Kinsey found at that time. The incidence depended strongly on the respondents' education level. For ages 16 to 20, the following incidence of premarital intercourse was found.

	Males	*Females*
Completed eighth grade or lower	85%	38%
Some high school or graduated	76%	32%
Some college	42%	17–19%

The data show a great disparity between the sexes and between what amounts to social-class divisions.

Hunt (1974) compared his national sample where possible to Kinsey's (late 1940s) data and found a general increase in permissiveness for sexual behavior. Some results of the comparisons were:

• Masturbation began earlier in Hunt's sample for both males and females and occurred more frequently. Further, more married people reported masturbation in 1972 than in Kinsey's samples.
• Kinsey found that over 25 percent of unmarried males (excluding those who were only grade-school educated) had not experienced intercourse by age 25; by 1972 the comparable figure was 3 percent.
• One-third of the females in Kinsey's sample had premarital intercourse by age 25; by 1972 the proportion had increased to over two-thirds.
• About 40 percent of Kinsey's sample of males engaged in oral sex with their wives; by 1972 incidence of oral sex had increased to about 60 percent. The increase was at all age levels, but greatest among young people.
• The incidence of homosexuality, sex with animals, and sadomasochistic acts had not changed.
• The overall incidence of extramarital intercourse had not changed, although it had become more common for both men and women under age 25.
• Sex as purely recreational behavior was very rare in Hunt's 1972 sample.

As with attitude change the change in sexual behavior has been most carefully documented for premarital intercourse. Some of the best surveys are summarized in Table 5-1. These data are arranged to show the percentage of people engaging in premarital intercourse at two or more survey dates. Even casual inspection of the data indicates that in every study the later the date, the larger the percentage of the sample experiencing premarital intercourse. The absolute level varies considerably from study to study, probably due to regional or age differences in samples or to some aspect of the research design. However, the trend toward greater expressed behavioral permissiveness is undeniable.

The study by Bell and Chaskes (1970) is of particular interest because it indicates that for females: (1) premarital intercourse is more likely for a serious relationship (like an engagement) than for a casual relationship (like dating), but (2) the increase in sex with a casual partner increased much more dramatically from 1958 to 1968 than the increase with a committed partner. Generally, this result is consistent with Hunt's (1974) findings of more diverse sexual activities. There has undoubtedly been some increase in casual sexual contacts, but the overwhelming majority of the sample members in Hunt's study stated that sex cannot be very satisfying without some emotional involvement between the partners.

The data for both attitude expression and actual behavior are consistent, suggesting greater permissiveness for a wide range of activities, but not for all activities. Similar consistency of results was obtained from an international sample of college students. In general students from England and Norway were more permissive than U.S. students, who were in turn somewhat more permissive than students from Canada and Germany (Luckey & Nass, 1969).

During Kinsey's era, men were supposed to be more sexually aggressive and women chaste. Actually, females were supposed to save themselves for marriage, and the issue of whether to remain a virgin or not

TABLE 5-1   Data from five studies on incidence of premarital intercourse

Authors	Type of sample	Sex of sample	Year of survey		
			Time 1	Time 2	Time 3
Bell and Chaskes (1970)	College students	Females only	1958	1968	
		Dating	10%	23%	———
		Going Steady	15%	28%	———
		Engaged	31%	39%	———
Vener and Stewart (1974)	Ages 13 to 17 years		1970	1973	
		Males	28%	33%	———
		Females	16%	22%	———
King, Balswick, and Robinson (1977)	College students		1965	1970	1975
		Males	65%	65%	74%
		Females	21%	37%	57%
Zelnik and Kantner (1977)	Ages 15 to 19 years	Females only	1971	1976	
		Whites	21%	31%	———
		Blacks	51%	63%	———
Hobart (1979)	Canadian English-speaking college and trade school students		1968	1977	
		Males	56%	73%	———
		Females	44%	63%	———

Note: Each study collected data on at least two occasions. The year the data were collected is shown in the columns headed *Time 1, Time 2,* and *Time 3.* Percentages of samples engaging in premarital intercourse are shown for year the data were collected.

troubled more than a few young women. The data summarized in Table 5-1 indicate that the mores of females are changing more rapidly than the mores of males, in part because a greater range for change existed for females. The change is so dramatic that some commentators suggest that the traditional double standard is dead, and that society is converging on a single standard of conduct for both sexes.

Is the Double Standard Endangered?

A study by Curran (1975) suggests that sexual mores are converging toward a single standard. College students completed the Heterosexual Behavior Inventory (Bentler, 1968a, 1968b), a standardized scale of 21 sexual behaviors arranged to increase in "severity." Each item is answered "yes" or "no." The items are shown in Table 5-2 in Bentler's original rank order. The percentages of "yes" responses obtained by Curran are shown for males and females. Curran's results are consistent with Bentler's earlier results. Further, the percentages are quite similar for males and females across the range of sexual activities with a few exceptions. A higher percentage of females had engaged in oral sex (items 16, 17, 18), possibly in an attempt to enjoy sexual activity while technically remaining a virgin (Curran, 1975, p. 193). Because of the highly similar ranking of both sexes on sexual activities, Curran suggested that the double standard is waning and that society is converging on a single standard.

A study of 231 dating couples by Peplau, Rubin, and Hill (1977) casts some doubt on this conclusion. The couples were college students from the Boston area who had been dating about eight months at the time the study began in 1972. The students' attitudes toward premarital sex were highly favorable, and in fact, 82 percent of the couples had experienced intercourse with each other. Nevertheless, the authors found considerable evidence for sexual role playing in which: (1) the man initiated sexual activity, and (2) the woman set limits for the couple. Sex was rated as the most important goal in the relationship by more men (28 percent) than women (9 percent). Among those couples having intercourse, the woman's attitudes and preferences tended to control when sex first began; among the 18 percent of the couples not having sex, the woman's preference was the controlling factor.

It is curious to find such liberal attitudes and high rate of sexual activity contrasted with the traditional roles of active male/passive female. One theory is that people's behavior follows social roles or scripts (Gagnon, 1977). Social scripts are rules of conduct that define the situation, the participants, and the plot. Sexual role playing is the following of a familiar, culturally defined set of guidelines for how sexual interactions should occur. Such rules about sex help coordinate this complex, interdependent behavior. If sexual scripts are socially determined, they should change over time as sexual freedom becomes more institutionalized. Initiation of sex and setting limits should gradually become equal across both sexes.

A very different theory, an evolutionary approach to sexuality, suggests that male initiative/female reticence may be an inherent aspect of our biological natures. Symons (1979) developed a strong argument that copulation is a female service to males, even when the female experiences as much pleasure as the male. We cannot debate these contrasting theories here. In part the question is empirical. If the sexual scripts change so that in a few generations women become equal to men in sexual initiatives, the evolutionary approach is incorrect. It is a fascinating question for future research.

TABLE 5-2   Percentage of "yes" respondents to sexual acts listed on the Heterosexual Behavior Inventory

| | *Respondents* | |
Abbreviated items	*Males*	*Females*
1. One minute continuous lip kissing	86	89
2. Manual manipulation of female breasts, over clothes	83	71
3. Manual manipulation of female breasts, under clothes	76	66
4. Manual manipulation of genitals, over clothes	76	68
5. Kissing nipples of female breast	66	59
6. Manual manipulation of female genitals, under clothes, by male	64	60
7. Manual manipulation of male genitals, over clothes, by female	57	52
8. Mutual manipulation of genitals	56	51
9. Manual manipulation of male genitals, under clothes, by female	50	52
10. Manual manipulation of female genitals to massive secretions	49	51
11. Sexual intercourse, ventral/ventral	44	37
12. Manual manipulation of male genitals to ejaculation, by female	37	41
13. Oral contact with female genitals, by male	32	42
14. Oral contact with male genitals, by female	31	42
15. Mutual manual manipulation of genitals to mutual orgasm	31	27
16. Oral manipulation of male genitals, by female	30	39
17. Oral manipulation of female genitals, by male	30	41
18. Mutual oral/genital manipulation	21	29
19. Sexual intercourse, ventral/dorsal	15	23
20. Oral manipulation of male genitals to ejaculation	23	27
21. Mutual oral manipulation of genitals to mutual orgasm	14	12

Adapted from "Convergence toward a Single Standard?" by J. P. Curran. In *Social Behavior and Personality*, 1975, *3*, 189–195. Reprinted by permission. The inventory items are reprinted with permission from "Heterosexual Behavior Assessment-I. Males," by P. M. Bentler. In *Behavior Research and Therapy*, 1968, *6*, 21–25. Copyright 1968, Pergamon Press, Ltd.

Was There a Revolution?

Our society is still in transition, and the story is not complete. Clearly there has been substantial attitude change and increased behavioral permissiveness. From one viewpoint it certainly seems as if revolutionary changes have occurred. However, Hunt (1974) believes that the new freedom does not displace basic institutional structures. According to Hunt, a true revolution would require three changes:

1. Displacement of vaginal coitus by other sex acts that serve as substitutes for coitus.
2. Increase in sex acts that alter the connection between sex and marriage, such as mate-swapping, swinging, and mutually agreed upon extramarital sex.
3. Increase in sex acts without emotional significance.

Hunt (1974) does not believe that these three conditions have occurred. We do not have a revolution, but a new freedom with permissiveness. However, a process of more radical change may be beginning. Peplau, Rubin, and Hill (1977) found three types of couples in their study.

1. *Traditional couples*—Sex is morally wrong for such couples unless it is sanctioned by marriage. Love is not a sufficient reason to have sex. In fact, abstinence indicates love and respect.
2. *Moderate couples*—Sex is okay for these couples as long as the two people love each other; a more enduring commitment is not necessary. Permissiveness with affection is the code phrase.
3. *Liberal couples*—Permissiveness without affection is the value code for these couples. Sex with love is desirable, but sex without love is quite acceptable. Such couples are capable of enjoying casual or recreational sex.

One surprise was that the duration of the relationship did not depend on which type of relationship the couple formed. We conjecture that if the percentage of liberal couples greatly increases in the years ahead, the sexual revolution will be a fact. If recreational sex should become normative, Hunt's criteria would substantially be met, and the society would become quite different from what it is now. Whether such a change is ultimately good or bad is an ethical issue, another story for another time.

Sexual Interactions

Sexual interactions are among the most complicated of human social interactions. Interaction begins with two persons, each with a unique set of desires, needs, expectations, tendency toward moral evaluation, and self-image or self-concept. A sexual interaction requires some degree of congruence between the various cognitive orientations of the two people and negotiation of the several behavioral stages of the actual sexual encounter. Part of this process involves the coordination of a complex interdependency between two bodies in contact, and the management of internal emotional arousal and the experience of pleasure. Sex is not simple! Things can go wrong at many points in sexual interactions.

The basis for sexual interactions begins with the individual person or, more precisely, with the person's self-concept and that facet of the self-concept concerned with sexual behavior.

The Sexual Self

In general, the *self-concept* may be defined as all the ways one experiences oneself as a being in the world and one's evaluations of those experiences. The sexual self-concept is all the ways one experiences and evaluates oneself as a sexual being. The emphasis is on *cognition,* the perceptual and thought processes by which people perceive, recognize, categorize, and evaluate the world around them. Thus the self-concept consists of all the belief and evaluative components of the many attitudes (Chapter 1) held about oneself, and the sexual self-concept consists of all the specific sexual attitudes that are part of the general self-concept.

We can categorize our existence into three general dimensions: *biophysical, personal,* and *social* (Victor, 1980). These dimensions refer to the self as a biological entity, the self as a whole person, and the self as an object of other people's responses, respectively. Each individual holds many self-attitudes corresponding to each of the three dimensions. Further, the attitudes that make up the sexual self-concept cut across these three dimensions. Thus each person has a set of attitudes toward his or her body in general (body image), the genitals, and various sex-related acts such as masturbation, intercourse, menstruation, and pregnancy.

Our bodily images of sexuality can profoundly affect the way we approach the personal and interpersonal aspects of sexual behavior. Our personal self-concept is affected by the way we accept the bodily aspect of our sexual nature. Many people comfortably accept sexuality as a part of their nature and like themselves as sexual beings. Such liking in turn feeds into a heightened sense of general self-esteem. Other people are socialized to believe that sex is in some way wrong. Such people may, as adults, develop a relatively constant feeling of *sex-guilt* for engaging in sexual activities (Mosher & Cross, 1971). Guilt is defined as anger directed against the self (Victor, 1980). Sex-guilt often leads to unhappy interpersonal relations, especially in marriage.

Social or interpersonal attitudes about sex refer to such things as norms for sexual attractiveness of other people, concepts of proper and improper masculine and feminine sexual behavior, attitudes about the relation between love and sexual expression, and so on. Naturally these interpersonal attitudes may affect actual sexual relationships.

At lower levels of the phylogenetic scale, sexual behavior is increasingly controlled by instinctual and hormonal influences. However, nearly all authorities agree that although a biological core in humans is given, this core is shaped in an infinite variety of ways by the modifiability of higher cortical centers called learning (Ford & Beach, 1951; Gagnon & Simon, 1973; Kinsey, Pomeroy, Martin, & Gebhard, 1953). Some societies are repressive; others are permissive. The particular channels of expression and repression in childhood help shape the nature of the adult sexual self-concept and sexual interactions.

All societies have some taboos on sexual expression. Some types of taboos are common across most societies.

1. *Sex is private.* The overwhelming majority of the world's peoples engage in sex in a secluded area. Very few of us have ever seen our parents (or anyone else for that matter) engage in sexual intercourse. There is some speculation that the need for privacy is an evolutionary adaptation for protection against predators (Symons, 1979). However, it is just as likely that social learning is the best explanation.

2. *Sex always has inhibitions.* The content of inhibitions varies widely. In some societies female breasts are salient parts of sexual anatomy; in other societies breasts are not important. It is significant that in societies where breasts are sex coded, they are covered; in societies without such coding breasts may be left uncovered. Sexual inhibitions are learned through two mechanisms, sex-guilt (discussed previously) and *shame*. Shame is fear of social disapproval and is created by ridicule, gossip, and in children by direct punishment. "Shame on you, Johnny, quit playing with yourself" may serve as the archetype for how shame is instilled into children and associated with their sexuality.

3. *Sex is associated with interpersonal avoidance.* Age-avoidance is very common (Money, 1980), especially physical contact and discussion between adults and children. If the ages are inappropriate in a certain way, sexual contact will result in a charge of statutory rape even though both individuals freely consented to sex. More commonly, adults avoid talking to children about sex, and it is recognized that we have a massive problem of inadequate sex education in our society.

Another common avoidance is cross-sex restrictions on talk and behavior. There is male talk about sex and female talk about sex, and the two styles of talk often differ considerably. Further, both types will differ from the polite mixed-sex version of sex-talk. The widespread segregation of public bathrooms and locker rooms implies that while exposure of the body or genitals to strangers of the same sex is acceptable, cross-sex exposure is not.

Finally, there is a general intimacy-avoidance in sexual matters in which age and cross-sex avoidance are special cases. Most people are very reticent to disclose the contents of their sexual histories to other people, and even their own sexual partners may receive only partial disclosure. Indeed, lack of communication to the partner of one's innermost desires is quite common. There are private aspects of sex even in sexual encounters. Such is the power of sexual taboos learned in childhood.

The various taboos and inhibitions on sexual expression become part of one's sexual self-concept as an adult. These facets of self would be expected to have a strong effect on the nature of sexual interactions in adulthood.

Sexual Interaction: An Overview

Money (1980) proposed that sexual interactions may be viewed as a set of three stages: *proception, acception,* and *conception.*

Proception refers to all the stimuli and responses, including fantasy, that men and women experience in their sexual interactions prior to sexual union. Generically, proception extended over time is called courtship and includes all the relationship issues involved in love (Chapter 4). "Proception is the phase of invitation, of solicitation and seduction, and of attraction—of being both attracted and attractive" (Money, 1980, p. 75). In an ongoing interaction the proceptive phase involves flirting, kissing, and touching preliminary to intercourse. The biological function of this phase appears to be to create in the organism a readiness for copulation.

In humans the eyes are the primary sense organ for sexual signalling. Males may depend somewhat more than females on visual stimulation for arousal, and females are somewhat more dependent on touch (Money, 1980; Symons, 1979). The importance of vision for sexual arousal may be related to the extensive amounts of sexual imagery that people have, imagery that is largely visual in nature.

In many other mammals the nose is the primary organ of proception. Females secrete pheromones during *estrus,* a relatively brief period of female receptivity that ordinarily coincides with the period of fertility for reproduction. Pheromones serve as powerful attractants to males of these species. Primate females secrete a general pheromone that is not species-specific. In fact, the pheromone secreted by an ovulating woman will, when smeared on a virgin female rhesus monkey, strongly excite the rhesus male. Human females do not experience estrus, although ovulation does occur in a regular monthly cycle. To date there is not firm evidence that proceptivity in women is associated with the monthly cycle. There is also no evidence that the pheromone is an attractant for the human male. Most likely, the nose was more important in an earlier stage of our ancestry, but our species has evolved to the point of dominant visual control of the proceptive sexual system.

Acception and conception involve the act of intercourse itself and its aftermath. "In the ordinary course of events, proception leads to acception, a two-way interaction of the penis and vulva, which receive one another. Acception, in the ordinary course of events, leads sooner or later to conception and parenthood" (Money, 1980, p. 73). What the eyes do for proception, touch does for acception. Touch is important during courtship and arousal, but it is by definition the main sensory system involved in sexual intercourse. Humans often overlook the importance of touching prior to sexual union. In other primate species individuals spend much time in *grooming* each other, which is stroking, combing, and scratching fur and skin. Grooming is related to sexual expression, social friendliness, and care of the young. According to Money humans engage in much grooming activity also, but we use terms such as hug, cuddle, tickle, squeeze, pet, rub, and so forth. Humans also use (nongenital) grooming in caring for the young and to express sociability, as well as for sexual purposes.

Fashions vary. A generation ago extensive grooming preliminaries to full coital union tended to be frowned upon. After Masters and Johnson (1966) there was increased attention on such activities (often called pleasuring or sensate focus by sex therapists) as an antidote for sex problems, a fad that may have been carried too far (Money, 1980). Nevertheless, deprivation of grooming by one's partner can be experienced as a tremendous loss, sometimes of greater importance than the loss of intercourse or orgasm. The habitual feel of one's partner, his or her "creatureness" is probably a powerful stimulant to the maintenance of the pair-bond. This aspect of sexual functioning probably has its roots in infancy, in the grooming of the infant by the mother in loving, caring, and feeding.

The zenith of the acception stage is the act of heterosexual coitus. The research of Masters and Johnson indicated that intercourse can be divided conceptually into four phases that are roughly comparable for males and females: excitement, plateau, orgasm, and resolution. These stages are averages across many people; any given individual may experience coitus quite differently. The stages are therefore descriptive, not prescribed requirements for "proper sex."

1. *Excitement phase.* The excitement and tension builds over time, increasing in intensity. Problems may occur when people differ in rate of increase in feelings. Many people use fantasy prior to and during intercourse as a means of enhancing excitement. For example, one study (Hariton & Singer, 1974) of married women found that nearly all women reported some imagery during intercourse, and over one-third had very frequent imagery.

2. *Plateau phase.* Excitement reaches a maximum which may be sustained for a shorter or longer period. Respiration, heart rate, and blood pressure are elevated, and perspiration may be intense. If this phase is not disrupted, orgasm usually occurs.

3. *Orgasmic phase.* This phase ordinarily lasts only a few seconds and results in an explosive release of pent-up sexual stimulation. Female orgasm is more variable than male orgasm, which is usually correlated with ejaculation of seminal fluids. Some women have two orgasmic responses in quick succession; some have a single extended orgasm; others have a long series of smaller orgasmic responses.

Masters and Johnson's work demonstrated that the clitoris is the central organ of orgasmic response in women. Freudian psychology has argued for a vaginal orgasm as being more sexually mature than a clitoral orgasm. The spread of sensation in the pelvic region may feel as if the orgasm originates deep within the vagina for many women. However, the physiological site for all female orgasms is undoubtedly the clitoris.

There are wide individual differences in the way people subjectively experience orgasm. However, because of the involuntary nature of orgasm, the attentional focus is drawn to the pelvic area. It seems reasonable therefore that the subjective experience of orgasm might not differ between males and females. Vance and Wagner (1976) had college students provide written descriptions of what an orgasm feels like. Judges then guessed at the sex of the writer. Professional judges achieved only chance accuracy in their guesses, suggesting that the experience of orgasm is indeed similar on the average for both sexes.

BOX 5-2 Descriptions of orgasms by males and females. It is interesting to try to guess whether a description was provided by a male or female. These 16 descriptions are from a larger set of 48. Expert judges did no better than chance accuracy. Answers for the 16 items in order are F, F, F, M, F, M, F, F, M, F, F, F, F, M, F, M. (*From "Written Descriptions of Orgasm: A Study of Sex Differences," by E. B. Vance and N. N. Wagner. In Archives of Sexual Behavior, 1976, 5, 87–98. Copyright 1976 by Plenum Publishing Corporation. Reprinted by permission.*)

The following statements are replies by both men and women to a request to describe what an orgasm feels like. For each, please indicate in the blank spaces provided whether you think the statement was written by a male or a female. Put an M for male and an F for female.

1. _____ A sudden feeling of lightheadedness followed by an intense feeling of relief and elation. A rush. Intense muscular spasms of the whole body. Sense of euphoria followed by deep peace and relaxation.

2. _____ Feels like tension building up until you think it can't build up any more, then release. The orgasm is both the highest point of tension and the release almost at the same time. Also feeling contractions in the genitals. Tingling all over.

3. _____ I often see spots in front of my eyes during orgasm. The feeling itself is so difficult to describe other than the most pleasurable of all sensory impressions. I suppose the words "fluttering sensation" describe the physical feeling I get. All nerve endings sort of burst and quiver.

4. _____ There is a great release of tensions that have built up in the prior stages of sexual activity. This release is extremely pleasurable and exciting. The feeling seems to be centered in the genital region. It is extremely intense and exhilarating. There is a loss of muscular control as the pleasure mounts and you almost cannot go on. You almost don't want to go on. This is followed by the climax and refractory states!

5. _____ An orgasm feels extremely pleasurable, yet it can be so violent that the feeling of uncontrol is frightening. It also is hard to describe because it is as if I am in limbo—only conscious of release.

6. _____ To me an orgasmic experience is the most satisfying pleasure that I have experienced in relation to any other type of satisfaction or pleasure that I've had which were nonsexually oriented.

7. _____ The period when the orgasm takes place—a loss of a real feeling for the surroundings except for the other person. The movements are spontaneous and intense.

8. _____ They vary a great deal depending on circumstances. If it's just a physical need or release it's OK, but it takes more effort to "get there." If you're really very much in love (at least in my case) it's so close at hand that the least physical expression by your partner, or slightest touch on the genitals brings it on. And then if the lovemaking is continued it repeats again and again. It's about 90 percent cortical or emotional and the rest physical. But one has to have the emotion or (in my case) I don't even want to begin to try.

9. _____ Obviously, we can't explain what it feels "like" because it feels "like" nothing else in human experience. A poetic description may well describe the emotions that go with it, but the physical "feeling" can only be described with very weak mechanical terminology. It is a release

that occurs after a period of manipulation has sufficiently enabled internal, highly involuntary spasms that are pleasurable due to your complete involuntary control (no control).

10. _____ It's like shooting junk on a sunny day in a big, green, open field.

11. _____ It is like turning a water faucet on. You notice the oncoming flow but it can be turned on or off when desired. You feel the valves open and close and the fluid flow. An orgasm makes your head and body tingle.

12. _____ An orgasm . . . located (originating) in the genital area, capable of spreading out further . . . legs, abdomen. A sort of pulsating feeling—very nice if it can extend itself beyond the immediate genital area.

13. _____ A build-up of tension which starts to pulsate very fast, and there is a sudden release from the tension and desire to sleep.

14. _____ Begins with tensing and tingling in anticipation, rectal contractions starting series of chills up spine. Tingling and buzzing sensations grow suddenly to explosion in genital area, some sensation of dizzying and weakening—almost loss of conscious sensation, but not really. Explosion sort of flowers out to varying distance from genital area, depending on intensity.

15. _____ A heightened feeling of excitement with severe muscular tension especially through the back and legs, rigid straightening of the entire body for about five seconds, and a strong and general relaxation and very tired relieved feeling.

16. _____ A tremendous release of built-up tension all at once lasting around five to ten seconds where a particular "pulsing" feeling is felt throughout my body along with a kind of tickling and tingling feeling.

Males and females do differ, however, in the uniformity with which they achieve orgasm during intercourse. Males are nearly always able to have an orgasm. Females are more variable. Some proportion of females have difficulty in obtaining enough stimulation during intercourse to trigger an orgasm. Kinsey and associates (1953) found that, among women who had no prior sexual experience or orgasm, only 60 percent achieved orgasm during the first year of marriage. Women who had intercourse with orgasm before marriage experienced orgasm in 95 percent of the cases during the first year of marriage, although not on every occasion. Fisher (1973) found that the most reliable predictor of orgasm in a woman was her feelings of love for her partner, something clearly not the case for males.

The past decade has led to an increased awareness that women are fully capable of having orgasm, but that many have difficulty some of the time. The way in which this knowledge affects current sexual interactions is not clear.

4. *Resolution phase.* This phase involves a decrease in sexual tension to the level of an unstimulated state. For males there is a recovery period during which restimulation is not possible. Masters and Johnson discovered that females can be restimulated again during the resolution phase. During the past few years this finding has caused much discussion of the possiblity of multiple orgasms in women. This possibility is true for some women, but for what proportion of women and how often is unknown.

The Social Context of Sexual Interactions

Sexual interactions occur within the fabric of ongoing social life. A couple does not just have sex, they *negotiate* it within the framework of their sexual *communication system.* Conflict over sexual matters requires resolution, just as conflict in other areas of life. Problems of boredom and the need for novel experience also beset long-term sexual couples. Fantasy and erotica may affect the sexual relationship, sometimes positively and occasionally negatively. A catch phrase of several years ago—"Make love, not war"—seemed unaware of the fact that coercion and aggression sometimes invade the sexual realm. In brief, sexuality does not occur in a vacuum, but is interwoven with all of life.

Sexual Communication

People must communicate to engage in sex, and they frequently communicate about sex. In some cases it may be as blunt as "Let's screw," but usually an invitation is more subtle—"Why don't we put the kids to bed early tonight?" Such subtle initiatives may be rebuffed ("Not tonight, dear, I have a headache") or missed entirely ("Good, then we can watch the X-rated movie"). Sexual communication is often aided by expectations or social scripts described previously (Gagnon, 1977). Such sexual scripts explain why most sex occurs at night in the bedroom, even though both people may be tired and not particularly interested. They allow the setting to communicate for them, and sometimes the messages are unclear or false.

The old stigma about not discussing sex currently continues in our society in more subtle forms. We can now talk about sex freely as a social phenomenon in many nonsexual settings. But very few people can reveal *all* their most intimate thoughts to their lover (or to anyone else). Box 5-3 lists an approximate hierarchy of increasingly intimate sexual communication. Some people will have trouble in all six areas. Very few people feel completely free to discuss details of sex fantasies or past sexual experiences, especially with their lovers.

> **BOX 5-3** Levels of sexual communication range from bodily self-disclosure to communicating past sexual experiences. An individual may have difficulties at any level. However, many people find communication of fantasy and past sexual experiences very difficult. Sex may remain private in several senses. (*Jeffrey S. Victor,* Human Sexuality: A Social Psychological Approach, © *1980, pp. 234–235. Reprinted by permission of Prentice-Hall, Inc., Englewood Cliffs, N.J.*)

1. Bodily self-disclosure. Bodily self-disclosure in erotic activities is the most obvious form of sexual self-disclosure. It can be a source of concern and personal reserve for people during initial sexual encounters. However, excessive modesty or body prudery can create difficulties for couples who have had sexual relations over decades. It is quite likely, for example, that many husbands and wives remain unfamiliar throughout their lives with the details of each other's genital anatomy. Because of sexual reserve, they remain unaware of genital areas of particular sexual sensitivity and the kinds of genital caresses which maximize erotic pleasure. Many couples even avoid sexual intercourse in the nude and neglect possible pleasures of erotic body exploration. Sexual reserve may also inhibit the sensual pleasures of touching and being touched as an expression of affection outside the confines of the bedroom.

2. Signaling sexual receptiveness. The signaling of sexual receptiveness involves the use of both verbal and nonverbal communication to indicate a desire or lack of desire for sexual activity. This is often a subtle and difficult matter when spouses do not have mutually frequent sexual desire. Many couples develop special codes of expression to indicate their receptiveness.

3. Communicating sexual responsiveness. The communication of sexual responsiveness involves verbal and nonverbal expressions of erotic pleasure. Such expressiveness can intensify the mutual pleasure of sexual partners via the effects of empathy.

4. Communicating sexual preferences. The communication of sexual preferences involves the communication of desires for kinds of caresses, sexual positions, and environments. Such communication is crucial in pacing the build-up of sexual excitement. It also provides feedback information which enables sexual partners to maximize each other's pleasure.

5. Communicating sexual fantasies. At an even more intimate level of sexual self-disclosure, sexual partners can disclose their per-

sonal sex fantasies. Some sex therapists suggest that the sharing of sex fantasies, even when involving socially condemned practices, can intensify mutual sexual arousal. It is doubtful that many married couples release their sexual reserve as far as sharing sex fantasies. Many individuals cannot openly face their own fantasies. Such intimate self-disclosure can be very threatening to many couples.

6. Communicating past sexual experiences. Finally, sexual self-disclosure may also involve the communication of past sexual experiences with others in premarital or extramarital affairs or in a previous marriage. This sort of self-disclosure may be particularly threatening, because it is likely to evoke feelings of sexual jealousy.

People differ in their need and ability for intimate contact and disclosure (McAdams & Powers, 1981). The traditional stereotypes of the strong, silent, self-sufficient male and the warm, emotionally supportive female do not suggest free and easy communication about sexual matters. Fortunately, these stereotypes are weakening somewhat, and people now probably have more intimate sexual discussions than at any time in the past. Such open communication is desirable because faulty communication is one cause of sexual conflict.

Sexual Conflicts

Sexual conflict, or at least sexual dissatisfaction, is common. Expectations about the pleasures of sex are high, and people believe that sexual pleasure should occur spontaneously, without prior knowledge, practice, or skill (Gagnon, 1977). We remain ambivalent about sex, as part of the general cultural uneasiness about pleasure. More recently, the norm of "male's right, woman's duty" has shifted radically to a norm of "equal rights to equal pleasure." Sexual pleasure has become an achievement goal. Women now feel guilty if they do not have orgasm regularly; men tend to interpret female orgasm as a sign of their own sexual competence. In general, anxiety about performance seems to have increased. These issues are further confounded by the political aspects of sexual rights and obligations in the current general trend toward female equality. The basis for many sexual conflicts clearly exists.

Sexual conflicts occur most often from disagreements over sexual preferences, unequal sexual satisfactions, and jealousy (see Chapter 4), according to Victor (1980). Also, conflicts from other areas of life spill over into the sexual arena. Frequency of sex declines from about three times per week in young couples to about once per week in couples in their fifties, although a recent survey suggests that the absolute frequency of sex is increasing (Westoff, 1974). One study found that over half the couples experienced unequal preferred frequencies of sex with males wanting a higher frequency (Levinger, 1966). Inequality of desired frequency plus the general decline with age suggests that the basic issue of "how often" is an important source of conflict.

Inequality of satisfaction is another source of conflict. The average time for sex is from ten to 20 minutes (Gagnon, 1977). Males tend to have orgasm faster than females, at least among young people, and problems of coordination of timing lead to feelings of frustration and inadequacy. Differences in desire to experiment with different coital positions and oral and anal sex also provide a basis for sexual arguments.

Rules of courtesy called etiquette govern our behavior in most social situations. Appleton (1981) believes that many sexual conflicts would be avoided if people simply used good manners in their sexual interactions. "There has been too much emphasis placed on the extremes of empathy vs narcissism, of concentrating on a relationship or on oneself" (Appleton, 1981, p. 88). Good manners will not solve all sexual conflicts, of course, but the mundane recommendation of a balance between satisfying self and satisfying the other makes good common sense.

Sexual Boredom and Novelty

Apparently any continuously repetitious behavior will become boring, even sex. Some people may actively try to vary their sexual routines, but larger numbers do not. One way to seek sexual novelty is to find a new sex partner. Kinsey et al. (1953) found that among married people by age 40, one-fourth of the women and half the men had at least one extramarital sexual experience. The incidence of extramarital sex may be increasing, especially among women under 25 (Hunt, 1974). Reasons for extramarital sex vary, but one study of male business executives (Johnson, 1974) found the desire for new sexual experience as one of the major reasons.

The need for new experience in the sexual realm is highly problematic. Even though sexual jealousy and negative attitudes toward extramarital affairs often lead to fear, guilt, and anxiety, large numbers of people continue to have such experiences. Among many other species diversity of sexual partners is the rule. One evolutionary argument is that because females are breeding near their capacity to reproduce, they have little to gain by mating with many males, but males can ensure genetic success—creating offspring—by mating with many females (Dewsbury, 1981). There is animal research indicating that a male totally satiated by a female may be able to copulate immediately with a new partner, a phenomenon called the Coolidge effect (see Box 5-4).

It is impossible to know to what extent human desire for sexual novelty is based on our evolutionary heritage. As in so many other

BOX 5-4   The Coolidge effect

There is a fable that goes as follows:

When Calvin Coolidge was president, he and his wife were visiting a farm. Each was taken on a separate tour. As she passed the chicken yard, Mrs. Coolidge noticed the proud rooster and asked her guide whether the rooster had sex more than once a day. "Oh yes, dozens of times," the guide replied. "Please tell that to the President," Mrs. Coolidge requested. Later as the President passed the chicken yard, he was told about the active rooster. "Same hen every time?" he asked. "Oh no, Mr. President, a different hen each time." The President nodded and said, "Please tell that to Mrs. Coolidge."

This bit of humor suggests the human need for sexual variety in the guise of an animal story. Novelty in sex partners may stimulate heightened sexual activity. In many species a male who has copulated to satiation with one female may be aroused to new sexual activity when a novel female is placed in the cage. The phenomenon is called the "Coolidge effect," even though the fable deals with the availability of many females. Presumably the rooster would not copulate dozens of times daily if only one hen was available. The literature on the Coolidge effect is fully reviewed by Dewsbury (1981).

behavioral systems, it is possible that a minimal biological basis exists, but that it is overshadowed by social learning, with its many derived symbolic meanings.

Sexual Fantasy and Erotica

Sexual fantasy or daydreams are very common, and in the modern world we are constantly bombarded by erotic materials, in advertising, movies, novels, magazines, and on television. We live in an eroticized environment. Further, in contrast with other species, it appears that humans have always created erotic artifacts, even in sex-repressive societies. Why is erotic imagery so frequently created and communicated? Byrne (1976) suggests several reasons: (1) erotic materials are a source of knowledge, especially in societies reluctant to talk to children about sex; (2) erotic fantasies are pleasurable in their own right; (3) the stimulation value of fantasy and erotic materials serve as aphrodisiacs to actual sexual activity; and (4) fantasy may supplement reality which is often more impoverished than the images the mind can construct.

In Western society erotic materials in the form of pornography have traditionally been a male preserve. Although it is true that males seek out such materials more often than females, when exposed to such materials in a laboratory setting, both men and women are equally aroused (Fisher & Byrne, 1978). Further, men and women do not differ quantitatively in amount of fantasy generated from imagining an erotic situation, although there are some qualitative differences (Carlson & Coleman, 1977). Physiological responses to erotica (Schmidt & Sigusch, 1970; Schmidt, Sigusch, & Meyberg, 1969) as well as fantasy are well established.

External erotic stimulation and internal erotic fantasies clearly have strong effects. But on what? The persistent attempts to censor erotic materials assume that such materials will affect overt behavior, possibly leading to promiscuity and the breakdown of the social order. The evidence suggests a very limited effect of erotic materials on overt behavior (Wrightsman & Deaux, 1981), and such effects are restricted to brief enhancement of routine sexual activities.

Sexual Aggression

Hostility and aggression are a part of social life. Therefore it is reasonable to expect aggression to be linked to sexuality on some occasions. The nature of the link between sex and aggression has been long debated. Freud thought that aggressive instincts and sexual instincts spill over into and reinforce each other. Violent sex is common among many species. However, Ford and Beach (1951) noted that intense fighting often functions for the release of eggs from the ovary, and that the mating will be sterile without a preliminary bout of painful aggressive behavior. Some evolutionists (for example, Symons, 1979) link aggression to the competition to reproduce. The most aggressive males will often win and thus transmit their genetic material down through the generations. In this way aggression may be selected as a correlate of sexual behavior over long time periods.

Human sexual aggression is common. People have sex for a variety of reasons, including anger and revenge. Less subtle is the phenomenon of forcible rape, a detested but frequent crime. In general rape is a crime committed by men against women, although homosexual rape (such as that which takes place in prisons) occurs with some frequency. The causes of rape are unclear. The common explanation until a decade ago was that rape occurred because of sexual deprivation. We now know that this answer is untrue because many rapists have regular sexual partners. According to Brownmiller (1975), rape, or fear of rape, is a political act which helps males dominate females and keep them subjugated. While this explanation may be far-fetched, rape occurs for reasons that often have little to do with sex. The desire to degrade and dominate is often a strong motive component.

Rape sometimes occurs incidentally in the context of another crime such as burglary. People often view sexuality as if it were property, to be guarded and doled out. Thus stealing sex forcibly may be in those instances another type of theft of property. Research on rape has increased dramatically during the past decade. The specific social influences that lead some men to rape are not yet fully clear. One thing is clear: the concept of *civilization* will remain part hypocrisy until forcible rape is eradicated from the human species.

During the recent past the aggressive content of pornographic films has increased. In fact, "snuff films" in which the female is killed, are popular. Many people fear that such explicit aggression mixed with sex will increase aggressive behavior in the society, including sexually aggressive acts such as rape. Laboratory evidence suggests that depictions of rape (Malamuth, Heim, & Feshbach, 1980) and exposure to erotica (Donnerstein, 1980; Donnerstein & Hallam, 1978; White, 1979) can increase aggressive responses. The story is complex, however, because some research has found that sexual arousal inhibits aggression (Malamuth, Feshbach, & Jaffe, 1977; Baron, 1978). Whether exposure to aggressive erotica in everyday life is related to actual aggression is unknown.

Summary

The study of sexuality is so connected with value issues that separation of facts from ethics is difficult. One central issue is whether sex is best within a love relationship or whether sexual experience without love is equally satisfactory. Many reasons can be given for either alternative. Ultimately, this choice is based on values; empirical research or facts cannot dictate an answer, although arguments pro and con will often seem factual.

Sexual behavior is complex because it exists and can be studied at different levels of analysis: biological, interpersonal, and societal. Sex has always had taboos associated with it, and those taboos prevented scientific research on sex until nearly the beginning of the twentieth century. Freud's theories and later Kinsey's descriptive research caused a furor because they challenged cherished assumptions about the nature of sexuality. By the time Masters and Johnson reported their work in the 1960s, the public had accepted sex research reasonably well. Today sex research is a vast industry that sprawls across many scientific disciplines.

During the past generation there has been an increase in sexual permissiveness, including more favorable expressions of attitudes and more overt activities. Premarital sexual intercourse has been studied more carefully and intensively than other types of sexual activity. Most studies show that the incidence of premarital sex has increased substantially from 1965 to 1980 for both sexes. Although the absolute level is still higher for males, females appear to be approaching parity rapidly. The double standard of the last generation may be endangered, although even among sexually liberal college samples there is evidence of traditional sexual role playing with males initiating and females setting limits. On balance the society may not have gone through a sexual revolution, but a serious rebellion against ancient traditions has surely occurred.

Sexual interactions are based on two persons, each with a complex of attitudes called the self-concept. The sexual self-concept is part of the general self-concept, and sexual self-images may affect sexual interactions. All societies socialize their young to hold some sexual taboos: the most common are secretiveness about sex, inhibitions on talk and action, and avoidance of sexual interaction with persons in certain social categories. Sexual interaction may be viewed as consisting of three progressive stages, *proception, acception,* and *conception.* Acception includes coitus. The research of Masters and Johnson suggests that the phases of intercourse—excitement, plateau, orgasm, and resolution—are roughly equivalent for both males and females. Females vary more physiologically in the way they experience orgasm, and they have orgasms less consistently than males during intercourse.

Sexual interactions occur within a more general social context. Communication about sex is often unclear, and many inhibitions to full sexual disclosure exist. Communication problems are one source of sexual conflicts. Different preferences in frequency, duration, and type of activity are other basic causes of sexual conflicts. People become bored and seek novelty in sex as in other areas of life. Novelty with a new partner is a common occurrence, and a substantial amount of extramarital sex occurs even though it often causes problems and is disapproved by the majority of people. Sexual fantasies and exposure to erotic materials are common and may enrich sex. Current evidence suggests that exposure to such materials will not lead to a breakdown of sexual mores. One cautionary note is the recent increase in aggression in pornographic films. Some authorities believe that such exposure can lead to greater general aggression in everyday life and to increased sexual aggression, such as rape. Laboratory evidence suggests aggressive erotica can enhance aggression under some conditions and inhibit it under other conditions.

PART THREE

Relating

Liking and loving are personal and interpersonal facets of intimate relation-ships. A relationship takes at least two people, and life is continually filled with the process of "relating" to others. In daily life, liking, loving and relating tend to come in one interconnected bundle. But it is reasonable to separate the concepts analytically, as we have done, to provide different perspectives on human relations. When we focus on a relationship, we seem to be dealing with an entity with a life of its own, comparable in some respects to a real, concrete person. Relationships begin and develop; sometimes they stabilize, and some-times they regress. Relationships also die, sometimes peacefully, sometimes violently. The analogy can easily be pushed to ridiculous extremes, but it does suggest that in everyday life, two people often treat their relationship as if it were a precious object in its own right, almost as if it were a third person.

Chapter 6 is concerned with processes of relationship initiation and develop-ment. Several general theoretical approaches are discussed, as well as more specific theories of mate selection. Because of its recent importance the notions of general exchange theory are developed at some length. Commitment is suggested as an important variable because it is involved in all the theories of relation-ships.

Marriage is perhaps the most important close relationship that the majority of people experience. Chapter 7 treats several aspects of marriage, starting with the primary vehicle by which marriages begin and continue—communication. One type of communication, self-disclosure, is particularly important. Conflict is common in marriage relationships, and several facets of conflict are explored. The important issues of power and marital decision making are also discussed. The chapter concludes with a broad consideration of the general issue of marital satisfaction.

Chapter 8 deals with a number of issues in contemporary relationships. The important topics of separation and divorce, and one modern consequence—

blended families—receive full discussion. Some of our current social turbulence seems due to changing conceptions about appropriate sex roles. One relatively new phenomenon resulting in part from changing sex roles is the dual-career couple. These topics conclude the chapter.

6

Initiating and Developing Relationships

Wild nights! Wild nights!
Were I with thee,
Wild nights should be
Our luxury!

Futile the winds
To a heart in port,
Done with the compass,
Done with the chart.

Rowing in Eden!
Oh! The sea!
Might I but moor
To-night in thee!

[Dickinson, 1959]*

The intense longing that forms the fabric of this poem shows that Emily Dickinson (reputed to be a shy New England spinster) knew more than a little about close relationships! Of course, not all our relationships are characterized by the fervor of Dickinson's poem. In fact, many of our daily encounters are brief and fall within the context of strict role relationships—for example, plumber to homeowner, doctor to patient, professor to student. Thus relationships exist in hundreds of casual daily encounters, in the structure of friendships, and within a romantic framework. The study of noncasual or intimate relationships has blossomed in recent years in the social sciences, partially because of a return to field research and, even more importantly, partially because of the major social changes that have affected interpersonal relationships. The potential for nuclear holocaust, the birth control pill, the rampant rise of inflation, and the no-fault divorce, to name a few developments, have caused modern relationships to be stress-tested on a daily basis.

Several theories of relationship development envision relationship structure and progress over time. These general theories serve as background for specific theories of mate selection. The marriage relationship is of great importance in the modern world and has received much research attention. Exchange theory receives special attention because it is presently the most widely used approach to the study of relationships. The nature of commitment, an important dimension of relationship maintenance, concludes the chapter.

*From *Selected Poems and Letters of Emily Dickinson*, by Robert N. Linscott. © 1959 by Doubleday & Company, Inc.

Theories of Relationship Development

Levels of Pair Relatedness

Levinger and Snoek (1972) proposed a theory of relationship development in which interpersonal relationships are located along a single
primary dimension of *relatedness*. At one end of the continuum there is
zero contact and zero relatedness; simply, most human beings do not
know one another. The first real point on the continuum at which P
(person) and O (other) have some measure of relatedness is: (1) *unilateral awareness*, where P is aware of and has formed some attitudes
toward O, but where there has been no interaction between them. At
the next point of (2) *surface contact* there is limited interaction between P
and O, but these actions tend to be independent rather than interdependent. (3) *Mutuality* marks the point at which at least modest interdependence characterizes the relationship. From this point on the continuum
the relationship becomes increasingly interrelated, interdependent, and
strongly attached. This relationship progress can be seen in Figure 6-1.

At level 1 awareness is unilateral. For instance, Jay and Daisy are
undergraduate students in an introductory psychology class. At the
beginning of the semester neither student noticed the other, but during
the third week of class, Daisy sits directly in front of Jay and impairs his
view of the professor. Jay is irritated and begins to have negative
thoughts about Daisy—for example, "Girls shouldn't be so tall." He
also has some positive thoughts, such as "She really has beautiful long
blond hair." Awareness has taken place! The importance of this initial
stage in relationship development is underscored by Berscheid and
Graziano (1979), who mention the need for perceptual attention of P to
O in the beginning of the acquaintance. Whether we call it awareness or
attention, clearly P must notice O before a relationship can possibly
begin.

If we proceed to level 2, we find surface contact. At this point, our
students Daisy and Jay might begin to develop a relationship. For instance, Jay might tap Daisy on the shoulder and ask her to move her
head slightly so that he can see the board. If Daisy smiles and accedes to
the request, Jay might make a point of striking up a conversation with
her after class. (Of course, this second move by Jay depends on a variety
of factors involved in attraction, which were discussed in Chapter 2.)
Even if Daisy and Jay begin to sit together during class and chat for a
few minutes after class ends, they are likely to focus on class-related
topics of conversation and to keep within the social roles appropriate to
the situation—namely, female college student and male college student.
Although each individual enacts his or her social role in a unique way,
this position on our continuum still offers just what its name implies,

surface contact. In this situation communication is limited to task-related concerns, and the individuals' knowledge of each other is rather superficial.

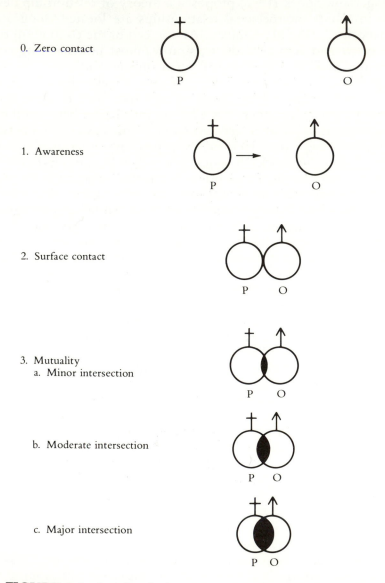

0. Zero contact

1. Awareness

2. Surface contact

3. Mutuality
   a. Minor intersection

   b. Moderate intersection

   c. Major intersection

FIGURE 6-1 Levels of relationship. *(Based on* Attraction in Relationship: A New Look at Interpersonal Attraction, *by G. Levinger and J. D. Snoek. Copyright © 1972 by General Learning Press. Copyright © 1978 by G. Levinger and J. D. Snoek. Reprinted by permission.)*

Perhaps, as we proceed to level 3, the area of mutuality, we should take another look at Daisy and Jay. When Jay missed the psychology midterm, Daisy became concerned and called Jay at the dorm to see if he was all right. It turned out that Jay was sick, but he appreciated Daisy's concern and impulsively invited her to see a movie the following weekend. The date went well, and Daisy and Jay found that they shared many common interests and did not run out of things to talk about during the evening. So they decided to date each other again. The students have begun interacting as persons with impact on each other, and they may well be on their way to real mutuality. By real mutuality or interdependence, we mean that "the partners have shared knowledge of one another, assume some responsibility for each other's outcomes, and at least begin to regulate their association upon a mutually agreed basis" (Levinger & Snoek, 1972, p. 8). Levinger and Snoek also mention shared attitudes and values, empathy, altruistic behaviors, and deepening affection as accompaniments to (and facilitators of) a deepening relationship. The need for mutuality in marriage prompts Lederer and Jackson (1968) to say that "shared behavior interlocks to form *mutual* respect and devotion. One spouse alone cannot achieve this relationship. Both must participate to the same degree" (p. 58). This mutuality is necessary to both the achievement and the maintenance of a level-3 relationship. Maintenance is also aided by commitment, social norms, and legal sanctions (such as marriage license or partnership contract). Relationships are characterized by stability of some factors and changes in other factors.

From levels 0 to 1 the probability of P meeting O is affected by proximity, climate (extreme weather patterns can be inhibiting to human interaction), socioeconomic variables (similarities versus differences in age, class, ethnic background), and personal characteristics (shy versus gregarious). From levels 1 to 2, these factors are still influential, as are the stimulus characteristics of O (for instance, attractiveness).

Since this is a building process, movement from levels 2 to 3 is influenced by all the above factors and additional ones such as P and O's liking for each other; satisfaction with their relationship; open communication based on trust; accommodation (mutuality); and attitude, value, and need compatibility. Levinger (1977) has extended his view of the levels of relatedness to include three aspects of Person/Other relationships that exist on level 3. "These include (1) *involvement,* which here refers to the size of the relationship intersection; (2) its *commitment,* which pertains to the strength of its boundaries, and (3) its *symmetry,* which refers to the relative equality of the two members' investments and rewards inside and outside the relationship" (p. 8). These conceptions are illustrated in Figure 6-2. Involvement, shown by the shaded area of the two circles, pertains to the content, the commonality of

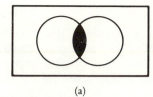 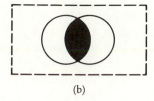

(a)   (b)

FIGURE 6-2   Relationships of (a) external restraint and (b) internal consent. *(Adapted from "The Embrace of Lives: Changing and Unchanging," by G. Levinger. In G. Levinger and H. L. Raush (Eds.),* Close Relationships: Perspectives on the Meaning of Intimacy. *Copyright © 1977 by the University of Massachusetts Press. Reprinted by permission.)*

time, interests, and behaviors of a pair. Commitment, shown by the thickness of the boundary around the shaded area of the two circles, refers to the degree of voluntary obligation which the pair's members feel toward each other. Although we use "commitment" in a voluntary sense, less–voluntary factors may also keep a relationship intact. This external constraint is shown by the thickness of the rectangular boundary around the two circles in (a). Symmetry refers to the equality or balance of the members' investment in the relationship, and although the circles are the same size and show perfect symmetry, such symmetry rarely occurs in real-life relationships. The relationship of mother to infant, while often very profound, may show great asymmetry.

Levinger has devoted considerable time to research on intimate relationships (see Levinger & Senn, 1967; Levinger, Senn, & Jorgensen, 1970), and in a recent study (Rands & Levinger, 1979) asked college students and senior citizens, two generations apart, to rate the likely occurrence of 30 different behaviors for each of 14 different pair relationships. The college students judged relationships between 22-year-old partners today, while the older raters described relationships as they were when the raters themselves were 22. The 14 relationships were considered across two major dimensions called "affective interdependence" and "behavioral interdependence." Although both groups of raters perceived affective and behavioral interdependence to increase as a relationship moved from casual to intimate, the younger raters estimated significantly higher rates of interaction for today's pairs, particularly for good friends and for close relationships. In addition the younger raters made significantly fewer distinctions between male and female actors in a relationship; behavior for them was less sex typed than for the older raters.

As we can see, relationships do not exist in isolation, but are influenced by the dyad's social and historical contexts, as well as by various interpersonal factors. Although admittedly rather general Levinger's conceptual levels of human relationships can be quite useful as we try to catalog the vast number of possible relationships.

Social Penetration Theory

This approach to the development of relationships is the most highly developed theory in this area (Altman & Taylor, 1973), and the conceptual structure is quite complex. Because the theory is highly cited and well developed, we present it in considerable detail as a major example of a theory of social behavior. Although social penetration theory has often been viewed as a theory of self-disclosure and will be discussed in that context in Chapter 7, it also encompasses all facets of verbal and nonverbal communication, use of the physical environment, and interpersonal perceptions. Altman and Taylor view relationships as having different levels of intimacy and as progressing through time in a systematic manner. The notion of progressive involvement is similar to that proposed by Levinger and Snoek. Perhaps the best definition of social penetration is given by Altman and Taylor themselves:

> Social penetration refers to (1) overt interpersonal behaviors which take place in social interaction, and (2) internal subjective processes which precede, accompany, and follow overt exchange. The term includes verbal, nonverbal, and environmentally oriented behaviors, all of which also have substantive affective/emotional components. Verbal behaviors include information exchanges; nonverbal behaviors involve use of the body, such as postures and positions, gestures, limb and head movements, facial expressions such as smiling, eye gaze, and so on. Environmentally oriented behaviors include spatial and personal distance between people and use of physical objects and areas. As these behaviors occur, they are preceded, accompanied, and followed by a series of subjective internal processes that occur within each individual. These involve the development of a subjective picture of what the other person is like, positive and negative feelings about the person, an estimation of how the other individual would behave in a variety of situations, and so forth [p. 5].

The occurrence of these various behaviors in a dyad and the interpretations of and reactions to the behaviors by the dyad members form the basis of social penetration. One basic premise of the theory is that the social penetration process is orderly and progresses over time through various stages. A second premise is based on exchange theory (which will be discussed later in the chapter) and states that since rewards and costs, or gains and losses, are present in every interpersonal relationship, the quantity and quality of such gains and losses are carefully weighed as the relationship advances. Altman and Taylor view relationship dissolution similarly to Levinger—namely, as a reverse of the relationship advancement process. This reverse process is characterized by movement from greater to lesser amounts and intimacy of interaction.

As part of their theory of social penetration, Altman and Taylor developed a simple model of personality structure, shown in Figure 6-3. Personality is seen as composed of an almost infinite number of ideas, attitudes, and feelings, represented by the smallest subdivisions in the figure. These individual items are organized into personality areas, shown by blocks A and B, which represent cohesive areas such as job or children. Within this structure the authors view personality in terms of the *breadth* dimension. *Breadth category* refers to the number of areas such as A or B which make up an individual's personality structure. *Breadth frequency* refers to the number of items within a single category—in a sense to the richness of the category. Taking breadth category and breadth frequency into account, one can develop *social penetration profiles*. For instance, suppose that as Daisy and Jay get to know one another, Jay reveals many facets of his personality to Daisy (high breadth category), but gives minimal information about each facet (low breadth frequency). Daisy, on the other hand, discusses only a few areas of her personality (low breadth category), but offers extensive information about each one (high breadth frequency). We thus can see essentially opposite profiles.

A second aspect of Altman and Taylor's personality conception is shown in Figure 6-3. The circles represent layers of the personality,

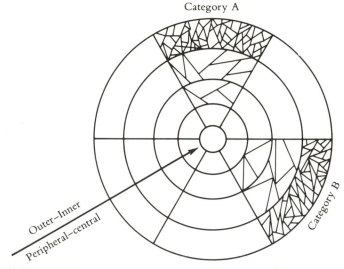

FIGURE 6-3   Model of personality structure. Categories A and B refer to topical or substantive areas of personality. The subparts refer to specific items within a topical area. The concentric circles represent layers of the personality. *(Adapted from* Social Penetration: The Development of Interpersonal Relationships, *by I. Altman and D. A. Taylor. Copyright © 1973 by Holt, Rinehart, and Winston. Copyright © 1981 by I. Altman. [New York: Irvington Publishers, Inc.] Reprinted by permission.)*

similar to the thin layers of an onion, and represent the *depth* dimension of personality, a dimension going from outside the circles to inside the core. Taylor and Altman, along with other personality theorists (for example, Rokeach, 1960), propose several key properties of the depth dimension:

1. Peripheral personality layers include an individual's biographical data, including sex, age, and personal history. Middle layers contain opinions and attitudes, and central layers contain emotions and notions about the self (core elements).
2. Those items contained in the central area of the personality influence great numbers of items in the middle and outside layers. Thus knowledge about an individual's central characteristics, such as interpersonal trust, might allow us to better determine his or her attitudes toward various religious and ethnic groups.
3. As we move toward the personality core, items become less common and visible and more unique and invisible. Thus we can readily determine an individual's preference in cars (a peripheral characteristic) by noting the type of car he or she drives, but we would have considerably more difficulty determining the individual's amount of self-esteem.
4. The greater the depth of a personality characteristic, the more likely it is to reflect a vulnerable aspect of the individual, such as a particular fear.
5. More socially undesirable items are thought to be located in central layers of the personality.
6. Finally, central personality aspects involve more trans-situational positive *and* negative personality characteristics (such as "I am scared of people" versus "I get nervous at cocktail parties") (Altman & Taylor, 1973).

The authors use ideas about both personality structure and actual behavior to explain *social penetration*. They view this process in much the same way as they view personality—that is, on the dimensions of breadth and depth. Breadth refers to the various personality areas that one person may show to another, whereas depth refers to the significance of the items within the areas. Altman and Taylor see communication (and other forms of interaction) occurring with greater variety of areas or breadth at the beginning of a relationship, gradually proceeding deeper as the relationship grows closer. In terms of Figure 6-3 this can be viewed as a pie or wedge shape, wide at the beginning, but narrowing and deepening as we proceed toward the center. Of course, since there are many varied aspects of personality, we will see many wedges as a relationship progresses.

Altman and Taylor propose many reward/cost factors that may accelerate the social penetration process. In assessing rewards and costs, dyad members evaluate the past in terms of comparable relationships and accrued experience, evaluate the present in terms of positives and negatives, and forecast the future based on progress of the existing relationship and likely outcomes.

A number of studies have examined the various features of social penetration theory in a variety of settings and within varying types and lengths of relationships (see, for example, Altman & Haythorn, 1967; Morton, 1978; Taylor, Altman, & Sorrentino, 1969).

In rounding out their original theory, Altman and Taylor attempted to combine their levels of personality with several rather abstract dimensions of the penetration process and derived four stages of relationship development.

Stage 1, *Orientation,* has our friends Daisy and Jay making polite conversation before and after psychology class. They utter stereotyped modes of response, and their verbal interaction is limited.

Stage 2, *Exploratory Affective Exchange,* occurs between casual friends and involves a somewhat greater revealing of self and more behavior unique to the persons involved. Daisy and Jay might be in this stage after their first or second date.

Stage 3, *Affective Exchange,* characterizes close friendships or romantic relationships when persons are open in their exchanges, offer positive and negative feelings and engage in affectionate and uniquely personal behaviors. If they pursue a relationship over an extended period of time, Daisy and Jay might enter this stage.

Stage 4, *Stable Exchange,* is said by the authors to be rarely achieved. "Stable exchange continues to reflect openness, richness, spontaneity, and so on in public areas. Very rarely are there mistakes or misunderstandings in the meaning of communications. . . . Dyad members know one another well and can readily interpret and predict the feelings and probable behavior of the other" (p. 140). Daisy and Jay have a long way to go!

Altman and Taylor's social penetration theory has undergone some recent revision. Although the original theory viewed relationships as unidirectional, always moving toward greater openness, Altman, Vinsel, and Brown (1981) suggest the possibility of alternating between superficial and intimate topics of communication and interaction throughout the life of a relationship. After examining the research and theory on territoriality, personal space, and crowding, Altman turned to *privacy* as a concept that could be usefully juxtaposed against social penetration and proposes a dialectical analysis of the two (1975). As we shall see throughout our discussion of relationships, relationships in the real world are less unidirectional than multifaceted. Although it is usually necessary to quantify relationships along particular dimensions in order to begin to examine them in detail (dimensions of mutuality, conflict, self-disclosure, and so on), such quantification sacrifices much of the relationship's complexity and richness.

In attempting to integrate the theoretical bases of social penetration and privacy regulation, Altman and his colleagues offer the concept of *interpersonal openness,* a significant factor in penetration theory, and *interpersonal closedness,* a factor regarded positively in privacy regulation research. In order to account for the behavioral fact that social relationships contain both openness and closedness, both accessibility and inaccessibility, the authors propose also the idea of *stability/change.* Thus, if we conceive them as relationship dimensions, we have *openness/closedness* and *stability/change.*

The authors offer an extensive description of the *dialectic* as it has been viewed throughout history, and, for their purposes, characterize dialectics by (1) the idea of opposition or polarity, (2) the unity of opposites, and (3) the dynamic, ever-changing relationships between opposites.

The idea of opposites is ubiquitous, appearing in Judeo/Christian religious values as good and evil, among the ancient Chinese philosophers as the *yin* (passive, dependent, nurturing, yielding) force and the *yang* (dominant, active, creative, aggressive) force, and emerging from Jungian personality theory as the *anima* (female force) and *animus* (male force) in every human personality.

The notion of the unity of opposites involves both synthesis and complementary balance of opposites and "assumes that opposites function in a complementary way as part of a unified system, that opposition does not involve complete exclusion of one or the other pole, and that there is a range of relationships between opposites, with no particular one, including equality or balance, being 'better' than any other one" (p. 24).

In presenting opposites as constantly changing, Altman et al. consider the biological/psychological perspective of the human organism always seeking stability or equilibrium versus an organism seeking novelty and change, perhaps eventually achieving a temporary equilibrium at a new level of experience.

After using dialectic processes to present the concepts of openness/closedness and stability/change, the authors offer several hypotheses based on an integration of theories of social penetration and privacy regulation:

1. Human social relationships are characterized by (1) forces toward contact or openness *and* forces toward separateness or closedness between participants and (2) forces toward stability or consistency *and* forces toward variety or change in relationships.
2. Social relationships do not strive toward an ultimate or ideal balance of openness and closedness or of stability and change.
3. Neither openness or closedness nor stability or change totally dominates a relationship.

Based on these interesting, though general, assumptions the authors propose a number of relevant research questions and even offer schematic representations of possible statistical outcomes when openness/closedness and stability/change are examined over time in interpersonal relationships. Although this theoretical integration will require a substantial amount of refinement and empirical investigation, it nevertheless offers a much-needed conceptual richness in the area of relationship development.

Dimensions of Relationships

A much-cited study by Wish, Deutsch, and Kaplan (1976) was conducted to document the basic dimensions that underlie people's perceptions of both *typical* and *their own* interpersonal relationships. This study offers a way of classifying different types of relationships, rather than a coherent theory of relationship development.

Wish and his colleagues tested nearly a hundred subjects recruited from the New York–Philadelphia area by having the subjects evaluate a total of 45 pair relationships: 25 typical relations and 20 of the subjects' own relations, including both past and present relationships, on 14 bipolar scales. Subjects were encouraged to think of each relationship in comprehensive terms, evaluating thoughts and feelings, behaviors, and communication. Multidimensional scaling techniques were used in analysis of the subjects' perceptions of the 45 relationships under consideration, and these analyses resulted in the development of four general dimensions of dyadic relationships. The four dimensions are (1) cooperative and friendly versus competitive and hostile, (2) equal versus unequal, (3) intense versus superficial, and (4) socioemotional and informal versus task-oriented and formal. (Subsequent research broke this fourth dimension into two dimensions, socioemotional versus task-oriented and formal versus informal.) The dimensions and some of the relationships are shown in Figure 6-4. It is interesting to note where different relationships are located on the various dimensions. In Figure 6-4a we see that a psychotherapist and patient relationship is perceived to be somewhat cooperative and friendly, but very unequal in terms of power and role, whereas a divorced couple is viewed as considerably more equal, but rather competitive and hostile. In Figure 6-4b, however, the psychotheraptist/patient and the divorced couple relationships differ somewhat in perceived intensity on the intense versus superficial dimension, but they are relatively alike on the socioemotional and informal versus task-oriented and formal dimensions.

General findings of the study reveal more variability of subjects' ratings of typical relations than their ratings of their own relations, reflecting at least partially the subjects' idealization of their personal relations. Subjects also tended to view childhood and adult relationships differently, allocating greater equality and cooperation but less intensity to their present adult relationships. In addition there was much higher subject agreement in ratings of relations evaluated as friendly rather than hostile; thus there was great individual variability in evaluating (and dealing with) hostility. Although the authors found some within-sample rating differences (between New York subjects and Philadelphia subjects), the finding of interest to us here is that the intensity dimension was of considerable importance to subjects' own relations but not to typical relations. This finding fits well with Altman and Taylor's theory of a relationship's depth increasing as social penetration takes place.

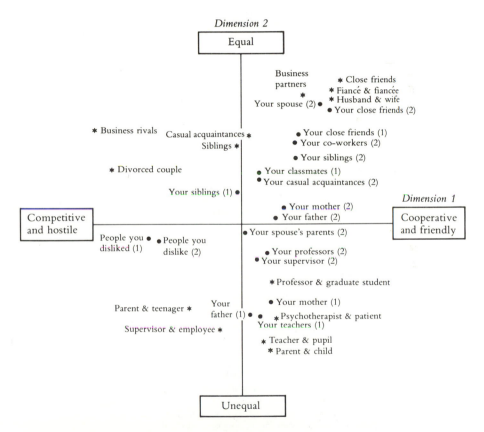

* Denotes a typical dyadic relation between the designated individuals.
● Denotes a relation between the subject and the designated individual.
The subject's childhood relations are indicated by a (1), while
the subject's current relations are indicated by a (2).

FIGURE 6-4a Dimensions (1) cooperative and friendly versus competitive and hostile and (2) equal versus unequal. *(Adapted from "Perceived Dimensions of Interpersonal Relations," by M. Wish, M. Deutsch, and S. J. Kaplan. In* Journal of Personality and Social Psychology, *1976, 33, 409–420. Copyright 1976 by the American Psychological Association. Reprinted by permission.)*

Wish and his colleagues have findings that are congruent with previous research on relationship dimensions (for example, Marwell & Hage, 1970), but that offer new and potentially useful dimensions for the study of interpersonal relationships.

At this point we will briefly mention social exchange theory, a theory based on principles proposed by Homans (1961) and Thibaut and Kelley (1959) and more recently modified by many social psychologists (Burgess & Huston, 1979). Exchange theory is currently widely used in

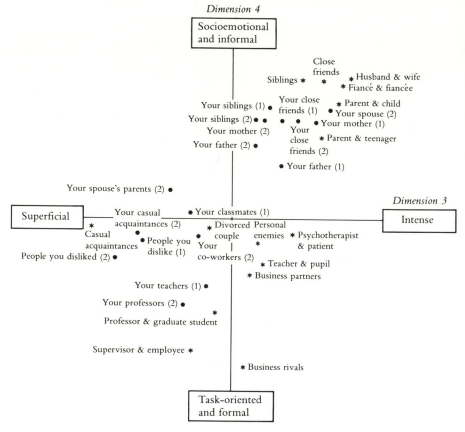

*Denotes a typical dyadic relation between the designated individuals.
•Denotes a relation between the subject and the designated individual.
  The subject's childhood relations are indicated by a (1), while
  the subject's current relations are indicated by a (2).

FIGURE 6-4b Dimensions (3) intense versus superficial and (4) socioemotional and informal versus task-oriented and formal. (*Adapted from "Perceived Dimensions of Interpersonal Relations," by M. Wish, M. Deutsch, and S. J. Kaplan. In* Journal of Personality and Social Psychology, *1976, 33, 409–420. Copyright 1976 by the American Psychological Association. Reprinted by permission.*)

analyses of relationship development and should logically be included in this section but because of its popularity, we will devote a later section of the chapter to exchange theory alone.

Theories of Mate Selection

Theories of relationship development describe general principles on which all types of relationships rest. There are also more specialized theories of relationship choice and progress in the institutionalized relationship called marriage. Poets, musicians, and philosophers have written for centuries about the process of marital choice, the means by which women and men decide to wed each other. Commonsense theories might include sheer proximity (the girl-next-door marrying the boy-next-door), basic economics (let's pool our resources; two can live as cheaply as one), or shotgun theory (responsible boy marries pregnant girl).

In many cultures, the notion of voluntary mate selection is irrelevant, because marriages are arranged by the bride and groom's respective parents. Politics (familial and societal) and economics form the bases of many arranged marriages, yet many such marriages may produce love and commitment once the marriage partners have truly established a relationship (Chapter 4). Although voluntary mate selection is clearly the present norm in most societies, in terms of historical time it is a relatively new norm (Gadlin, 1977). Nevertheless, theories of mate selection form very compelling grist for the researcher's mill, and whenever the topic of mate selection is introduced, the first name mentioned is usually that of Robert Winch.

Complementary Needs

Winch's theory of complementary needs in mate selection (Winch, 1952; Winch, Ktsanes, & Ktsanes, 1954) is derived from motivation theories, primarily Murray's (1938) need schema, which focus on the organism's drive to obtain gratification of physical and psychic needs. The basic hypothesis of Winch's theory is that "in mate-selection each individual seeks within his or her field of eligibles for that person who gives the greatest promise of providing him or her with maximum need-gratification" (1954, p. 242). A second hypothesis is that P (person) will seek O (other) who has a need structure that is *complementary* rather than *similar* to P's own need structure. For example, suppose that Jay is a talkative, somewhat aggressive person who likes to be the center of attention, and Daisy is nurturant, admiring, and a good listener. Voila! The needs are complementary.

Winch defines *need* as simply a goal-directed drive to transform an unsatisfactory situation in a certain direction, so that the situation can become satisfactory. For his study Winch adapted a list of needs from

Murray's original classification; the needs considered were abasement, achievement, approach, autonomy, deference, dominance, hostility, nurturance, recognition, status aspiration, status striving, and succorance. Also examined were general personality traits of anxiety, emotionality, and vicariousness. The needs and traits were evaluated in terms of overt/covert expression and were viewed both in the marriage relationship and in all other situations. Winch defined complementariness as occurring when the needs of P and O that are gratified in their relationship (1) are different in *kind* from one another, or (2) different in *intensity* from one another (see Chapter 2).

Winch, in his first hypothesis regarding mate selection, used the term *field of eligibles,* meaning the group of potentially marriageable persons within P's frame of reference. A field of eligibles or potential mates is likely to be confined to a certain geographic area (close to P) and might likely include individuals who are similar to P with respect to social characteristics, such as race, religion, educational level, and social class. Although Winch proposed complementarity of needs in couples as the basis for mate selection, he recognized that similarity of partners on social characteristics may define the field of eligibles.

Although his study is a much-cited one, Winch's methodology was far from sophisticated by today's standards. Winch's sample consisted of 25 married undergraduate students at Northwestern University and their spouses. Couples were fairly homogeneous with respect to social variables, had been married less than two years, and had no children. They were evaluated on three bases: (1) a structured need interview, (2) a case-history interview, and (3) an abbreviated psychological projective test. The data drawn from the need interview alone formed most of the basis for Winch's conclusions. After examining 388 interspousal need correlations, Winch and his colleagues found that the number of interspousal correlations which were significant in the hypothesized direction exceeded the number of such correlations expected by chance, and thus they claimed moderate support for their theory. They found that their subjects tended to select mates whose needs were complementary rather than similar to their own.

Needs and Values

Winch's study, though far from definitive, is still given modest attention and provided one of the bases for Kerckhoff and Davis's (1962) study of need complementarity and value consensus in mate selection. The authors administered measures of need complementarity and value consensus to 103 college-age dating couples and then retested 94 of the couples with a shortened questionnaire seven months after initial testing. The independent variables in the study were (1) consensus between dating partners on family values and (2) degree of need complementarity, and the dependent variable of interest was progress of the relationship toward permanence. The two hypotheses of the study were:

1. Degree of value consensus is positively related to progress toward a permanent union.
2. Degree of need complementarity is positively related to progress toward a permanent union.

In examining the data the authors found that the first hypothesis was supported, while the second was not. However, when the length of relationship was considered (long-term relationships being defined as longer than 18 months and short-term as shorter than 18 months), the patterns changed. The relationship between value consensus and relationship progress was still significant for the short-term couples (as for the whole sample), but not for the long-term couples. The reverse was true for need complementarity, however, with complementarity related to progress toward permanence for the long-term couples (on two out of three measures), but not for short-term couples. To reconcile the seemingly contradictory directions in their data, Kerckhoff and Davis proposed a *sequential filtering theory,* whereby similarity of social status variables is important in the early stages of mate selection, consensus on personal and family values emerges in importance later on, and need complementarity is most significant when the relationship has progressed for a considerable length of time. In line with this theory Winch's subjects were all married couples who had presumably been in their respective relationships for a substantial time period and thus would be concerned with need complementarity.

The Kerckhoff-Davis study stood as a respectable theoretical and methodological model for the investigation of ongoing dyadic relationships until Levinger, Senn, and Jorgensen's (1970) attempted replication of the earlier study. A total of 330 steadily attached couples were recruited from two state universities and were assessed using the measures which had been employed by Kerckhoff and Davis and with several additional measures. The couples were tested twice during the school year and were divided into long-term and short-term couples.

Although about 60 percent of the couples indicated relationship progress during the months between the first and second testing sessions, neither value consensus nor need compatibility was shown to be related to such progress. Although Levinger and his colleagues performed a variety of statistical tests on the data, none of the additional tests confirmed the Kerckhoff-Davis findings. In fact, analyses revealed that the best predictors of a couple's relationship progress at second testing was their own estimate of their progress at the first testing. The individual partners themselves were thus more effective at predicting their relationship progress than were any of the more elaborate written measures.

Levinger and his colleagues proposed that the divergent findings might well have resulted from instability of the measuring device as well as changes in the courtship process during the years intervening between the earlier and later studies. They also proposed that a pair relationship does pass through a series of stages, one series relating to the manner in which the partners discover one another and the other series relating to the construction of a joint enterprise or pair communality. If this is indeed the case, the two different series or themes in relationships would have to be assessed with very different measures according to Levinger.

Stimulus–Value–Role Theory

Murstein's (1976) stimulus–value–role (SVR) theory is in some respects similar to Kerckhoff and Davis's filter theory; indeed, Murstein refers to SVR as "an exchange-process-filter theory." Murstein describes SVR theory thus:

> The theory is an exchange one, positing that, in a relatively free choice situation, attraction and interaction depend on the exchange value of the assets and liabilities each of the parties brings to the situation. The kinds of variables that influence the course of development of the relationship can be classified under three categories: stimulus, value comparison, and role. The variables are operative during the entire course of courtship, but they are maximally influential at different stages of courtship, and each of the three stages reflects by its name the kind of variables most influential during that period (for example, stimulus variables are most influential in the stimulus stage) [p. 107].

In setting the scene for his discussion of courtship stages Murstein describes the context of the relationship as an *open* or *closed* field (similar to Winch's field of eligibles). An open-field encounter occurs when a man and woman do not know each other and are placed in a situation where they are free to choose whether or not they wish to interact. An example of an open-field situation would be the large introductory psychology class in which our students Daisy and Jay first met. A closed situation would be a small study group composed of Daisy and Jay and a few other students. The latter environment almost requires that the members interact and get to know one another at least to a limited degree.

The type of field or setting can make a substantial difference in which stimulus variables are important during the beginning of a relationship. Surface factors such as physical attractiveness, voice and speech patterns, coordination, and mode of dress are all more influential when the encounter is in an open field and when all P knows about O is what he or she can see or hear at a distance. A closed field allows individuals to notice surface characteristics but also to learn about another person's attitudes and feelings, to share ideas, and to communicate on a variety of levels.

Remembering Murstein's definition of SVR theory, if a couple has fairly equal stimulus variables (similar balances of assets and liabilities), they may progress to the value comparison stage of courtship. Murstein incorporates interests, attitudes, beliefs, and sometimes needs under

BOX 6-1   This theory of mate compatibility is based on the complementarity of sibling roles (order of birth). The information is based on the proposition that we will form better marriage relationships if we have the same rank and sex relationship to our spouse that we had to our siblings, and that these relationships will function best if they are complementary. Thus the most complementary relationship is that of an *older brother of younger sisters* who marries a *younger sister of older brothers*. The former is used to being responsible and protective while the latter is supportive and admiring. Similarly, an *older sister of younger brothers* would provide the necessary concern and nurturance for a somewhat dependent *younger brother of older sisters*. The least complementary relationship would include *two only children*, since neither partner would be familiar in interacting with a same or opposite sex sibling. Both partners would need to learn new roles. (*Adapted from* Family Constellations (3rd ed.), *by W. Toman, 1976.*)

BIRTH ORDER AND MATE SELECTION: COMPLEMENTARITY OF SIBLING ROLES—MOST TO LEAST

Type of complementarity	*Relationship example*
Partners are complementary in both rank and sex.	An older brother with younger sisters marries a younger sister with older brothers.
Partners are complementary in rank but have a conflict in sex.	An older brother of younger sisters marries a younger sister of older *sisters* (no sex complementarity).
Partners are complementary in sex but have a conflict in rank.	An older brother of a younger sister marries an older sister of a younger brother (no rank complementarity).
Partners have complete conflicts in rank and sex.	The youngest of three brothers marries the youngest of three sisters.
One partner is an only child, while the other partner has at least one opposite-sex sibling.	An older sister of a younger brother marries an only child.
Both partners are only children.	No opportunities for complementarity.

values and views this stage as one of verbal information gathering. Self-disclosure is particularly important during this stage of relationship development, because it is the primary means by which P and O can actually compare their values. The stimulus stage can perhaps be thought of as an *awareness* period, the value comparison stage as an *affective* period, and the role stage as a *behavioral* period. The role stage is a crucial one, for it is here that P and O can compare the ways they actually behave toward each other with the ways they would like to behave toward each other. If for a moment we can place Daisy and Jay in Murstein's role stage, we may observe that Jay desires a wife who will be quiet and demure, while Daisy, though quiet in personal settings, is a competitive, aggressive tiger in the classroom. Jay may also find that although he likes to think of himself as both confident and fair minded, he is unreasonably resentful end even jealous of Daisy's academic attainments. So we can see that actual behavior—the bottom line of the relationship—is most influential in the role stage. However, although the stages are progressive, there is a great deal of overlap between them.

Murstein has conducted considerable research on SVR theory, gathering data periodically from 1964 to 1972 on over 200 courting couples. Various paper-and-pencil measures were used, some of which were focused on the individual and some of which were focused on the relationship. Although Murstein has discussed his findings at considerable length (Murstein, 1971, 1974a, 1976), the extensiveness of his research hypotheses and the complexity and redundancy of his data preclude a detailed discussion here. His findings did indicate that in addition to the social characteristics, which have been shown in many studies to be similar for courtship partners, variables such as physical attractiveness, value similarity, role-compatibility, self-acceptance, sex-drive, and several other factors also influence mate selection. His data also showed that males have a more powerful role than do females in affecting courtship progress.

Basically, Murstein has developed a fairly comprehensive theory of mate selection, adapting various aspects of existing theories and giving due attention to exchange principles. His attempt to gather relationship data from real-world couples is certainly a laudable effort, although his research findings have been subject to mixed reviews (see, for example, Rubin & Levinger, 1974), which we will consider later. First, however, we will briefly discuss another theory, Lewis's PDF theory.

Premarital dyadic formation

Lewis (1972, 1973) developed a theory of *premarital dyadic formation* (PDF) rather than a theory of actual mate selection, though the two are closely linked. He proposed six pair processes that couples progressively experience throughout the duration of dating and courtship.

These processes and subprocesses are shown in Figure 6-5. We include this list not because is is particularly unusual, but because it offers a fairly complete picture of a healthy, satisfying intimate dyadic relationship. Although he explicitly does not say that this is a stage theory, with a couple needing to pass through stage one before they can go on to stage two, Lewis does believe that a couple who has successfully fulfilled the first process (A—similarity perception) should be more successful at fulfilling B, the next process.

To test his theory, Lewis analyzed questionnaire data gathered from 91 couples at the beginning and end of a two-year period. Sixty-one couples had continued their relationships; 30 relationships had been dissolved. Lewis's basic prediction was that couples who had moved well through process A at the time of initial testing would also show good movement through process B at the second testing. Conversely, couples who had not completed A-type tasks at initial testing would also do poorly at B-type tasks at later testing. Basically, couples doing well would move ahead through the processes, and couples doing poorly would not. On a series of tests for differences in couples' task accomplishments between initial testing and later testing, the pronounced differences between continuing couples and dissolved couples

A.   The achievement by pairs of perceiving similarities in each other's
   1.   sociocultural background
   2.   values
   3.   interests
   4.   personality

B.   The achievement of pair rapport, as evidenced in a pair's
   1.   ease of communication
   2.   positive evaluations of the other
   3.   satisfaction with pair relationships
   4.   validation of self by the other

C.   The achievement of openness between partners through a mutual self-disclosure

D.   The achievement of role-taking accuracy

E.   The achievement of interpersonal role-fit, as evidenced by a pair's
   1.   observed similarity of personalities
   2.   role complementarity
   3.   need complementarity

F.   The achievement of dyadic crystallization, as evidenced by a pair's
   1.   progressive involvement
   2.   functioning as a dyad
   3.   boundary establishment
   4.   commitment to each other
   5.   identity as a couple

FIGURE 6-5 Processes of dyadic formation. *(From "A Developmental Framework for the Analysis of Premarital Dyadic Formation," by R. A. Lewis. In* Family Process, *1972,* 11, *17–48. Copyright 1972 by* Family Process. *Reprinted by permission.)*

caused Lewis to claim empirical support for his PDF theory. Although the theory is appealing in many ways, other researchers have leveled various criticisms at Lewis's findings (for example, Murstein, 1976; Rubin & Levinger, 1974).

Indeed, Rubin and Levinger (1974) evaluated the theories of both Murstein and Lewis in one succinct critique, accusing the theorists not of poor theorizing, but of providing poor support for their respective theories: "Our argument with Lewis, as with Murstein, then, is not that his framework is false, but rather that it has been presented in a false light" (p. 230). The critics focused on Murstein's theory as a sequential one and questioned his assignment of all his subject couples to the role stage of development and his subsequent analyses of data in terms of the role stage. Murstein answered his critics (1974a) by emphasizing the *exchange* aspects of SVR theory and by defending his assignment of couples to the role stage. Lewis was criticized by Rubin and Levinger primarily because he did not provide sufficient data to support the notion that his six processes occur in any kind of sequential order. Lewis (1975) answered by stating that the processes are not in absolute sequential order, but that although one need not complete process A to go on to process B, one could more satisfactorily complete process B if one has gone through process A.

If the academic interchange we have just described sounds a bit like a tennis game, with the ball consistently (or monotonously) hit back and forth between theorist and critic, our readers have a fairly accurate picture of much of the process of theory development. It is wise to remember that, even though many of the theories we present seem somewhat simplistic, they have evolved from a rather strenuous conceptual process. In other words, it may look easy, but it's not!

Although we have discussed the major theories of mate selection, research studies continue to survey more specific aspects of dyad formation and mate selection (such as Hieger & Troll, 1973, on romantic love in mate selection; Melton & Thomas, 1976, on instrumental versus expressive values in mate selection). The topic of who marries whom will undoubtedly intrigue theorists and researchers for a long time.

Exchange Theory, or Life Is a Tradeoff

Basic Concepts

An *exchange* is defined as the "act of giving or taking one thing in return for another as an equivalent, i.e. a trade or barter" (Webster, 1953). Although this definition appears rather straightforward, Webster goes on for 30 more lines trying to cover some of the myriad aspects of exchange. So also have many psychologists and sociologists taken the simple concept of barter or exchange and woven elaborate theories around it (for example, Blau, 1964; Homans, 1961; Thibaut & Kelley,

1959). Before we consider these theories, however, let us look at exchange in everyday terms—enter Daisy and Jay.

Daisy: Jay, I'm really nervous about the psychology midterm next week. I think I understand most of the material, but attribution theory still confuses me. Could you study with me on Saturday afternoon?

Jay: Daisy, you're being ridiculous! You know you have the highest grades in the class on all the quizzes. Why study for the midterm at all? Besides, I'm playing basketball on Saturday afternoon.

Daisy: Be serious! I'd panic completely if I didn't study. Please help me. Why don't you come over for dinner on Saturday night and then we'll study after that?

Jay: Okay. That's fine with me!

This conversation offers an example of exchange on several levels. Although there is an exchange of feelings, attitudes, and information, our particular focus is the exchange of behaviors. Daisy wants to get help from Jay, but he is unwilling to give up his planned activity, and so she suggests an alternative time for the help and offers to cook dinner, perhaps as a way of compensating him. Jay agrees. This negotiation process really involves a fairly sophisticated assessment of potential help (reward), potential inconvenience (cost), and potential compensation (reward).

Do you know a couple whom you think are really mismatched? Maybe he is smart and good-looking and his girlfriend is a real loser? Or she is outgoing and attractive and her boyfriend has an IQ of minus ten! Exchange theory would assume that in both cases the apparently unappealing partner is likely to have some hidden virtues (maybe deeply hidden) that make the relationship a fairly equal one. Social stereotypes such as the beautiful young girl who marries an aged tycoon or the aspiring junior executive who makes a play for the boss's unmarried daughter are rather blatant examples of exchange in human relationships: the exchange of beauty for money or of power for intimacy.

Although exchange theory as a theory of the marketplace has been in use for centuries, formal exchange theory has achieved popularity only in the last twenty years (see Blau, 1964; Homans, 1961; Thibaut & Kelley, 1959). The basic concepts of exchange theory are succinctly outlined by Secord and Backman (1964) and include reward, cost, outcome, and comparison level.

A *reward* is a reinforcement, or something which contributes to an individual's gratification. A *cost* is not only a negative or punishing occurrence, but also consists of the value of rewards that are foregone by choosing one item rather than another. The term *outcome* refers to the rewards minus the costs incurred in a particular situation or interaction. If rewards are larger than costs, we have assets; if costs exceed rewards, we have liabilities. The final concept is *comparison level,* which is a level of expectation for an interaction based on an individual's perceptions of both optimal and probable interaction outcomes.

Exchange theory can explain why similarity between persons leads to mutual attraction, because similarity of social characteristics and values provides high rewards and low costs to the dyad members. Similarity of abilities and personality traits may be rewarding also, though complementary traits may be rewarding in some instances. High opportunity for interaction may lead to liking, because costs remain low. In any case exchange theory integrates and clarifies much of the data on interpersonal attraction (Secord & Backman, 1964; see also Chapter 2).

Certain other aspects of exchange theory are particularly applicable to dyadic relationships. The principle of *bargaining* involves the negotiation of rewards and costs, with both individuals concerned trying to motivate each other to produce the desired behavior. We might describe Daisy and Jay's latest encounter as a bargaining process, with Daisy attempting to provide enough rewards for Jay to overcome his costs and thus motivate him to reward her in turn (by helping her study). Intimate relationships may progress because of an ever-increasing level of bargaining, with one person giving progressively greater rewards to the other, and the other person responding in kind.

Variations in a relationship over time may be caused by changes in rewards and costs. Reward/cost changes may occur because of (1) past exchanges, which influence current reward/cost values, (2) changes in personal characteristics of the dyad members, (3) introduction of new rewards and costs, (4) developmental factors within the relationship, or (5) associations with other behaviors which have different reward/cost values. As we can see, reward/cost factors are very amenable to change, and Thibaut and Kelley (1959) emphasized comparison level as a standard for assessing changes in rewards and costs. They suggest that the comparison level will rise as the outcomes (rewards minus costs) of the partners rise and will fall if the outcomes decline. Dyad members may well adjust successfully to such increases and decreases, unless a member believes that his or her options *outside* the relationship are better than the options *inside*. Thibaut and Kelley (1959) refer to outside options as the *comparison level for alternatives*. To better understand concepts concerning rising and falling comparison levels and comparison level for alternatives, we will view them in everyday terms:

1. Comparison level   The profit I'm entitled to or my
                                            share

2. As profits go up, so do com-   The more I get, the more I want
   parison levels (expectations)

3. As profits go down, so do   If I don't expect anything, I can't
   comparison levels   be disappointed

4. The relationship may continue,   Is the grass greener on the other
   unless realistic alternatives   side?
   have better comparison levels

Up to this point we have been focusing most carefully on the process of exchange, but one of Homans's (1961) major concepts, *distributive justice,* refers to relative amounts of rewards and costs, and specifically to the balance of rewarding outcomes for P and O. Schematically, distributive justice prevails when:

$$\frac{\text{P's rewards less P's costs}}{\text{P's investments}} = \frac{\text{O's rewards less O's costs}}{\text{O's investments}}$$

We see that what is important here is not the actual amounts of P's and O's profitable outcomes, but rather the relative amount. For example, two female college friends may have greatly different social lives. Pat may be much sought after and have her choice of dates every weekend. Janie, on the other hand, rarely gets invited out and then usually by a rather unappealing fellow. But Janie does not envy Pat and does not herself feel rejected by men. She has observed that Pat spends a lot of time trying to look attractive: she exercises, diets, and devotes long hours to applying makeup and styling her hair. Janie, on the other hand, puts virtually no effort into her rather ordinary physical appearance; she spends the time in other ways. Thus Janie and Pat each feel that in terms of dates they get what they deserve. Essentially that is distributive justice. Of course individuals do not always feel fairly treated by life and may handle their sense of inequity in various ways, such as attempting to alter inputs or outcomes in the situation, mentally distorting actual inputs and outcomes, trying to influence the behavior (inputs and outcomes) of the other person in the situation, or leaving the situation altogether. If Janie felt that her situation was unfair in comparison to Pat's, she might increase the time spent on improving her own physical appearance or simply try to get asked out on more dates, decide that her social life is exactly the way she wants it, try to get Pat to become more careless about her appearance or harrass her about dating too much and ignoring her studies, or even move out of the dorm where Pat is living. We all like to think that life is reasonably fair, and when it is not fair, we will work hard to make it so (or at least make it seem so).

Current Research in Exchange Theory

Exchange theory provides the basis for considerable research on various aspects of intimate relationships. If we consider some of the theories of relationship development and mate selection, we can see that they fit within the exchange framework.

Levinger and Snoek's levels of pair relatedness provide for progress from awareness to interaction to mutuality, and this progress occurs because of reward/cost outcomes in the dyad. As positive interaction outcomes increase, a pair moves from superficial interaction to intimate interaction and mutuality; however, if outcomes are poor, the relationship regresses or terminates.

Much the same behavior occurs in Altman and Taylor's social penetration process. As a couple exchanges information on a variety of topics at the beginning of a relationship (breadth), the members also are evaluating rewards and costs in the interaction. If the reward outcomes are sufficient, the pair may progress to more significant levels of interaction (depth), but if costs are too high, the process is reversed.

Winch's theory of complementarity in mate selection is a classic example of exchange, because partners are hypothesized to bring opposite needs to the relationship and since each partner is supposed to reward the other by meeting his or her needs.

Kerckhoff and Davis have proposed that certain items are more important in a relationship at certain times, and that these items occur in sequence. In fact, dyad partners evaluate rewards and costs within one stage of the relationship before they move on to the next stage. Murstein explicitly refers to his stimulus–value–role (SVR) theory as a process/exchange theory, since partners must experience a positive exchange of stimulus variables in order to move to the value stage, where again values must be positive and rewarding overall for the persons to test out their role relationships in the next stage. Even Lewis's processes of dyadic formation would appear to require extensive exchanges before they could be successfully completed by an individual couple.

One recent sophisticated attempt to enlarge the scope of exchange theory (Kelley, 1979) proposes that all intimate relationships be considered in terms of both the partners' individual costs and benefits and their shared costs and benefits. If Jay and Daisy are in a close interdependent relationship, Daisy does not look at things merely as costs and benefits to her as an individual. She takes into consideration Jay's costs and benefits as well. Thus she is sometimes motivated to compromise on a given issue (such as what movie to see) so that both she and Jay can be pleased. What might have been a cost to her actually turns out to be a benefit to both of them. Kelley (1979) represents these behaviors in a matrix format.

Foa and Foa (1976) have developed a *resource theory* of exchange, stating that partners in a love relationship exchange many resources in addition to money. The Foas' list of resources includes love, status, information, goods, services, and money and allows the exchange relationship to be thought of in fairly broad terms.

In their recent commentary on social exchange factors in the development of relationships, Huston and Burgess (1979) note that several changes occur as partners move into an intimate relationship. The partners interact more frequently and in more situations. They obviously want to be physically close to each other, and the level of physical and emotional intimacy deepens. Social inhibitions tend to drop, and there is freer expression of both positive and negative feelings. The partners become increasingly aware of each other's attitudes and values, develop their own unique style of communication, and become stable and habitual in their interactions. Liking, loving, and trust grow mutually, and at some point the partners begin to function as a couple rather than as two individuals. Each person's investment in the relationship is very great, and each feels that his or her happiness is linked to the continued existence of the relationship. Therefore in their perceptions their relationship becomes unique and irreplaceable.

Braiker and Kelley (1979) examined the role of conflict in the development of close relationships, finding that dimensions of love, conflict, ambivalence, and maintenance characterized couples as they moved from casual dating to serious dating to engagement. The influence of the dimensions varied with the courtship stage in which a couple was located, and, interestingly, the love and conflict dimensions appeared basically unrelated to each other (debunking the myth that the higher the level of conflict, the lower the level of love). We shall discuss this study in conjunction with conflict in Chapter 7.

Interdependence in relationships was addressed by Huesmann and Levinger (1976) as they applied sophisticated mathematical concepts to incremental changes in relationships over time, and by Scanzoni (1979a), who viewed relationship development in terms of (1) exploration, moving to (2) expansion, and stabilizing with (3) commitment. Berscheid and Graziano (1979) have studied attentional processes in relationship development, using a motivational framework, and have made the point that persons who are dependent on one another will make a great effort to think well about the partner, whether or not that is realistic.

Ridley and Avery (1979) view the pair relationships within a *social network,* stating that the pair can be influenced by the size of the network as well as by its density, complexity, location, and climate. The authors observe that social exchanges take place not only between the pair's members but also between the dyad itself and its social network. When we understand that P has an individual social network, O has an individual social network, and the P–O dyad has its own unique social network, we begin to get some idea of the complexity of social network analyses.

Although we have mentioned only a few of the topics under consideration in current research on exchange theory and intimate relationships, many scholars are pursuing this area of study (for example, Carson, 1979; Foa & Foa, 1972; Levinger, 1979; Levinger & Raush, 1977).

Equity Theory

An extension of exchange theory receiving considerable attention in recent years is *equity theory,* formulated by Walster, Berscheid, and Walster (1973, 1976). The four basic propositions of equity in summary form are:

Proposition I: Individuals try to maximize outcomes, with outcomes defined as rewards minus costs.
Proposition IIA: Groups maximize collective reward by developing accepted systems for apportioning rewards and costs among members.
Proposition IIB: Groups generally reward members for equitable treatment and generally punish members who behave inequitably.
Proposition III: When individuals find themselves in an inequitable relationship, they become distressed; the greater the inequity, the greater distress felt.
Proposition IV: Individuals in an inequitable relationship will attempt to eliminate their distress by restoring equity. The greater the inequity, the harder they will try to restore equity.

We can illustrate these propositions with a few simple examples based on the now-familiar relationship between Daisy and Jay.

Proposition I: Both Jay and Daisy will try to get as much out of their relationship as possible.
Proposition IIA: Daisy and Jay will try to come to a mutually acceptable balance of rewards and costs in their relationship.
Proposition IIB: Daisy and Jay will get along well as long as each perceives he or she is receiving fair treatment from the other. If either perceives unfairness, he or she will become hostile.
Proposition III: If Daisy and Jay perceive their relationship to be inequitable, each will become distressed, whether he or she is the one who is *under*rewarded or the one who is *over*rewarded.
Proposition IV: Both Daisy and Jay will try to restore equity to their relationship if they feel it is unequal.

Although these examples do not include all the variations on the theme of equity and inequity, they should serve the purpose of exposing the basic principles of exchange and equity theories. (A comprehensive review of equity theory can be found in Walster, Walster & Berscheid, 1978.)

Some people believe that exchange theory does not fully explain close relationships. For example, in Chapter 4 we discussed Clark and Mills's (1979; Mills & Clark, 1982) distinction between exchange and communal relationships. Gains and losses perceived as equal are seen as the basis for exchange, and response to the other person's need is seen as the basis for communality. Clark and Mills propose that communality most often characterizes romantic love and family relationships. McDonald (1981) considers the exchange process in stable marital relationships. He believes that simple exchange is inadequate for such relationships and that the partners' social structure, the duration of the relationship, and the partners' trust in and commitment to each other all affect the marital exchange process.

Commitment: A Force in Relationship Progress

Intreat me not to leave thee, or to
Return from following after thee:
For whither thou goest, I will go;
And where thou lodgest, I will lodge:
Thy people shall be my people, and
Thy God my God: Where thou diest,
Will I die, and there will I be buried:
The Lord do so to me, and more also,
If ought but death part thee and me.

The Bible, Ruth 1:16, 17

This passage is an eloquent statement on the meaning of commitment in a relationship. Though it is often read during marriage ceremonies, it did not originate in a romantic relationship; rather, the words were spoken by Ruth, a young widow, to her mother-in-law, Naomi. Commitment can characterize many kinds of relationships, from friendship to kin relationships to marriage. We discuss some of the general definitions of commitment and theory and research focused on commitment in intimate male/female relationships.

A Definition of Commitment

Although Kiesler (1971) confines his attention to how commitment affects individuals in regard to attitude change, some of his basic assumptions about commitment are quite interesting:

Assumption 1:   A person tries to attain consistency between his or her attitudes and behaviors.

Assumption 2:   The effect of commitment is to make a behavior or situation less subject to change.

Assumption 3:   The greater the degree of commitment, the more powerful the commitment's effects.

Assumption 4:   Commitment may be increased by increasing the explicitness, importance, or irrevocability of the act, increasing the number of acts performed, or increasing the free choice perceived by the person in doing the act.

Kiesler points to the power that commitment may have to keep an individual from changing an attitude or cognition; the same mechanism is at work in an intimate relationship. For instance, we might rewrite assumption 4 to read: commitment to the courtship relationship may be increased by a couple being seen together more in public, going to some significant family and professional activities together, restricting dating only to each other, dating more frequently, or having either relationship member offer to terminate the relationship so that the other person can be free.

Blau (1964), one of the early exchange theorists, refers to commitment in typical reward/cost terms—that is, "the establishment of exchange relations involves making investments that constitute commitments to the other party" (p. 98). If rewards and commitment both increase, the relationship will progress, but Blau notes the curious fact that one person's increasing commitment may either increase the partner's love or cause the partner to completely lose interest in the relationship. Why? Blau concludes that commitments must be mutual and fairly balanced for a relationship to continue developing. If one person is much more involved in the relationship, the other may well feel trapped and then try to withdraw. Undoubtedly, most exchange and equity theorists would agree with Blau that a relationship requires a sound balance between partners in respect to commitment, as well as other factors.

Secord and Backman (1964) view commitment as occurring during a certain stage of friendship formation. The first stage of friendship formation includes *sampling and estimation,* initial encounter and estimate of likely future costs and rewards; *bargaining,* a negotiation process; *commitment,* a process of concentrating one's energy within the relationship and reduced comparison of the relationship with other options; and *institutionalization,* or the public and private confirmation of the dyad as both legitimate and exclusive. These authors thus view commitment as part of the courtship process rather than as an end-point.

As noted previously, Levinger views commitment as influenced both by the internal consent of the dyad members, but also by the external restraints imposed by society. Internal consent involves voluntary focus of resources into the relationship and relinquishing competitive relationships; it implies a flow of energy into the relationship. External restraints may be anything from powerful urging by friends and family that a couple continue their relationship to the negative emotional and economic factors associated with a divorce. Levinger points out that the manifestations and perhaps even the nature of commitment may be changing in contemporary society, and this proposition is echoed by Jesse Bernard (1972) in her book on marriage. Noting that commitment may range from spiritual vows to property arrangements, she states that "wide as the variety of forms of marriage commitment may be, the contents usually consist of some combination or permutation of two fundamental dimensions of the marital relationship: exclusivity and permanence" (p. 86). Bernard also conjectures that even these fundamental properties of commitment are undergoing changes and that our society may evolve to *degrees of marriage*, rather than an all-or-nothing status. Although she does not necessarily endorse the transformation in commitment, Bernard recognizes that life is a tradeoff and that marriage patterns which offer fewer economic guarantees for women may also offer greater opportunities for women's professional growth and may offer less power but more nurturance opportunities for men.

One example of an alternative type of commitment is discussed in a book by Constantine and Constantine (1973) on group marriage. The authors focus on multilateral or group marriage (usually two couples), where emphases on commitment and stability in many ways reflect the traditions of monogamy. Although their material may be considered controversial, their major thesis, that group marriage can (indeed, does) offer an alternative to traditional monogamy, appears to fit in with Levinger's and Bernard's ideas about changes in commitment.

Research on Commitment

Johnson (1973) observed that commitment has been sporadically studied in a wide variety of contexts, from social influence and conformity to courtship. His interviews of married and cohabiting students revealed that married students were more strongly committed to maintaining their relationships and perceived more social pressure to maintain them. Although married couples did not perceive any greater costs to terminating their relationships than did cohabiting couples, the married couples did have more complex relationships in terms of shared property and investments.

One difficulty in conducting research on commitment is the lack of quantification of the concept in such a way as to make it researchable. Leik and Leik (1976) proposed a mathematical model to monitor relationship processes as a dyad moves from *no involvement*, to *strict exchange*, to *confidence*, to *commitment* (a state in which no alternative relationships are being considered). The concept of commitment as a state or process in which alternative reward/cost ratios are no longer considered is a pervasive one (Secord & Backman, 1964), although exclusivity is not required for commitment according to Rosenblatt (1977), who combines various concepts and relevant research findings on commitment and suggests areas for future exploration. He defines commitment as a person's avowed intention to maintain a relationship and goes on to describe factors precipitating change in commitment, such as change in a couple's professional circumstances or changes in the availability of relationships with other people. He appears to be more comfortable saying what commitment is *not* rather than what it is. Rosenblatt points to a few accepted occurrences, such as marriage ceremonies and the birth of children, which serve to increase marital commitment (Levinger might call them external constraints). Marriage ceremonies require considerable investment of time and money and are usually very public. How often has an uncertain bride or bridegroom panicked immediately before the wedding only to follow through with the ritual because of social convention? And how often does that same individual convert his or her premarital panic into post-ceremony confidence? The advent of children can also at least appear to increase a couple's commitment to the relationship, sometimes merely by the time and energy required to attend to a new baby.

Commitment can be viewed as part of the relationship development process, but it is also an ongoing theme in a relationship, and as such provides a link to Chapter 7, in which we will consider other relationship themes, such as communication and conflict.

Summary

Relationship development is a process which has impact on all of us. Levinger and Snoek's levels of relationship include awareness, surface contact, and mutuality, with relationships existing on the mutuality level also characterized by varying degrees of involvement, commitment, and symmetry. Relationship qualities and boundaries may be viewed rather differently by people of widely different ages. Social penetration theory proposes that relationship development is progressive and orderly, beginning with a fairly broad array of communication topics and superficial behaviors at the beginning of a relationship, but moving toward greater depth and intimacy as the relationship continues into closeness. Recent theory development by Altman and his colleagues, however, proposes that social penetration is not a unidirectional process, but rather is composed of openness-penetration forces and closedness-privacy forces which exert varying amounts of influence in the relationship at various times. Wish, Deutsch, and Kaplan empirically derived a classification for relationships which contains dimensions labeled (1) cooperative and friendly versus competitive and hostile, (2) equal versus unequal, (3) intense versus superficial, and (4) socioemotional and informal versus task-oriented and formal.

Mate selection represents one type of relationship initiation and development. Winch's theory of complementary needs proposes that although persons may be more likely to initially meet each other because they have similar social characteristics, they will select potential mates who are different, but complementary. Kerckhoff and Davis's study, however, found that a period of value consensus preceded assessment of couples' need complementarity. Murstein's stimulus–value–role theory also views mate selection as a stage process, with importance shifting from stimulus characteristics to value comparisons to assessment of role compatibility as the relationship develops. Lewis emphasized the importance of processes rather than stages in his premarital dyadic formation theory.

Exchange theory is a very general approach to relationships, stressing the importance of rewards, costs, outcomes, and comparison levels as dyad members negotiate their relationship. It is a broad development, ranging from Homans's concept of distributive justice to Walster et al.'s equity theory. Equity theory deals primarily with dyad members' attempts to maintain equitable balance of costs and rewards.

Commitment usually refers to both the intention and behavior which maintain a relationship, and it can be difficult to examine empirically. We have much more conjecture than concrete fact about commitment. However, many scholars appear to agree that the manifestations and perhaps even the basic nature of commitment may be changing in contemporary society or at least in male/female pairing relationships.

7

The Marriage Relationship

The most complex, contradictory, sometimes joyous and sometimes bittersweet of human relationships is the marriage relationship. There probably is no other relationship for which our expectations are so high. Certainly, the parent/child relationship is demanding and frequently one-sided, with mothers and fathers expected to be nurturing, supportive, understanding, and self-sacrificing. But children grow up; then parents get the chance to be people again. The marriage relationship, on the other hand, is supposed to go on forever. The relationship between the clergy and their congregations is another demanding one, with expectations by the congregation that the cleric will be all-knowing, all-giving, and personally above reproach, but clergy and congregation do not have to stare at each other across the breakfast table every morning. Married people do. One other relationship invites comparison—that between therapist and client. Therapists are expected to have all the virtues of a good parent and also be brilliant and non-judgmental. That's the bad news! The good news is that they only need to present this model of perfection to a client for one hour at a time. Married couples get to spend long hours together doing things like cleaning house or camping in a tent with the kids during the rainiest week in July.

If you have any doubts about the demands we put on marriage, reflect on a few of the words used in traditional marriage ceremonies. In some situations, men and women look at each other and promise:

to have and to hold—comfort, be intimate with
to love and to cherish—regard highly, protect, take care of
in sickness and health—through all the bad times
forsaking all others—being intimate emotionally and sexually only with each other
as long as life lasts—forever

Still other religious groups hold up very high ideals for married love, such as the love held by Jacob for Rachel in the Old Testament. Jacob worked seven years for Rachel's hand and said that the seven years were as short as seven days because he loved her so much. Such expectations are rather difficult to meet.

As we discussed in Chapter 4, the romantic mystique that surrounds intimate relationships such as marriage is also a form of expectation, emphasizing such attributes as beauty, gallantry, physical attraction, and sexual fulfillment. Although modern romantic traditions trace most directly to courtly love of medieval Europe, love relationships were also idealized in ancient times:

I am the rose of Sharon, and the lily of the valleys.
As the lily among thorns, so is my love among the daughters.
As the apple tree among the trees of the wood,
So is my beloved among the sons.

I sat down under his shadow with great delight,
And his fruit was sweet to my taste.
My beloved is mine, and I am his.

The Bible, Song of Solomon 2:1–3, 16

When we combine the attributes of romantic love with the emotional and behavioral expectations of church and culture and then throw in for good measure the tremendous stresses of modern urban society, it is not surprising that so many marriages die, but rather that so many survive!

Why marriage? One might question why we have chosen to deal with marriage specifically rather than with intimate relationships in general. Our reasoning is twofold: first, many close relationships are relevant to us as human beings, including parent/child relationships, friendships, and premarital love relationships. Each type of relationship has its own unique importance and has been extensively written about. The array of existing information is so vast that it cannot be condensed into one volume, let alone one or two book chapters. Thus we felt it necessary to select one relationship to represent intimate relationships, and only marriage seems to contain many of the qualities of other relationships and yet also to offer unique attributes and interactional situations.

In addition marriage is a topic of particular interest to most of us. Although we cannot discuss all aspects of marriage, we will present many important ones. Because of its pervasive impact on nearly all marital situations, marital communication will be our first area for study.

Communication in Couples

Basic Communication Processes

We have probably all seen or heard the story of the American tourist in a foreign country who, when he cannot be understood by the local citizens, resorts to speaking louder and louder—in English! This situation represents a failure to communicate. If the tourist is persistent, he may resort to gestures such as pointing, or he may try finally to get a third person to translate for him. In many ways this situation is representative of a marriage where one spouse does not feel heard (much less understood) by the other spouse and so begins talking louder. If talking fails, the first spouse may resort to gestures (nonverbal behavior) such as pouting or throwing things, and if that does not promote understanding, a translator (family member, friend, marriage counselor) may be called in.

Both verbal and nonverbal behavior are important components of communication, and several studies have revealed that there are distinct differences between happy and unhappy married couples in terms of nonverbal behaviors such as eye contact and touching (Beier & Sternberg, 1980; Vincent, Friedman, Nugent, & Messerly, 1979). However, since nonverbal behavior has been comprehensively discussed in Chapter 3, our focus here will be on verbal marital communication. Most verbal behavior has both a *content* (or informational) component and an *affective* (or emotional) one. Morton, Alexander, and Altman (1976) view communication as the primary means by which individuals define relationships and as the vehicle for negotiation of control. The authors discuss the complexities of both the communication process and the negotiating process; partners in a relationship usually vary over time in the control or influence which they exert. Although the authors state that verbal disclosure, nonverbal behaviors, and environmental action are all necessary to the process of relationship definition, they grant primary importance to self-disclosure, a process we will consider in depth.

Another interesting perspective on the communication process is provided by Krauss and Weinheimer (1966), who devised a study that examined delivery of a message and feedback. They found that the amount of concurrent, approving feedback which the listener was able to give the message-sender greatly influenced the length of the message; the more feedback given, the *shorter* the message. In other words the sender was able to speak less when he or she felt understood. All of us know couples in which one person does nearly all the talking and the other person hardly gets a word in edgewise. Although our first response is often to condemn the talker for monopolizing the conversation, Krauss and Weinheimer's research might indicate that if we could induce the quiet person to verbally acknowledge more of what the partner is saying, the relationship might show greater balance in communication. In some cases, however, one partner may be quite apprehensive about talking to the other. Although some persons have a generalized communication apprehension, one recent study (Powers & Hutchinson, 1979) offered the proposition that "spouse communication apprehension is distinct from the personality trait of general communication apprehension" (p. 94). Although spouses can be fearful of communicating for many reasons, often couples are inept rather than afraid during their verbal interactions. Two persons frequently view the same situation quite differently. Watzlawick, Beavin, and Jackson (1967) use the term *punctuation* to refer to the way in which a marriage partner assigns importance to specific events in an interaction. For instance, suppose Scott and Sandy are in bed together, and Sandy suggests that they have sex. Scott says he thinks that would be fun, but he needs some time to get warmed up. Sandy observes that he's been taking longer to get warmed up lately and wonders if he's beginning to lose interest in her. Scott protests that he still loves her as much as ever, but instead of getting warmed up, Scott gets upset. Thereupon Sandy becomes convinced she's being rejected and turns away. Scott doesn't try to stop her, because he doesn't have tangible proof of his love for her.

So how does each *punctuate* the interaction? Sandy believes that Scott rejected her suggestion (and her) and that her subsequent responses merely reflected her sadness at the rejection. Scott, on the other hand, believes that when he made a simple request for patience, Sandy replied by pressuring him, and thus that his subsequent sexual unresponsiveness merely reflected his reaction to her pressure tactics. Each spouse puts the importance or exclamation point for triggering the unsatisfactory interaction on the other spouse. Who is right?

It is easy to appreciate the subtlety with which communication often occurs. It has even been said that one cannot *not* communicate (Lederer & Jackson, 1968), meaning that everything between two intimate people is a form of communication. However, one of the clearest and most powerful ways for marriage partners to communicate is through self-disclosure.

Self-Disclosure

The Nature of Self-Disclosure

Self-disclosure refers to telling another about oneself, to honestly offering one's thoughts and feelings for the other's perusal, hoping that truly open communication will follow. Sidney Jourard (1964) was the first psychologist to develop the area of self-disclosure for detailed discussion and research, and his name is still strongly associated with the area. Jourard believed that when we hide our innermost being from others, we tend to lose touch with ourselves and induce physical illness and interpersonal estrangement. Jourard felt that the physical and psychological health of individuals as well as relationships depends largely on the ability of self-disclosure to strip away restrictive social masks.

The phenomenon of self-disclosure has most often been studied as it occurs in a two-person relationship, since disclosure is usually judged to be more intimate in a pair than in a larger group (for example, Taylor, De Soto, & Lieb, 1979). Social penetration theory (Altman & Taylor, 1973), discussed in connection with relationship development, includes self-disclosure as the primary vehicle for relationship progression. Breadth of disclosure on many topics is greater in the initial stage of a relationship, but the depth or intimacy of topics increases (while breadth may decrease) as the relationship continues.

Rubin (1973) has been concerned with the variability of self-disclosure across situations and has developed a theory based on *trust* and *modeling* (the case in which one person serves as a model for the other). Modeling is most influential when self-disclosure is at a superficial or moderate level, but trust becomes an issue at more intimate levels of self-disclosure. Rubin has also dealt with a *stranger effect* in self-disclosure, finding people often very willing to disclose themselves intimately to others whom they will never see again. Rubin continues to be a strong spokesman for studying self-disclosure in naturalistic or real-world settings (see Rubin, 1976; Rubin & Shenker, 1978).

Major self-disclosure theories incorporate aspects of reciprocity and exchange theories. The basic premise of reciprocity theory as applied to self-disclosure is that *self-disclosure begets self-disclosure* (Jourard, 1964), and this has been confirmed in various laboratory experiments (Ehrlich & Graeven, 1971; Jourard, 1971). However, self-disclosure appears to be more flexible in well-established friendships (Derlega, Wilson, & Chaikin, 1976), a finding which has important implications for married couples. In fact, Morton (1978) found spouses to be less reciprocal in self-disclosure than strangers, although other research has shown spouses to be highly reciprocal (for example, Hendrick, 1981; Komarovsky, 1967). Exchange theory emphasizes the costs and benefits in interpersonal relationships, and in marriage there is almost constant, direct one-to-one exchange. Cozby (1972) proposed a curvilinear relationship between reciprocity and self-disclosure, stating that in an ongoing intimate relationship the rewards of reciprocal self-disclosure increase to a certain point, but increasing intimacy causes self-disclosure to become too threatening (costly), so reciprocity ceases to operate. In a similar vein Gilbert (1976) suggested that there is an apparent dichotomy between security and intimacy needs in a marriage, with security threatened by self-disclosure though intimacy is fostered by it.

Self-disclosure has also been examined in relation to concepts such as interpersonal liking and personality adjustment. As noted in Chapter 2, the relationship between liking and self-disclosure is not always a direct one, because liking can be affected by the intimacy (Worthy, Gary, & Kahn, 1969), the content (Hoffman-Graff, 1977), and the timing (Wortman, Adesman, Herman, & Greenberg, 1976) of the disclosure. Although direct links between disclosure and personality factors have not been substantiated, some research suggests that highly disclosing persons are better adjusted than people who disclose less (Jourard, 1971; Strassberg, Anchor, Gabel, & Cohen, 1978).

Some of the most interesting but most contradictory research has been conducted in the area of sex differences and self-disclosure. Several studies have indicated that women disclose more than do men (Chelune, 1977; De Forest & Stone, 1980; Hendrick, 1981; Stokes, Fuehrer, & Childs, 1980), and other studies revealed no major sex differences in self-disclosure (Feigenbaum, 1977; Komarovsky, 1974). What seems to be as important as the possibility of sex differences in actual amount of disclosure given is the fact that men and women do appear to differ in terms of the target person to whom they will disclose (Jourard, 1971; Komarovsky, 1974).

We can easily see that self-disclosure is a complicated process which varies across relationships and situations. We find that under some conditions—but not all—there are sex differences in self-disclosure, with females disclosing more than males. Self-disclosure is often reciprocal, with an individual responding to another's self-disclosure with similar levels of disclosure, but this may happen more often with strangers than with intimate others. Factors such as trust, modeling, or the desire for equity may influence reciprocity, but after a certain point of self-disclosure is reached, the costs of intimacy may escalate so that reciprocity no longer operates. Perhaps this explanation governs self-disclosure in a long-term relationship such as marriage. Self-disclosure varies through the chronological development of a relationship, according to Altman and Taylor, increasing in depth as it decreases in breadth, so it may well mean different things to the marriage partners at different times. In any case self-disclosure needs to be studied from a multidimensional approach (Altman et al., 1981; Gilbert & Whiteneck, 1976). As we discuss self-disclosure in married couples, we will observe that the varied patterns and themes of self-disclosure become even more complex.

Couples Communicating

Jill: I'm upset you are upset.
Jack: I'm not upset.
Jill: I'm upset that you're not upset that I'm upset you're upset.
Jack: I'm upset that you're upset that I'm not upset that you're upset that I'm upset, when I'm not.
Jill: You put me in the wrong.
Jack: I am not putting you in the wrong.
Jill: You put me in the wrong for thinking you put me in the wrong.
Jack: Forgive me.
Jill: No.
Jack: I'll never forgive you for not forgiving me [Laing, 1970, p. 21].

Although R. D. Laing is depicting very dysfunctional marital communication, he also makes a good point about very average communication—much of it is based on guesswork, attributions, and mind reading (when one spouse says to the other "I shouldn't have to tell you that; you should know!").

One of the most valuable aspects of the self-disclosure process is that, when it's done well, it takes a lot of the guesswork out of interpersonal communication. Various researchers have been interested in couples' self-disclosure patterns. Shapiro and Swensen (1969) tested subjects to see what they knew about their spouse and what they believed their spouse knew about them. The authors found that disclosure perceptions by one spouse correlated more highly with the other spouse's knowledge of attitudes and opinions and body and sex and less highly with work or studies or personality. They also found that spouses often knew more about each other than had actually been disclosed, confirming the assumption that spouses learn from behavioral observation.

In looking at how class differences affect marital self-disclosure, Mayer (1967) found that middle-class wives disclosed more than lower-class wives, with more disclosure directed to husbands (and professionals) and less to relatives. Middle-class wives tended to see self-disclosure as a corrective instrumental process to gain a definite objective, but lower-class wives saw it as a means to ventilate emotions or gain support. Class differences in self-disclosure had also been found by Komarovsky (1967), who gathered voluminous sociological data from Northeastern working-class families in the late 1950s. Komarovsky defined communication as willingness to share oneself with one's spouse, and she found high reciprocity between spouses' levels of self-disclosure, whether high or low, and determined that the main inhibitors to self-disclosure were disinterest and lack of responsiveness in one's spouse.

In recent years more researchers have become interested in the relationship of self-disclosure to marital satisfaction. Both Navran (1967) and Bienvenu (1970) have developed research instruments to assess marital communication and have found a positive relationship between effective communication and satisfaction in marriage. Miller, Corrales, and Wackman (1975) found that reciprocal styles of high disclosure were most satisfactory for couples; Burke, Weir, and Harrison (1976) offered several interesting findings. First, individuals who stated specific motivation to disclose did in fact disclose more. One's spouse was the person most often turned to with problems, and the greater the likelihood of disclosure, the greater were both marital and general life satisfaction. The reasons for not disclosing to the spouse were different for husbands and wives. Wives who did not disclose said that they did not want to bother their husbands or that their husbands would not understand, and husbands who did not disclose said they wanted to separate home from work or that their wives *could* not understand.

Hendrick (1981) administered two marital satisfaction instruments and Taylor and Altman's (1966) Social Penetration Scale (a self-disclosure scale) to 51 couples and found not only a positive relationship between a couple's marital satisfaction and self-disclosure, but also a positive relationship between each individual spouse's self-disclosure and the other spouse's marital satisfaction. In other words, the more the wife disclosed, the more satisfied the husband reported himself to be and vice versa. Hendrick also found a negative relationship between self-disclosure and years of marriage that supported previous findings (Jourard, 1971).

Since it appears that self-disclosure and marital satisfaction are indeed positively related, the task of helping couples communicate more effectively is an important one, and communication training courses for couples are becoming widespread. Birchler, Weiss, and Vincent (1975) observed differences between distressed and nondistressed couples in terms of verbal and nonverbal behaviors and problem-solving skills. Happily married couples exhibited a greater number of positive verbal and nonverbal behaviors and fewer negative ones. Interestingly, both happy and unhappy couples tended to communicate less easily than did stranger couples. Unfortunately, we often tend to be more polite and pleasant with strangers than with those to whom we are close.

The answer to improving marital communication may not lie simply in increasing the total amount of self-disclosure. How much self-disclosure is good—or even necessary? Total self-disclosure is risky. Simmel's observation was that "only those individuals can give themselves wholly without danger who cannot wholly give themselves, because such individuals contain an inexhaustible reservoir of latent psychological possessions, but less creative persons by their complete psychological abandon run the risk of coming to face one another with empty hands" (cited in Komarovsky, 1967, p. 143). Perhaps conditional self-disclosure is the answer. Komarovsky (1967) found one type of couple who was unhappy even though their level of disclosure was very high; these couples frequently disclosed negative material. The type rather than the amount of disclosure seemed to make the difference, and in these unhappy situations wives were more likely than husbands to disclose negative feelings. Similar findings by Levinger and Senn (1967) showed that marital satisfaction was more highly related to disclosure of positive rather than negative information, with frequency of negative disclosure higher in unhappy couples. Satisfied couples tended to disclose about positive, important things, and less-happy couples talked about negative things of every level of importance. Perhaps, as the authors propose, "For the average couple, selective disclosure of feelings seems more beneficial to marital harmony than indiscriminate catharsis" (p. 246).

Gilbert (1976) has suggested the possibility of a curvilinear relationship between marital satisfaction and self-disclosure that fits logically with Cozby's (1972) notion of a curvilinear relationship between reciprocity and self-disclosure and with findings showing self-disclosure to decrease with marriage length (Hendrick, 1981; Jourard, 1971). As we discussed earlier, Gilbert proposed that self-disclosure may be affected by both the security and intimacy needs in the marriage relationship, and while disclosure may promote intimacy in the beginning stages of a relationship, the security of the partners in an advanced relationship may be threatened by self-disclosure that is too revealing (or too negative). For example, if Scott and Sandy are in the early stages of a romantic relationship, it may help their relationship progress if they disclose fairly fully to each other about past romantic attachments, offering comments (from a safe distance, of course) about what was wrong and what was right in these now concluded affairs. It is another matter, however, if Scott and Sandy are deeply involved and one partner tells the other about his or her strong *present* attraction to someone else. The first information is not threatening; the second information is. We are not arguing at this point about the value of the second disclosure and whether such information should or should not be offered. We are merely pointing out that, if it is offered, it may seriously affect the relationship. However, as Gilbert points out, "The issue in disclosure for optimal husband–wife relations may be in learning how to deal with information, disappointments and conflicts at the far end of the disclosure continuum, where the risk is high" (1976, p. 229).

To this point we have been concerned with the tremendous demands placed on marital relationships by our society and with communication, one means by which married couples can improve and maintain their relationships. We have focused on self-disclosure because it is a central factor in interpersonal communication, and it continues to maintain an important position in social-psychological research. By now we all recognize that relationships are very difficult to quantify, so it will come as no surprise that *conflict,* the next relationship theme, is a very complex issue.

Conflict in Marriage

Though questions of physical and economic survival are the significant problems we might expect to cause trouble for couples, conflict is often related to small issues rather than large ones. Marriage counselors are all too familiar with "I can't stand her in the morning; she wakes up fast and I wake up slowly," or "He's a slob; he drops his clothes wherever he takes them off and then expects me to clean up after him." Such issues in and of themselves do not destroy a relationship, but the accumulation of issues and the way in which they are handled can make or break a marital bond. Before we discuss contemporary theory and research regarding marital partners and conflict, we need to understand some general ideas about conflict itself.

Conflict in General

The topic of social conflict has been studied by philosophers, historians, economists, and social scientists of all types, many of whom have made substantial contributions to our understanding of conflict and none of whom has been able to resolve human conflict. A general but clear outline of conflict relationships has been offered by Brickman (1974), although interested readers may also pursue the topic elsewhere (for example, Deutsch, 1969; Holmes & Miller, 1976). Brickman proposes a situational definition of conflict, stating that "conflict exists in situations in which parties must divide or share resources so that, to some degree, the more one party gets the less others can have" (p. 1). Such a definition is basically phrased in exchange terms. Brickman distinguishes between conflicts over what course of action to take in order to achieve a given goal and conflicts over which of several goals would be the best one (or ones) to achieve. Brickman structures conflict relationships into four categories: (1) *unstructured conflict relationships,* which have no rules or constraints, (2) *partially structured conflict relationships* characterized by competition and bargaining, (3) *fully structured conflict relationships* governed by strict rules and norms (often on a moral level), and (4) *revolutionary conflict,* or conflict over the rules of conflict. According to the author, the first three categories can be compared to Rapoport's (1960) description of fights, games, and debates.

> For Rapoport, fights are conflicts in which each party has the aim of eliminating the antagonist entirely. Games are conflicts in which each party has the aim of winning as much as possible from the other. Debates are conflicts in which each party has the aim of persuading the other to agree with the first party's views [Brickman, 1974, p. 17].

Marital conflict occurs in all three situations, ideally beginning with debates, which have formal (moral) rules, but more frequently occurring in games in which the competition is strong and each partner may try to bargain in order to maximize his or her outcomes. Unfortunately, married couples also engage in unstructured conflict, Rapoport's "fights," in which each partner may appear to really want to eliminate the other partner entirely. Such elimination sometimes may almost occur, as will be apparent when we discuss spouse abuse.

Although Brickman comments on conflict resolution strategies only briefly, many of these strategies are very useful for couples in conflict. Strategies include introduction of shared goals; partners role playing each other's point of view; gradual compromise, with one partner giving up a little and then the other partner responding in kind; and careful limitation of the conflict to the issue involved. The last item is particularly important for couples, because they may begin arguing about a particular issue, but can quickly spiral into a shouting match about money, sex, in-laws, and who did what to whom ten years earlier. It is helpful to understand that there are different types of conflict and that different methods of conflict resolution can be applied to the various situations. As we have seen, conflict is ubiquitous in human relationships; unfortunately, marriage seems to be no exception. We will focus on the *why* and *how* of conflict but will first briefly note the *who, what, when,* and *where* of marital conflict.

Who is involved in marital conflict? The marriage partners are the primary protagonists in arguments, though children are usually affected, and sometimes in-laws, other relatives, or friends become involved. *What* is involved in marital conflict? Verbal and nonverbal (nonviolent) behavior usually constitute the conflict situation, although it has become apparent in recent years that physical violence can play an important role in marital disagreement. *When* and *where* does conflict occur? Conflict situations can occur anytime, anywhere, from the supermarket to the bridge table, from the front lawn to the bedroom. However, the majority of marital conflict situations probably take place in the relative privacy of the home rather than in public. The *why* and the *how* of marital conflict are more complex and have been the subject of recent social-psychological research.

Marriage Conflict: Why?

Couples appear to engage in conflict for a great variety of reasons, but most of these reasons can be reduced to some sort of conflict of interest on an emotional or behavioral level. Braiker and Kelley (1979) conceptualize close relationships as involving high *interdependence* in terms of personal feelings and attitudes, specific behaviors, and social norm and role-related preferences, and such interdependence causes complexity of mutual rewards and costs. Ideally, each partner's rewards and costs are fair; however, unfairness frequently occurs and can set the stage for conflict. "In the absence of conflict of interest, the relationship proceeds beautifully; given conflict of interest, the pair either works around it or breaks off interaction completely" (Braiker & Kelley, 1979, p. 159). Although this either–or statement sounds deceptively simple, additional research by Kelley demonstrates the complexities of couples' attempts to deal constructively with conflict. Orvis, Kelley, and Butler (1976) examined the different causes of conflict identified by the male and female members of 41 young, heterosexual couples. The study was designed to find out what kinds of reasons each partner would give for certain kinds of behavior that might occur in the relationship; each person discussed his or her own behavior and the partner's behavior and own and partner's differing reasons for why the behavior occurred. Because of the nature of the study, many behaviors discussed were negative. There were basic differences in how partners viewed behaviors, with persons tending to view their own behaviors as more likely to be governed by situational or environmental causes and tending to view the partner's behavior as governed by ongoing personality characteristics or basic attitudes. Thus, if Sandy and Scott are supposed to meet for dinner and Sandy is an hour late, she will say "I'm sorry I'm late, but there was some special work at the office I just had to finish," but Scott might say "You're just inconsiderate of me; you always put me second to your work." She believes the cause of her tardiness is situational, a "one-shot" deal. Scott believes her lateness is chronic and indicates a pervasive disregard for him and his welfare.

The Orvis et al. study also showed some interesting sex differences in how reasons or causes are assigned. Subjects tended to see a woman as the more dependent, weaker partner and to view her behaviors as caused by the environment, other people, lack of ability, and insecurity about the relationship. The only two types of causes given significantly more frequently for men's behaviors were that the behavior would have either good direct or good indirect results. Thus men were seen as more actively and productively controlling the situation. Another sex difference involved the numbers of behaviors described by the partners. Women tended to assign fewer behaviors to their partners, while men assigned more behaviors to their partners. Because most of the behaviors were negative, both men and women thus saw more negative behaviors having been performed by women. These results were confirmed by Hendrick (1981), who found that, although husbands and wives agreed on the problems that wives contributed to the marriage relationship, there was very low agreement on the problems that husbands contributed. Further inspection of the findings revealed that both husbands and wives tended to blame wives for the marital problems. One possible explanation for this difference in assigning responsibility for marital problems may well reside in the traditional sex roles in marriages, since wives have traditionally assumed responsibility for keeping marriages functioning smoothly and have often accepted a major share of the blame for marital problems.

Although Orvis and his colleagues presented their evidence in great detail, showing how specific behaviors are perceived differently by dyad members and thus how easily conflict may result from nearly any behavior, most interesting for our purposes is the statement "Attributional conflicts [conflicts about causes] will generally be irresolvable" (p. 380). If in fact most arguments about the reasons for certain behaviors cannot be resolved, we may well ask "Why argue at all?" Orvis et al. believe that such conflicts serve to increase each partner's knowledge about self and about the other partner and to set some patterns and rules for continuing negotiation in the couple. Thus it may be less important that the disagreeing partners ultimately *agree* on a specific issue than that they *agree to disagree*. The necessity for agreeing to disagree is also emphasized by Morton et al. (1976) in their discussion of relationship definition.

In an extension of Orvis et al.'s (1976) study of conflict in couples, Passer, Kelley, and Michela (1978) used sophisticated statistical techniques to determine the general dimensions which could provide a framework for the various causes or reasons given by the 41 young couples for their behaviors. In this second study for half the subjects the authors described each cause or reason as believed by the *actor* (the person doing the behavior) and for the other half of the subjects, described each reason as believed by the *partner* (the other member). The type of negative behavior supposedly committed was varied also (sins of omission versus sins of commission). Analyses produced a single two-dimensional solution for the actor condition and another two-dimensional solution for the partner condition. These dimensions are shown in Figures 7-1a and 7-1b. The dimensions for the actor condition are (1) positive attitude toward partner versus negative attitude toward partner and (2) unintentional versus intentional. The dimensions for the partner condition are the same for dimension 1 and for dimension 2 are circumstances or states versus actor's traits. We can see that a very important dimension, carried across both conditions, is the positive or negative attitude the actor is perceived to hold for the partner. The other dimensions, although not identical, are similar, because both refer to situational or unplanned occurrences as compared with characteristic or planned occurrences.

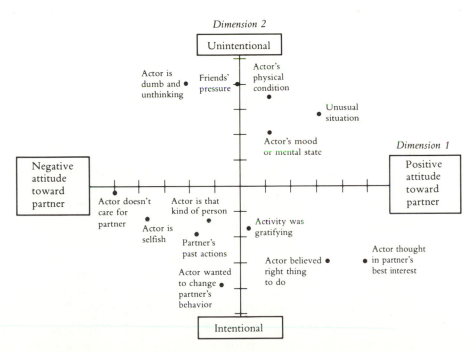

FIGURE 7-1a   Dimensions for actor condition; perceived dimensions underlying behaviors. *(Adapted from "Multidimensional Scaling of the Causes for Negative Interpersonal Behavior," by M. W. Passer, H. H. Kelley, and J. L. Michela. In* Journal of Personality and Social Psychology, *1978, 36, 951–962. Copyright 1978 by the American Psychological Association. Reprinted by permission.)*

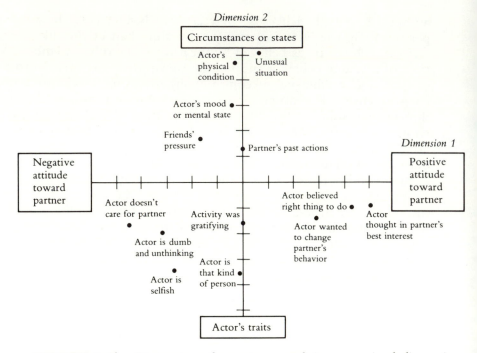

FIGURE 7-1b Dimensions for partner condition; perceived dimensions underlying behaviors. *(Adapted from "Multidimensional Scaling of the Causes for Negative Interpersonal Behavior," by M. W. Passer, H. H. Kelley, and J. L. Michela. In* Journal of Personality and Social Psychology, *1978, 36, 951–962. Copyright 1978 by the American Psychological Association. Reprinted by permission.)*

Much interpersonal conflict is produced because the various behaviors which persons commit and the broader dimensions underlying these behaviors are perceived very differently by the members of a pair.

Specifically, open attributional [causal] conflict occurs when there is conflict between the actor and the partner about how the actor's behavior is to be evaluated. It is on those occasions when the actor's explanation implies a more favorable evaluation of the behavior than does the partner's that attributional disagreement and communication about it are anticipated by the two persons [Kelley, 1979, p. 107].

Since the individuals in an intimate relationship attempt to identify causes for their own behavior as well as their partner's, the opportunities for error in perceptions and inferences are many.

Recent research on conflict in marriage has continued to focus on spouses' causal attributions (for example, Fichten, 1980; Madden & Janoff-Bulman, 1981). Madden and Janoff-Bulman interviewed 32 married women and found that women who were more satisfied with their marriages tended to blame themselves more than their husbands for marital conflict and to view themselves as having considerable power to resolve conflict. Fichten carried conflict research a step further when she allowed couples to view videotapes of their own previously recorded interactions. Couples' perceptions of the interactions were assessed before and after watching the videotape, and basically the perceptions did not change. Partners held onto their perceptions even though the videotape might have revealed things to be somewhat different from what the partners had thought. The philosophy seemed to be "My mind's made up—don't confuse me with the facts!"

We have discussed why couples are in conflict and have seen that partners tend to view situations very differently and to often be unwilling to change their views. Views that are both discrepant and firmly held are bound to cause conflict! However, it is not enough to know why conflict occurs. We also need to know *how* it occurs.

Marriage Conflict: How?

Although we mentioned earlier that marital conflict can be manifested both verbally and nonverbally, several recent social-psychological studies focus primarily on verbal behavior. Birchler and his colleagues (1975) found that distressed couples communicated more negative and fewer positive behaviors than did nondistressed couples. Billings (1979) noted that distressed couples offered more negative and fewer positive cognitive, problem-solving acts. Distressed couples also exhibited greater reciprocity of negative behaviors, and "among some distressed couples, the proportion of hostile communications escalates as the conflict continues" (p. 374). Thus one way in which conflict occurs and is perpetuated in married couples is through negative, often punishing verbal exchanges that may just keep getting worse the longer a couple continues to talk. Koren, Carlton, and Shaw (1980) gathered both questionnaire and observation data from distressed and nondistressed couples, again finding that distressed couples were more critical of each other and were less responsive to each other's suggestions. Since both types of couples proposed about the same number of solutions to try to resolve the conflicts, it appears that distressed couples will try as hard as nondistressed couples to resolve conflict but will be much less effective in doing so. When the authors surveyed the couples' satisfaction with their marriages as well as their satisfaction with the outcomes of various conflict situations, they found that a spouse's satisfaction with his or her marriage predicted later satisfaction with a conflict situation's outcome. In other words, if Scott is content with his marriage, he is likely to be satisfied with the outcome of any particular conflict situation. However, if he believes his marriage to Sandy is in trouble, he is less likely to feel satisfied with their way of resolving a particular conflict.

Negative feelings are pervasive and affect nearly every interaction. An important and highly related point made by these authors was that "one of the overriding impressions of the nondistressed couples in the sample was their concern for maintaining the relationship in spite of the opposing viewpoints provided by the procedure" (p. 467). Although such couples might disagree vehemently, they conveyed the strong assumption that the marriage itself was not at any risk in the conflict. Productive, healthy conflict or fighting in a relationship requires well-established rules for fair fighting and a substantial amount of basic security about the strength of the marriage bond itself (Bach & Wyden, 1968). One partner may feel more secure than the other partner in conflict situations. Douglas (1980) found that happily married couples used behavior-control strategies such as positive feedback or the promise of positive outcomes to increase a partner's behavior during nonconflict situations. However, couples used negative control strategies such as negative feedback and threats of negative outcomes to decrease a partner's behavior in a conflict situation. In addition, when the conflict took place in a very intimate rather than less intimate situation, wives attempted to increase total behaviors while husbands tried to decrease them. The husbands thus appeared to be less comfortable with very intimate conflict situations. The fact that people have difficulty with conflict is certainly not new information; in the Wish et al. (1976) study we discussed in Chapter 6, subjects had much greater difficulty categorizing unfriendly, hostile relationships than friendly ones. Some persons deal with conflict by avoiding it altogether, as Knudson, Sommers, and Golding (1980) learned in their examination of conflict resolution in 33 married couples. The couples were interviewed, initially videotaped during a role play of a conflict situation, and were then interviewed again while watching the videotape of their role play. Basically, the couples who had actively engaged in trying to resolve the conflict during the role play (whether they actually reached final agreement or not) showed greater agreement and greater understanding of each other during the final interview. Couples who avoided the conflict, either by leaving the room or by refusing to negotiate actively with each other, showed less actual agreement and resolution with each other during the final interview. Interestingly, however, some of the couples who had decreased actual agreement said they believed that their agreement had increased, thus displaying an apparent perceptual distortion of the true situation. This finding is important in light of what we said earlier about agreeing to disagree, because the couples who tried to resolve the conflict showed greatest progress not in actual agreement, but in increasingly accurate perceptions and increased understanding of each other. Rands, Levinger, and Mellinger (1981) collected data on conflict resolution and marital satisfaction from 244 married couples and from it developed a typology of marriage types.

Couples who were very intimate and had little conflict were the most satisfied with their marriages; couples who had little intimacy and high conflict were the least satisfied.

The area of conflict is highly relevant for those who study marriage. Although we know a bit about why and how conflict occurs, the difficulties involved in doing reliable research on couples are considerable (Peterson, 1977), and our approaches to reducing such conflict are all too limited.

Conflict in Action: Abuse

"There is no personal gratification from seeing someone close to you that's black and blue, with busted lips and a knocked-out tooth trying to hide it with dark glasses" (Geracimos, 1976, p. 53). Thus speaks a self-described woman-beater as he reviews his former relationships with women. Although such aggression is present in both sexes, battering of wives by husbands is the phenomenon which occurs more frequently.

Wife-beating or battering is not new. It has been part of the larger problem of inequality between the sexes, for "the existence of civil and religious laws giving men superior rights over women nurtured the belief—born in the dim past in the smoke-filled caves of primitives— that men also had the right to beat their wives" (Langley & Levy, 1977, p. 32). Male dominance has been supported by the total culture, with all the major religious works authorizing men's dominance over women and a body of knowledge such as British common law giving husbands the power to punish wives. Wives, along with children and property, have, throughout history, belonged to men to do with as they wished. Judge Blackstone, a noted English jurist, "recorded the English 'Rule of Thumb', which referred to a husband's right to chastise his wife with a whip or rattan no bigger than his thumb, in order to enforce the salutary restraints of domestic discipline" (Langley & Levy, 1977, p. 34). Conditions slowly improved in the legal system as women were allowed to own property, accorded voting rights, and in most cases treated as full citizens, yet wife-battering has continued to flourish. Why?

Langley and Levy offer several reasons why husbands beat their wives, and these factors may be loosely grouped into personality disturbances, environmental stresses, and social norms.

Mental illness, alcohol and drugs, and difficulties with communication, sex, self-image, and the threat of change can all be thought of as personality problems. For our purpose of describing husbands who beat their wives, we can consider these personality problems as severely limiting the alternatives a man sees in dealing with others, particularly with his wife. He may feel powerless to use any alternative but the one most available—violence. Negotiation processes may have been tried without success, and the negative verbal and nonverbal communication patterns that we described earlier in cool psychological terms have deteriorated into hot hostility: shouting, name-calling, and, finally, physical abuse. Although environmental stresses can cause constant frustrations, particularly for lower socioeconomic groups—and wife-beating does occur somewhat more frequently among disadvantaged people—it distinctly crosses all class lines. It is as common in the suburbs as in the inner city! Public acceptance of violence and the use of violence to solve problems, *violence as an acceptable social norm,* contributes to the prevalence and also the continuation of wife-battering, because the problem is cyclical. Just as abused children often grow up to become abusive parents, so also do boys raised by a battering father often grow up to beat their wives. And girls who grow up seeing their mothers cowering in fear are more likely to themselves become battered wives.

A nearly universal question concerns why wives allow such battering to continue. "Why don't they get out?" is a frequent question. Wives stay with abusive husbands for many reasons. Economic dependency is a big factor, because many battered wives are approaching middle age, have several children and few marketable skills. Some women are legitimately fearful of trying to support themselves, skeptical of their chances of getting economic help from an ex-husband, and reluctant to obtain public assistance. Varied economic reasons are matched by varied emotional ones. A traditionally raised battered wife may feel guilty, like a failure. The husband batters, but the wife feels responsible. In some cases a battered wife may genuinely love her husband and prefer being beaten to being alone, or she may hope that he will change or that things will get better. Each battered wife has her own complex reasons for remaining in her situation. In addition, wives often contribute to the system that exists in battering. They may verbally abuse their husbands, thus precipitating physical violence to themselves, or they may in some cases actually physically abuse their husbands.

Those who are concerned with the severe marital conflict resulting in spouse abuse have been instrumental in achieving crisis intervention training for police officers who deal with family violence, proposing punitive legal action against wife abusers, and establishing shelters to provide safe, temporary housing for battered wives and their children. Although wife-battering is now receiving some public attention, as long as sexual inequality is part of the fabric of our society such conflict will undoubtedly continue.

Marital conflict is complex. Although it typically involves a conflict of interest or difference of opinion, it can range from clear statements of disagreement to subtle nonverbal negatives, from civilized debate to primitive violence. The need for research on the causes and more particularly the cures of marital conflict is considerable. Issues clearly related to conflict are decision making and power, about which much research has been done.

Marital Power and Decision Making

The fact that the major proportion of marital power is seen to reside with husbands rather than wives allows such things as wife abuse to continue almost unchecked. Before we discuss the research that has focused on marital power, we will briefly survey general theories of power, negotiation, and decision making.

Power and Bargaining

Most social psychologists would accept a definition of *power* as the ability of one person to influence another in terms of behavior. If we view *authority* as the right to influence another, we can consider power as the ability to exercise that right successfully. In their classic description of the bases of social power, French and Raven (1968) propose five types of social power: reward, coercive, legitimate, referent, and expert.

Reward power denotes one person's (P) ability to reward another person (O) for a certain behavior. If P can offer O various rewards, as well as prevent various punishments from occurring, then P may be able to influence O. *Coercive power* refers to P's ability to administer punishments to O if O fails to produce a certain behavior. Coercive power is sort of the flip side of reward power. *Legitimate power* is defined by French and Raven as the internalized values and beliefs held by O which dictate that he or she "should" be amenable to P's influence. In a sense legitimate power gives P the authority to influence O, at least as far as O is concerned. *Referent power* is given to P by O because O wants to be like P. Attraction is one important source of referent power, because "the greater the attraction, the greater the identification and consequently the greater the referent power" (p. 267). The final source of power, *expert power,* refers to O's belief that P has knowledge about a certain area, is in fact an "expert" in that area. Expert power is what you as a student grant to us as authors, if you believe what we write. Although there are many ways to look at social power, the types of power just listed appear frequently in any social-psychological discussion of power and are transposed into marital terms in Box 7-1.

Another model of power was developed by Michener, Lawler, and Bacarach (1973), who examined undergraduates' perceptions of adversary and target power on the bases of (1) damage (the amount the adversary could inflict on the target); (2) probability (likelihood of adversary using his or her power); (3) blockage (how effectively the target can block an attack); and (4) retaliation (the target's power to hurt

BOX 7-1   Five marital vignettes, based on French and Raven's (1968) bases of social power.

SOCIAL POWER AS MARITAL POWER

Type of Power	*Example*
Reward power	Sandy implies to Scott that she will be very loving and sexual if he agrees to buy a new sofa.
Coercive power	Scott refuses to buy the sofa, and Sandy says she won't have sex with him for a week.
Legitimate power	Sandy wants to begin taking a college course at night, but Scott protests that he wants/needs her at home. Sandy agrees, believing that he has the right to demand that she stay home.
Referent power	Scott talks to his boss, a man he likes and respects, about Sandy's wish to take a class. The boss supports Sandy's right to do what she wishes; Scott reevaluates his own position.
Expert power	Scott and Sandy seek marriage counseling, and when the counselor suggests that Sandy stop using sex as a weapon and that Scott stop trying to control Sandy, both partners listen carefully and agree.

---

the adversary). The authors found that all four variables were important in determining an adversary's power and that three out of the four influenced perceptions of the target's power. We can easily put this power model into a marital situation where one spouse may threaten the other with a negative action. The second spouse may weigh the likelihood of action as well as his or her own abilities to deter the action or to respond in kind. Such power assessments occur on a daily basis.

Bargaining, or negotiation, is intimately involved with power and is summarized by Rubin and Brown (1975) in five characteristics:

1. At least two persons are involved.
2. There is a conflict of interest.
3. The persons are engaged in a voluntary relationship.
4. There is required a division or exchange of resources.
5. The proposals and counterproposals that are made are sequential.

Although the process of negotiation is a complex one and has been described at length in books and articles, the characteristics named are sufficient for our understanding negotiation in marriage. Many people in fact object to viewing an intimate relationship in such marketplace terms as exchange, power, or bargaining, but these words accurately describe much of the ongoing interaction in an intimate couple.

In order to look at the bargaining process in marriage, let us suppose that Scott and Sandy are discussing Sandy's wish to return to college on a part-time basis. The first three criteria for bargaining have been met, because two persons are engaged in the discussion, a conflict of interest is involved, and the persons are willingly (if somewhat angrily) talking. Scott says that he does not wish Sandy to return to school because she will be away two nights each week and because on those nights he would be responsible for child care and dinner preparation. Sandy reiterates her desire to go to school and says that she will plan meals for the nights she is away so that dinner can be served with minimum effort on Scott's part. Scott agrees to take some responsibility for serving dinner, but urges Sandy to take one class rather than two so that she will only be away from home at school one night per week. Sandy realizes that it is important for her and Scott to have time together in the evening, so she volunteers to give up her weekly evening bridge game with friends so that she and Scott can spend more time together. Scott then agrees to support Sandy's returning to school two nights a week.

We can see that there has been an exchange of resources through a series of proposals and counterproposals, and though neither Scott nor Sandy has obtained all they initially desired, both have achieved a satisfactory compromise. Bargaining that results in compromise is usually a constructive way for spouses, as well as other persons or social systems, to make decisions. It is, however, only one aspect of decision making. Decision making involves choices. It involves having one or more persons choose a course of action. The choice itself may be influenced by various power questions, as well as by the opportunities for and the results of various bargaining strategies. An important point made by Olson, Cromwell, and Klein (1975) is that "family power occurs in the context of a non-zero-sum game, where all participants may win or lose, more often than it occurs in the context of a zero-sum game, where only one can win" (p. 236).

Marital Power

Although men are perceived to hold and to exert more power than women (Kahn, in press), some underlying research biases in the study of power must be explored. One methodological problem with power research is that it has often been based on data gathered only from wives (Safilios-Rothschild, 1970). Women have traditionally been more available and more willing to participate in studies than have men, but wives can only draw half the marriage picture.

Another bias in this research has been scholars' reliance on the resource theory of power, which views power as positively related to income, prestige, social status, and education. The person in the pair (or group) who holds the greatest quantities of these resources holds also the greatest amount of power, according to resource theory. Safilios-Rothschild (1976) points out the need to list all a couple's positive resources (such as love, sex, and companionship) when looking at power and resultant decision making. Safilios-Rothschild accepts the basic exchange orientation of resource theory, but extends her ideas to cover all related rewards (socioeconomic and affective), many related costs, and the alternative relationships that may be available to the spouses. Gottman and his colleagues (Gottman, Notarius, Markman, Bank, & Yoppi, 1976) examined marital decision making of distressed and nondistressed couples, and their conclusions fit within an exchange theory framework. In that study, distressed and nondistressed couples did not differ in their communication intentions (both types of couples attempted to communicate positive and negative behaviors in about the same ratios), but a nondistressed spouse was more likely to see his or her partner's behavior as positive than was a distressed spouse. In addition, communication differences between the two types of couples were more likely to occur during some task involving a great deal of conflict. Gottman, et al. proposed a bank-account model of marriage, in which a nondistressed marriage has a higher amount of positive deposits than negative withdrawals. This allows a nondistressed couple to depart from complete reciprocity in such things as self-disclosure and affectionate behaviors (they don't have to keep score) and to make allowances for each other during stress periods or times of moodiness. This is really a conceptual extension of exchange theory, which itself emphasizes more of a strict tradeoff. Various other researchers have also examined marital power within a social exchange theory framework (for instance, see Osmond, 1978).

One of the more interesting studies of marital power was a field study (Strodtbeck, 1974) conducted in the late 1940s in the Arizona–New Mexico area with three distinctly different cultural groups: Navaho Indians, homesteading farmers, and Mormon workers. The experimental procedure required each couple to engage in several decision-making situations, and outcomes were analyzed on the basis of the decision-making process itself, as well as on the spouse who won the greater number of decisions in the pair. It was found that the spouse who talked the most made the most decisions. It was also found that Mormon husbands made a significantly greater number of decisions than Mormon wives (Mormon families being traditionally patriarchal), farm couples had fairly egalitarian decision-making procedures, and Navaho wives made more decisions than Navaho husbands (Navaho women traditionally have had favored positions in their culture). In this study the power to make decisions is rather clearly related to one's power in the family and in the larger culture.

Stewart and Rubin (1974) examined power in dating couples and found that men's *hope of power* (motivation to get power) was inversely related to both their own and their partner's satisfaction with the current intimate relationship. Hope of power was also inversely related to a man's love and liking for his partner. Basically, this means that the more strongly a man wants power, the less satisfied he is likely to be with his current love relationship and the more likely he is to experience somewhat chronic instability in his opposite-sex relationships. Winter, Stewart, and McClelland (1977) also looked at the power motive, this time in married couples, and found that a husband's need for power was inversely associated with his wife's career achievement. At least in this study, it appears that power-oriented men either do not initially seek out or do not positively reinforce career-oriented women. Of course, as Kahn (in press) points out, power and influence are integral parts of the traditional male sex-role stereotype, and competition for this power and influence is not likely to be welcomed from a female partner. In fact, women may not always want a great deal of power in an intimate relationship, as Corrales (1975) found in a study of the marital satisfaction of young couples in early marriages. Marriages that were husband dominated in terms of authority appeared to provide the greatest marital satisfaction for husbands and wives, and marriages that were egalitarian in the area of control provided the most satisfaction. For both authority and control, wife-dominated marriages offered the least satisfaction for both spouses.

Husband–wife difference in power strategies have been reported by various authors (such as Kipnis, 1976). Both differential sex-role socialization and power differences between the sexes have been proposed as reasons for sex differences in the use of power. Using French and Raven's (1968) definitions of bases of social power, Raven, Centers, and Rodrigues (1975) surveyed power in couples. One significant finding was that women were much more likely to attribute expert power to their husbands than men were likely to attribute such power to their wives. Men, on the other hand, granted that their wives had referent power, because "they are part of the same family and should see eye-to-eye with their wives" (p. 224).

To further examine sex differences, Falbo and Peplau (1980) evaluated the association between gender, sexual orientation, egalitarianism, and power strategies in a sample of 50 heterosexual women, 50 heterosexual men, 50 lesbians, and 50 male homosexuals. After assessing various power strategies and coding them into categories, the authors constructed the model of power strategies shown in Figure 7-2. This two-dimensional model has *direct/indirect* as one dimension and *bilateral/unilateral* as the other dimension. Direct influence involves telling and

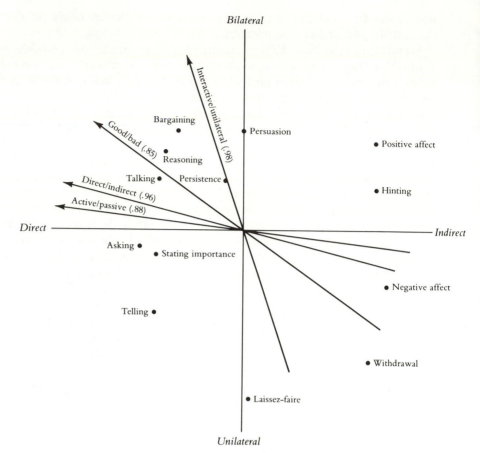

FIGURE 7-2   This two-dimensional model of power strategies includes a direct/indirect dimension and a bilateral/unilateral dimension. *(Adapted from "Power Strategies in Intimate Relationships," by T. Falbo and L. A. Peplau. In* Journal of Personality and Social Psychology, *1980, 38, 618–628. Copyright 1980 by the American Psychological Association. Reprinted by permission.)*

talking; indirect implies hinting or pouting. Bilateral influence involves discussion and negotiation; unilateral indicates nonnegotiable independent action.

The primary finding of the study is that although gay men and women do not differ significantly from one another in their use of power strategies, heterosexual men and women do differ, with men more likely to report using direct and bilateral strategies and women more likely to report using indirect and unilateral strategies. Although these findings to some extent parallel earlier findings on gender differences in power use, women's use of unilateral strategies is somewhat new. Perhaps, as Falbo and Peplau hypothesize, women do not have high expectations of being able to influence their partners and so learn to behave unilaterally, without approval or agreement. We might also suggest that the feminist movement has motivated women to behave more independently, even though it has not clearly increased women's actual power either in or out of intimate relationships.

Power issues clearly continue to be part of intimate relationships. Power and conflict are tied together in many instances, and Kahn (in press) hypothesizes that some men who feel their power threatened by women will resort to the use of more coercive (violent) power tactics. Perceptions of power are clearly related to decision making, because the more powerful partner (either in terms of socioeconomic or emotional resources) has the greater decision-making ability. However, an observer cannot assess real power in a couple just by observing who makes the most decisions. Safilios-Rothschild (1976) distinguishes between *orchestration power* and *implementation power,* the former involving important and infrequent decisions and the latter involving unimportant and time-consuming decisions. Also, who decides how decisions will be made? If a wife decides that the husband can make all social-arrangement decisions, which spouse really has the decision-making power? Olson and Cromwell (1975) underscore the need to use both observational and self-report research methods to gain an accurate picture of power and decision making in a couple.

We have discussed communication, conflict, and power and have moved inexorably toward the point at which all these variables meet—marital satisfaction.

Marital Satisfaction at Present

Historical Development

Marital satisfaction (also called marital adjustment or marital happiness) has been examined by researchers (usually sociologists) for the past several decades, but the rise in divorce during recent years has caused increasing interest in marital satisfaction by mental health and social science professionals. Marital satisfaction is an all-encompassing term that can include many variables: happiness in and adjustment to the marriage; agreement on values, priorities, and family "rules" for the marriage partners; frequency of sexual intercourse; frequency and severity of arguments; regret or absence of regret about the marriage itself; emotional involvement with children; and any number of other feelings, verbal expressions, and behaviors that characterize evaluation of a relationship. Most research in this area has focused primarily on prediction of marital satisfaction. In other words, what combination of the variables just listed, as well as related items, can either raise or lower marital satisfaction?

A seminal work in this area, *Predicting Adjustment in Marriage* (Locke, 1951), employed both questionnaires and interviews and discovered that factors such as conflicts, courtship, parental influences, and sexual behavior were positively related to marital adjustment. Locke and Wallace's (1959) construction of a short marital adjustment scale, in which they used the most discriminating items from six previous scales, was a significant step in research development in marital satisfaction, and the scale is still in active use. Length of marriage is thought to affect marital satisfaction, and Luckey (1966) noted that the longer couples had been married, the fewer favorable qualities one spouse saw in the other and the less highly one spouse believed the other to be evaluated by other people. In other words, disillusionment seemed to have occurred. Luckey also found that marital satisfaction was positively related to shorter marriage, getting married later, obtaining more education, and having fewer children.

Howard and Dawes (1976) developed a simple method of predicting marital satisfaction. They instructed couples to keep track of the number of times they had sexual intercourse and the number of times they had arguments during a period of 35 consecutive days. They found that occurrences of intercourse minus occurrences of arguments effectively predicted marital happiness. Thornton's (1977) replication of this study found both occurrences of sexual intercourse and occurrences of arguments to be good separate predictors of an individual's marital satisfaction.

Earlier we outlined the importance of communication in marriage and the positive relationship of such factors as self-disclosure to overall marital satisfaction. Some researchers have taken a communication–systems approach to improving a marriage relationship and increasing marital satisfaction. Bockus's (1975) paradigm is a feedback loop, with constant needs assessment, goal setting, implementation of changes, and evaluation going on within marriage. Sherwood and Scherer (1975) also take a process focus, advocating preventive maintenance for couples. They believe that open communication, information sharing, stability, and willingness to renegotiate the marriage contract are all necessary to reduce marital disruption. Still another study found that couples could be taught to improve their communication and thence their relationship by open speaking and empathic listening (D'Augelli, Deys, Guerney, Hershenberg, & Sborofsky, 1974).

We can see that prediction of marital satisfaction is a complex issue. Not only do premarital factors such as socioeconomic background, education, and parental influences affect satisfaction, so do postmarital occurrences such as the number of children and the quality of ongoing marital communication.

The Curvilinearity Issue

A curvilinear relationship between length of marriage and marital satisfaction has been shown in several studies (for example, Rollins & Cannon, 1974), with satisfaction rising in the years immediately following marriage, then falling during the middle or child-rearing years, and rising again later in the marriage. Spanier, Lewis, and Cole (1975) found some evidence of curvilinearity in their study of three subsamples of couples from three different geographical areas, but they pointed out that the methodological problems involved in cross-sectional research (research where different groups are sampled at the same time) may bias the data and that longitudinal research (research where the same group is sampled at different times) is to be much preferred. Spanier continued his research on the subject and eventually developed a marital adjustment scale (1976), incorporating the best items from several previously used scales.

Rollins and Cannon (1974) replicated two earlier studies of marital satisfaction and found that, in spite of various assessment problems in the study, a curvilinear pattern of satisfaction did emerge. In seeking to explain their result, the authors drew upon the research of Burr (1973) concerning problems of role strain as they affect a couple through the life cycle. Although we will discuss role strain (as well as role conflict and role incompatibility) in our detailed discussion of changing sex roles in Chapter 8, we will describe it here as the stress an individual experiences when he or she has difficulty coping with various role expectations. Rollins and Cannon point out that role stresses and strains are created and intensified by work pressures, family responsibilities, and social obligations, factors that are all likely to be particularly intense during the middle, child-rearing years of the marriage and family life cycle, a period that research reveals as somewhat low in marital satisfaction. During later years, when careers are usually well established and children have been "launched" into their own independent lifestyles, a couple's role pressures decrease, and marital satisfaction is likely to rise again. In some sense having an empty nest may well be a positive step toward having a full life! The authors thus reason that role strain is a variable that may mediate between family life cycle and marital satisfaction, and they propose research that will look directly at role strain and marital satisfaction. "A more direct focus on the antecedents of role strain in terms of the family career would probably have much more theoretical and practical value than further attempts to find out more definitively the relationship between stages of the family life cycle and marital satisfaction" (Rollins & Cannon, 1974, p. 281). In another study role strain in an individual is correlated with decreased sexual satisfaction both in couples seeking some type of therapy and in nonpatient couples (Frank, Anderson, & Rubinstein, 1979). Lower levels of role strain are found in nonpatient than in patient couples, but even in these so-called "normal" couples, greater role pressure means less sexual pleasure.

Sex Differences in Marital Satisfaction

It appears that men and women experience marriage—and marital satisfaction—in somewhat different ways. Bernard (1972) describes this differential experience as "his" and "her" marriages and states that "there is by now a very considerable body of well-authenticated research to show that there really are two marriages in every marital union, and that they do not always coincide" (p. 5). Corsini (1956) was one of the first researchers to point out that different variables predict marital satisfaction for wives and husbands. In a more recent analysis, Wills, Weiss, and Patterson (1974) had couples rate each other's behavior over a two-week period, including both instrumental (task-type) behaviors and affective (emotional) behaviors. Behaviors were rated on two dimensions: instrumental/affective and displeasurable/pleasurable. In terms of displeasurable behaviors, instrumental and affective behaviors equally affected husbands and wives. For pleasurable behaviors, however, a wife's instrumental behaviors were more important to her husband, but a husband's affective behaviors were more important to his wife. Since husbands have traditionally been expected to be more instrumental or task oriented and wives are supposed to be emotional or affective, this study showed that each spouse desired behavior from the other that was contrary to sex-role expectations.

To put this in concrete terms, let's assume that we have viewed Scott and Sandy rather traditionally up to this time. We have seen Sandy be affectionate and openly demonstrative with Scott, even though he is a bit shy. We have also seen Scott take command in certain situations and perform specific tasks around the house such as paying the bills and cutting the grass. If they had participated in Wills et al.'s study, results would show that Scott really wants Sandy to do task behaviors such as paying the bills, and Sandy wants Scott to be openly warm and affectionate. Each spouse wants the other to give behaviors that the other person is not really "trained" to give. Each may thus hold unrealistic expectations for the spouse, may be frequently disappointed, and may experience reduced marital satisfaction. We have discussed the Wills et al. study in some detail, even though it has considerable methodological problems (such as a very small sample) because its results reflect the wide-ranging expectations that most spouses have for each other, expectations which often cannot be met.

Although extensive reviews of marital satisfaction research have been conducted (for example, Riskin & Faunce, 1972), our purpose is to point out some of the important factors which influence marital satisfaction, whether in "his" marriage or "hers," as well as to discuss how marital satisfaction may change over the family life cycle. To briefly note a few of the methodological difficulties in conducting marital satisfaction research, we might remember that recruitment of subjects is more difficult, because both partners must agree to participate in any research project. Two heads may be better than one, but they are also harder to get!

Another issue involves how and where to study couples. It is rather difficult to see couples in their homes, at least for a substantial length of time, but, if they are interviewed in a laboratory setting, the atmosphere is often formal and stilted, and spouses may not interact naturally. Research with couples has most often involved questionnaires or other paper-and-pencil instruments, although behavioral observation and even video- or audiotaping of couples has become a more favored technique in recent years.

Another problem in marital research is that many different kinds of professionals do such research, and different professionals ask different questions. Analytically trained clinicians may be interested in spouses' early-childhood experiences. Cognitive-behaviorists will assign homework tasks and assess how various positive and negative rewards may affect spouses' behaviors and subsequent marital satisfaction. A structural family therapist may well look at an entirely different set of variables. We thus have a variety of couples, research settings, test instruments and methods, and researchers. It is small wonder then that we still have so many questions about how to achieve and then maintain marital satisfaction.

Summary

Communication, both verbal and nonverbal, is an important component of marriage, and quantity and quality of communication have been found to differentiate between happy and unhappy couples. Self-disclosure is of great significance in communication and was developed conceptually by Jourard. Social penetration theory includes self-disclosure as the primary method of relationship progression, and self-disclosure is believed to be influenced by variables such as trust, modeling, reciprocity, and intimacy. Women appear to be more highly disclosing than men in many situations, although self-disclosure has been found to be strongly related to marital satisfaction for both wives and husbands. Couples' communication can sometimes be improved through education or counseling, and selective self-disclosure has been suggested as a way to help communication.

Marital conflict usually involves a conflict of interest between spouses and can range from unstructured conflict, sometimes called fights, where each spouse may try verbally or nonverbally to get the other, to structured conflict or debates, where very reasonable and civilized behavior may be exercised. Marital conflict occurs in many different situations and may often involve misperceptions by one partner of the causes of the other partner's behavior. One important outcome of productive conflict is that the partners agree to disagree, though misperceptions can be resistant to change. Marriage conflict can occur when communication becomes more negative than positive or when spouses believe that the marriage itself is in jeopardy, and spouses may actually try to decrease communication behaviors in a highly intimate conflict situation. An extension of marital conflict is wife abuse, which was briefly discussed in terms of historical development and present existence.

Bases of social power include reward, coercive, legitimate, referent, and expert power, which can also be thought of as bases for marital power. Bargaining is also an important factor in marriage processes. Exchange theory offers a framework for marital power research, and the spouse with the greatest number of socioeconomic resources has often been assumed to be the most powerful spouse. Men's attainment of power has often precluded women's attainment of power, but the women's movement may change that somewhat. Husbands and wives have been perceived as holding different kinds of social power, and heterosexual men and women may use different power strategies. Both observational and self-report research techniques should be used in further studies of marital power and of marriage in general.

Scholars have become more interested in marital satisfaction during recent years because of the rising divorce rate. Factors such as conflict, parental influence, sexual behavior, length of marriage, number of children, and education have all been related to marital satisfaction. Communication also is significantly related to marital happiness. Marital satisfaction often has a curvilinear relationship with length of marriage, and although there are some methodological problems with marital satisfaction studies, curvilinearity may be influenced by role strain, which mediates between family life cycle and marital satisfaction. Men and women experience marriage—and marital satisfaction—quite differently, so both spouses must participate in any kind of marital satisfaction research.

8

Issues in Contemporary Relationships

What do we know about divorce? Although that may appear to be a rhetorical question, it is not. Because of the frequency of divorce in society, you are very likely to have personal knowledge of divorce, either as children in a family in which the parents have been divorced or as relatives or friends of a divorcing couple. Some of you may even be divorced yourselves. In any case you probably know firsthand the mixed feelings, the pain and loss, and the revitalization that may accompany divorce. This book has discussed at considerable length the means by which relationships are forged and maintained. Another dimension of relationship progress is relationship failure and subsequent dissolution, and many of the issues that we have studied in regard to relationship development will prove equally relevant to relationship disintegration (that is, social exchange, communication, conflict). We will discuss some of the major causes as well as consequences of divorce, and we will look at an increasingly common phenomenon, the blended family.

Separation and Divorce

Prevalence of Marital Disruption

Although none of us would deny that divorce is steadily increasing, actual divorce statistics vary from source to source. However, whether one of four, one of three, or one of two marriages ends in divorce, divorce is clearly a major social issue. As they survey historical patterns of marriage and divorce in the United States over the past 50 years, Norton and Glick (1979) note that the divorce rate has substantially increased overall, as the first-marriage and remarriage rates have declined. People are tending to marry later and to produce fewer children. The number of divorces is to some degree balanced by the number of remarriages, however, so that "four out of every five people who go through a first divorce remarry, most within three to five years of their final decree" (Norman, 1980, p. 44). Thus divorce does not appear to be a repudiation of the structure of the family so much as the repudiation of a particular marital partner.

Although divorce has been a historical reality in the United States since Colonial times (Scanzoni, 1979b), marriage was considered inviolable by both ecclesiastical (church) and secular courts, and divorces were granted reluctantly. Desertion was one method used to end an unhappy marriage, if a divorce proved to be too difficult to obtain. Scanzoni points out that Colonial women lacked the social and economic resources increasingly available to modern women; thus, for that reason alone, women were less likely to sue for divorce than they are now. Husbands were in a better position to obtain alternatives to an unhappy situation. However, as women came to be considered less as the "property" of the husband and more as "partners" in the relationship, they also became more likely than men to petition for divorce. By 1975, 73 percent of all divorces in the United States were granted to the wife (Norton & Glick, 1979).

Causes of Marital Disruption

Divorce occurs across all socioeconomic levels, although lower socioeconomic groups are hit proportionately harder by it. Individuals with limited education, low professional status, and low income (often people who marry at a very young age) are those who will divorce more frequently and who may take longer to remarry. Furstenberg (1979) relates premarital pregnancy to marital instability, both because it disrupts the courtship process and cuts short a premarital stage of development and because it acts as a limiting force on economic success. Pope and Mueller (1979) believe that there is some evidence for intergenerational transmission of marital instability, though research findings are somewhat mixed. This will perhaps remain a question until the present generation of children who are growing up in divorced households begin to succeed or fail in their own marriages.

Levinger (for example, 1979a, 1979b) views marital dissolution in the same framework in which he views relationship development (see Chapter 6). He describes spouses as persons who are involved in an interdependent, cohesive relationship. These qualities are intensified by spouses' attraction for one another and for the relationship, with attraction (rewards) to marriage consisting of "(1) material rewards, derived from income and ownership; (2) symbolic rewards, obtained from family status and mutual similarity; and (3) affectional rewards, associated with companionship and sexual enjoyment" (Levinger, 1979a, p. 44). Interdependence and cohesiveness are lessened by the costs of the relationship as well as by competing attractions (rewards) outside the relationship. In addition to attractions the relationship is maintained by barriers to dissolution such as social pressure to stay married, mutual economic investments, fear of children's reactions to dissolution, and so on. In a purely exchange-theory sense, spouses who experience either high attraction (reward) to each other and/or who perceive strong barriers (costs) to marital dissolution are likely to remain married. Spouses who experience either low rewards or high costs in relating to each other and who perceive few costs to dissolution are likely to divorce. In addition spouses' perceptions of likely alternative attractions may also influence the reward/cost balance.

Relationship dissolution has been examined by various researchers (for example, Harvey, Wells, & Alvarez, 1978; Hill, Rubin, & Peplau, 1979) in the context of intimate but not marital relationships. In one study Harvey and his colleagues extensively interviewed persons who were going or living together, primarily to assess how each individual felt about areas of conflict in his or her relationship and then to predict

FIGURE 8-1 Some relationships seem to have greater costs than rewards. *(Copyright, 1980, Jules Feiffer. Reprinted with permission of Universal Press Syndicate. All rights reserved.)*

how his or her partner would feel about those same areas. Although male and female partners showed considerable similarity in how they perceived conflict in the relationship, there were also some definite sex differences. Males attributed greater conflict potential to sexual incompatibility and to disloyalty, while females attributed more significance to financial problems and to stresses associated with work and educational activities. What is perhaps more significant is that

> males showed inaccuracy in: (a) overestimating females' attribution of importance to sexual incompatibility; (b) underestimating females' attribution of importance to financial factors; and (c) underestimating females' attribution of importance to stress associated with work or educational activities. Females showed inaccuracy in underestimating males' attribution of importance to sexual incompatibility and the influence of important events; also, females overestimated males' attribution of importance to financial problems and stress associated with work or educational activities [Harvey et al., 1978, p. 247].

The critical factor here is not that partners disagree about causes of conflict but that *partners do not know how much they disagree.* Partners make assumptions about each other and then often act on those assumptions without checking to see if they are accurate. Hill, Rubin, and Peplau (1979) found that college couples tended to sever their relationships during natural "breaks," such as summer vacation or the period between quarters or semesters. Not surprisingly, the partner who was less emotionally involved in the relationship was the one who usually initiated the breakup, though women were more likely to end relationships, whether they were the less—or the more—involved partner. Actual reasons for severing a relationship can vary from fear of conflict (including physical abuse) to poor communication, unsatisfactory sex, boredom, financial problems, one partner's involvement with someone else outside the relationship, and on and on. Just as no two persons are exactly alike, so no two divorces are exactly the same.

The Course of Marital Dissolution

The dissolution of a marriage is usually not undertaken lightly, and separation or divorce may be discussed for several years before it actually occurs. Separation does not itself always lead to divorce; Levinger (1979b) found that, in one midwestern sample, couples who had not physically separated at the time of filing for divorce were more likely to dismiss the divorce proceedings and stay together than were separated couples. Thus physical separation seems to propel a couple closer to dissolution, or as Levinger suggests, separation removes one more barrier to a subsequent divorce.

Various authors (for example, Cherlin, 1979; Levinger, 1979b) have noted that a higher income on the part of the husband increases the likelihood of marital stability, though income by the wife may have the opposite effect. Since women may be more likely than men to end relationships under any circumstances, when women have viable economic alternatives to being supported by a husband, they may elect to divorce.

After a couple has decided to seek a divorce (or during the decision-making process), they are likely to consult professionals such as lawyers, clergy, and psychotherapists. After extensive interviews with all three types of professionals, Kressel, Lopez-Morillas, Weinglass, and Deutsch (1979) found that lawyers tended to experience the greatest amount of role strain, perhaps because of their more intense involvement in the adversarial aspects of the divorce process. The authors describe six basic stances taken by attorneys, described in Box 8-1. All three types of professionals agreed that divorce is an unfolding process, beginning with (1) the establishment of a working alliance between all parties involved and continuing with (2) information gathering, (3) improving the emotional climate (therapists and clergy are more comfortable establishing such things as emotional cooling-off periods), and (4) decision making and planning. It is in the last area that lawyers can actively help clients work on the nuts and bolts of establishing a divorce agreement and planning for the future. Many professional groups have begun offering various types of counseling to aid divorcing couples in navigating the hazardous waters of the divorce process, and the Roman Catholic Church has been quite helpful in planning programs to aid in postdivorce adjustment (Kressel et al., 1979).

BOX 8-1   Six basic stances of divorce attorneys. *(Adapted from "Professional intervention in divorce: The views of lawyers, psychotherapists, and clergy," by K. Kressel, M. Lopez-Morillas, J. Weinglass, and M. Deutsch. In G. Levinger and O. C. Moles (Eds.),* Divorce and separation. *New York: Basic Books, 1979.)*

The Undertaker	Believes that the job is thankless and unpleasant and may feel little respect for the client.
The Mechanic	Believes that technical competence is all that is required and stays quite uninvolved with the client.
The Mediator	Tries to negotiate a rational compromise without putting clients in an adversary position.
The Social Worker	Takes into account the client's postdivorce adjustment and the total social welfare of the family.
The Therapist	Engages the client emotionally as well as legally; frequently approves of mental health professionals and disapproves of the traditional legal system.
The Moral Agent	Clear, nonneutral involvement with clients and an attempt to get the "right" outcome, particularly for the children.

Although divorce can certainly be an agonizing process, much of the emotional trauma occurs after the actual divorce, when real feelings of loss take place. During the divorce pragmatic and often far-reaching decisions must be made in relation to economic support, property division, and custody of minor children. Although the stories of acrimonious property settlements, in which one partner tries to take the other to the cleaners, are legion, many couples do not have a lot of property to divide. In addition, two households cannot be maintained as cheaply as one, so, after a divorce occurs, at the very least two sets of rent and utilities must be paid. Although a divorced woman may well seek full-time employment outside the home, her earning potential is probably considerably less than that of her ex-husband, so, even though the family expenses may double, the family income will not. Thus "in 1976, 52 percent of children in female-headed families were in families with incomes below the poverty level" (Bane, 1979, p. 283). Economic problems are accompanied by issues of custody and visitation, which we will consider as we look at the consequences of divorce for the parties involved.

Consequences of Marital Dissolution

In their comprehensive overview of marital disruption as a source of stress, Bloom, Asher, and White (1978) review the research linking divorce and separation to a wide variety of emotional and physical disorders and propose some conceptual explanations for these links. First, marital status (and by implication disruption) has been consistently linked to psychological disturbance. Adult admission rates to psychiatric facilities are highest among the divorced and separated, and the relationship between marital disruption and psychiatric distress is somewhat stronger for men than for women, contrary to common expectations.

In terms of physical disturbance, victims of marital disruption (widowed, separated, and divorced) had higher rates of illness and disability than did married or never-married persons, and higher rates of alcoholism and incidence of automobile accidents occur among maritally disrupted persons (Bloom et al., 1978). Suicide, homicide, and disease mortality have all been linked to marital disruption. Persons who have incurred the loss of a loved one through death or divorce are "significantly overrepresented among those who commit suicide and . . . significantly underrepresented among those who attempt it" (p. 873). Deaths from tuberculosis, cirrhosis of the liver, some types of cancer, diabetes mellitus, arteriosclerotic heart disease, and other coronary disease all occur more frequently to those who have experienced some type of marital disruption. Factors such as financial difficulties, problems with children, sexual problems, feelings of failure and shame, needing to go to work (usually faced by the single mother), and loneliness (usually faced more strongly by the noncustodial parent, most often the father) will undoubtedly create differing levels of stress in nearly all who face them.

Robert Weiss (1979), who has conducted extensive research with divorced persons, notes that, even when love, friendship, and all the other positive feelings between ex-spouses disappear, a strong *attachment* still exists, a bond that cannot be described as positive or negative but one that persists well beyond the point of divorce. Of course divorce is not a simple action occurring at a single point in time. Bohannan (1970) views divorce as a complex event involving at least six different kinds of separation: (1) legal divorce, (2) emotional divorce (losing a once-loved one), (3) economic divorce, (4) coparental divorce (when children are involved), (5) community divorce (including the couple's social network), and (6) psychic divorce (concerning the individual's attempt to be independent and self-secure). Given the complexity of the process, one can easily understand why real adjustment to divorce can take a long time.

Bloom and his colleagues note that research has been much more successful in linking marital disruption to stress-related disorders than in showing exactly why such disruption causes disorder, though four possible hypotheses are proposed. First, the *premarital-disability* hypothesis proposes that people with physical or emotional disorders before marriage are less likely to marry or, if they marry, are less likely to achieve a successful relationship. Second, the *postmarital-disability* hypothesis suggests that disabilities that arise after marriage will increase marital disruption. Third, the *protective-marriage* hypothesis posits that the status of marriage somehow reduces an individual's vulnerability to certain diseases. This concept does not account for the fact that never-married persons tend to be healthier than those who have experienced marital disruption. If marriage is a panacea, how do never-married persons manage to stay well? The fourth hypothesis is the *stressor concept,* which states that marital disruption is a major source of physical and psychic stress, and it is to this hypothesis that Bloom et al. give greatest attention, noting that "for both men and women, married persons were less depressed than persons in all other marital status categories" (p. 882). Several researchers have concluded that marital disruption is just one of many stressful life events (both positive and negative) that cause the individuals involved to experience a variety of physical and emotional disorders. Although various disabilities are likely to exist in an individual marriage and may well contribute to marital disruption, disruption may also exacerbate previously existing disabilities.

One aspect of the stress caused by marital disruption is the economic problems mentioned earlier. For divorced men who continue to support their families, expenses seem never ending. The contemporary cost of living and rising inflation strain upper-middle-class incomes, but wreak havoc on lower incomes. Although some fathers continue to be active in economically supporting their children, "the resources men bring to families are for the most part withdrawn following the divorce" (Kohen, Brown, & Feldberg, 1979, p. 234). When support is not forthcoming, women must rely on their own economic success in the work world (usually much more limited than men's success) or on social service agencies such as welfare (Aid to Families with Dependent Children). And no economic help comes without strings attached. Money is often used as a source of power, whether by the welfare department or by an ex-spouse.

Bane (1979) estimates that, based on present divorce rates, about 30 percent of the children growing up in the 1970s will experience parental divorce. In 1976 alone there were more than 1 million divorces, averaging 1.08 children per divorce, so that over 1 million children were affected by divorce in the span of a single year. Research on the effects of divorce on children has proliferated as divorce rates have accelerated (for example, Hetherington, Cox, & Cox, 1979; Kelly & Wallerstein, 1976), and several findings have emerged. As Weiss (1979) points out, at the present time over 90 percent of minor children are entrusted to the mother, while the father receives custody less than 10 percent of the time. Contrary to popular television and movie mythology, most custody decisions are made outside the courtroom, and Gersick (1979) discovered that in many "cases where fathers took custody, it was with the mothers' pre-trial consent" (p. 321). Although a man's relationships in his family of origin appeared to affect his seeking of custody, Gersick did not find fathers with custody to have more actively participated in child rearing before the divorce than did fathers without custody.

In comparing children in the custody of the father, children in the custody of the mother, and children from intact families, Santrock and Warshak (1979) found no major differences between the children in their levels of mature and socially competent behavior. However, in divorced families children who lived with the same-sex parent appeared better adjusted than children who lived with the opposite-sex parent. In other words, boys did better with father custody and girls with mother custody. In addition, all children fared better when the parenting was authoritative (warm, clear rule-setting, extensive verbal exchanges) rather than authoritarian or laissez-faire. In his discussion of the historical patterns of adjudication of custody, Weiss (1979) suggests that present practices of custody and visitation are less than successful, though the newer approach of *joint custody* has yet to prove much better. Basically, a child needs something after a divorce that he or she may not have had before the divorce—a good relationship with each of the parents individually and at least a reasonably supportive relationship *between* the parents.

As he discusses the stresses of single parenting, Weiss notes the almost superhuman effort required to keep a family functioning. By the time a parent has coped with employment, child care, housework and cooking, home repairs and maintenance, homework, medical and dental appointments, and the like and then gone on to nurture, listen to problems, arbitrate disputes, and read bedtime stories, there may be little or no energy available to interact with extended family and friends, to initiate new intimate relationships, or even find a little quiet, private time. Although the parent–child relationships may be quite satisfying and family life conflict free and rewarding, the task of the single parent is still a monumental one.

In discussing the changes in family structure that accompany divorce and that may affect children, Longfellow (1979) mentions the absence of the father, the effects of single motherhood, conflict in the family, quality of parent–child relationships, parents' mental health, and family support networks. The issue of conflict is a complex one, since children fare worse in intact families with high conflict levels than in divorced families with lower conflict levels. Longfellow also points out that, because children react differently to stressful life events during different developmental periods, researchers must take a child's age (and stage) into account when assessing the child's response to divorce. Table 8-1 presents some typical reactions to parental divorce by children of varying ages.

Hetherington, Cox, and Cox (1979) conducted a study over time of the effects of divorce on children's play patterns and social interactions and found that, although there initially were disruptions of play and social interactions, these effects lessened over time. Immediately following divorce, both boys and girls showed less maturity and imagination in their play and a greater degree of unhappiness. Improvement was seen over the two-year time span, however, with girls exhibiting greater improvement. Hess and Camara (1979) evaluated children from divorced and intact families and discovered that "For divorced and intact groups combined, the relationships among family members appeared to be more potent influences on child behavior than was marital status. The negative effects of divorce were greatly mitigated when positive relationships with both parents were maintained. The child's relationship with the non-custodial parent (father) was as important as the continuing relationship with the mother" (pp. 79–80). In other words, if children can continue to maintain positive close relationships with both parents, they may achieve successful academic and social adjustment. Although a high level of conflict between the parents (whether married or divorced) may stress the child, the parents' relationship with each other is a less critical factor than the child's relationship with each parent. Perhaps because there are many ways in which a child can receive emotional and social support without being part of an

TABLE 8-1   Reaction to parental divorce by children of varying ages

Ages	Reaction
Preschool, 2½–6 years	Fear, confusion, and blame of self. Difficulty in expressing feelings.
Early elementary, 7–8 years	Easier expression of fear, sadness, and loss. Anger at parents, but hope for reconciliation.
Later elementary, 9–10 years	More realistic understanding, but anger and outrage at parents. Divided loyalties.
Adolescence, 13–18 years	The most openly upset. Feel anger, shame, and sadness. Relate to both parents. Re-examine own values.
Adult children	The same feelings as adolescents, though may not be similarly expressed. Parental divorce hurts at any age.

Based on "Divorce in Context: Its Impact on Children," by C. Longfellow. In G. Levinger and O. C. Moles (Eds.), *Divorce and separation*. New York: Basic Books, 1979.

intact family, Kulka and Weingarten (1979) found very modest differences in adult adjustment between persons who were from intact families and persons who had experienced a parental separation or divorce before age 16. Divorce is a stressful experience, but it does not have to be a disabling one.

Although the phrase *broken home* has been in use for many years, Ahrons (1980) has coined the term *binuclear family* to more aptly and positively describe a family that has been transformed by divorce, and, as we noted earlier, a degree of attachment does exist between former spouses, both because of deep emotional bonds and present-day shared concerns about finances and children. It is better for the children if their parents get along fairly well (Weiss, 1979), and a tolerant, conflict-free relationship is certainly better for the ex-spouses themselves. Yet much ambivalence usually remains regarding a former partner, and there seems to be no uniform consensus about what these relationships should be like (Goetting, 1980). The complexity is increased greatly if or when one of the spouses remarries; if there are children involved, the total family group becomes part of a rapidly increasing phenomenon in the United States, the blended family.

Blended Families

Definitions

Any discussion of the topic of blended families must necessarily begin with definitions, because even the phrase *blended families* may be new to many readers. Reconstituted families, blended families, stepfamilies—all basically the same entity—make up nearly 15 percent of all families in the United States according to recent statistics (Visher & Visher, 1979). Yet the millions of stepchildren and stepparents are almost completely ignored by our culture, and the intact nuclear family is the model touted in most situations. Stepfamilies or blended families, as we will refer to them, can differ among themselves. One family may have a natural father with his children and a stepmother without previous children; another family may consist of a man and a woman, each with children, who marry and combine families. There are many types of blended families, and these in turn differ from other types of family patterns. A comparison of several family structures is shown in Table 8-2. Although blended families share characteristics with other family types, they have many unique properties. One major issue for the blended family, as for the single-parent one, is the need to confront the pain and loss of separation by death or divorce. When a parent dies, the loss is irrevocable, and mechanisms for grieving are fairly clear cut. Though the situation cannot be said to be easier than that which occurs after divorce, it is at least clearer. When parents divorce, however, children often continue to relate to both parents and must necessarily

TABLE 8-2 Family structures in the United States

	Stepfamilies	Nuclear families	Single-parent families	Adoptive families	Foster families
	Biological parent elsewhere.	—	Biological parent elsewhere.	Biological parent elsewhere.	Biological parent elsewhere.
	Virtually all members have recently sustained a primary relationship loss.	—	All members have recently sustained a primary relationship loss.	The children have sustained a primary relationship loss.	The children have sustained a primary relationship loss.
	An adult couple in the household.	An adult couple in the household.	—	Usually an adult couple in the household.	Usually an adult couple in the household.
	Relationship between one adult (parent) and child predates the marriage.	—	—	Relationship between one adult (parent) and child predates the marriage *where stepchildren are adopted.*	—
	Children are members in more than one household.	—	Children may be members in more than one household.	—	Children may be members in more than one household.
	One adult (stepparent) not legally related to a child (stepchild).	—	—	—	The adults have no legal relationship to the child.

Note: The terms *biological parent* and *natural parent* are used synonymously as are the terms *nuclear family* and *intact family.*

From *Stepfamilies: A Guide to Working with Stepparents and Stepchildren,* by E. B. Visher and J. S. Visher. Copyright © 1979 by Brunner Mazel, Inc. Reprinted by permission.

deal with continuing feelings of loss. Children may fantasize the reuniting of their parents and may work actively to get their parents back together. When this is not possible, youngsters may play one parent off against the other for various reasons or may sabotage new relationships of one or both parents. Most of us are resistant to drastic changes in our personal relationships and our general lifestyles, and children are no exception. Thus the addition of new parents, siblings, grandparents, and other extended family may not be welcome—at least initially.

There has been a minimum amount of research on blended families during the past decade, though much more research will undoubtedly be directed to this area in the future. Visher and Visher (1979), in their comprehensive survey of blended families, summarize the research in the following manner:

1. At the present time one half million adults become stepparents each year in the United States.
2. One of every six American children under 18 is a stepchild.
3. There is a positive correlation between socioeconomic status and stepfamily success.
4. Studies of adults indicate that individuals growing up in stepfather families do not differ in measures of social functioning from individuals growing up in nuclear families.
5. Stepmother–stepchild relationships are much more tentative and difficult than stepfather–stepchild relationships.
6. Stepsibling relationships are relatively good, especially when there is a half-sibling to join the two groups together.
7. Stepfamilies experience more psychological stress than do intact families.
8. Stepmothers have difficulties with the negative *Stepmother* image [pp. 48–49].

Typical Problems in Blended Families

Although blended families have all the typical problems of any family—such as parent–child conflict, shortage of money, and sibling rivalry—blended families are uniquely stressed by *mythology*. One of the primary myths is the *bad-stepmother* myth (Schulman, 1979), which arises in large measure from fairy tales such as "Cinderella" and "Snow White." In the first story the stepmother is portrayed as an insensitive, slave-driving shrew who blatantly favors her two "natural" daughters over her stepdaughter. In the second story the stepmother is so jealous of her stepdaughter's youth and beauty that she arranges to have the girl murdered. What a terrible indictment of stepmothers! And how unfair! Schulman notes that, whether there has been a death or a divorce, "the stepmother is a newcomer to an already formed relationship and is seen both as a rescuer as well as an intruder into the father–child dyad"

(p. 214). If a stepmother tries diligently to create a homelike atmosphere and meet the needs of the stepchild, she is accused of trying to take the natural mother's place. If she takes a less-involved, laissez-faire position, she may be blamed for not caring.

It is not our goal here to paint a completely gloomy picture of the role of stepmother, but the problems facing her are real. Perhaps the biggest trap of stepmothering is trying to be perfect. If one tries to love one's stepchildren instantly and completely and then create a tightly knit happy family where everyone is supremely content all the time, one is doomed to fail. There is no perfect blended family, just as there is no perfect intact family.

Men in stepfamilies have their own set of problems. The mythology surrounding stepfathers is less prevalent than that surrounding stepmothers, though the mean, brutal stepfather is certainly an image some people hold. Fathers are very often put into the role of disciplinarian, and this can mean problems with stepchildren if discipline precedes the establishment of a friendly relationship. A stepfather needs to have a friendly and at least somewhat secure relationship with his stepchildren before he can effectively discipline them without causing great family conflict. Men may feel considerable guilt if they live with stepchildren but have only visitation periods with their own natural children, and this can create the *superdad* myth, in which the father tries to pack a month's worth of play and loving into each day or weekend visit. The natural children may be overwhelmed, and the stepchildren may look on with envy. As with stepmothers, stepfathers need to frame realistic expectations of themselves and everyone else in the family. They need to accept the limits placed on them as stepfathers and/or as fathers without primary custody of their natural (biological) children. Men who live with both their natural children and their stepchildren have a particular challenge to work out their relationships with each individual child in a satisfactory manner. Visher and Visher (1979) point out that the changing sex roles in the United States, which are causing some men to be more accepting of their nurturance tendencies, are likely to hold positive prospects for blended families.

Although men and women clearly need to deal with their parent roles in a blended family, they also need to deal with their roles as spouses. Each spouse has come from a different family background with different rules and norms. In addition, each has had a primary bond with another marriage partner for whom there may still be some feelings of attachment. Although positive bonds between a mate and his or her ex-spouse may be threatening to a new spouse, as we noted earlier, such bonds have profound effects on the emotional stability of the children. Financial problems may be particularly accentuated for the blended family, because there may well be alimony and child support payments flowing both into and out of the family, and these payments may not balance. Often there is less income than outgo. And of course the normal parenting problems may be exacerbated in the blended family. Perhaps the most important aspect of the couple's relationship is the strength of the marital bond. The varying stresses of a blended family can only be handled successfully when the marital bond is healthy, unlike intact families, when very marginal marriages can still accompany a fairly successful family system.

Children in a blended family differ from the adults in the family in one major respect: the children did not *choose* a blended family. The adults made the choices, and the children had to accept them. Although they confront problems of unreasonable expectations of themselves and their parents and the complex logistics of living in a blended family, children are particularly concerned by feelings of loss and questions of loyalty and belongingness. If they successfully complete the mourning process that should follow loss, the children still need to learn that love and loyalty can be given to two different households and two different sets of parents. A child can feel affection for a noncustodial parent, a custodial parent, and a stepparent without having to feel guilty. Of course the level of friendliness (or conflict) between ex-spouses determines to a great extent a child's freedom to love (or at least like) everyone. If ex-spouses are hostile to each other and/or to each other's new spouses, the children involved are likely to have considerable difficulty in handling their own feelings positively. Although we have focused to a great degree on the problems of blended families, such families may offer positive benefits to children in the form of an additional extended family and new role models and relationships that can greatly enrich the child's life experience.

Supports for Blended Families

Although many families develop their own social support network via family, friends, and neighbors, many blended families turn to religious and mental health professionals for help in coping. Therapy can be helpful, beginning with the couple and extending to the children and perhaps even to the ex-spouses. Such sessions may focus on communication, family rules, or eradicating myths and on establishing a realistic basis for cooperation. Parent education or support groups can help parents feel less alone and can also offer new strategies for maintaining a blended family. In addition, books dealing with blended families (such as Noble & Noble, 1977; Roosevelt & Lofas, 1976; Visher & Visher, 1979) can offer both comfort and clarity. Although much of the therapeutic work with a blended family may stress solving practical family problems, there must be a concomitant recognition that feelings of anger, love, guilt, loss, and fear need to be dealt with also. Emily and John Visher, themselves members of a blended family, have compiled a commonsense list of guidelines for stepfamilies, reproduced in Box 8-2.

(Text continues on p. 243.)

BOX 8-2 Guidelines for stepfamilies. (*From* Stepfamilies: A Guide to Working with Stepparents and Stepchildren, *by E. B. Visher and J. S. Visher. Copyright © 1979 by Brunner/Mazel, Inc. Reprinted by permission.*)

GUIDELINES FOR STEPFAMILIES

1. It is difficult to have a new person or persons move into your "space," and it is difficult to be the "new" person or people joining a preexisting group. For these reasons it helps to cut down feelings involved with "territory" if families can start out in a new house or apartment.

2. Parent-child relationships have preceded the new couple relationship. Because of this, many parents feel that it is a betrayal of the parent-child bond to form a primary relationship with their new partner. A primary couple relationship, however, is usually crucial for the continuing existence of the stepfamily, and therefore is very important for the children as well as for the adults. A strong adult bond can protect the children from another family loss, and it also can provide the children with a positive model for their own eventual marriage relationship. The adults often need to arrange time alone to help nourish this important couple relationship.

3. Forming new relationships within the stepfamily can be important, particularly when the children are young. Activities involving different subgroups can help such relationships grow. For example, stepfather and stepchildren might do some project together; or stepmother and a stepchild might go shopping together.

4. Preserving original relationships is also important and can help children experience less loss at sharing a parent. So at times it is helpful for a parent and natural children to have some time together, in addition to stepfamily activities.

5. Caring relationships take time to evolve. The expectation of "instant love" between stepparents and stepchildren can lead to many disappointments and difficulties. If the stepfamily relationships are allowed to develop as seems comfortable to the individuals involved, then caring between step-relatives has the opportunity to develop.

6. Subsequent families are structurally and emotionally different from first families. Upset and sadness are experienced by the children and at times by the adults as they react to the loss of their nuclear family or to the loss of a dream of a perfect marriage. Acceptance that a stepfamily is a new type of family is important. It is also very helpful to recognize that this type of family pattern can provide the opportunity for children and adults to grow and mature and lead satisfying lives. Many upsetting behaviors may result from these feelings of insecurity and loss.

7. Because children are part of two biological parents they nearly always have very strong pulls to both of these natural parents. These

divided loyalties often make it difficult for children to relate comfortably to all the parental adults in their lives. Rejection of a stepparent, for example, may have nothing to do with the personal characteristics of the stepparent. In fact, warm and loving stepparents may cause especially severe loyalty conflicts for children. As children and adults are able to accept the fact that children can care for more than two parental adults, then the children's loyalty conflicts can diminish and the new step-relationships improve. While it may be helpful to the children for the adults to acknowledge negative as well as positive feelings about ex-spouses, children may become caught in loyalty conflicts and feel personally insecure if specific critical remarks are made continuously about their other natural parent.

8. Courteous relationships between ex-spouses are important, although they are very difficult for many adults to maintain. If such a relationship can be worked out it is especially helpful to the children. In such instances the children do not get caught in the middle between two hostile parents, there is less need for the children to take sides, and the children are better able to accept and utilize the positive elements in the living arrangements.

Direct contact between the adults can be helpful since it does not place the children in the sometimes powerful position of being message carriers between their natural parents. Although it may be strained, many ex-spouses are able to relate in regards to their children if the focus is kept on their mutual concern for the welfare of the children.

9. Children as well as adults in a stepfamily have a "family history." Suddenly these individuals come together and their sets of "givens" are questioned. Much is to be gained by coming together as a stepfamily unit to work out and develop new family patterns and traditions. During these "family negotiation sessions" the feelings and ideas of all members are important, regardless of age. Many creative solutions can be worked out as a family.

Even when the individuals are able to recognize that patterns are not "right" or "wrong" it takes time and patience to work out satisfying new alternatives. Values (the underlying approach to life in general ways of doing things) do not shift easily. Within a stepfamily different value systems are inevitable because of different previous family histories, and tolerance for these differences can help smooth the process of stepfamily integration. Needs (specific ways individuals relate together, individual preferences, etc.) can usually be negotiated more quickly than can general values. Having an appreciation for and an expectation of such difficulties can make for more flexibility and relaxation in the stepfamily unit. Negotiation and renegotiation are needed by most such families.

10. Being a stepparent is an unclear and at times difficult task. The

wicked stepmother myth contributes to the discomfort of many women, and cultural, structural and personal factors affect the step-parent role. Spouses can be very helpful to one another if they are able to be supportive with the working out of new family patterns. Step-parenting is usually more successful if stepparents carve out a role for themselves that is different from and does not compete with the natural parents.

While discipline is not usually accepted by stepchildren until a friendly relationship has been established (often a matter of 18 to 24 months), both adults do need to support each other's authority in the household. The natural parent may be the primary disciplinarian ini-tially, but when that person is unavailable it is often necessary for that parent to give a clear message to the children that the stepparent is acting as an "authority figure" for both adults in his or her absence.

Unity between the couple is important to the functioning of the stepfamily. When the couple is comfortable with each other, differ-ences between them in regards to the children can sometimes be worked out in the presence of the children, but at no time does it work out for either children or adults to let the children approach each adult separately and "divide and conquer." When disciplinary action is necessary, if it is not kept within the stepfamily household many resentful feelings can be generated. For example, if visitation rights are affected, the noncustodial parent is being included in the action without his or her representation. Such a punishment, then, may lead to difficulties greater than the original behavior that caused the disciplinary action.

11. Integrating a stepfamily that contains teenagers can be particu-larly difficult. Adolescents are moving away from their families in any type of family. In single-parent families teenagers have often been "young adults," and with the remarriage of a parent they may find it extremely difficult or impossible to return to being in a "child" posi-tion again.

Adolescents have more of a previous "family history" and so they ordinarily appreciate having considerable opportunity to be part of the stepfamily negotiations, although they may withdraw from both natural parents and not wish to be part of many of the "family" activities.

12. "Visiting" children usually feel strange and are outsiders in the neighborhood. It can be helpful if they have some place in the house-hold that is their own; for example, a drawer or a shelf for toys and clothes. If they are included in stepfamily chores and projects when they are with the stepfamily they tend to feel more connected to the group. Bringing a friend with them to share the visit and having some active adult participation in becoming integrated into the

neighborhood can make a difference to many visiting children. Knowing ahead of time that there is going to be an interesting activity, stepfamily game of Monopoly, etc., can sometimes give visiting children a pleasant activity to anticipate.

Noncustodial parents and stepparents often are concerned because they have so little time to transmit their values to visiting children. Since children tend to resist concerted efforts by the adults to instill stepfamily ideals during each visit, it is comforting to parents and stepparents to learn that the examples of behavior and relationships simply observed in the household can affect choices made by all the children later in their lives when they are grown and on their own.

13. Sexuality is usually more apparent in stepfamilies because of the new couple relationship, and because children may suddenly be living with other children with whom they have not grown up. Also there are not the usual incest taboos operating. It is important for the children to receive affection and to be aware of tenderness between the couple, but it may also be important for the couple to minimize to some extent the sexual aspects of the household, and to help the children understand, accept, and control their sexual attractions to one another or to the adults.

14. All families experience stressful times. Children tend to show little day-to-day appreciation for their parents, and at times they get angry and reject their natural parents. Because stepfamilies are families born of loss, the mixture of feelings can be even more intense than in intact families. Jealousy, rejection, guilt, and anger can be more pronounced, and therefore expectations that the stepfamily will live "happily ever after" are unrealistic. Having an understanding and acceptance of the many negative as well as positive feelings can result in less disappointment and more stepfamily enjoyment.

15. Keeping even minimal contact between adults and children can lead to future satisfaction since time and maturity bring many changes. With some communication between stepfamily members satisfying interpersonal relationships often develop in the future when children become more independent in their relationships with both natural parents and with stepparents.

A central theme in the guidelines is to be patient, flexible, and tolerant, both of oneself and of others. Blended families are stressful and complicated, but they are here to stay. And, as the Vishers note, "probably the most significant gain for the members of a stepfamily is the opportunity to rekindle a faith in close interpersonal relationships as they experience and share in the remarriage of two adults" (p. 259).

A potent social and political force of the past two decades, closely connected to the topics we are considering, is the feminist movement. It has helped to produce the present changing male/female sex roles in the United States.

Some Words about Sex Roles

Although some observers of contemporary relationships between men and women ascribe the increases in separation and divorce to the rising visibility of the women's movement and the accompanying changes in sex roles, others see an opposite causal relationship, with separation and divorce resulting in situations that require changes in traditional sex roles. In fact, there is an interactive relationship between sex-role changes and many of the aspects of modern society such as open marriage, dual-career couples, increases in divorce, and the women's movement. We cannot be sure exactly "what causes what," but we know that all the factors are related to each other.

Prescribed Sex Roles

One definitional distinction we will make is between *gender identity* and *gender role* or *sex role*. *Gender identity* refers to the individual's emotional and intellectual awareness of being either male or female. Except on rare occasions, it corresponds to the individual's biological sex characteristics, and it is believed to be complete by about age three (Gagnon & Greenblat, 1978). *Gender role* or *sex role* refers to the personality characteristics, attitudes, and behaviors that a society ascribes to a particular sex. Although societies see gender identities similarly (that is, a penis denotes maleness, whether in Samoa or Syracuse), gender roles may be viewed differently (for instance, European men are allowed to be emotional, but American men are not). *Sexual role* is another aspect of this composite and is concerned with the sexual inclinations and behaviors an individual constructs on the basis of a usually already-established gender identity and gender role. There may not always be congruence between these aspects of an individual, because a person may have clear male biological characteristics, a stable identity of maleness, the role performance of accepted male attributes, and the sexual role of desiring other males rather than females (the traditionally accepted sexual choice). Thus there is a discrepancy in *sexual* role.

Few people would argue that boys and girls are raised in exactly the same way in our society. Even before birth, distinctions are made between boys and girls, such as "The baby's so active, it must be a boy" or "You're carrying high, so it must be a girl." Considerable evidence exists that in the United States more people want to have boys than girls—at least for the first child (Unger, 1979). Infants may be treated somewhat differently on the basis of sex, since various research indicates that mothers tend to look at and talk to girl infants more frequently during the first six months of life and to touch boy infants more frequently during the same period (Gagnon & Greenblat, 1978). However, after six months, girls are touched more and are encouraged to stay closer to the mother than are boys. As infants become toddlers and then young children, sex-typed behavior is usually encouraged by the parents and later by the society at large. Boys play with trucks and blocks; they are active, noisy, and curious. They have bedrooms painted in bold colors and designed with lines and angles. Girls play with dolls and toy kitchens; they are passive, quiet, and content. They have bedrooms painted in pastel colors and designed with curves and ruffles.

At very early ages children begin sex typing themselves and others, thereby continuing the patterns their parents have set. As they enter school, new norms for sex stereotyping may emerge. Children with minimal sex typing may be forced to learn that boys don't cook and girls don't play football. On the other hand, youngsters with maximal sex typing may be surprised to learn that both boys and girls get dirty playing soccer together in physical education class. As if parents and children themselves are not enough to maintain traditional sex roles, we can add many teachers, written educational materials, and the media, particularly television. For the most part television portrays males as heroes, or at least central figures, but women too often are portrayed as mere companions or as the semiliterate figures who deal with the problems of floor-wax buildup or ring around the collar.

For the readers who feel we are being inaccurate and/or polemical in the way we are presenting this material, we suggest the following task: At home this evening watch at least one hour of prime-time television. Take a sheet of paper and make four columns, labeled "positive" and "negative" for females and "positive" and "negative" for males (see Table 8-3). As you view the television programs and commercials during this time, put a slash mark in the column for "female–positive" whenever a female says or does something positive and a mark in the "male–positive" column whenever a male behaves in a positive manner. Record negative behaviors in the same way. When you are finished

TABLE 8-3   Television portrayals of women and men

Females		Males	
Positive	*Negative*	*Positive*	*Negative*

watching, tally your results. We suspect that you will find males to be presented much more positively and females more negatively!

Although there clearly are sex differences between females and males, these differences are not always those we would expect to see. Some of the important conclusions from Maccoby and Jacklin's (1974) extensive review of the literature on psychological differences and similarities between females and males are shown in Box 8-3.

As our progressively more sex-typed girls and boys grow into adulthood, they begin transferring their attention from individual growth to relationship formation. Over 85 percent of American females and a slightly smaller percentage of males marry. Although marriage is reputed to be a healthy way to live, it appears to be healthier and more

BOX 8-3   Similarities and differences between females and males. (*Based on* The Psychology of Sex Differences, *by E. E. Maccoby and C. N. Jacklin. Stanford, Calif.: Stanford University Press, 1974.*)

Unfounded beliefs about sex differences
1. Girls are more social than boys.
2. Girls are more suggestible than boys.
3. Girls have lower self-esteem.
4. Girls are better at role learning and simple repetitive tasks, boys at tasks that require higher-level cognitive processing.
5. Boys are more analytic.
6. Girls are more affected by heredity, boys by environment.
7. Girls lack achievement motivation.
8. Girls are auditory, boys are visual.

Rather well established sex differences
1. Girls have greater verbal ability than boys.
2. Boys excel in visual–spatial ability.
3. Boys excel in mathematical ability.
4. Boys are more aggressive.

Questions that are still open
1. Girls and boys differ significantly in tactile sensitivity.
2. Girls and boys differ significantly in fear, timidity, and anxiety.
3. Girls and boys differ significantly in activity level.
4. Girls and boys differ significantly in competitiveness.
5. Girls and boys differ significantly in dominance.
6. Girls and boys differ significantly in compliance.
7. Girls and boys differ significantly in nurturance and maternal behavior.

productive for men than for women. In various studies discussed by Unger (1979), married men are shown to be healthier and more professionally productive than single men, while never-married women rate higher than married women. Although women may be somewhat freer to remain single now that *spinsterhood* is a seldom-used word and women alone are not necessarily seen as society's rejects, statistics indicate that marriage is still the choice of the majority. And marriage can restrict options, particularly for women. Children growing up in traditional families will usually see the father as a more powerful figure than the mother, and once again the view that maleness is more valuable than femaleness is passed on to a new generation.

Nowhere are the different perceptions held of men and women more clear than in the work world. Sherman (1976) points out in her commentary on femininity and competence that it is not "supposed that females in fact are not competent. The point is that in many ways they are *not expected to be* competent" (p. 183). However, as more and more women are employed outside the home, competence in a variety of situations is becoming increasingly important. (Let us clearly note that competence inside the home has always been important, though not always valued).

For the most part women have been less successful than men in the work world in terms of both position and economic benefits. Although this situation has been ascribed to women's inferiority or to women's fear of achievement and success, more and more research seems to indicate that societal and institutional sexism is responsible for much of the career inequity between females and males (see, for example, Forisha, 1978; Unger, 1979). Discrimination exists in the business world, where women are seen as less appropriate for positions of authority, in the academic world, where female professors are patronized and male professors are promoted, and in the white-collar clerical force, where the secretary often trains her boss. But to state the obvious is easy; to change the existing system is extremely difficult.

One way for women to begin getting a piece of the action in the work world is by playing by men's rules in order to achieve success. More women than ever before are enrolled in medical school, law school, and graduate programs (especially in business), realizing that higher education is one proven vehicle for gaining success. Women are also moving into formerly exclusively male-dominated vocations in the skilled trades and utility companies, relying on their agility and physical strength as well as their verbal skills. Women are also beginning to be more willing to travel as part of their jobs and to turn over aspects of child care and home management to their husbands or to paid household help. In other words, women are taking more initiative in trying to increase their own options.

Changing Sex Roles

The women's movement, which began in the 1960s, is really a re-surgence of an earlier push for social change manifested in this century by women's getting the right to vote. One difference that characterizes the contemporary women's movement is the great visibility given it by the media. Whether women are running for Congress or are marching on Washington to protest nuclear arms, they are both vocal and visible. One point that has been underlined by feminism is that women want options to the traditional sex roles previously assigned to them.

Women make up a substantial part of the work force, and the number of working women is increasing. Part of that increase represents choice and part necessity. Most single women are self-supporting, and the steadily rising cost of living requires many women to work outside the home. As we noted earlier, divorced mothers nearly always have to be employed. Now women can choose to work with less of a social stigma than was attached to working before. The day-care movement offers limited help, although it certainly has a long way to go before it can present viable child-care opportunities for all the women who need them. Many women who choose to stay at home with their own young children are choosing also to care for other young children of women who are employed outside the home. Options such as flexible time (in which employees set their own hours within a normal 40-hour week) and shared jobs (two people working part-time sharing one full-time job) have also made working more feasible for women. Job-sharing and, more frequently, flex-time are also popular with men.

The women's movement is only one aspect of changing sex roles, since *men's liberation* has emerged in recent years. Traditional male roles have often required the expression of competition, aggressiveness, and constant competence, along with the suppression of emotions and most affiliative relationships. Jourard (1964) discussed what he considered to be the lethal aspects of maleness in terms of the suppression of emotion and the restrictions on self-disclosure. If women have not been allowed to be strong, men have certainly not been allowed to be weak. And both sexes have been poorly served. Pleck notes that, although men have traditionally expected women to defer to their authority, "the modern male's expectation that women soothe his wounds and re-plenish his emotional reserves places different demands on women, but ones at least equally limiting" (1976, p. 157). Pleck discusses various views of the problems and stresses in the contemporary male role, noting that traditional masculine traits and behaviors may be difficult to attain in modern life, but they are seen as highly desirable by many people. On the other hand, Pleck argues that there may be inherent stresses in a role that has always required males to be instrumental (task-oriented) and now requires them to be expressive (person-oriented) as well. Perhaps a restructuring of the male role is what is needed and perhaps, as Pleck states, "Males need deeper emotional contact with other men and with children, less exclusive channeling of their emotional needs to relationships with women, and less dependence of their self-esteem on work than the modern male role allows" (p. 161). If one adopts this perspective, then changes in masculine roles are seen as necessary not only because the women's movement is bringing about changes in women that require changes in men, but also because men deserve more emotional richness and expressive alternatives than have heretofore been available to them.

Changes in the ways in which traditional masculine and feminine roles are viewed is closely linked to the study of *androgyny*. The androgynous person combines positive qualities of both masculinity and femininity; thus on a simplistic level the androgynous female is both nurturing and competent, and the androgynous male is both competent and nurturing. Psychological androgyny has been studied by various scholars (for instance, Bem, 1974; Spence & Helmreich, 1978), and certain interesting results have been found. Masculinity and femininity have been shown to be independent rather than opposite; thus individuals do not have to be *either* masculine or feminine, they can be high or low in *both*. Masculinity and femininity are clearly multifaceted (Helmreich, Spence, & Holahan, 1979). Because androgynous females and males are more likely to be able to engage in cross-sex behaviors than are strictly sex-typed persons, and because androgynes may function more effectively in certain social situations than strictly sex-typed persons (Ickes & Barnes, 1978), some amount of androgynous behavior may be desirable for all individuals.

The women's movement, men's liberation, and psychological androgyny are also related to changes in performance of sex roles in regard to children, housework, and dual careers. Although Unger (1979) discusses research that shows that marital satisfaction and couple communication are higher for couples where both spouses are employed, she also notes that "men whose wives work outside the home may be subject to greater stress than men whose wives work only within it" (p. 291) because greater responsibility for housework and child care often fall to the man with a working wife. In actual fact, women still carry the greatest burden of domestic work, whether or not they are employed outside the home. A recent study (Albrecht, Bahr, & Chadwick, 1979) indicates that, although there may have been some democratization of traditional family roles over recent decades, changes in family role definitions occur at different rates for different roles, and some roles have undergone very little change.

Looking Ahead

When one looks at recent changes in relationships between women and men, one can be awed either by the amount that has been accomplished or the amount that still remains to be done. Bernard (1976) discusses several theoretical models for sex-role change, noting that changing social norms may cause social behaviors to change and vice versa. Various crises (such as the economic stresses that accompany rising inflation) may induce social change, or change may occur because of a conversion phenomenon (for example, the militant antifeminist female who is forced to go to work because of death or divorce and after finding herself discriminated against because of her sex, becomes an equally vocal feminist supporter). One of Bernard's important contributions is her reply to the question of what will come of all this role changing, androgyny, and affirmative action.

Would all roles have a 50–50 sex composition or would they still retain the present sex composition? We cannot know the answer until we try. But, in my opinion, neither the present nor a 50–50 composition would result. There are some occupational roles that many more people would continue to aspire to than there are individuals who are qualified to perform them. Astronauts and ballerinas require not only motivation but also special talents. But assuming both motivation and talent, what could we expect? Something like this, I would guess. In occupation A, a preponderance of men; in occupation C, of women; but for a vast and increasing range of occupations a rough equality or minimal balance one way or the other. The situation of women in occupation A and of men in occupation C, now so often quite devastating, would hopefully be mollified by educational processes in the nature of sex-typed behavior. In family roles an analogous allocation of functions by sex is expectable, some men preferring domestic functions and some women, "provider" functions, but a—still indeterminate—proportion willing to assume or to share either or both.

The restructuring of sex roles in our society today is much like the breakup of the old estates system and the emergence of the capitalist class system that came with industrialization. In both cases what looked to conservatives like an eternal, natural, even divinely instituted system was attacked by seemingly mad, certainly misguided, revolutionaries or innovators. We can see now that industrialization could never have been possible if the old regime had remained unchallenged. If everyone had had to know his or her station in life and accept it unquestioningly, the mobility and flexibility demanded by industrialization would have been greatly retarded if not altogether prevented.

An old sex-role structure had to be shaken up also to prepare for the changes technology was producing then and continues to produce today. . . . The feminist movement was required to help us see what is actually happening in our society today and to redefine sex roles to meet these new conditions. Changing sex-specialized norms and sex-typed behavior is not a take-it-or-leave-it option. It is a fundamental imperative. The question is not whether to do it but rather how to do it [Bernard, 1976, pp. 221–222].★

One aspect of changing sex roles is the dual-career couple. Dual-career couples are sometimes viewed as glamorous, affluent, and continuously successful. The following brief vignettes will illustrate the fantasy and reality of the dual-career couple (adapted from Hall & Hall, 1979).

Fantasy couple: The Talbots—Friday evening.

(The couple, both psychologists, are sipping martinis in their quiet, book-filled study.)

Linda: Lord, what a wonderful day! We wrapped up the plans for the new psychology clinic without a hitch, and we have unlimited funds to refurbish the building.

Paul: Good for you! I've had quite a day too. I had two articles accepted by *The American Psychologist,* and one of them is going to be a lead article. Also, no revisions required.

Linda: So we both had victories today! How about celebrating with a nice candlelight dinner tonight, just the two of us? We can live dangerously with one of our bottles of 1962 Lafitte, some chamber music on the stereo, and . . . who knows what?

Paul: That would be wonderful, darling! And then let's get up early tomorrow morning and spend the day on the boat.

Linda: Wonderful!

A nice fantasy. Unfortunately, most dual-psychologist couples do not live like that. To set the record straight, let's look at a few minutes in the lives of a more realistic dual-career couple, the Hendricks.

Reality couple: The Hendricks—Friday evening.

(Both spouses are psychologists. Susan walks in the door perspiring, wrinkled, and late. Clyde is already home.)

Susan: How was your day, honey?

Clyde: I'm not sure. . . . There's talk going around the department about a reorganization in the university. I don't know what that's going to mean for me. There may be an increase in the teaching load. It's all up in the air right now, of course, but I think we really ought to talk about what we would do if . . . .

Susan: Clyde, can we talk about it some other time? I mean, I can't worry about some uncertain future right now. It's after six, dinner isn't even started, and I have a briefcase full of case notes to write.

★From "Change and Stability in Sex-Role Norms and Behavior," by J. Bernard. In *Journal of Social Issues,* 1976, *32*(3), 207–223. Copyright 1976 by Plenum Publishing Corporation. Reprinted by permission.

Mark needs a present for Harris's birthday tomorrow, Rachel has soccer practice in the morning, and . . . .

Clyde: Okay! We'll save it. Besides, I guess there are more immediate things to think about. Like the notice in the mail today about our checking account being overdrawn again. We've got to get better organized. Also, we can get the air conditioning fixed tomorrow, but it will cost time and a half.

Susan: Well, we don't really have a choice. Don't forget that we have a party to go to tomorrow night.

Clyde: The party? I completely forgot. Your group practice has the most boring parties I've ever been to.

Susan: I know. Maybe we can go late and leave early!

(And so it goes . . .)

The Dual-Career Couple

"He works. She works. But how does the relationship work?" These words from the cover of Hall and Hall's (1979) book on the dual-career couple offer a parsimonious description of what this topic area is all about. In the past few years, the dual-career couple has become a popular topic among social scientists and other related professionals. Of course, couples in which both partners are employed outside the home have been common for a number of years, but only recently have they become a hot item. The increase in dual-career couples has been attributed to (1) the influence of the feminist movement, (2) increasing availability of higher education and professional training for women, and (3) the pressures of soaring inflation and rising expenses that necessitate two incomes. We believe that all three of these factors (as well as several others) have contributed to the growing number of couples in which both spouses work, and we have touched on some of these factors in our section on changing sex roles. However, our interest here is not so much on *why* dual-career couples exist as on *how* the dual-career couple manages to maintain the often delicate balance of family and career involvements—and what happens when the balance gets tipped! We will first briefly note some definitions and statistics about dual careers, and will then go on to discuss factors influencing the career and the relationship.

Definitions

Although the phrase *dual-career* seems self-explanatory, we use it to refer only to those couples in which each partner has a career or profession that is intrinsically rewarding, that requires considerable education or training as well as dedication and involvement, and that offers promise of continued professional growth and advancement.

In contrast, the *dual-worker* couple has both spouses employed in jobs that have fixed parameters of time and involvement as well as a fairly fixed limit for growth or promotion.

The *two-person career* is a rather different entity and refers to a career such as oil company executive, hospital administrator, or politician, in which one spouse (usually the husband) is hired to fill a position that requires considerable commitment on the part of the other spouse (usually the wife). For example, a man may be hired to administer a community hospital; this involves management of hospital systems, hiring and firing of personnel, and frequent contact with governing board members and perhaps with the community at large. This man's wife may be expected to support the hospital through volunteer work, participation in a number of related community activities, and entertainment of administrative staff, medical staff, board members, and community leaders. Thus, if both persons perform their designated roles, we have a *two-person career,* or two for the price of one! Vast numbers of families have both spouses working, and many of these families include very young children. So much for the myth of the traditional nuclear family, where the father is employed and the mother is a full-time homemaker. Just as the cottage with a picket fence has been overshadowed by the planned community and the condo, so also is the traditional family at least equated in numbers by dual-career/worker families.

Psychological Issues

Norms and values change slowly—often more slowly than real behaviors. We noted in our discussion of changing sex roles that, although many women and men are changing their conceptions of their own abilities and are going on to try to reshape their destinies, the social system often seems intent on maintaining the status quo. Inertia exists in any social system, and it thus requires more energy to change a situation than to leave it just as it is. Change may be better, but maintenance is easier. Thus we find the media, particularly television and magazines, showing men in corporate offices or at home washing the car, but women are waxing the floor or serving Kool-Aid to an army of children. The few advertisements that actually consider women in executive positions frequently mimic the perfume ad in which a lovely blonde can "bring home the bacon—fry it up in a pan—and never let *him* forget he's a man" and thus epitomize the *Superwoman* myth. This fantasy says that, if a woman only runs hard enough, fast enough, and long enough, she can be a brilliant executive, a mother who is uniformly wise, just, and loving, and a wife who combines the virtues of gourmet cooking, gourmet sex, and breathtaking beauty! Some women exhaust themselves trying to maintain the myth; even if neither spouse subscribes to it, both husband and wife have expectations of themselves and of each other that concern their careers and their relationship.

Career Issues

Spouses' careers may harmonize to a greater or lesser degree, depending on logistical matters such as work time and traveling required, on career stage, how each partner ranks career versus family, similarity of careers, and the flexibility and autonomy within careers (Hall & Hall, 1979).

If spouses are both in beginning stages of careers, intensity and pressure are likely to be quite high. Each spouse works long hours, thrives on professional stimulation, and hopes for the pot of gold at the end of the rainbow—for example, a vice presidency, a partnership, or tenure. Spouses may be quite competitive at this stage, particularly if they are in similar fields, although similar careers can also increase partners' understanding and support of each other. If spouses' careers are at different stages, the partner who has progressed farther may be able to assume greater home and family responsibilities during the time when the other partner has a professional growth spurt.

If both partners rank family life as more important than career, work conflicts are likely to be reduced. This may also occur if one partner puts family first and the other partner places career in the first spot (complementarity). However, if both partners give career top priority, there may well be conflict, particularly if they have children (Hall & Hall, 1979).

Flexibility and autonomy are particularly important for dual-career couples, because household repairmen, school programs, and children's illnesses do not follow a predictable schedule. Academics and certain self-employed professionals such as lawyers and physicians may have considerable autonomy and flexibility and thus may be particularly able to function in a dual-career situation. Although we mentioned earlier that spouses in similar careers may be singularly supportive of one another, similar careers tend to have similar peak times. For example, two professors may function in a dual-career marriage very well, except during midterms and finals, and two tax accountants may be adoring most of the time, but mutually antagonistic from January 15 to April 15. A recent study by Ferber and Huber (1979) indicated that highly educated persons (Ph.D.s) who have Ph.D. spouses may be penalized by the spouse's attainment. Male Ph.D.s with Ph.D. wives were found to be less productive in terms of journal articles published and professional offices held. Female Ph.D.s with Ph.D. husbands, on the other hand, did not suffer in terms of productivity, but did show greater career disruptions due to having children, and geographical relocation because of the husband's job. Broschart (1978) found similar results for women, with Ph.D. mothers achieving less professional rank than single or married-but-childless Ph.D. women, although the mothers were no less professionally productive. The lower rank was due to childbearing and relocation.

Dual-career couples carry heavy workloads that may engender considerable stress, and some authors have hypothesized that husbands of career women may experience heightened stress and resulting illness, though Booth (1979) found no differences in measurements of physiological stress between men whose wives were employed and those whose wives remained at home. In fact, on the three measures that showed some differences, husbands of working wives were actually shown to be happier and healthier.

One aspect of dual-career marriage that is not as happy or healthy is salary. In a recent review of relevant literature, Bryson and Bryson (1980) noted that employed wives average considerably less annual income than employed husbands. Discrepancies between married women's and married men's incomes seem to result from three major factors: differences in background and training, occupational roles and choices, and organizational discrimination against women. Being married is positively related to men's incomes but negatively related to women's incomes. In addition, amount of education and grades in college are more strongly related to income for males and unmarried females than for married women. The authors pointed out that wives who work part time are paid less per hour than wives who work full time, but the opposite is true for husbands. Career interruptions due to having children and to geographical relocation tend to depress women's careers, and "moves for husbands [are] accompanied by higher salaries, whereas moves for wives [result] in lower salaries" (Bryson & Bryson, p. 5).

Nepotism is also an issue, particularly in academic institutions, and many universities and corporations are reluctant to hire two spouses. Interestingly, in a study which they conducted of dual-career psychologist couples, Bryson and Bryson found that couples employed at the same institution were more productive than couples who worked separately. As in other research these authors found that in couples who begin with approximately the same career potential, husbands tend to succeed much more than do wives. In addition, although wives are more productive than single employed psychologists, unfortunately this productivity does not result in heightened job stability or income.

It appears that dual-psychologist couples, as most dual-career couples, adhere to familial and societal sex-role stereotypes in which women assume greater household and child care responsibilities and subordinate their careers to the careers of their husbands. Married career women may have glimpsed the promised land, but they have not yet set foot in it.

Relationship Issues

A dual-career marriage is like any marriage in that it includes the normal stresses and joys that affect any marital relationship, including issues of communication, commitment, conflict, sexual compatibility, and so on. However, dual-career aspects influence these typical factors and also produce additional ones.

In our discussion of marital power, we found that husbands are usually perceived as more powerful than wives in some of the major decision-making areas, though marital power may in fact be fairly well balanced. Winter, Stewart, and McClelland (1977) measured men's need for power when the men were undergraduate college students and compared this with demographic information obtained about the men and their wives 14 years later. The researchers found that a husband's need for power was negatively associated with his wife's career level; thus the greater the man's power needs, the lower the woman's career achievement. Although it may be that men with high power needs and women with low career needs are more likely to marry each other, the authors favor the explanation that a man's need for power may actually limit his wife's need or ability to achieve in the work world.

The sheer amount of work required by dual-career families necessitates some sharing of family and household responsibilities, though the sharing is often far from equal. Some couples attempt to divide responsibilities, but along rather traditional sex-role lines, with husbands attending to house repairs and outdoor work and wives assuming responsibility for cooking, cleaning, and laundry. Other couples divide chores on the basis of the unique skills and preferences of each spouse, so that a husband might cook when a wife cuts the grass (Mortimer, 1978; Rapoport & Rapoport, 1971). Although responsibilities may be allocated to each spouse at a given point in time, continuous exchange and negotiation of specific items occurs, because things rarely go exactly as planned. Equal partitioning of responsibility is more fiction than fact for dual-career couples, because the number of tasks may be divided equally, but wives spend a greater actual amount of time performing those tasks. Pleck (1979) notes research that documents employed wives as "experiencing a substantial *overload* in their combinations of work and family roles as compared to their husbands" (p. 485). Mortimer (1978) points out that women are usually responsible for children-related situations such as illness, dentist appointments, and teacher conferences and reports that "in one study, only a single truly egalitarian family was found in a sample of 51 dual-career couples" (p. 11). Role overload or strain was found to be related to marital satisfaction in both clinical and nonclinical couples (Frank, Anderson, & Rubinstein, 1979). The greater the role strain, the lower the marital satisfaction.

Commitment is an issue for all married couples, but it has some unique properties for the dual-career couple. Spouses who are professionally successful and self-sustaining have considerable independence; they do not need each other to survive, as was often the case for traditional couples. A wife can support herself; a husband can cook and do his own laundry. Knowledge of these capabilities may cause spouses to hedge their bets, knowing that the relationship is not essential to survival. And a full commitment to each other may not be made.

Because of the stresses on dual-career couples, such couples need support; this support usually comes from other couples in similar situations. Since most of society presses against the lifestyle changes and role reallocation required to make dual-career marriages workable and satisfying, new support-systems must be created and maintained (Lein, 1979). The problem with this idea is that dual-career couples lack the necessary time to build such support systems; thus they must borrow time from other activities or people. The dual-career couple is a complex entity that will increase in numbers and perhaps complexity in the years ahead.

The Future

One of the most important questions for the future is how we promote changes in men's conception of their roles. In a sense women have begun changing their roles fairly rapidly and hoping men are going to catch up. Scanzoni (1979) proposes three strategies to change men's roles prior to and subsequent to marriage. *Self-interest strategy* involves getting men to recognize how it would be in their best interest to widen their own roles in a more egalitarian direction. *Prosocial or altruistic strategy* involves convincing men that it is right and just that women and men have equal options and share equal responsibilities. The third strategy, *negotiation,* requires that women learn about conflict and bargaining and then negotiate with men for changes the women seek. Such changes would undoubtedly include more equal sharing of household duties and child care in the case of the dual-career couple.

One dual-career lifestyle that has infrequently come under scrutiny is the dual-career couple whose members live apart (Gross, 1980). Talking with 43 partners in such marriages, Gross found that living apart was something to be endured for a given time rather than a viable alternative lifestyle that could be happily continued indefinitely. Women seemed somewhat more comfortable than men with living apart, perhaps because they were enjoying a full career equality that had not always been possible for them. Couples who were older, had been married longer, and in which at least one partner had an established career found living apart to be a bit less stressful. Younger couples seemed to use traditional marriage as a standard of comparison and found less stress in the logistics of living apart, but more stress in the power issue of whose career ought to be subordinate to whose. Younger spouses "confronted each other directly (sometimes playfully, sometimes accusingly), with the question, 'Who left whom?'" (Gross, p. 572). Although the development of more egalitarian values may decrease some of the stresses for couples, it is unlikely that any two people who marry because they want to be together will be entirely satisfied to be apart.

Many changes must occur before dual-career couples can really get the most from their lives. Employers must become more flexible, child care more available, and society much more liberated and open in how it defines women's and men's roles.

Summary

Separation through death or divorce affects a significant proportion of marriages in the United States. Although divorce has been an option since Colonial times, it is only in recent decades that it has become so widespread. Divorce crosses all socioeconomic lines, but persons with limited education, low professional status, and low income experience divorce more frequently and remarry less often. In exchange theory terms persons who experience more rewards from marriage and who anticipate greater costs from a divorce are more likely to stay married. Conflict, poor communication, unsatisfactory sex, boredom, financial problems, extramarital relationships, and many other factors can cause divorce. Spouses may frequently disagree as to the problems in a relationship, and the female relationship partner is the one more likely to initiate the breakup. Higher income by a husband is a barrier to divorce, and higher income by a wife may make a divorce more likely. Financial difficulties usually accompany divorce, because two households cannot be maintained as cheaply as one, and many female-headed single-parent households have incomes below the poverty level. Various psychological and physical illnesses may accompany marital disruption. Research indicates that, although children may manifest some psychological and behavioral stress shortly after a divorce, within two years most of the negative effects have abated. Custody of minor children is usually given to the mother, although more fathers are seeking custody, and joint-custody arrangements have increased. A friendly, conflict-free relationship between ex-spouses, though hard to maintain, has significant positive impact on a child's emotional well-being.

Reconstituted or blended families are a reality, though the media give them little attention. Myths about wicked stepmothers and stepfathers create special problems for blended families, as do unrealistic expectations for family intimacy. Flexibility, tolerance, and patience by the adults in a blended family help the children adjust more easily. Our society needs to increasingly recognize blended families as a viable entity.

Traditional sex-role typing begins before birth and continues through childhood into adulthood. Boys are encouraged by parents, teachers, society as a whole, and ultimately by their peers to be active, aggressive, and instrumental. Girls are encouraged by the same forces to be quiet, passive, and expressive. Although there are reputed to be many more psychological differences between males and females than actually exist, statements about sex differences are used to maintain traditional sex roles. In traditional families men have been the wage earners and women the caretakers of children and household. However, social changes precipitated by the women's movement, as well as economic pressures of modern society, have caused many women to work. Although sex discrimination clearly exists in the work world, many observers see the need for change, for economic if not for humanitarian reasons. Women's liberation may also mean men's liberation, so that as women are free to be both nurturant and competent, men will be free to be both competent and nurturant.

One contemporary phenomenon related to changing sex roles is the dual-career couple. Dual-career couples are somewhat different from dual-worker couples because of greater career investment and more opportunities for advancement. Dual-career spouses may be competitive in their careers or be quite understanding and supportive of each other, depending on the career stage and career commitment of each partner. Responsibilities of child care and housework are exacerbated by the stresses of two careers, though women put more time into family-related work than do men. Dual-career husbands may participate fairly fully in family labor, but wives more often than husbands lose career momentum from childbirth and from geographical relocation due to a spouse's job change. Role strain is a problem for both dual-career wives and husbands. Some dual-career couples live apart so that each partner can maximize his or her career, but this is not a satisfactory long-term solution for most couples.

Both individual and societal norms will need to change regarding separation and divorce, blended families, sex roles, and dual-career couples. Human behavior is already changing; it is time for human values to catch up.

Research Issues in Attraction, Love, and Intimate Relationships

In this book we attempt to integrate areas of study that have been quite disparate: attraction, researched in depth by social psychologists; love, about which nearly everyone purports to know something; and intimate (or close) relationships, which are beginning to be studied by scholars from various disciplines. These three topics are conceptually coherent, but a wide range of research methods and theoretical approaches has been used to study them. Students have differing backgrounds in the logic and methods of scientific research. Therefore an overview will be useful for many students, especially because of the many different types of research summarized in the book. Basic issues of theory, hypotheses, and measurement receive detailed attention. These abstract issues are made more concrete by use of the similarity–attraction relation discussed in Chapter 2, and the theoretical explanations of similarity and attraction described in Chapter 1. Some of the special issues involved in studying the relatively new area of intimate relationships are also presented in overview, including a survey of the methods of research that have been used and ethical issues involved in such research.

Theory, Hypotheses, and Measurement

We discuss many ideas, concepts, research, and folk proverbs about attraction, love, and relationships. For example, *birds of a feather flock together* is a folk proverb that expresses a hypothesis about interpersonal attraction. Stated more formally, the hypothesis might be phrased:

> The more similar two people are on any of a variety of characteristics, the more strongly they will be attracted to each other.

Each of the questions in Box 1-1 of Chapter 1 can, with some effort, be transformed into a scientific research hypothesis in the same way.

Suppose that we have formally stated a research question as a carefully phrased hypothesis. What next? We would like to know if the hypothesis is true or sometimes true. To find out we have to do research to get the answers. There are many types of research; case studies, field studies, laboratory experiments, analysis of documentary materials, and so on. In much social psychology research, such as research on attraction, the laboratory experiment is the most common research method. Sociologists also do research on attraction. They tend to do surveys that study such phenomena as attitudes, values, and practices about such things as friendship, mate selection, courtship styles, and the like.

In the study of interpersonal attraction, as in other areas of scientific research, scholars take a systematic approach to developing knowledge. One major concern is to explain interpersonal attraction, how it occurs, in what circumstances, and between what types of people. This quest is sometimes phrased: "What are the causes or determinants of interpersonal attraction?" When asked in this way, attraction is the dependent variable, and the causes are the independent variables, as noted in Chapter 2. The same general approach can be taken to develop a systematic knowledge base about love and intimate relationships.

In seeking the causes of phenomena, scientists often find it useful and interesting to develop *theories* about the phenomena. Specific *hypotheses* are drawn or deduced from the theory for testing. Scientific hypothesis testing nearly always involves *measurement*.

Theories and Hypotheses

A theory is a set of assumptions which purport to explain a phenomenon of interest. The phenomenon may be a specific piece of behavior (for instance, sneezing) or a broad and varied range of life (such as attraction). From the basic assumptions or premises, consequences are deduced that can be tested in some way. These consequences are usually called hypotheses and occasionally theorems. Theories that follow this format are referred to as formal deductive theories (Hendrick & Jones, 1972). Very few theories have been fully formalized, but the scheme serves as a model for the construction of good theories.

There are several aspects to a well-developed theory.

1. The core of the theory is a set of basic *concepts* with which the theory is concerned. To be useful as a scientific theory, each concept must be given a verbal definition, the meaning of which is agreed upon by a community of researchers. Further, most of the concepts must be given an *operational definition*. Such a definition is a rule by which we can point to or mark off quantities of the concept as it manifests itself in

the world. Thus a good operational definition provides measurement procedures for the concept.

As an example we stipulate several concepts from which we hope to develop a (demonstration) theory of attraction.

Reality contact: A human propensity to know and experience accurately what is happening in the world.

Prediction: A human ability to anticipate events which have not yet occurred. Prediction may vary in its degree of accuracy.

Reality: The world out there. The world of things and nature is called physical reality. The world of human relationships is called social reality.

Competence: An internal state of good feeling because one is able to deal successfully with some aspect of the world.

Social comparison: An act by which one measures oneself against another on some selected attribute.

Similarity: The extent to which two people are at the same point on some attribute dimension. The extent can range from dissimilar to identical.

Attraction: Liking.

2. The basic concepts are combined with each other to form a set of propositions. A *proposition* is any statement, either verbal or mathematical, that relates at least two concepts to each other. The set of propositions is what is meant by the assumptions of the theory. They are the core statements. These basic sentences have several names: assumptions, postulates (in mathematics), and premises (in logic).

A high act of creativity is required to come up with a good set of propositions. The theorist is free to construct any type of theory. There are few rules on how to succeed in building an outstanding system of postulates.

Let us take the concepts defined earlier and see if we can cast them into a reasonable set of propositions. We construct the following six propositions:

- People appraise *reality* by trying to stay more or less continuously in *reality contact*.
- Previous *reality contact* in a given situation enables people to make *predictions* about that situation.
- *Prediction* that is successful causes positive feelings of *competence;* unsuccessful prediction causes feelings of incompetence.
- *Social comparison* may be used as a mode of *prediction*.
- *Similarity* is a dimension that affects *prediction;* the more similar, the more precise the prediction.
- *Reality contact* is the experiential basis for *attraction*.

These propositions seem more or less reasonable, even though they are stated in rough verbal form. For better or worse we will consider them as basic axioms of our budding theory. Note that each proposition relates two of the concepts in one way or another.

3. From these basic propositions we wish to derive some interesting hypotheses. There are several rules of reasoning ("laws of logic") by which propositions may be related to each other. One is the *law of the syllogism,* which says that if A implies B, and B implies C, then A must also imply C. Each of the hypotheses above is considered to be in the format of "something implies something." For some of the propositions, we assume that it is reasonable for the direction to be reversed; that is, A implies B, but B can imply A also.

Consider the following pair of propositions. "Similarity implies prediction" and "Prediction implies reality contact." By the law of the syllogism, "Similarity implies reality contact." This (somewhat peculiar) deduction is a hypothesis. We may use it to draw out more deductions. Consider: "Similarity implies reality contact" and "Reality contact implies attraction." Therefore by the law of the syllogism "Similarity implies attraction."

This last hypothesis we have deduced is of considerable interest. In fact, it is logically identical to the similarity–attraction hypothesis based on the "birds of a feather" proverb. A great deal of research has been done to test the similarity–attraction hypothesis. Of course, our theory is somewhat artificial in that we knew some of the basic propositions that would be required in order for the hypothesis to be deduced. The ideas about social comparison and reality come from Festinger's (1954) theory of social comparison processes. The assumption on competence stems from White's (1959) theory of effectance motivation. Both ideas put together in this way do result in a general prediction of similarity causing attraction.

There are other sets of propositions that might also entail the similarity–attraction hypothesis. One upshot is that it is difficult to claim absolute support for any one theory. It takes a preponderance of evidence from many tests of theories before one can decide if one theory is really superior to another. Nevertheless, the example is useful to illustrate the general process of theory construction and hypothesis formation.

After the hypothesis is created, we must set up research procedures to test it. Research procedures involve creating experiments (and other types of research) and measurement operations.

Hypothesis Testing

The central purpose in testing the hypothesis is to find out if the two concepts are actually related to each other in the way that the proposition says that they are. The degree of precision in the statement of the proposition can vary from nebulous to quantitative exactness. Some examples of increasing exactness are:

1. Similarity is *associated* with attraction.
2. Similarity is *positively correlated* with attraction.
3. Similarity is related to attraction by $y = 2x + 1$, where y is attraction, x is similarity, and the numbers are mathematical constants.

The first statement merely says that the two concepts somehow "go together." Statement 2 says that as similarity changes, the attraction changes proportionally in the same direction. In general, the higher the similarity score, the higher the attraction score. The third statement provides an exact *prediction* of attraction if the similarity score is known. For example, if the similarity score is 2, the attraction score is predicted to be 5; if similarity is 4, attraction is predicted to be 9.

The goal of many sciences is to write propositions in mathematical form because it allows the two concepts to be linked together with exact precision. The hypothesis of statement 3 says that, if you create or specify different magnitudes of similarity between two people, you can predict exactly how well they will like each other. Several different values of attraction and similarity are shown in Figure A-1, where they are related by $y = 2x + 1$. If exact predictions can be made, the hypothesis can more easily be verified or falsified. If the attraction scores are not those predicted by the equation, the hypothesis is false; if the attraction scores are as predicted, the hypothesis is confirmed.

In social research it is seldom possible to make exact predictions with equations. Researchers have to be satisified with statements like "increases in similarity lead to increases in attraction." It is implicit in the statement that the researcher expects a *causal relation;* that is, that similarity is one cause of attraction. The statement can be translated as "increases in similarity *cause* increases in attraction."

One way of testing the hypothesis is to construct an experiment. An experimenter will try to create a situation in which the presumed causal factor is changed or varied. Any concept that is defined so that it can be varied from a low to high amount is called a *variable*. Since the experimenter believes that similarity is the causal variable, he or she will try to create or manipulate different degrees of similarity as an independent variable to see if the variation results in different degrees of attraction as the dependent variable.

There are many situations an experimenter might create as a basic scenario for the manipulation of attraction. First, a dimension of similarity has to be selected. The experimenter might select attitude similarity/dissimilarity on several attitude topics as the dimension to manipulate. Suppose that you fill out an attitude rating scale on a variety of topics. Afterward you are given a copy of the same scale purportedly filled out by someone else. You are asked to rate how much you would like or dislike that person, based on the person's attitude profile.

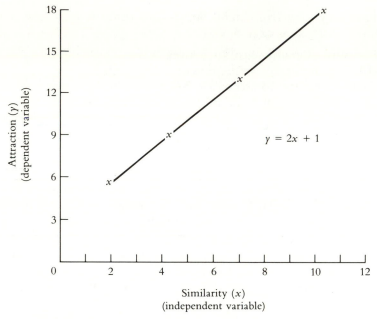

FIGURE A-1   The graph shows that similarity values plotted on the bottom (abscissa) of the graph predict attraction values plotted on the left side (ordinate) by the equation $y = 2x + 1$. A graph shows the form of the relationship through a wide range of values. Such a precise relationship is a mathematical function. The equation $y = 2x + 1$ is a positive linear relation, which means that the graph plots as a straight line of increasing values. There are as many types of functions as there are types of equations, although the search for linear relations between concepts is most common in social science. Note that well constructed scales of measurement are required to have well defined empirical relations.

Suppose that the attitude profile is very similar to your own profile. After rating the person, you inspect a second attitude scale completed by still another person. This profile is very dissimilar to your own profile.

If the attitude–similarity hypothesis is correct, you should find the person similar to yourself in attitudes as more likable than the dissimilar person. Such results have been found in many experiments (for example, Byrne, 1971).

One point of interest in the hypothetical experiment is that the experimenter created only two degrees (also called *levels*) of attitude similarity, very similar and very dissimilar. That is the minimum number of levels that can be used. The reason is that at least two levels are required in order to see if *changes* in attraction scores occur. Stated differently, two levels of similarity is the minimum variation in the manipulated independent variable that can be used in order to observe variation or change in the dependent variable of attraction. Of course such a basic framework does not constitute a mathematical function, but an analogy is created that is good enough to allow the experimenter to infer whether or not a causal relation exists.

This type of outcome is shown in panel A of Figure A-2. Two levels of attitude similarity (very dissimilar and very similar) are plotted on the abscissa. Assume that attraction was rated on a seven-point rating scale as shown on the ordinate. Attraction to the dissimilar person is in the disliking range, and attraction to the similar person is in the liking range. The two points of the graph are joined by a straight line for convenience to show the changes in attraction scores from a very dissimilar to a very similar other person.

Similarity is only one cause of attraction. There are probably many other causes. In modern research it is common to study the simultaneous effects of two (or more) independent variables on one dependent variable. To do so the experimenter manipulates two (or more) independent variables in an experiment and assesses their joint effect on the dependent variable. Panel B in Figure A-2 illustrates this conception. Attitude similarity was manipulated in the same way as described for panel A. However, in addition, the experimenter attached a photograph of the other people to the attitude scales that they had completed. The

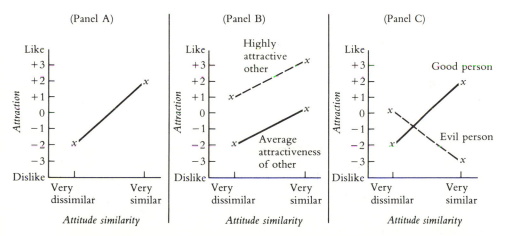

FIGURE A-2 The three panels illustrate typical results in similarity–attraction experiments. Most experiments manipulate only two (or a few) levels of the independent variable. In the three examples only two levels are created, very similar and very dissimilar. Graphs can be plotted, but they are not true mathematical functions because the independent variable does not have true quantitative values. Panel A shows the results when one independent variable is manipulated. Panel B shows the results for two independent variables. Panel C shows an interaction effect of two independent variables on attraction.

experimenter had observed that physically attractive people seemed to be better liked than ugly people. It seemed reasonable that beauty is a causal factor in attraction. So, in addition to the hypothesis that "attitude similarity causes attraction," the experimenter wanted to test a second hypothesis, that "beauty causes attraction."

In order to test both hypotheses, the experimenter had to create a minimum of four *experimental conditions*. They were: an attitudinally dissimilar person of average physical beauty, an attitudinally similar person of average physical beauty, an attitudinally dissimilar person of high physical beauty, and an attitudinally similar person of high physical beauty.

The plot of the results for attraction scores in panel B shows that both hypotheses were confirmed. Increases in similarity cause increased attraction. Increases in physical beauty also result in increased attraction, as shown by the displacement upward of the parallel line for the physically attractive person. In this case the addition of a good-looking photograph adds an increment to the liking ratings. Similarity and physical appearance are said to be *additive* in their effects on attraction ratings. The experimenter concluded that both similarity and physical appearance are causal variables that determine attraction and that their effects operate independently of each other.

Two independent variables sometimes have a mutual influence on each other. Stated differently, two independent variables do not always operate independently of each other in determining a dependent variable. Panel C of Figure A-2 illustrates this situation. In this case the experimenter manipulated attitude similarity the same way as previously. However, biographic information was added to other people's attitude scales. Two of the others were described as good people, and the remaining two were described as evil. In the latter case information was given that the two others had been convicted of a particularly gruesome murder. The attraction scores plotted in panel C show that, for the good persons, the typical similarity–attraction result holds true. However, for the evil persons, the relationship is reversed. The evil person similar in attitudes is highly disliked, and more so than the evil person dissimilar in attitudes. This reversal is called an *inverse relationship;* increases in the independent variable cause decreases in the dependent variable.

This reversal is intuitively plausible. Usually, people similar to us in attitudes and values are highly rewarding. However, to hear that a very similar person has committed a brutal murder is likely to be highly threatening. We may well reject such a person vigorously and dislike him or her intensely. A very dissimilar person should be rejected less vigorously. After all, such behavior is what one might expect from an individual who holds such perverted attitudes! Such people are incomprehensible to us, therefore noncomparable.

The pattern of results in panel C is called an *interaction effect*. The independent variables of attitude similarity–dissimilarity and good/evil of the others are said to *interact* in determining attraction ratings. Such interaction effects in experiments make prediction and explanation more complicated. Such interaction effects are, in fact, rather common in social research; unfortunately, the world is not always simple in the way it operates.

Measurement

The need for careful measurement has been obvious in most of the previous discussion. Unless concepts can be operationalized by some type of measurement procedure, the relationship between two concepts in a hypothesis cannot be established. When we think of measurement, we usually think of objects such as yardsticks or physical scales to measure length or weight. Unfortunately, psychological attributes cannot be measured so easily. There is no way that a direct yardstick can be used on variables such as attraction, beauty, and goodness. However, a less rigorous type of measurement is possible.

It is conventional to categorize four types of measurement scales. A *nominal scale* is a device to sort objects into categories: males and females, religious and irreligious, and Democrats and Republicans, for example. The categories cannot be ordered (greater than, better than) with respect to each other. An *ordinal scale* is a type of measure in which increasing numbers on the scale indicate increasing size of the attribute being measured. However, the distances between scale points are not standardized. For example, let A, B, C, and D be a scale of increasing units. We know that B is greater than A, C greater than B, and D greater than C. But we do not know how these differences compare to each other. In an *interval scale* the differences between the scale marks are constant and one unit of scale difference is the same as any other unit of scale difference. However, an interval scale does not have a true zero point. A *ratio scale* has a true zero point and equal units of measurement. Measurement of length by a yardstick is ratio measurement. All operations of arithmetic can be performed on ratio measurements. For length, for example, division of one length by another is possible (that is why such scales are called ratio scales).

Most measurements in social research are at the ordinal level. For example, in Figure A-2 two scale points are arbitrarily drawn for the independent variable (very dissimilar and very similar). The two points could have been drawn closer together or farther apart. The seven-point attraction scale shown on the ordinate is drawn in equal step units, but the scale is in fact ordinal; there is no assurance that the distances between the numbers are *psychologically* equal to each other. Nevertheless, ordinal measurement is often sufficient to discover causal relations. All that is required is that as scale numbers increase the dimension measured is greater than the quantity measured by smaller scale numbers. Of course, mathematical functions cannot be computed when only ordinal scales exist. Nevertheless, this analogue approach, as illustrated in Figure A-2, indicates that substantial bodies of knowledge can be discovered with ordinal scales. We do the best we can with what we've got.

Analyzing Close Relationships

Several recently published books address the complexities of close relationships (for example, Burgess & Huston, 1979; Hinde, 1979; Levinger & Raush, 1977) and more will undoubtedly follow. Close or intimate relationships are relevant to all of us; therefore their study has wide appeal. When we speak of close relationships we often think of man–woman romantic relationships, and we use the marital dyad as the prototype of an intimate relationship. However, there are many kinds of close relationships—mother–infant, father–son, therapist–client, friend–friend—and all these relationships merit systematic study.

Approaches to Investigation

Robert Hinde (1979), a British scholar, makes a strong case for the study of relationships. He first attempts to describe the dimensions along which relationships may be viewed, dimensions such as the content and process of dyadic interactions, similarity versus complementarity, intimacy, and commitment. He also notes relationship dynamics that deserve study such as conflict, power, and feedback processes as well as some of the various theoretical approaches used in the study of relationships, including dissonance and balance theories, learning paradigms, and exchange theories. He offers a useful comment on parent–child relationships as the basis for future adult relationships. Hinde's book may be more useful as a professional statement of the major importance of the study of relationships than as a text, since the book reflects Hinde's rather idiosyncratic view of the topic and also largely ignores the methodological problems involved.

Harvey (in press), on the other hand, succinctly grapples with the knotty issues of research methods, primarily descriptive and causal analyses, which are used to study relationships.

Descriptive analysis involves the recording of events which occur in the dyad; it is a process of recording, labeling, and describing. The most frequently used type of descriptive analysis is the *self-report,* whereby a researcher asks one or both dyad members to describe aspects of themselves, their partner, and the relationship on either a questionnaire or psychological test, in a diary, or in a tape-recorded interview. *Behavioral observation* of a couple by an observer can be used alone or in conjunction with self-report data. These methods have been both praised and criticized, the former because of their practicality and because they go right to the source of the data, the subjects themselves. Criticism is based on the inevitable distortion and biases that affect the subjects' responses as well as the researcher's observations and that may impair the validity of the data gathered. Another type of behavioral measure that could prove useful in the future would be the documentation of events related to a relationship such as physical illnesses or career changes (promotions, demotions).

Another descriptive method is *simulation,* which may use a combination of self-report and behavioral observation techniques. Simulational techniques are typically used in a laboratory setting in which dyad members may role play current relationship issues, take part in structured problem-solving or conflict-resolution situations, and generally try to behave as if they were in a real-life interaction. In a strict sense the interaction is real, but the setting is not. Role play was used by Raush, Barry, Hertel, and Swain (1974) to study marital interaction, and Gottman (1979) and his colleagues have used simulation techniques as well as behavioral observation of couples both at home and in the laboratory as the basis for developing his structural model of family interaction. Although simulation techniques can be accused of artificiality and thence of questionable validity, simulation methods can be better controlled than purely naturalistic observation and can offer behavioral evidence that cannot be gleaned from strictly self-report data. Harvey concludes his discussion of descriptive analysis by cautioning the reader that, although a multimethod approach (both self-report and behavioral observation) to the study of relationships appears to be increasingly favored by researchers, theoretical bases and appropriate statistical treatment are essential if any research methods are to yield valid and reliable data.

Causal analysis has been used by relationship researchers in a much more limited way than has descriptive analysis, because it is very difficult to show causality in a relationship where variables influence each other in a sometimes circular, sometimes multidirectional fashion. Although longitudinal, cross-sectional, and retrospective developmental designs have all been used in the relationship area with some success (for instance, Hill, Rubin, & Peplau, 1976; Levinger, Senn, & Jorgensen, 1970), these methods have some of the same kinds of validity and reliability problems as do self-report and behavioral observation techniques. Although innovative statistical techniques such as path analysis and cross-lagged panel correlation offer considerable promise in establishing the effectiveness of causal analysis, because the study of close relationships is so complex emotionally, behaviorally, and ethically, investigators will probably continue to use all the analytic methods available.

Ethical Issues

In the study of close relationships, it is particularly important for investigator and participants to have good rapport and a basis of trust. Because the research context is quite personal and may include testing sessions or interviews conducted over months or even years, all those involved may come to know one another quite well. During lengthy interviews or observation sessions, particularly when held in a participant couple's home, greater intimacy may evolve between investigators and participants than was expected or even desired. Such intimacy could affect the participants' responses and/or the investigator's perceptions of responses and behaviors; thus Harvey (in press) suggests the use of multiple trained investigators as well as reliability checks on the data. The relationship between investigator and participants needs to be good, but not too good.

An additional ethical concern is the point at which couples' research may become couples' counseling. Rubin and Mitchell (1976) have noted that academic researchers may become change agents in the relationships they study. By asking couples certain pointed questions and by prompting them to evaluate and discuss their relationships, researchers may influence the relationships toward continuation or termination. For that reason Rubin and Mitchell conclude that researchers must fully inform potential participants about the research procedures and at least some of the possible effects of participation (such as increased discussion by a couple of their relationship). Researchers must also bear some responsibility for the long-term effects of the study on a couple. In addition, researchers need to develop some of the counselor's skills in person perception, communication, problem solving, and conflict resolution. Although the investigation of close relationships is surely research, "Whenever research touches on important areas of the participants' lives, the processes of research and of counseling are likely to merge" (Rubin & Mitchell, 1976, p. 25).

References

Adams, G. R. Physical attractiveness research: Toward a developmental social psychology of beauty. *Human Development,* 1977, *20,* 217–239.

Ahrons, C. R. Divorce: A crisis of family transition and change. *Family Relations,* 1980, *29,* 533–540.

Ainsworth, M. D. S. The development of infant–mother attachment. In B. M. Caldwell & H. N. Ricciuti (Eds.), *Review of child development research* (Vol. 3). Chicago: University of Chicago Press, 1973.

Albrecht, S. L., Bahr, H. M., & Chadwick, B. A. Changing family and sex roles: An assessment of age differences. *Journal of Marriage and the Family,* 1979, *41,* 41–50.

Allport, G. W., & Odbert, H. S. Trait names: A psycho-lexical study. *Psychological Monographs,* 1936, *47,* (Whole No. 211).

Altman, I. *The environment and social behavior: Privacy · personal space · territory · crowding.* Monterey, Calif.: Brooks/Cole, 1975.

Altman, I. & Haythorn, W. W. The ecology of isolated groups. *Behavioral Science,* 1967, *12,* 169–182.

Altman, I., & Taylor, D. A. *Social penetration: The development of interpersonal relationships.* New York: Holt, Rinehart & Winston, 1973.

Altman, I., Vinsel, A., & Brown, B. B. Dialetic conceptions in social psychology: An application to social penetration and privacy regulation. In L. Berkowitz (Ed.), *Advances in experimental social psychology* (Vol. 14). New York: Academic Press, 1981.

Anderson, N. H. Likableness ratings of 555 personality-trait words. *Journal of Personality and Social Psychology,* 1968, *9,* 272–279.

Appleton, W. S. Bedroom etiquette. *Medical Aspects of Human Sexuality,* 1981, *15*(3), 77; 84; 86; 88.

Archer, R. L., & Burleson, J. A. The effects of timing of self-disclosure on attraction and reciprocity. *Journal of Personality and Social Psychology,* 1980, *38,* 120–130.

Argyle, M., & Dean, J. Eye contact, distance and affiliation. *Sociometry,* 1965, *28,* 289–304.

Aronson, E. Some antecedents of interpersonal attraction. In W. J. Arnold & D. Levine (Eds.), *Nebraska symposium on motivation* (Vol. 17). Lincoln: University of Nebraska Press, 1969.

Aronson, E., & Cope, V. My enemy's enemy is my friend. *Journal of Personality and Social Psychology,* 1968, *8,* 8–12.

Aronson, E., & Linder, D. Gain and loss of esteem as determinants of interpersonal attractiveness. *Journal of Experimental Social Psychology*, 1965, *1*, 156–171.

Aronson, E., Willerman, B., & Floyd, J. The effect of a pratfall on increasing interpersonal attractiveness. *Psychonomic Science*, 1966, *4*, 227–228.

Asch, S. E. Forming impressions of personality. *Journal of Abnormal and Social Psychology*, 1946, *41*, 258–290.

Bach, G. R., & Wyden, P. *The intimate enemy*. New York: Avon, 1968.

Backman, C. W., & Secord, P. F. The effect of perceived liking on interpersonal attraction. *Human Relations*, 1959, *12*, 379–384.

Baldassare, M. Human spatial behavior. *Annual Review of Sociology*, 1978, *4*, 29–56.

Bane, M. J. Marital disruption and the lives of children. In G. Levinger & O. C. Moles (Eds.), *Divorce and separation*. New York: Basic Books, 1979.

Baron, R. A. Aggression-inhibiting influence of sexual humor. *Journal of Personality and Social Psychology*, 1978, *36*, 189–197.

Bar-Tal, D. & Saxe, L. Perceptions of similarly and dissimilarly attractive couples and individuals. *Journal of Personality and Social Psychology*, 1976, *33*, 772–781.

Baumeister, R. F. A self-presentational view of social phenomena. *Psychological Bulletin*, 1982, *91*, 3–26.

Beach, F. A. It's all in your mind. *Psychology Today*, 1969, *3*(2), 33–35; 60.

Beier, E. G., & Sternberg, D. P. Marital communication. *Journal of Communication*, 1977, *27*(3), 92–97.

Bell, R. R., & Chaskes, J. B. Premarital sexual experience among coeds, 1958 and 1968. *Journal of Marriage and the Family*, 1970, *32*, 81–84.

Bem, S. L. The measurement of psychological androgyny. *Journal of Consulting and Clinical Psychology*, 1974, *42*, 155–162.

Bentler, P. M. Heterosexual behavior assessment—I. Males. *Behaviour Research and Therapy*, 1968, *6*, 21–25. (a)

Bentler, P. M. Heterosexual behavior assessment—II. Females. *Behaviour Research and Therapy*, 1968, *6*, 27–30. (b)

Bermant, G. Response latencies of female rats during sexual intercourse. *Science*, 1961, *133*, 1771–1773.

Bernard, J. *The future of marriage*. New York: World, 1972.

Bernard, J. Change and stability in sex-role norms and behavior. *Journal of Social Issues*, 1976, *32*(3), 207–223.

Berscheid, E., Dion, K., Walster, E., & Walster, G. W. Physical attractiveness and dating choice: A test of the matching hypothesis. *Journal of Experimental Social Psychology*, 1971, *7*, 173–189.

Berscheid, E., & Graziano, W. The initiation of social relationships and interpersonal attraction. In R. L. Burgess & T. L. Huston (Eds.), *Social exchange in developing relationships*. New York: Academic Press, 1979.

Berscheid, E., & Walster, E. *Interpersonal attraction*. Reading, Mass.: Addison-Wesley, 1969.

Berscheid, E., & Walster, E. A little bit about love. In T. L. Huston (Ed.), *Foundations of interpersonal attraction*. New York: Academic Press, 1974. (a)

Berscheid, E., & Walster, E. Physical attractiveness. In L. Berkowitz (Ed.), *Advances in experimental social psychology* (Vol. 7). New York: Academic

Press, 1974. (b)

Bienvenu, M. J. Measurement of marital communication. *The Family Coordinator,* 1970, *19,* 26–31.

Billings, A. Conflict resolution in distressed and nondistressed married couples. *Journal of Consulting and Clinical Psychology,* 1979, 47, 368–376.

Birchler, G. R., Weiss, R. L., & Vincent, J. P. Multimethod analysis of social reinforcement exchange between maritally distressed and nondistressed spouse and stranger dyads. *Journal of Personality and Social Psychology,* 1975, *31,* 349–360.

Birdwhistell, R. L. *Kinesics and context.* Philadelphia: University of Pennsylvania Press, 1970.

Blau, P. M. *Exchange and power in social life.* New York: Wiley, 1964.

Bloom, B. L., Asher, S. J., & White, S. W. Marital disruption as a stressor: A review and analysis. *Psychological Bulletin,* 1978, *85,* 867–894.

Bockus, F. A systems approach to marital process. *Journal of Marriage and Family Counseling,* 1975, *1,* 251–258.

Bohannan, P. (Ed.). *Divorce and after.* Garden City, N.Y.: Doubleday, 1970.

Booth, A. Does wives' employment cause stress for husbands? *The Family Coordinator,* 1979, *28,* 445–449.

Booth, A., & Hess, E. Cross-sex friendship. *Journal of Marriage and the Family,* 1974, *36,* 38–47.

Bowlby, J. The nature of the child's tie to his mother. *International Journal of Psychoanalysis,* 1958, *39,* 350–373.

Braiker, H. B., & Kelley, H. H. Conflict in the development of close relationships. In R. L. Burgess & T. L. Huston (Eds.), *Social exchange in developing relationships.* New York: Academic Press, 1979.

Brickman, P. Rule structures and conflict relationships. In P. Brickman (Ed.), *Social conflict.* Lexington, Mass.: D. C. Heath, 1974.

Brink, J. H. Effect of interpersonal communication on attraction. *Journal of Personality and Social Psychology,* 1977, *35,* 783–790.

Brockner, J., & Swap, W. C. Effects of repeated exposure and attitudinal similarity on self-disclosure and interpersonal attraction. *Journal of Personality and Social Psychology,* 1976, *33,* 531–540.

Broschart, K. R. Family status and professional achievement: A study of women doctorates. *Journal of Marriage and the Family,* 1978, *40,* 71–76.

Browning, E. B. Sonnet XLIII. *The poetical works of Elizabeth Barrett Browning,* Cambridge edition. Boston: Houghton Mifflin, 1974.

Brownmiller, S. *Against our will: Men, women, and rape.* New York: Simon & Schuster, 1975.

Brunner, L. J. Smiles can be back channels. *Journal of Personality and Social Psychology,* 1979, *37,* 728–734.

Bryson, J. B., & Bryson, R. *Salary and job performance differences in dual career couples.* Paper presented at the meeting of the American Psychological Association, Montreal, September, 1980.

Buber, M. *I and thou* (2nd ed.). New York: Scribner, 1958.

Bullough, V. L. *Sexual variance in society and history.* Chicago: University of Chicago Press, 1976.

Burgess, R. L., & Huston, T. L. (Eds.). *Social exchange in developing relationships.* New York: Academic Press, 1979.

Burke, R. J., Weir, T., & Harrison, D. Disclosure of problems and tensions experienced by marital partners. *Psychological Reports, 1976, 38,* 531–542.

Burr, W. R. *Theory construction and the sociology of the family.* New York: Wiley, 1973.

Byrne, D. Attitudes and attraction. In L. Berkowitz (Ed.), *Advances in experimental social psychology* (Vol. 4). New York: Academic Press, 1969.

Byrne, D. *The attraction paradigm.* New York: Academic Press, 1971.

Byrne, D. Sexual imagery. In J. Money & H. Musaph (Eds.), *Handbook of sexology.* Amsterdam: Exerpta Medica, 1976.

Byrne, D. Social psychology and the study of sexual behavior. *Personality and Social Psychology Bulletin, 1977, 3,* 3–30. (a)

Byrne, D. Sexual changes in society and in science. In D. Byrne & L. A. Byrne (Eds.), *Exploring human sexuality.* New York: Harper & Row, 1977. (b)

Byrne, D., & Byrne, L. A. (Eds.). *Exploring human sexuality.* New York: Harper & Row, 1977.

Byrne, D., & Clore, G. L., Jr. Effectance arousal and attraction. *Journal of Personality and Social Psychology Monograph, 1967, 6*(4, Part 2, Whole No. 638).

Byrne, D., Clore, G. L., Jr., & Worchel, P. Effect of economic similarity–dissimilarity on interpersonal attraction. *Journal of Personality and Social Psychology, 1966, 4,* 220–224.

Byrne, D., Griffitt, W., & Stefaniak, D. Attraction and similarity of personality characteristics. *Journal of Personality and Social Psychology, 1967, 5,* 82–90.

Byrne, D., & Nelson, D. Attraction as a linear function of proportion of positive reinforcements. *Journal of Personality and Social Psychology, 1965, 1,* 659–663.

Cappella, J. N. Mutual influence in expressive behavior: Adult–adult and infant–adult dyadic interaction. *Psychological Bulletin, 1981, 89,* 101–132.

Carlson, E. R., & Coleman, C. E. H. Experiential and motivational determinants of the richness of an induced sexual fantasy. *Journal of Personality, 1977, 45,* 528–542.

Carson, R. C. Personality and exchange in developing relationships. In R. L. Burgess & T. L. Huston (Eds.), *Social exchange in developing relationships.* New York: Academic Press, 1979.

Cartwright, D., & Zander, A. (Eds.). *Group dynamics: Research and theory* (3rd ed.). New York: Harper & Row, 1968.

Cash, T. F., & Derlega, V. J. The matching hypothesis: Physical attractiveness among same-sexed friends. *Personality and Social Psychology Bulletin, 1978, 4,* 240–243.

Chaiken, S. Communicator physical attractiveness and persuasion. *Journal of Personality and Social Psychology, 1979, 37,* 1387–1397.

Chapman, A. J., Smith, J. R., Foot, H. C., & Pritchard, E. Behavioural and sociometric indices of friendship in children. In M. Cook & G. Wilson (Eds.), *Love and attraction.* Oxford: Pergamon, 1979.

Chelune, G. J. Sex differences, repression-sensitization and self-disclosure: A behavioral look. *Psychological Reports, 1977, 40,* 667–670.

Cherlin, A. Work life and marital dissolution. In G. Levinger & O. C. Moles (Eds.), *Divorce and separation.* New York: Basic Books, 1979.

Cialdini, R. B., & Richardson, K. D. Two indirect tactics of image management: Basking and blasting. *Journal of Personality and Social Psychology*, 1980, *39*, 406–415.

Clanton, G., & Smith, L. G. (Eds.). *Jealousy*. Englewood Cliffs, N.J.: Prentice-Hall, 1977.

Clark, M. S., & Mills, J. Interpersonal attraction in exchange and communal relationships. *Journal of Personality and Social Psychology*, 1979, *37*, 12–24.

Clayton, R. R., & Bokemeier, J. L. Premarital sex in the seventies. *Journal of Marriage and the Family*, 1980, *42*, 759–775.

Clore, G. L., & Byrne, D. A reinforcement-affect model of attraction. In T. L. Huston (Ed.), *Foundations of interpersonal attraction*. New York: Academic Press, 1974.

Clore, G. L., Wiggins, N. H., & Itkin, S. Gain and loss in attraction: Attributions from nonverbal behavior. *Journal of Personality and Social Psychology*, 1975, *31*, 706–712.

Cohen, S. *Social and personality development in childhood*. New York: Macmillan, 1976.

Connor, J. Olfactory control of aggressive and sexual behavior in the mouse (Mus musclus L.). *Psychonomic Science*, 1972, *27*, 1–3.

Constantine, L., & Constantine, J. M. *Group marriage*. New York: Collier Books, 1973.

Corrales, R. G. Power and satisfaction in early marriage. In R. E. Cromwell & D. H. Olson (Eds.), *Power in families*. New York: Halsted Press, 1975.

Corsini, R. J. Multiple predictors of marital happiness. *Marriage and Family Living*, 1956, *18*, 240–242.

Cottrell, N. B., & Epley, S. W. Affiliation, social comparison, and socially mediated stress reduction. In J. M. Suls & R. L. Miller (Eds.), *Social comparison processes*. Washington, D.C.: Hemisphere, 1977.

Cozby, P. C. Self-disclosure, reciprocity and liking. *Sociometry*, 1972, *35*, 151–160.

Curran, J. P. Convergence toward a single sexual standard? *Social Behavior and Personality*, 1975, *3*, 189–195.

Dabbs, J. M., Evans, M. S., Hopper, C. H., & Purvis, J. A. Self-monitors in conversation: What do they monitor? *Journal of Personality and Social Psychology*, 1980, *39*, 278–284.

Daher, D. M., & Banikiotes, P. G. Interpersonal attraction and rewarding aspects of disclosure content and level. *Journal of Personality and Social Psychology*, 1976, *33*, 492–496.

D'Augelli, A., Deys, D., Guerney, B., Hershenberg, B., & Sborofsky, S. Interpersonal skill training for dating couples. *Journal of Counseling Psychology*, 1974, *21*, 385–389.

Davis, J. D. Self-disclosure in an acquaintance exercise: Responsibility for level of intimacy. *Journal of Personality and Social Psychology*, 1976, *33*, 787–792.

Davis, K. E., & Todd, M. Friendship and love relationships. In K. E. Davis (Ed.), *Advances in descriptive psychology* (Vol. 2). Greenwich, Conn.: JAI Press, 1982.

De Forest, C., & Stone, G. L. Effects of sex and intimacy level on self-disclosure. *Journal of Counseling Psychology*, 1980, *27*, 93–96.

Derlega, V. J., Wilson, M., & Chaikin, A. L. Friendship and disclosure reciprocity. *Journal of Personality and Social Psychology*, 1976, *34*, 578–582.

Dermer, M., & Pyszczynski, T. A. Effects of erotica upon men's loving and liking responses for women they love. *Journal of Personality and Social Psychology*, 1978, *36*, 1302–1309.

Dermer, M., & Thiel, D. L. When beauty may fail. *Journal of Personality and Social Psychology*, 1975, *31*, 1168–1176.

Deutsch, M. Conflicts: Productive and destructive. *Journal of Social Issues*, 1969, *25*(1), 7–41.

Dewsbury, D. A. Effects of novelty on copulatory behavior: The Coolidge effect and related phenomena. *Psychological Bulletin*, 1981, *89*, 464–482.

Dickinson, E. Wild nights. In R. N. Linscott (Ed.), *Selected poems and letters of Emily Dickinson*. Garden City, N.Y.: Doubleday, 1959.

Dion, K. The incentive value of physical attractiveness for young children. *Personality and Social Psychology Bulletin*, 1977, *3*, 67–70.

Dion, K., Berscheid, E., & Walster, E. What is beautiful is good. *Journal of Personality and Social Psychology*, 1972, *24*, 285–290.

Donnerstein, E. Aggressive erotica and violence against women. *Journal of Personality and Social Psychology*, 1980, *39*, 269–277.

Donnerstein, E., & Hallam, J. Facilitating effects of erotica on aggression against women. *Journal of Personality and Social Psychology*, 1978, *36*, 1270–1277.

Douglas, M. *Behavior control by happily-married couples in conflict situations*. Paper presented at the meeting of the American Psychological Association, Montreal, September, 1980.

Ebbesen, E. B., Kjos, G. L., & Konecni, V. J. Spatial ecology: Its effects on the choice of friends and enemies. *Journal of Experimental Social Psychology*, 1976, *12*, 505–518.

Ehrlich, H. J., & Graeven, D. B. Reciprocal self-disclosure in a dyad. *Journal of Experimental Social Psychology*, 1971, *7*, 389–400.

Ekman, P. Universals and cultural differences in facial expressions of emotion. *Nebraska Symposium on Motivation*, 1972, *19*, 207–283.

Ekman, P., Friesen, W. V., & Ancoli, S. Facial signs of emotional experience. *Journal of Personality and Social Psychology*, 1980, *39*, 1125–1134.

Ekman, P., Friesen, W. V., & Tomkins, S. S. Facial affect scoring technique: A first validity study. *Semiotica*, 1971, *3*, 37–58.

Elliott, G. C. Some effects of deception and level of self-monitoring on planning and reacting to a self-presentation. *Journal of Personality and Social Psychology*, 1979, *37*, 1282–1292.

Ellis, H. *Studies in the psychology of sex* (1899). New York: Random House, 1936.

Ellsworth, P. C., Carlsmith, J. M., & Henson, A. The stare as a stimulus to flight in human subjects. *Journal of Personality and Social Psychology*, 1972, *21*, 302–311.

Exline, R. V. Visual interaction: The glances of power and preference. *Nebraska Symposium on Motivation*, 1972, *19*, 163–206.

Falbo, T., & Peplau, L. A. Power strategies in intimate relationships. *Journal of Personality and Social Psychology*, 1980, *38*, 618–628.

Fast, J. *Body language*. New York: M. Evans, 1970.

Feigenbaum, W. M. Reciprocity in self-disclosure within the psychological interview. *Psychological Reports*, 1977, *40*, 15–26.

Ferber, M., & Huber, J. Husbands, wives, and careers. *Journal of Marriage and the Family*, 1979, *41*, 315–325.

Festinger, L. Informal social communication. *Psychological Review*, 1950, *57*, 271–282.

Festinger, L. A theory of social comparison processes. *Human Relations*, 1954, *7*, 117–140.

Fichten, C. *It's all your fault: Videotape and spouse's causal attributions*. Paper presented at the meeting of the American Psychological Association, Montreal, September, 1980.

Figley, C. R. Tactical self-presentation and interpersonal attraction. In M. Cook & G. Wilson (Eds.), *Love and attraction*. Oxford: Pergamon, 1979.

Fishbein, M., & Ajzen, I. *Belief, attitude, intention and behavior: An introduction to theory and research*. Reading, Mass.: Addison-Wesley, 1975.

Fisher, S. *The female orgasm: Psychology, physiology, fantasy*. New York: Basic Books, 1973.

Fisher, W. A., & Byrne, D. Sex differences in response to erotica? Love versus lust. *Journal of Personality and Social Psychology*, 1978, *36*, 117–125.

Foa, E. B., & Foa, U. G. Resource theory of social exchange. In J. W. Thibaut, J. T. Spence, & R. C. Carson (Eds.), *Contemporary topics in social psychology*. Morristown, N.J.: General Learning Press, 1976.

Folkes, V. S., & Sears, D. O. Does everybody like a liker? *Journal of Experimental Social Psychology*, 1977, *13*, 505–519.

Foot, H. C., Smith, J. R., & Chapman, A. J. Non-verbal expressions of intimacy in children. In M. Cook & G. Wilson (Eds.), *Love and attraction*. Oxford: Pergamon, 1979.

Ford, C. S., & Beach, F. A. *Patterns of sexual behavior*. New York: Harper & Row, 1951.

Forisha, B. L. *Sex roles and personal awareness*. Morristown, N.J.: General Learning Press, 1978.

Franck, K. A. Friends and strangers: The social experience of living in urban and non-urban settings. *Journal of Social Issues*, 1980, *36*(3), 52–71.

Frank, E., Anderson, C., & Rubinstein, D. Marital role strain and sexual satisfaction. *Journal of Consulting and Clinical Psychology*, 1979, *47*, 1096–1103.

French, J. R. P., & Raven, B. The bases of social power. In D. Cartwright & A. Zander (Eds.), *Group dynamics: Research and theory* (3rd ed.). New York: Harper & Row, 1968.

Freud, S. *Three contributions to the theory of sex*. New York: Dutton, 1962. (Originally published, 1905.)

Freud, S. [New introductory lectures on psychoanalysis] (J. Strachey, Ed. and trans.). New York: Norton, 1965. (Originally published, 1933.)

Furstenberg, F. F. Premarital pregnancy and marital instability. In G. Levinger & O. C. Moles (Eds.), *Divorce and separation*. New York: Basic Books, 1979.

Gadlin, H. Private lives and public order: A critical view of the history of intimate relations in the United States. In G. Levinger & H. L. Raush (Eds.), *Close relationships: Perspectives on the meaning of intimacy*. Amherst, Mass.: University of Massachusetts Press, 1977.

Gagnon, J. H. Sex research and social change. *Archives of Sexual Behavior*, 1975, *4*, 111–141.

Gagnon, J. H. *Human sexualities*. Glenview, Ill.: Scott, Foresman, 1977.

Gagnon, J. H., & Greenblat, C. S. *Life designs: Individuals, marriages and families*. New York: Scott, Foresman, 1978.

Gagnon, J. H., & Simon, W. *Sexual conduct: The social sources of human sexuality*. Chicago: Aldine, 1973.

Gardner, L. I. Deprivation dwarfism. *Scientific American*, 1972, *227*(1), 76–82.

Geer, J. H. Direct measurement of genital responding. *American Psychologist*, 1975, *30*, 415–418.

Geer, J. H., Morokoff, P., & Greenwood, P. Sexual arousal in women: The development of a measurement device for vaginal blood flow. *Archives of Sexual Behavior*, 1974, *3*, 559–564.

Geracimos, A. How I stopped beating my wife. *Ms.*, 1976, *5*(2), 53.

Gergen, K. J. Social psychology as history. *Journal of Personality and Social Psychology*, 1973, *26*, 309–320.

Gersick, K. E. Fathers by choice: Divorced men who receive custody of their children. In G. Levinger & O. C. Moles (Eds.), *Divorce and separation*. New York: Basic Books, 1979.

Gilbert, S. Self-disclosure, intimacy and communication in families. *The Family Coordinator*, 1976, *25*, 221–231.

Gilbert, S., & Whiteneck, G. G. Toward a multidimensional approach to the study of self-disclosure. *Human Communication Research*, 1976, *2*, 347–355.

Goetting, A. Former spouse-current spouse relationships: Behavioral expectations. *Journal of Family Issues*, 1980, *1*, 58–81.

Goffman, E. On cooling the mark out: Some aspects of adaptation to failure. *Psychiatry*, 1952, *15*, 451–463.

Goldman, W., & Lewis, P. Beautiful is good: Evidence that the physically attractive are more socially skillful. *Journal of Experimental Social Psychology*, 1977, *13*, 125–130.

Gottman, J. *Marital intervention: Experimental investigations*. New York: Academic Press, 1979.

Gottman, J., Notarius, C., Markman, H., Bank, S., & Yoppi, B. Behavior exchange theory and marital decision making. *Journal of Personality and Social Psychology*, 1976, *34*, 14–23.

Gouldner, A. W. The norm of reciprocity: A preliminary statement. *American Sociological Review*, 1960, *25*, 161–178.

Gray, J. G. *The warriors: Reflections on men in battle*. New York: Harper & Row, 1959. (Perennial Library Edition, 1973.)

Griffitt, W. Environmental effects on interpersonal affective behavior: Ambient effective temperature and attraction. *Journal of Personality and Social Psychology*, 1970, *15*, 240–244.

Griffitt, W., & Veitch, R. Hot and crowded: Influence of population density and temperature on interpersonal affective behavior. *Journal of Personality and Social Psychology*, 1971, *17*, 92–98.

Gross, H. E. Dual-career couples who live apart: Two types. *Journal of Marriage and the Family*, 1980, *42*, 567–576.

Hall, E. T. *The hidden dimension*. New York: Doubleday, 1966.

Hall, F. S., & Hall, D. T. *The two-career couple*. Reading, Mass.: Addison-Wesley, 1979.

Hall, J. A. Gender effects in decoding nonverbal cues. *Psychological Bulletin*, 1978, *85*, 845–857.

Hariton, B. E., & Singer, J. L. Women's fantasies during sexual intercourse. *Journal of Consulting and Clinical Psychology*, 1974, *42*, 313–322.

Harlow, H. F. *Learning to love*. New York: Jason Aronson, 1974.

Harlow, H. F., & Harlow, M. K. Learning to love. *Scientific American*, 1966, *54*, 244–272.

Harlow, H. F., & Harlow, M. K. The young monkeys. In P. Cramer (Ed.), *Readings in developmental psychology today*. Del Mar, Calif.: CRM Books, 1970.

Harrison, A. A., & Saeed, L. Let's make a deal: An analysis of revelations and stipulations in lonely hearts advertisements. *Journal of Personality and Social Psychology*, 1977, *35*, 257–264.

Hartup, W. W., & Lempers, J. A problem in life-span development: The interactional analysis of family attachments. In P. B. Baltes & K. W. Schaie (Eds.), *Life-span developmental psychology: Personality and socialization*. New York: Academic Press, 1973.

Harvey, J. H. Research methods. In E. Berscheid, A. Christensen, J. Harvey, T. Huston, H. Kelley, G. Levinger, E. McClintock, A. Peplau, & D. Peterson (Eds.), *The psychology of close relationships*, in press.

Harvey, J. H., Wells, G. L., & Alvarez, M. D. Attribution in the context of conflict and separation in close relationships. In J. H. Harvey, W. Ickes, & R. F. Kidd (Eds.), *New directions in attribution research* (Vol. 2). Hillsdale, N.J.: Erlbaum, 1978.

Hayduk, L. A. Personal space: An evaluative and orienting overview. *Psychological Bulletin*, 1978, *85*, 117–134.

Heider, F. *The psychology of interpersonal relations*. New York: Wiley, 1958.

Helmreich, R. L., Spence, J. T., & Holahan, C. K. Psychological androgyny and sex role flexibility: A test of two hypotheses. *Journal of Personality and Social Psychology*, 1979, *37*, 1631–1644.

Hendrick, C., & Brown, S. R. Introversion, extraversion, and interpersonal attraction. *Journal of Personality and Social Psychology*, 1971, *20*, 31–36.

Hendrick, C., & Jones, R. A. *The nature of theory and research in social psychology*. New York: Academic Press, 1972.

Hendrick, C., & Page, H. Self-esteem, attitude similarity, and attraction. *Journal of Personality*, 1970, *38*, 588–601.

Hendrick, S. S. Self-disclosure and marital satisfaction. *Journal of Personality and Social Psychology*, 1981, *40*, 1150–1159.

Herman, J. Father–daughter incest. *Professional Psychology*, 1981, *12*, 76–80.

Hess, R. D., & Camara, K. A. Post-divorce family relationships as mediating factors in the consequences of divorce for children. *Journal of Social Issues*, 1979, *35*(4), 79–96.

Hetherington, E. M., Cox, M., & Cox, R. Play and social interaction in children following divorce. *Journal of Social Issues*, 1979, *35*(4), 26–49.

Hieger, L. J., & Troll, L. A three-generation study of attitudes concerning the importance of romantic love in mate-selection. *Gerontologist*, 1973, *13*(3, Part 2), 86. (Abstract)

Hill, C. T., Rubin, Z., & Peplau, L. A. Breakups before marriage: The end of 103 affairs. *Journal of Social Issues*, 1976, *32*(1), 147–168.

Hill, C. T., Rubin, Z., & Peplau, L. A. Breakups before marriage: The end of 103 affairs. In G. Levinger & O. C. Moles (Eds.), *Divorce and separation*. New York: Basic Books, 1979.

Himmelfarb, S., & Eagly, A. H. *Readings in attitude change.* New York: Wiley, 1974.

Hinde, R. A. *Towards understanding relationships.* London: Academic Press, 1979.

Hobart, C. W. Changes in courtship and cohabitation in Canada, 1968–1977. In M. Cook & G. Wilson (Eds.), *Love and attraction: An international conference.* New York: Pergamon, 1979.

Hofer, M. A. (Ed.). *Parent-infant interaction.* Ciba Foundation Symposium 33. New York: American Elsevier, 1975.

Hoffman-Graff, M. Interviewer use of positive and negative self-disclosure and interviewer-subject sex pairing. *Journal of Counseling Psychology,* 1977, *24,* 184–190.

Holmes, J. G., & Miller, D. T. Interpersonal conflict. In J. W. Thibaut, J. T. Spence, & R. C. Carson (Eds.), *Contemporary topics in social psychology.* Morristown, N.J.: General Learning Press, 1976.

Homans, G. C. *The human group.* New York: Harcourt & Brace, 1950.

Homans, G. C. *Social behavior: Its elementary forms.* New York: Harcourt, Brace & World, 1961.

Howard, J. W., & Dawes, R. M. Linear prediction of marital happiness. *Personality and Social Psychology Bulletin,* 1976, *2,* 478–480.

Huesmann, L. R., & Levinger, G. Incremental exchange theory: A formal model for progression in dyadic social interaction. In L. Berkowitz & E. Walster (Eds.), *Advances in experimental social psychology* (Vol. 9). New York: Academic Press, 1976.

Hunt, M. *Sexual behavior in the 1970s.* Chicago: Playboy Press, 1974.

Huston, T. L., & Burgess, R. L. Social exchange in developing relationships: An overview. In R. L. Burgess & T. L. Huston (Eds.), *Social exchange in developing relationships.* New York: Academic Press, 1979.

Huston, T. L., & Levinger, G. Interpersonal attraction and relationships. In M. R. Rosenzweig & L. W. Porter (Eds.), *Annual review of psychology* (Vol. 29). Palo Alto, Calif.: Annual Reviews, 1978.

Ickes, W., & Barnes, R. D. Boys and girls together—and alienated: On enacting stereotyped sex roles in mixed-sex dyads. *Journal of Personality and Social Psychology,* 1978, *36,* 669–683.

Insko, C. A. *Theories of attitude change.* New York: Appleton-Century-Crofts, 1967.

Insko, C. A., & Adewole, A. The role of assumed reciprocation of sentiment and assumed similarity in the production of attraction and agreement effects in P-O-X triads. *Journal of Personality and Social Psychology,* 1979, *37,* 790–808.

Johnson, H. J. *Executive life-styles.* New York: Crowell, 1974.

Johnson, M. P. Commitment: A conceptual structure and empirical application. *Sociology Quarterly,* 1973, *14,* 395–406.

Jones, E. *The life and work of Sigmund Freud: Years of maturity 1901–1919* (Vol. 2). New York: Basic Books, 1955.

Jones, E. E. *Ingratiation.* New York: Appleton-Century-Crofts, 1964.

Jones, E. E., & Gordon, E. M. The timing of self-disclosure and its effect on personal attraction. *Journal of Personality and Social Psychology,* 1972, *24,* 358–365.

Jones, E. E., & Pittman, T. S. Toward a general theory of strategic self-presentation. In J. Suls (Ed.), *Psychological perspectives on the self* (Vol. 1). Hillsdale, N.J.: Erlbaum, 1982.

Jourard, S. M. *The transparent self.* Princeton, N.J.: Van Nostrand Reinhold, 1964.

Jourard, S. M. *Self-disclosure: An experimental analysis of the transparent self.* New York: Wiley, 1971.

Kahn, A. The power war: Male response to power loss under equality. *Psychology of Women Quarterly,* in press.

Kaplan, H. S. *The new sex therapy.* New York: Brunner/Mazel, 1974.

Kasarda, J. D., & Janowitz, M. Community attachment in mass society. *American Sociological Review,* 1974, *39,* 328–339.

Kelley, H. H. *Personal relationships: Their structures and processes.* Hillsdale, N.J.: Erlbaum, 1979.

Kelly, B., & Wallerstein, J. S. The effects of parental divorce: Experiences of the child in early latency. *American Journal of Orthopsychiatry,* 1976, *46*(1), 25–32.

Kenrick, D. T., & Cialdini, R. B. Romantic attraction: Misattribution versus reinforcement explanations. *Journal of Personality and Social Psychology,* 1977, *35,* 381–391.

Kenrick, D. T., & Johnson, G. A. Interpersonal attraction in aversive environments: A problem for the classical conditioning paradigm? *Journal of Personality and Social Psychology,* 1979, *37,* 572–579.

Kerckhoff, A. C., & Davis, K. E. Value consensus and need complementarity in mate selection. *American Sociological Review,* 1962, *27,* 295–303.

Kiesler, C. A. *The psychology of commitment.* New York: Academic Press, 1971.

King, K., Balswick, J. C., & Robinson, I. E. The continuing premarital sexual revolution among college females. *Journal of Marriage and the Family,* 1977, *39,* 455–459.

Kinsey, A. C., Pomeroy, W. B., & Martin, C. E. *Sexual behavior in the human male.* Philadelphia: Saunders, 1948.

Kinsey, A. C., Pomeroy, W. B., Martin, C. E., & Gebhard, P. H. *Sexual behavior in the human female.* Philadelphia: Saunders, 1953.

Kipnis, D. *The powerholders.* Chicago: University of Chicago Press, 1976.

Knudson, R. M., Sommers, A. A., & Golding, S. L. Interpersonal perception and mode of resolution in marital conflict. *Journal of Personality and Social Psychology,* 1980, *38,* 751–763.

Koestenbaum, P. *Existential sexuality: Choosing to love.* Englewood Cliffs, N.J.: Prentice-Hall, 1974.

Kohen, J. A., Brown, C. A., & Feldberg, R. Divorced mothers: The costs and benefits of female family control. In G. Levinger & O. C. Moles (Eds.), *Divorce and separation.* New York: Basic Books, 1979.

Komarovsky, M. *Blue-collar marriage.* New York: Vintage Books, 1967.

Komarovsky, M. Patterns of self-disclosure of male undergraduates. *Journal of Marriage and the Family,* 1974, *36,* 677–686.

Koren, P., Carlton, K., & Shaw, D. Marital conflict: Relations among behaviors, outcomes, and distress. *Journal of Consulting and Clinical Psychology,* 1980, *48,* 460–468.

Kosok, M. The phenomenology of fucking. *Telos,* 1971, No. 8, 64–76.

Krafft-Ebing, R. von. *Psychopathia sexualis* (1886). Philadelphia: F. A. Davis, 1894.

Krauss, R. M., & Weinheimer, S. Concurrent feedback, confirmation, and the encoding of referents in verbal communication. *Journal of Personality and Social Psychology*, 1966, *4*, 343–346.

Krebs, D., & Adinolfi, A. A. Physical attractiveness, social relations, and personality style. *Journal of Personality and Social Psychology*, 1975, *31*, 245–253.

Kressel, K., Lopez-Morillas, M., Weinglass, J., & Deutsch, M. Professional intervention in divorce: The views of lawyers, psychotherapists, and clergy. In G. Levinger & O. C. Moles (Eds.), *Divorce and separation*. New York: Basic Books, 1979.

Kulka, R. A., & Weingarten, H. The long-term effects of parental divorce in childhood on adult adjustment. *Journal of Social Issues*, 1979, *35*(4), 50–78.

La Gaipa, J. J. Testing a multidimensional approach to friendship. In S. Duck (Ed.), *Theory and practice in interpersonal attraction*. London: Academic Press, 1977.

Laing, R. D. *Knots*. New York: Pantheon, 1970.

Landy, D., & Sigall, H. Beauty is talent: Task evaluation as a function of the performer's physical attractiveness. *Journal of Personality and Social Psychology*, 1974, *29*, 299–304.

Langley, R., & Levy, R. C. *Wife beating: The silent crisis*. New York: Dutton, 1977.

Lasswell, M., & Lobsenz, N. M. *Styles of loving: Why you love the way you do*. New York: Doubleday, 1980.

Lederer, W. J., & Jackson, D. D. *Mirages of marriage*. New York: Norton, 1968.

Lee, J. A. *The colors of love: An exploration of the ways of loving*. Don Mills, Ontario: New Press, 1973. (Popular Edition, 1976.)

Leik, R. K., & Leik, S. K. Transition to interpersonal commitment. In R. L. Hamblin & J. H. Kunkel (Eds.), *Behavior theory in sociology*. New Brunswick: Transaction, 1976.

Lein, L. Male participation in home life: Impact of social supports and breadwinner responsibility on the allocation of tasks. *The Family Coordinator*, 1979, *28*, 489–495.

Levinger, G. Systematic distortion in spouses' reports of preferred and actual sexual behavior. *Sociometry*, 1966, *29*, 291–299.

Levinger, G. A three-level approach to attraction: Toward an understanding of pair relatedness. In T. L. Huston (Ed.), *Foundations of interpersonal attraction*. New York: Academic Press, 1974.

Levinger, G. The embrace of lives: Changing and unchanging. In G. Levinger & H. L. Raush (Eds.), *Close relationships: Perspectives on the meaning of intimacy*. Amherst, Mass.: University of Massachusetts Press, 1977.

Levinger, G. A social psychological perspective on marital dissolution. In G. Levinger & O. C. Moles (Eds.), *Divorce and separation*. New York: Basic Books, 1979. (a)

Levinger, G. Marital cohesiveness at the brink: The fate of applications for divorce. In G. Levinger & O. C. Moles (Eds.), *Divorce and separation*. New York: Basic Books, 1979. (b)

Levinger, G., & Raush, H. L. (Eds.). *Close relationships*. Amherst, Mass.: University of Massachusetts Press, 1977.

Levinger, G., & Senn, D. J. Disclosure of feelings in marriage. *Merrill-Palmer Quarterly*, 1967, *13*, 237–249.

Levinger, G., Senn, D. J., & Jorgensen, B. W. Progress toward permanence in courtship: A test of the Kerckhoff-Davis hypotheses. *Sociometry*, 1970, *33*, 427–443.

Levinger, G., & Snoek, J. D. *Attraction in relationship: A new look at interpersonal attraction*. Morristown, N.J.: General Learning Press, 1972.

Lewis, M., & Rosenblum, L. A. (Eds.). *The effect of the infant on its caregiver*. New York: Wiley, 1974.

Lewis, R. A. A developmental framework for the analysis of premarital dyadic formation. *Family Process*, 1972, *11*, 17–48.

Lewis, R. A. A longitudinal test of a developmental framework for premarital dyadic formation. *Journal of Marriage and the Family*, 1973, *35*, 16–25.

Lewis, R. A. A reply to Rubin and Levinger's critique of Lewis' test of the PDF developmental framework. *Journal of Marriage and the Family*, 1975, *37*, 9–11.

Lickona, T. A cognitive–developmental approach to interpersonal attraction. In T. L. Huston (Ed.), *Foundations of interpersonal attraction*. New York: Academic Press, 1974.

Locke, H. J. *Predicting adjustment in marriage*. New York: Holt, 1951.

Locke, H. J., & Wallace, K. Short marital-adjustment and prediction tests: Their reliability and validity. *Marriage and Family Living*, 1959, *21*, 251–255.

Longfellow, C. Divorce in context: Its impact on children. In G. Levinger & O. C. Moles (Eds.), *Divorce and separation*. New York: Basic Books, 1979.

Lott, A. J., & Lott, B. E. The role of reward in the formation of positive interpersonal attitudes. In T. L. Huston (Ed.), *Foundations of interpersonal attraction*. New York: Academic Press, 1974.

Luckey, E. B. Number of years married as related to personality perception and marital satisfaction. *Journal of Marriage and the Family*, 1966, *28*, 44–48.

Luckey, E. B., & Nass, G. D. A comparison of sexual attitudes and behavior in an international sample. *Journal of Marriage and the Family*, 1969, *31*, 364–379.

Maccoby, E. E., & Jacklin, C. N. *The psychology of sex differences*. Stanford, Calif.: Stanford University Press, 1974.

Madden, M. E., & Janoff-Bulman, R. Blame, control, and marital satisfaction: Wives' attributions for conflict in marriage. *Journal of Marriage and the Family*, 1981, *43*, 663–674.

Malamuth, N. M., Feshbach, S., & Jaffe, Y. Sexual arousal and aggression: Recent experiments and theoretical issues. *Journal of Social Issues*, 1977, *33*(2), 110–133.

Malamuth, N. M., Heim, M., & Feshbach, S. Sexual responsiveness of college students to rape depictions: Inhibitory and disinhibitory effects. *Journal of Personality and Social Psychology*, 1980, *38*, 399–408.

Marwell, G., & Hage, J. The organization of role relationships: A systematic description. *American Sociological Review*, 1970, *35*, 884–900.

Masters, W. H., & Johnson, V. E. *Human sexual response*. Boston: Little, Brown, 1966.

Masters, W. H., & Johnson, V. E. *Human sexual inadequacy*. Boston: Little, Brown, 1970.

Mayer, J. E. Disclosing marital problems. *Social Casework*, 1967, *48*, 342–351.

McAdams, D. P., & Powers, J. Themes of intimacy in behavior and thought.

Journal of Personality and Social Psychology, 1981, *40,* 573–587.

McDonald, G. W. Structural exchange and marital interaction. *Journal of Marriage and the Family,* 1981, *43,* 825–839.

Melton, W., & Thomas, D. L. Instrumental and expressive values in mate selection of black and white college students. *Journal of Marriage and the Family,* 1976, *38,* 509–517.

Mettee, D. R., & Aronson, E. Affective reactions to appraisal from others. In T. L. Huston (Ed.), *Foundations of interpersonal attraction.* New York: Academic Press, 1974.

Mettee, D. R., & Wilkins, P. C. When similarity "hurts": The effects of perceived ability and a humorous blunder upon interpersonal attractiveness. *Journal of Personality and Social Psychology,* 1972, *22,* 246–258.

Michener, H. A., Lawler, E. J., & Bacarach, S. B. Perception of power in conflict situations. *Journal of Personality and Social Psychology,* 1973, *28,* 155–162.

Middlebrook, P. N. *Social psychology and modern life* (2nd ed.). New York: Knopf, 1980.

Middlemist, R. D., Knowles, E. S., & Matter, C. F. Personal space invasions in the lavatory: Suggestive evidence for arousal. *Journal of Personality and Social Psychology,* 1976, *33,* 541–546.

Miller, C. E., & Norman, R. M. G. Balance, agreement, and attraction in hypothetical social situations. *Journal of Experimental Social Psychology,* 1976, *12,* 109–119.

Miller, S., Corrales, R., & Wackman, D. B. Recent progress in understanding and facilitating marital communication. *The Family Coordinator,* 1975, *24,* 143–152.

Mills, J., & Clark, M. S. Exchange and communal relationships. In L. Wheeler (Ed.), *Review of personality and social psychology* (Vol. 3). Beverly Hills, Calif.: Sage, 1982.

Money, J. *Love and love sickness: The science of sex, gender difference, and pair-bonding.* Baltimore, Md.: Johns Hopkins University Press, 1980.

Moreno, J. L. *Who shall survive?* Washington, D.C.: Nervous and Mental Diseases Monograph, No. 58, 1934.

Morris, D. *Intimate behavior.* New York: Random House, 1971.

Mortimer, J. T. Dual-career families—a sociological perspective. In S. S. Peterson, J. M. Richardson, & G. V. Kreuter (Eds.), *The two-career family: Issues and alternatives.* Washington, D.C.: University Press of America, 1978.

Morton, T. L. Intimacy and reciprocity of exchange: A comparison of spouses and strangers. *Journal of Personality and Social Psychology,* 1978, *36,* 72–81.

Morton, T. L., Alexander, J. F., & Altman, I. Communication and relationship definition. In G. R. Miller (Ed.), *Annual reviews of communication research* (Vol. 5). Beverly Hills, Calif.: Sage, 1976.

Mosher, D. L., & Cross, H. J. Sex guilt and premarital sexual experiences of college students. *Journal of Consulting and Clinical Psychology,* 1971, *36,* 27–32.

Murray, H. A. *Explorations in personality.* New York: Oxford University Press, 1938.

Murstein, B. I. A theory of marital choice and its applicability to marriage adjustment. In B. I. Murstein (Ed.), *Theories of attraction and love.* New York: Springer, 1971.

Murstein, B. I. Physical attraction and marital choice. *Journal of Personality and Social Psychology*, 1972, *22*, 8–12.

Murstein, B. I. Clarification of obfuscation on conjugation: A reply to a criticism of the SVR theory of marital choice. *Journal of Marriage and the Family*, 1974, *36*, 231–234. (a)

Murstein, B. I. *Love, sex, and marriage through the ages*. New York: Springer, 1974. (b)

Murstein, B. I. *Who will marry whom?* New York: Springer, 1976.

Murstein, B. I. Mate selection in the 1970s. *Journal of Marriage and the Family*, 1980, *42*, 777–792.

Murstein, B. I., & Christy, P. Physical attractiveness and marriage adjustment in middle-aged couples. *Journal of Personality and Social Psychology*, 1976, *34*, 537–542.

Nahemow, L., & Lawton, M. P. Similarity and propinquity in friendship formation. *Journal of Personality and Social Psychology*, 1975, *32*, 205–213.

Navran, L. Communication and adjustment in marriage. *Family Process*, 1967, *6*, 173–184.

Newcomb, T. M. *The acquaintance process*. New York: Holt, Rinehart & Winston, 1961.

Noble, J., & Noble, W. *How to live with other people's children*. New York: Hawthorne, 1977.

Noller, P. Misunderstandings in marital communication: A study of couples' nonverbal communication. *Journal of Personality and Social Psychology*, 1980, *39*, 1135–1148.

Norman, M. The new extended family. *The New York Times Magazine*, Nov. 23, 1980, pp. 26–29; 44; 46; 53–54; 147; 162; 166; 173.

Norton, A. J., & Glick, P. C. Marital instability in America: Past, present, and future. In G. Levinger & O. C. Moles (Eds.), *Divorce and separation*, New York: Basic Books, 1979.

Olson, D. H., & Cromwell, R. E. Methodological issues in family power. In R. E. Cromwell & D. H. Olson (Eds.), *Power in families*. New York: Halsted Press, 1975.

Olson, D. H., Cromwell, R. E., & Klein, D. M. Beyond family power. In R. E. Cromwell & D. H. Olson (Eds.), *Power in families*. New York: Halsted Press, 1975.

Orvis, B. R., Kelley, H. H., & Butler, D. Attributional conflict in young couples. In J. H. Harvey, W. J. Ickes, & R. F. Kidd (Eds.), *New directions in attribution research* (Vol. 1). Hillsdale, N.J.: Erlbaum, 1976.

Osgood, C. E., Suci, G. J., & Tannenbaum, P. H. *The measurement of meaning*. Urbana, Ill.: University of Illinois Press, 1957.

Osmond, M. W. Reciprocity: A dynamic model and a method to study family power. *Journal of Marriage and the Family*, 1978, *40*, 49–61.

Passer, M. W., Kelley, H. H., & Michela, J. L. Multidimensional scaling of the causes for negative interpersonal behavior. *Journal of Personality and Social Psychology*, 1978, *36*, 951–962.

Patterson, M. L. An arousal model of interpersonal intimacy. *Psychological Review*, 1976, *83*, 235–245.

Peplau, L. A., & Perlman, D. Blueprint for a social psychological theory of loneliness. In M. Cook & G. Wilson (Eds.), *Love and attraction*. Oxford: Pergamon, 1979.

References

Peplau, L. A., Rubin, Z., & Hill, C. T. Sexual intimacy in dating relationships. *Journal of Social Issues*, 1977, *33*(2), 86–109.

Peterson, D. R. A functional approach to the study of person–person interactions. In D. Magnusson & N. S. Endler (Eds.), *Personality at the crossroads: Current issues in interactional psychology*. Hillsdale, N.J.: Erlbaum, 1977.

Phillips, D., & Judd, R. *How to fall out of love*. New York: Fawcett, 1978.

Pleck, J. H. Men's family work: Three perspectives and some new data. *The Family Coordinator*, 1979, *28*, 481–488.

Pope, H., & Mueller, C. W. The intergenerational transmission of marital instability: Comparisons by race and sex. In G. Levinger & O. C. Moles (Eds.), *Divorce and separation*. New York: Basic Books, 1979.

Powers, W. G., & Hutchinson, K. The measurement of communication apprehension in the marriage relationship. *Journal of Marriage and the Family*, 1979, *41*, 89–95.

Price, R. A., & Vandenberg, S. G. Matching for physical attractiveness in married couples. *Personality and Social Psychology Bulletin*, 1979, *5*, 398–400.

Rabbie, J. Differential preference for companionship under stress. *Journal of Abnormal and Social Psychology*, 1963, *67*, 643–648.

Rands, M., & Levinger, G. Implicit theories of relationship: An intergenerational study. *Journal of Personality and Social Psychology*, 1979, *37*, 645–661.

Rands, M., Levinger, G., & Mellinger, G. D. Patterns of conflict resolution and marital satisfaction. *Journal of Family Issues*, 1981, *2*, 297–321.

Rapoport, A. *Fights, games and debates*. Ann Arbor: University of Michigan Press, 1960.

Rapoport, R., & Rapoport, R. *Dual career families*. Baltimore: Penguin, 1971.

Raush, H. L., Barry, W. A., Hertel, R. K., & Swain, M. A. *Communication, conflict, and marriage*. San Francisco: Jossey-Bass, 1974.

Raven, B. H., Centers, R., & Rodrigues, A. The bases of conjugal power. In R. E. Cromwell & D. H. Olson (Eds.), *Power in families*. New York: Halsted Press, 1975.

Reis, H. T., Nezlek, J., & Wheeler, L. Physical attractiveness in social interaction. *Journal of Personality and Social Psychology*, 1980, *38*, 604–617.

Ridley, C. A., & Avery, A. W. Social network influence on the dyadic relationship. In R. L. Burgess & T. L. Huston (Eds.), *Social exchange in developing relationships*. New York: Academic Press, 1979.

Riskin, J., & Faunce, E. E. An evaluative review of family interaction research. *Family Process*, 1972, *11*, 365–455.

Robinson, P. A. *The modernization of sex*. New York: Harper & Row, 1976.

Rodin, M. J. Liking and disliking: Sketch of an alternative view. *Personality and Social Psychology Bulletin*, 1978, *4*, 473–478.

Rokeach, M. *The open and closed mind: Investigations into the nature of belief systems and personality systems*. New York: Basic Books, 1960.

Rollins, B., & Cannon, K. Marital satisfaction over the family life cycle: A reevaluation. *Journal of Marriage and the Family*, 1974, *36*, 271–282.

Roosevelt, R., & Lofas, J. *Living in step*. New York: Stein & Day, 1976.

Rosenblatt, P. C. Needed research on commitment in marriage. In G. Levinger & H. L. Raush (Eds.), *Close relationships: Perspectives on the meaning of intimacy*. Amherst, Mass.: University of Massachusetts Press, 1977.

Rubin, Z., & Brown, B. R. *The social psychology of bargaining and negotiation*.

New York: Academic Press, 1975.

Rubin, Z. Measurement of romantic love. *Journal of Personality and Social Psychology*, 1970, *16*, 265–273.

Rubin, Z. *Liking and loving: An invitation to social psychology*. New York: Holt, Rinehart & Winston, 1973.

Rubin, Z. From liking to loving: Patterns of attraction in dating relationships. In T. L. Huston (Ed.), *Foundations of interpersonal attraction*. New York: Academic Press, 1974.

Rubin, Z. Naturalistic studies of self-disclosure. *Personality and Social Psychology Bulletin*, 1976, *2*, 260–263.

Rubin, Z. *Children's friendships*. Cambridge, Mass.: Harvard University Press, 1980.

Rubin, Z., & Levinger, G. Theory and data badly mated: A Critique of Murstein's SVR and Lewis's PDF models of mate selection. *Journal of Marriage and the Family*, 1974, *36*, 226–231.

Rubin, Z. & Mitchell, C. Couples research as couples counseling. *American Psychologist*, 1976, *31*, 17–25.

Rubin, Z., & Shenker, S. Friendship, proximity, and self-disclosure. *Journal of Personality*, 1978, *46*, 1–22.

Saegert, S., Swap, W., & Zajonc, R. B. Exposure, context, and interpersonal attraction. *Journal of Personality and Social Psychology*, 1973, *25*, 234–242.

Safilios-Rothschild, C. The study of family power structure: A review of 1960–1969. *Journal of Marriage and the Family*, 1970, *32*, 539–552.

Safilios-Rothschild, C. A macro- and micro-examination of family power and love: An exchange model. *Journal of Marriage and the Family*, 1976, *38*, 355–362.

Santrock, J. W., & Warshak, R. A. Father custody and social development in boys and girls. *Journal of Social Issues*, 1979, *35*(4), 112–125.

Sarnoff, I., & Zimbardo, P. Anxiety, fear and social affiliation. *Journal of Abnormal and Social Psychology*, 1961, *62*, 356–363.

Scanzoni, J. Social exchange and behavioral interdependence. In R. L. Burgess & T. L. Huston (Eds.), *Social exchange in developing relationships*. New York: Academic Press, 1979. (a)

Scanzoni, J. Strategies for changing male family roles: Research and practice implications. *The Family Coordinator*, 1979, *28*, 435–442. (b)

Schachter, S. *The psychology of affiliation*. Stanford: Stanford University Press, 1959.

Schachter, S. The interaction of cognitive and physiological determinants of emotional state. In L. Berkowitz (Ed.), *Advances in experimental social psychology* (Vol. 1). New York: Academic Press, 1964.

Schachter, S., & Singer, J. E. Cognitive, social and physiological determinants of emotional state. *Psychological Review*, 1962, *69*, 379–399.

Schaffer, H. R. *The growth of sociability*. Baltimore: Penguin, 1971.

Scheflen, A. E. Quasi-courtship behavior in psychotherapy. *Psychiatry*, 1965, *28*, 245–257.

Schmidt, G., & Sigusch, V. Sex differences in responses to psychosexual stimulation by film and slides. *Journal of Sex Research*, 1970, *6*, 268–283.

Schmidt, G., Sigusch, V., & Meyberg, V. Psychosexual stimulation in men: Emotional reactions, changes of sex behavior, and measures of conservative attitudes. *Journal of Sex Research,* 1969, *5* 199–217.

Schulman, G. L. Myths that intrude on the adaptation of the stepfamily. In G. K. Phelan (Ed.), *Family relationships.* Minneapolis, Minn.: Burgess, 1979.

Secord, P. F., & Backman, C. W. *Social psychology.* New York: McGraw-Hill, 1964.

Segal, M. W. Alphabet and attraction: An unobtrusive measure of the effect of propinquity in a field setting. *Journal of Personality and Social Psychology,* 1974, *30,* 654–657.

Seligman, C., Fazio, R. H., & Zanna, M. P. Effects of salience of extrinsic rewards on liking and loving. *Journal of Personality and Social Psychology,* 1980, *38,* 453–460.

Seyfried, B. A. Complementarity in interpersonal attraction. In S. Duck (Ed.), *Theory and practice in interpersonal attraction.* London: Academic Press, 1977.

Seyfried, B. A., & Hendrick, C. When do opposites attract? When they are opposite in sex and sex-role attitudes. *Journal of Personality and Social Psychology,* 1973, *25,* 15–20.

Shaffer, D. R. *Personality and social development.* Monterey, Calif.: Brooks/Cole, 1979.

Shaffer, D. R., & Sadowski, C. This table is mine: Respect for marked barroom tables as a function of gender of spatial marker and desirability of locale. *Sociometry,* 1975, *38,* 408–419.

Shapiro, A., & Swensen, C. Patterns of self-disclosure among married couples. *Journal of Counseling Psychology,* 1969, *16,* 179–180.

Shelley, D. S. A., & McKew, A. Pupillary dilation as a sexual signal and its links with adolescence. In M. Cook & G. Wilson (Eds.), *Love and attraction.* Oxford: Pergamon, 1979.

Sherman, J. A. Social values, femininity, and the development of female competence. *Journal of Social Issues,* 1976, *32*(3) 181–195.

Sherwood, J., & Scherer, J. J. A model for couples: How two can grow together. *Small Group Behavior,* 1975, *6,* 11–18.

Shulman, N. Life cycle variation in patterns of close relationships. *Journal of Marriage and the Family,* 1975, *37,* 813–821.

Sigall, H., & Landy, D. Radiating beauty: Effects of having a physically attractive partner on person perception. *Journal of Personality and Social Psychology,* 1973, *28,* 218–224.

Simmel, G. Sociology of the senses: Visual interaction. In R. E. Park & E. W. Burgess (Eds.), *Introduction to the science of sociology.* Chicago: University of Chicago Press, 1924.

Skinner, B. F. *The behavior of organisms: An experimental analysis.* New York: Appleton-Century-Crofts, 1938.

Skinner, B. F. *Science and human behavior.* New York: Macmillan, 1953.

Smith, R. J., & Knowles, E. S. Affective and cognitive mediators of reactions to spatial invasions. *Journal of Experimental Social Psychology,* 1979, *15,* 437–452.

Snyder, M. The self-monitoring of expressive behavior. *Journal of Personality and Social Psychology,* 1974, *30,* 526–537.

Snyder, M. Self-monitoring processes. In L. Berkowitz (Ed.), *Advances in experimental social psychology* (Vol. 12). New York: Academic Press, 1979.

Snyder, M. Impression management: The self in social interaction. In L. S. Wrightsman & K. Deaux (Eds.), *Social psychology in the 80s* (3rd ed.). Monterey, Calif.: Brooks/Cole, 1981.

Snyder, M., & Cantor, N. Thinking about ourselves and others: Self-monitoring and social knowledge. *Journal of Personality and Social Psychology,* 1980, *39,* 222–234.

Snyder, M., Tanke, E. D., & Berscheid, E. Social perception and interpersonal behavior: On the self-fulfilling nature of social stereotypes. *Journal of Personality and Social Psychology,* 1977, *35,* 656–666.

Solomon, S., & Saxe, L. What is intelligent, as well as attractive, is good. *Personality and Social Psychology Bulletin,* 1977, *3,* 670–673.

Sommer, R. *Personal space: The behavioral basis of design.* Englewood Cliffs, N.J.: Prentice-Hall, 1969.

Spanier, G. B. Measuring dyadic adjustment: New scales for assessing the quality of marriage and similar dyads. *Journal of Marriage and the Family,* 1976, *38,* 15–25.

Spanier, G. B., Lewis, R. A., & Cole, C. L. Marital adjustment over the family life cycle: The issue of curvilinearity. *Journal of Marriage and the Family,* 1975, *37,* 263–275.

Spence, J. T., & Helmreich, R. L. *Masculinity and femininity: Their psychological dimensions, correlates and antecedents.* Austin, Texas: University of Texas Press, 1978.

Stapleton, R. E., Nacci, P., & Tedeschi, J. T. Interpersonal attraction and the reciprocation of benefits. *Journal of Personality and Social Psychology,* 1973, *28,* 199–205.

Stewart, A. J., & Rubin, Z. The power motive in the dating couple. *Journal of Personality and Social Psychology,* 1974, *34,* 305–309.

Stokes, J., Fuehrer, A., & Childs, L. Gender differences in self-disclosure to various target persons. *Journal of Counseling Psychology,* 1980, *27,* 192–198.

Stone, L. *The family, sex and marriage in England 1500–1800.* New York: Harper & Row, 1977.

Strassberg, D. S., Anchor, K. N., Gabel, H., & Cohen, B. Client self-disclosure in short-term psychotherapy. *Psychotherapy: Theory, Research and Practice,* 1978, *15,* 153–157.

Strodtbeck, F. L. Husband–wife interaction over revealed differences. In P. Brickman (Ed.), *Social conflict.* Lexington, Mass.: D. C. Heath, 1974.

Symons, D. *The evolution of human sexuality.* New York: Oxford University Press, 1979.

Taylor, D. A., & Altman, I. *Intimacy-scaled stimuli for use in studies of interpersonal relationships* (Res. Rep. No. 9, MF022.01.03-1002). Bethesda, Md.: Naval Medical Research Institute, 1966.

Taylor, D. A., Altman, I., & Sorrentino, R. Interpersonal exchange as a function of rewards and costs and situational factors: Expectancy confirmation–disconfirmation. *Journal of Experimental Social Psychology,* 1969, *5,* 324–339.

Taylor, R. B., De Soto, C. B., & Lieb, R. Sharing secrets: Disclosure and discretion in dyads and triads. *Journal of Personality and Social Psychology,* 1979, *37,* 1196–1203.

Tedeschi, J. T. Attributions, liking, and power. In T. L. Huston (Ed.), *Foundations of interpersonal attraction.* New York: Academic Press, 1974.

Tennov, D. *Love and limerence: The experience of being in love.* New York: Stein & Day, 1979.

Thibaut, J. W., & Kelley, H. H. *The social psychology of groups.* New York: Wiley, 1959.

Thornton, B. Toward a linear prediction model of marital happiness. *Personality and Social Psychology Bulletin*, 1977, *3*, 674–676.

Toman, W. *Family constellations* (3rd ed.). New York: Springer, 1976.

Tyler, T. R., & Sears, D. O. Coming to like obnoxious people when we must live with them. *Journal of Personality and Social Psychology*, 1977, *35*, 200–211.

Unger, R. K. *Female and male.* New York: Harper & Row, 1979.

Vance, E. B., & Wagner, N. N. Written descriptions of orgasm: A study of sex differences. *Archives of Sexual Behavior,* 1976, *5*, 87–98.

Vannoy, R. *Sex without love: A philosophical exploration.* Buffalo, N.Y.: Prometheus Books, 1980.

Vener, A. M., & Stewart, C. S. Adolescent sexual behavior in middle America revisited: 1970–1973. *Journal of Marriage and the Family,* 1974, *36*, 728–735.

Victor, J. S. *Human sexuality: A social psychological approach.* Englewood Cliffs, N.J.: Prentice-Hall, 1980.

Vincent, J. P., Friedman, L. C., Nugent, J., & Messerly, L. Demand characteristics in observation of marital interaction. *Journal of Consulting and Clinical Psychology,* 1979, *47*, 557–566.

Vinsel, A., Brown, B. B., Altman, I., & Foss, C. Privacy regulation, territorial displays, and effectiveness of individual functioning. *Journal of Personality and Social Psychology,* 1980, *39*, 1104–1115.

Visher, E. B., & Visher, J. S. *Stepfamilies: A guide to working with stepparents and stepchildren.* New York: Brunner/Mazel, 1979.

Walster, E. The effect of self-esteem on romantic liking. *Journal of Experimental Social Psychology,* 1965, *1*, 184–197.

Walster, E. Passionate love. In B. I. Murstein (Ed.), *Theories of attraction and love.* New York: Springer, 1971.

Walster, E., Aronson, V., Abrahams, D., & Rottmann, L. Importance of physical attractiveness in dating behavior. *Journal of Personality and Social Psychology,* 1966, *4*, 508–516.

Walster, E., Berscheid, E., & Walster, G. W. New directions in equity research. *Journal of Personality and Social Psychology,* 1973, *25*, 151–176.

Walster, E., Berscheid, E., & Walster, G. W. New directions in equity research. In L. Berkowitz & E. Walster (Eds.), *Advances in experimental social psychology: Equity theory: Toward a general theory of social interaction* (Vol. 9). New York: Academic Press, 1976.

Walster, E., & Walster, G. W. *A new look at love.* Reading, Mass.: Addison-Wesley, 1978.

Walster, E., Walster, G. W., & Berscheid, E. *Equity: Theory and research.* Boston: Allyn & Bacon, 1978.

Watzlawick, P., Beavin, J. H., & Jackson, D. D. *Pragmatics of human communication: A study of interactional patterns, pathologies, and paradoxes.* New York: Norton, 1967.

Weeks, D. G., Michela, J. L., Peplau, L. A., & Bragg, M. E. Relation between loneliness and depression: A structural equation analysis. *Journal of Personality and Social Psychology,* 1980, *39*, 1238–1244.

Weiss, R. S. Issues in the adjudication of custody when parents separate. In G. Levinger & O. C. Moles (Eds.), *Divorce and separation.* New York: Basic Books, 1979.

Werner, C., & Parmelee, P. Similarity of activity preferences among friends: Those who play together stay together. *Social Psychology Quarterly*, 1979, *42*, 62–66.

Westoff, C. Coital frequency and contraception. *Family Planning Perspectives*, 1974, *6*, 136–141.

White, L. A. Erotica and aggression: The influence of sexual arousal, positive affect, and negative affect on aggressive behavior. *Journal of Personality and Social Psychology*, 1979, *37*, 591–601.

White, R. W. Motivation reconsidered: The concept of competence. *Psychological Review*, 1959, *66*, 297–333.

Wills, T. A., Weiss, R. L., & Patterson, G. R. A behavioral analysis of the determinants of marital satisfaction. *Journal of Consulting and Clinical Psychology*, 1974, *42*, 802–811.

Winch, R. F. *The modern family*. New York: Holt, 1952.

Winch, R. F. *Mate selection: A study of complementary needs*. New York: Harper & Brothers, 1958.

Winch, R. F., Ktsanes, T., & Ktsanes, V. The theory of complementary needs in mate-selection: An analytic and descriptive study. *American Sociological Review*, 1954, *19*, 241–249.

Winter, D. G., Stewart, A. J., & McClelland, D. C. Husband's motives and wife's career level. *Journal of Personality and Social Psychology*, 1977, *35*, 159–166.

Wish, M., Deutsch, M., & Kaplan, S. J. Perceived dimensions of interpersonal relations. *Journal of Personality and Social Psychology*, 1976, *33*, 409–420.

Worthy, M., Gary, A. L., & Kahn, G. M. Self-disclosure as an exchange process. *Journal of Personality and Social Psychology*, 1969, *13*, 59–63.

Wortman, C., Adesman, P., Herman, E., & Greenberg, R. Self-disclosure: An attributional perspective. *Journal of Personality and Social Psychology*, 1976, *33*, 184–191.

Wrightsman, L. S., & Deaux, K. *Social psychology in the 80s*. Monterey, Calif.: Brooks/Cole, 1981.

Zajonc, R. B. Attitudinal effects of mere exposure. *Journal of Personality and Social Psychology Monograph Supplement*, 1968, *9*(2, Part 2), 1–27.

Zelnik, M., & Kantner, J. F. Sexual and contraceptive experience of young unmarried women in the United States, 1976 and 1971. *Family Planning Perspectives*, 1977, *9*, 55–71.

Name Index

Subject Index